Saints, Clergy and Other Religious Figures
on Film and Television, 1895–2003

# Saints, Clergy and Other Religious Figures on Film and Television, 1895–2003

ANN C. PAIETTA

McFarland & Company, Inc., Publishers

*Jefferson, North Carolina, and London*

Ann Paietta is also the author of
*Access Services: A Handbook* (McFarland, 1991)

LIBRARY OF CONGRESS CATALOGUING-IN-PUBLICATION DATA

Paietta, Ann Catherine, 1956–
Saints, clergy and other religious figures on film
and television, 1895–2003 / Ann C. Paietta.
p. cm.
Includes bibliographical references and index.

ISBN 0-7864-2186-X (softcover : 50# alkaline paper) ∞

1. Saints in motion pictures. 2. Clergy in motion pictures.
3. Saints on television. 4. Clergy on television. 5. Religion in motion pictures.
6. Religion on television. 7. Motion pictures—Catalogs.
8. Television programs—Catalogs. I. Title.
PN1995.9.S234P35 2005 791.43'682—dc22 2005014050

British Library cataloguing data are available

Cover image: Geraldine Chaplin in *Mother Teresa* (1997)

Manufactured in the United States of America

*McFarland & Company, Inc., Publishers
Box 611, Jefferson, North Carolina 28640
www.mcfarlandpub.com*

For Charles and Lillian Paietta

# Contents

# Introduction

The portrayal of religious figures — saints, priests, clergy, nuns, ministers, rabbis, preachers, missionaries, monks, and other spiritual leaders — dates back to the very beginnings of motion pictures and television. Films drew on everyday life, as well as history, drama, and literature, for their depictions of these figures. There is little doubt that the media have had a strong influence on how society views religious leaders, and that movies and television have shaped our perception of them. Filmmakers did not create the stereotypes, but movies do embellish society's preexisting feelings.

From early on, films and television dealt with religious subjects, and conversely, religious groups attempted to influence the content and approach of film and television. Groups of all stripe realized the power of motion pictures to sway public opinion. Photographic film was invented by an Episcopal priest, and one of the first photographic films shown was the 1898 version of *Oberammergau (The Passion Play)*.

Since their inception motion pictures have been a constant source of controversy in the debate on morals in society. The Motion Picture Production Code of 1930 required that films showing bad behavior — like the film *Angels with Dirty Faces* (1938), with its hoodlums and criminal gangs — compensate with uplifting moral lessons. The code also required that religious characters in films be treated with respect, and it encouraged films that were more heartwarming than mind-expanding. Clergy were allowed some struggles in their personal dealings but were more likely to handle troubles effortlessly, as if by God's blessing.

Examples of early films showing religious figures include *After the Battle* (1898), which depicted scenes of nurses and a priest giving last rites to soldiers on the battlefield, and *The Monks* (1898), which showed a monk smoking a cigar and accidentally burning his sleeping friend. *Attack on a Mission Station* (1900) featured a missionary barricading his house against Chinese forces in the Boxer rebellion and eventually being saved. Over the years, religious figures have been portrayed as heroes, villains, mad men, ineffectual buffoons, money grubbers, snobs, humanitarians, drunks, saints, saviors, weak-willed molesters, and murderers. The recent American Film Institute list of 100 favorite heroes and villains included, under heroes, Father Edward Flanagan of *Boys Town* (1938), and, under villains, Reverend Harry Powell of *The Night of the Hunter* (1955). Religious figures in both movies and television tend toward being either miraculously pure or despicably evil and hypocritical. While there are exceptions, generally Hollywood figures are either saints or sinners, either laboring against all odds for good, or financially pursuing a crusade hate and bigotry while overwhelmed by sexual repression. Some early silent films did portray the sexual angst in ministers; examples include *Rain* (1932) and *Hallelujah* (1929).

The nature of Roman Catholic priesthood, with its vows and rules, offers many dramatic possibilities. Many plots have revolved around a priest learning a murderer's identity or some other secret in the confessional and not being able to tell, even when their own life is threatened. Also, the vow of celibacy creates sexual conflict seen in many plots. Today more films deal with Roman Catholic priests and the sexual abuse of children. For example, *The Boys of St. Vincent* (1992) and *The Boys of St. Vincent: 15 Years Later* (1993) examine that issue in great detail.

Compared to other religious figures, the rabbi is underrepresented in films and on television. Nevertheless, plenty of cinematic rabbis exist—for the traditional principled leader (*None Shall Escape*, 1944) to wisecracking go-getter—(*Bye Bye Braverman*, 1968) to modern young man coming to grips with his career (*Keeping the Faith*, 2000).

The religious figure as a character is at home in all types of films or any television series. Whether it is a western, mystery or detective, war, comedy, or horror film, religious figures fit easily into any genre. In fact, religious figures often are characters in nonreligious plots, where the setting could be anything else. One example is the television series *Father Dowling Mysteries*, where the parish house could easily just have been a hospital with doctors instead of a church.

Television and movies have created many memorable fictional clergy, such as Father Chuck O'Malley in *Going My Way* (a 1944 film that spun off a 1962–63 TV series) and *The Bells of St. Mary's* (1945) or Father Mulcahy from the long-running television series *M*A*S*H*. Both of these priests were popular characters and almost "regular" people. Screen nuns such as Sister Bertrille from TV's *The Flying Nun* or Sister Mary Benedict of *The Bells of St. Mary's* also have become cultural icons.

Religious figures have been portrayed both positively and negatively in films since the silent era. Some of the most memorable negative images in films include Reverend Isaiah Jenkins, an escaped convict posing as a minister in *Body and Soul* (1925), and Robert Mitchum as the psychopathic preacher Reverend Harry Powell in *Night of the Hunter* with "hate" and "love" tattooed on his fingers. Humphrey Bogart showed us the opposite: When men and women impersonate religious figures they are transformed into selfless people, as in *The Left Hand of God* (1955).

Female religious figures' portrayals have been less severe than their male counterparts. Unlike priests, nuns are rarely portrayed as drunk or evil. Nuns as central characters were largely absent from movies until the 1940s. Mother Superior Sister Mary Benedict from *The Bells of St. Mary's* was one of the first portrayals of nuns on screen. Ingrid Bergman, Loretta Young, Celeste Holm, Lilia Skala, and Deborah Kerr were all nominated for Academy Awards while playing nuns on screen. With few exceptions, nuns were angelic or eccentric characters. There were some exceptions. For example, in *Black Narcissus* (1947), the Anglican nuns were quite disturbed and sexual frustration bubbled just under the surface. Nun impersonators, such as Shirley MacLaine in *Two Mules for Sister Sara* (1970) or Whoopi Goldberg in *Sister Act* (1992), were usually allowed a few flaws.

Saints on the screen include Joan of Arc, the subject of many films since 1895, whose appeal continues across national, cultural, and gender boundaries even today. Besides the 1895 production, her story has been told in Méliès' 1897 *Jeanne d'Arc* (406), Cecil B. DeMille's 1917 *Joan the Woman*, Carl Theodor Dreyer's classic *La Passion de Jeanne d'Arc* (1928), Luc Besson's *The Messenger* (1999), *Joan of Arc* (1948) with Ingrid Bergman, and Robert

Bresson's *Procés de Jeanne d'Arc* (1962), to name some of the films based on her life. St. Francis has also been the subject of many films.

Over 900 films and television series are described in this book. Taken together, they have much to say about the long history of religious figures in movies and television series.

## THE ORGANIZATION OF THE BOOK

The selected films and television series fall into one of these three categories:

1. A religious figure plays a prominent role in a film.
2. A religious figure has a recurring role on a television series.
3. A character is posing as a religious figure in either a film or a television depiction.

Included in this book are films (both U.S. and foreign releases) from the 1890s through 2003, prime time television series (both U.S. and foreign), and made-for-television films. U.S. government films, soap operas, and documentaries are excluded.

Part I, Theatrical and Made for Television Films, contains credits, annotations, and detailed discussion of the plot and religious figures. The titles are arranged alphabetically, word-by-word; articles are ignored at the beginning of titles. The films are serially numbered from 1 to 919. Foreign-language releases are alphabetized under their original titles: English translations of these titles appear as cross-references.

Part II, Television Series, predominantly covers regularly scheduled programs. The series are listed alphabetically by the titles by which they are most commonly known (which sometimes differ from their official titles). The series are serially numbered from 920 to 979.

The Annotated Bibliography lists relevant articles and books on religious figures in films and television.

The Name Index is of religious figures; the names of real people are italicized.

The Subject Index categorizes the films and series (for example, World War II, missionaries, supernatural, HIV, and nursing). Many of the films and series are listed under several subject categories.

# Abbreviations

| | |
|---|---|
| AA | Allied Artists |
| AA | Anglo-Amalgamated Films |
| AB | Associated British |
| ABC | American Broadcasting Corporation |
| ABF | Associated British Film |
| ABFD | Associated British Film Distributors |
| ABPC | Associated British Picture Corporation |
| AIP | American International Pictures |
| AP&D | Associated Producers and Distributors |
| B&D | British and Dominions Film Corporation |
| BBC | British Broadcasting Corporation |
| BFI | British Film Institute |
| BIP | British International Pictures |
| BL | British Lion Film Corporation |
| B&W | Black and White |
| C | Color |
| CBS | Columbia Broadcasting System |
| DUK | Do-U-Know Film Productions |
| EMI | Electrical and Musical Industries |
| FBO | Film Booking Offices |
| FN | First National Pictures |
| GAS | George Albert Smith Films |
| GFD | General Film Distributors |
| HBO | Home Box Office |
| IFD | Independent Film Distributors |
| HMO | Health Maintenance Organization |
| JMG | Jury-Metro-Goldwyn |
| KTC | Kinematograph Trading Company |
| m | Minutes |
| MGM | Metro-Goldwyn-Mayer |
| NBC | National Broadcasting Corporation |
| P&C | Phillips and Carroll |
| PBS | Public Broadcasting System |
| PRC | Producers Releasing Corporation |
| RFD | Rank Film Distributors |
| RKO | Radio-Keith-Orpheum |
| TCF | 20th-Century Fox |
| TV | Television |
| TVM | Television Movie |
| UA | United Artists Film Corporation |
| UFA | Universum Film Aktiengesellschaft |
| UI | Universal International Pictures |
| US | United States |
| W&F | Woolf and Freedman |
| YCC | Yorkshire Cinematograph Company |

# Theatrical and
# Made for Television Films

1. **The Abdication.** Warner. UK. 1974. 103m. C. *Producer*: Robert Fryer, James Cresson *Director*: Anthony Harvey *Writer*: Ruth Wolff *Cast*: Peter Finch, Liv Ullmann, Cyril Cusack, Paul Rogers, Graham Crowden, Michael Dunn, Kathleen Byron, Lewis Fiander, Harold Goldblatt, Tony Steedman, Noel Trevarthen, Richard Cornish, James Faulkner, Edward Underdown

In 1654, the Pope's successor Cardinal Azzolino (Peter Finch) falls in love with Queen Christina (Liv Ullmann) of Sweden when teaching her Catholicism. She decides to give up her throne and convert.

2. **The Abduction of Saint Anne.** ABC. (TV). US. 1975. 72m. C. *Producer*: John Wilder *Director*: Harry Falk *Writer*: Edward Hume *Cast*: Robert Wagner, E. G. Marshall, Lloyd Nolan, Kathleen Quinlan, William Windom, James Gregory, A. Martinez, Ruth McDevitt, Alfred Ryder, George McCallister, Tony Young, Martha Scott, Victor Mohica, Patrick Conway, Roy Jenson

A detective and a Roman Catholic bishop (E. G. Marshall), from the Vatican, team up to investigate the miraculous powers of a seventeen year old girl Anne Benedict (Kathleen Quinlan) who is being held captive in her father's home by her ill father and the mob. Also known as *They've Kidnapped Anne Benedict*.

3. **Absolution.** Enterprise Pictures. UK. 1981. 95m. C. *Producer*: Elliott Kastner, Danny O'Donovan *Director*: Anthony Page *Writer*: Anthony Shaffer *Cast*: Richard Burton, Dominic Guard, David Bradley, Billy Connolly, Andrew Keir, Willoughby Gray, Preston Lockwood, James Ottaway, Brook Williams, Jon Plowman

Father Goddard (Richard Burton) is a stern devout priest teacher at a Catholic boarding school for boys. Two resentful students use the secrecy of the confessional to drive him to an unwittingly killing. The film was completed in 1979 but shelved until 1981.

4. **Abuna Messias.** Generalcine. Italy. 1939. 96m. B&W. *Producer*: Alessandro F. Gagna *Director*: Goffredo Alessandrini *Writer*: Goffredo Alessandrini, Vittorio Cottafavi *Cast*: Camillo Pilotto, Enrico Glori, Mario Ferrari, Amedeo Trilli, Berchè Zaitù Taclè, Hipólito Silvestre, Franz Sala, Roberto Pasetti, Corrado Racca

King Menelik (Enrico Glori) is pleased with the work that Cardinal Guglielmo Massata named Abuna Messias (Camillo Pilotto) and the Franciscan monks are doing in Ethiopia converting natives to Christianity. Abuna Atanasio (Mario Ferrari), head of the native Coptic Church, is jealous of Messias and asks Menelik to expel him, when he refuses a war starts. Also known as *Cardinal Messias*.

5. **The Accused.** Film Productions International. US/UK. 1957. 83m. C. *Producer*: Burton Martin, Lloyd Young *Director*: Michael Audley, Gilbert Gunn *Writer*: H. Kenn Carmichael, Lloyd Young *Cast*: Eartha Kitt, Juano Hernandez, John McIntire, Sidney Poitier, Patrick Allen, Earl Cameron, Gerard Heinz, Helen Horton, Clifton Macklin, Ewen Solon, Marne Maitland, Lockwood West, Francis Matthews

In colonial Africa, American missionary Bruce Craig (John McIntire) influences workers' representative Obam (Sidney Poitier) who is torn between duty and his brother's terrorist/freedom fighting gang. Also known as *The Mark of the Hawk*.

**6. Act of the Heart.** UI. Canada. 1970. 103m. C. *Producer:* Paul Almond, Jennings Lang *Director & Writer:* Paul Almond *Cast:* Geneviève Bujold, Donald Sutherland, Monique Leyrac, Billy Mitchell, Suzanne Langlois, Sharon Acker, Ratch Wallace, Jean Duceppe, Gilles Vigneault, Eric House

A religious woman Martha Hayes (Geneviève Bujold) from rural Canada moves to Montreal to earn money for her parents. She finds housing with a woman seeking a tutor for her son. Even though she is a Protestant she sings in the Catholic Church choir. Father Michael Ferrier (Donald Sutherland), an Augustinian monk, chooses her to sing a solo. He teaches her about the order and St. Augustine's association with the flaming heart. She soon falls in love with him. Russell the boy she is tutoring dies in a hockey accident. Martha is so upset that she rushes to Father Ferrier where their argument about God ends in making love. He leaves the order and they live together. Michael attempts a social crusade but it goes nowhere. He tells Martha that only an act of the heart will draw attention to his cause. Without his knowledge, Martha pours gasoline on her head and sets herself on fire. Also known as *Acte du Coeur*.

**Acte du coeur** *see* **Act of the Heart**

**7. Adventure in Baltimore.** RKO. US. 1949. 89m. B&W. *Producer:* Richard H. Berger *Director:* Richard Wallace *Writer:* Lionel Houser *Cast:* Robert Young, Shirley Temple, John Agar, Albert Sharpe, Josephine Hutchinson, Charles Kemper, Johnny Sands, John Miljan, Norma Varden, Carol Brannan

The story of a Protestant minister's family living in 1905 Baltimore. Dr. Andrew Sheldon (Robert Young) is an understanding father and minister. His aspiring artist and budding suffragette daughter Dinah (Shirley Temple) is experiencing many growing pains that teenagers face in life.

**8. Les Adventures de Rabbi Jacob.** TCF. France. 1973. 100m. C. *Producer:* Bertrand Javal *Director:* Gérard Oury *Writer:* Josy Eisenberg, Gérard Oury, Danièle Thompson *Cast:* Louis de Funès, Suzy Delair, Marcel Dalio, Claude Giraud, Renzo Montagnani, Janet Brandt, André Falcon, Xavier Gélin, Henri Guybet, Popeck

A bigoted Frenchman Victor Pivert is forced to impersonate Rabbi Jacob (Louis de Funès) while running from a group of assassins. Accompanying him also dressed as a Rabbi is Mohamed Larbi Slimane (Claude Giraud), an Arab rebel leader. The real Rabbi Jacob is a beloved figure returning to France after 30 years in the United States. Confusion reigns. Also known as *The Mad Adventures of Rabbi Jacob*.

**9. The Adventures of Robin Hood.** Warner. US. 1938. 102m. C. *Producer:* Hal B. Wallis *Director:* Michael Curtiz, William Keighley *Writer:* Norman Reilly Raine, Seton J. Miller *Cast:* Errol Flynn, Olivia De Havilland, Basil Rathbone, Claude Rains, Patric Knowles, Eugene Pallette, Alan Hale, Melville Cooper, Ian Hunter, Una O'Connor, Herbert Mundin, Montagu Love, Leonard Willey, Robert Noble, Kenneth Hunter, Robert Warwick, Colin Kenny, Lester Matthews, Harry Cording, Howard Hill, Ivan Simpson

The classic tale of Robin Hood (Errol Flynn) and His Merry Men of Sherwood Forest. Friar Tuck (Eugene Pallette) is there to assist Robin as he fights injustices and woos Maid Marian (Olivia De Havilland).

**10. The African Queen.** UA. US/UK. 1951. 105m. C. *Producer:* Sam Spiegel *Director:* John Huston *Writer:* James Agee, John Huston, C. S. Forester (novel) *Cast:* Humphrey Bogart, Katharine Hepburn, Robert Morley, Peter Bull, Theodore Bikel, Walter Gotell, Peter Swanwick, Richard Marner

In Africa during World War I, a gin drinking riverboat captain Charlie Allnut (Humphrey Bogart) comes across a missionary brother-sister team. Reverend Samuel Sayer (Robert Morley) and his spinster sister Rose (Katharine Hepburn) lead natives at the First Methodist Church. Charlie warns them about the impending war in Europe, but they refuse to leave the village. Soon German troops invade and burn down the huts while

Samuel loses his mind and soon collapses. When the Reverend Samuel Sayer dies, Charlie agrees to help the strait-lace Rose Sayer get to safety. Rose has other plans and convinces Charlie to attack an enemy warship the Louisa. Eventually they fall in love and learn each other's first name. Finally, they succeed in their plan to sink the German ship the Louisa. In 1977, a television version starring Mariette Hartley and Warren Oates aired.

**11. After the Battle.** S. Lubin. US. 1898. B&W.

The Sisters of Charity and members of the Red Cross Society care for wounded soldiers after a fierce battle. Also visible is a priest giving the sacrament of Last Rites to the dying and dead being carried from the field

**12. Against the Wind.** GFD. UK. 1948. 96m. B&W. *Producer*: Michael Balcon *Director*: Charles Crichton *Writer*: J. Elder Wills, Michael Pertwee *Cast*: Robert Beatty, Jack Warner, Simone Signoret, Gordon Jackson, Paul Dupuis, Gisèle Préville, John Slatter, Peter Illing, James Robertson Justice, Sybilla Binder, Héléne Hansen, Eugene Deckers, Andre Morell

After undergoing spy and saboteur training in London, Canadian priest, Father Phillip (Robert Beatty), a Scot with knowledge of explosives, Belgian girl trying to forget a lost love, an elderly man who undergoes a facial operation, and others are sent to Germany to destroy records and rescue an important person,

**13. Agnes of God.** Columbia. US. 1985. 98m. C. *Producer*: Patrick Palmer, Norman Jewison *Director*: Norman Jewison *Writer*: John Pielmeier (play) *Cast*: Jane Fonda, Anne Bancroft, Meg Tilly, Anne Pitoniak, Winston Rekert, Gratien Gelinas, Guy Hoffman, Gabriel Arcand, Francoise Faucher

A court-appointed psychiatrist, Dr. Martha Livingston (Jane Fonda), is sent to investigate whether a young novice nun, Sister Agnes (Meg Tilly), accused of giving birth and then killing her baby, is fit to stand trial. Sister Agnes claims it's a virgin birth. The main conflict is between Mother Superior Miriam Ruth (Anne Bancroft) and Dr.

Livingston. Mother Superior wants Sister Agnes left alone while the psychiatrist wants to help Sister Agnes regain her sanity and uncover the truth. Mother Superior is a very religious woman with a past as a wife and mother and knowledge of the world.

**14. The Agony and the Ecstasy.** TCF. US. 1965. 138m. C. *Producer & Director*: Carol Reed *Writer*: Irving Stone (novel), Philip Dunne *Cast*: Charlton Heston, Rex Harrison, Diane Cilento, Harry Andrews, Alberto Lupo, Adolfo Celi, Venantino Venantini, John Stacy, Fausto Tozzi, Maxine Audley, Tomas Milian

Film focuses on sculptor/painter Michelangelo (Charlton Heston) and Pope Julius II (Rex Harrison). The Pope commissions Michelangelo to create 40 statues for his tomb. Later the Pope asks him to paint the ceilings of the Sistine Chapel. Initially, Michelangelo says no that he is not a painter but later changes his mind. Soon he becomes frustrated and leaves, but he does return to paint after a revelation. The Pope fearing death in battle asks Michelangelo to preview the painting but is denied by Michelangelo. When the wounded Pope returns to Rome, Michelangelo convinces him to visit the chapel. The Pope is awed by the artwork.

**15. Agostino d'Ippona.** EMC. Italy. 1972. 121m. C. *Producer*: Francesco Orefici *Director*: Roberto Rossellini *Writer*: Carlo Cremona, Marcella Mariani, Jean-Dominique de la Rochefoucauld, Roberto Rossellini, Luciano Scaffa *Cast*: Dary Berkani, Virgilio Gazzolo, Cesare Barbetti, Bruno Cattaneo, Leonardo Fioravanti, Dannunzio Papini, Beppe Mannaiuolo, Livio Galassi, Fabio Garriba, Giuseppe Alotta

The life story of Saint Augustine of Hippo (Dary Berkani). Augustine was the Bishop of Hippo, a North African region during the last days of the Roman Empire. Also known as *Augustine of Hippo*.

**16. Aguirre, der Zorn Gottes.** New Yorker Films. Germany. 1972. 90m. C. *Producer, Director & Writer*: Werner Herzog *Cast*: Klaus Kinski, Helena Rojo, Del Negro, Ruy Guerra, Peter Berling, Cecilia Rivera, Daniel Ades, Edward Roland, Armando Polanah

The opening text attributes this story to the diary of a Spanish monk Brother Gaspar de Carvajal (Del Negro). A group of Pizzaro's men are sent to find the city of gold 'El Dorado.' Spanish soldier Don Lope de Aguirre (Klaus Kinski) in 1560 led a mutiny against his Spanish commander Pedro de Ursua (Ruy Guerra) in Peru. With a small group of soldiers he attempts to lay claim to an empire of his own in the jungle. The conquistadores endure whirlpools, Indian attacks, and rebellions within themselves. Also known as *Aguirre, the Wrath of God*.

**Aguirre, the Wrath of God** *see* **Aguirre, der Zorn Gottes**

**Aimsir Padraig** *see* **In the Days of St. Patrick**

**17. ¡Al diablo con este cura!** Argentina. 1967. 96m. C. *Producer*: Celestino Anzuola *Director*: Carlos Rinaldi *Writer*: Ulises Petit de Murat *Cast*: Luis Sandrini, Ubaldo Martínez, Elizabeth Killian, Iris Marga, Virginia Lago, Eduardo Rudy, Enzo Viena, Ricardo Bauleo, Diana Ingro

Comedy about a down-to-earth priest pitted against insensitive people in a high-class neighborhood. Also known as *To Hell with This Priest*.

**18. Aleksandr Nevsky.** Amkino. Russia. 1938. 112m. B&W. *Director*: Sergei M. Eisenstein, Dmitri Vasiliev *Writer*: Sergei M. Eisenstein, Pyotr Pavlenko *Cast*: Andrei Abrikosov, Nikolai Arsky, Serge Blinikov, Nikolai Cherkasov, Anna Danilova, Vladimir Erschiov, Lev Fenin, Vera Ivasceva, Ivan Lagutin, Varvara Massalitinova, Nicholas Okhlopkov, Vasili Novikov, Dmitri Orlov, Naum Rogozhin

Based on the life of Alexander Nevsky (c. 1220–1263) who became a Russian national hero and a saint of the Orthodox Church. Prince Alexander arouses the peasantry to bear arms in defense of Russia in the early 1200s. Also known as *Warrior of Russia* and *Alexander Nevsky*.

**The Alienist** *see* **O Alienista**

**19. O Alienista.** New Yorker Films. Brazil. 1970. 100m. C. *Director & Writer*: Nelson Pereira dos Santos *Cast*: Nildo Parente, Isabel Ribeiro, Arduíno Colasanti, Irene Stefânia, Leila Diniz, Gabriel Archanjo, Manfredo Colassanti

Based on a Brazilian tale. During the 17th century a new priest arrives at a Brazilian town to get the upper class villagers back to the rundown church. He builds an asylum to house the alienated and mad people. Although he seems to want to do good things, he also uses the asylum to lock up people who do not agree with his ways or religion. Eventually the entire town ends up in the asylum. Also known as *The Alienist* and *Um Asilo muito louce*.

**All About My Mother** *see* **Todo sobre mi madre**

**20. Gli Altri racconti di Canterbury.** Transeuropa Film. Italy. 1972. *Director & Writer*: Mino Guerrini *Cast*: Alida Rossano, Mirella Rossi, Eleonara Vivaldi, Francesco Angelucci, Roberto Borelli, Mariana Camara, Fortunata Cecilia, Teodoro Corrà, Assunta Costanzo

Dramatizes six different tales in which one tells the story of a woman who seeks comfort with a monk to escape a husband who beats her. Also known as *The Other Canterbury Tales*.

**21. L'Altro inferno.** Film Concept Group. Italy. 1980. 88m. C. *Producer*: Arcangelo Picchi *Director*: Bruno Mattei *Writer*: Claudio Fragasso, Bruno Mattei *Cast*: Franca Stoppi, Carlo De Mejo, Francesca Carmeno, Susan Forget, Franco Garofalo, Paola Montenero, Sandy Samuel, Andrea Aureli

A young priest Father Valerio (Carlo De Mejo) investigates a series of bizarre and brutal murders at a convent. Could it be the work of Satan? Or perhaps a deranged person? Also known as *The Other Hell*.

**22. Amateur.** Sony Pictures Classics. US/UK/France. 1994 105m. C. *Producer*: Hal Hartley, Ted Hope *Director & Writer*: Hal Hartley *Cast*: Isabelle Huppert, Martin Donovan, Elina Lowensohn, Damian Young, Chuck Montgomery, Dave Simonds, Pamela Stewart

Isabelle (Isabelle Huppert), an ex-nun of 15 years, is waiting for her mission from God by making her living writing pornography. She meets Thomas (Martin Donovan), a confused amnesiac and together they set out to discover his past, which is that he used to be a pornographer.

**23. Amen.** Kino International. France/Germany/Romania/US. 2002. 126m. C. *Producer:* Claude Berri, Andrei Boncea, Michele Ray-Gavras *Director:* Costa-Gavras *Writer:* Costa-Gavras, Jean-Claude Grumberg, Rolf Hochhuth (play) *Cast:* Ulrich Tukur, Mathieu Kassovitz, Ulrich Mühe, Michel Duchaussoy, Ion Caramitru, Marcel Iures, Friedrich von Thun, Antje Schmidt, Angus MacInnes

A young Jesuit priest Ricardo Fontana (Mathieu Kassovitz) with ties to the Vatican and a chemist and SS Lieutenant Kurt Gerstein (Ulrich Tukur) fight to reveal the truth about the systematic murder of interred Jews. The lieutenant has witnessed the chemical, zyklon B, he's helped perfect actually used on people. The film and play are based on actual events with Kurt Gerstein a real-life person. Ricardo Fontana is a fictitious character who represents a composite of those priests willing to fight for the truth.

**24. Amityville Horror.** American International. US. 1979. 117m. C. *Producer:* Ronald Saland, Elliot Geisinger *Director:* Stuart Rosenberg *Writer:* Sandor Stern, Jay Anson (book) *Cast:* James Brolin, Margot Kidder, Rod Steiger, Don Stroud, Natasha Ryan, K.C. Martel, Meeno Peluce, Michael Sacks, Helen Shaver, Val Avery, Amy Wright, Murray Hamilton, John Larch, Irene Dailey

Tells the supposedly true story of the Lutz family who move into a possessed home in Amityville, New York. The family turns to family priest Father Delaney (Rod Steiger) for help. Father Delaney believes that the house is haunted and he attempts to perform an exorcism. The evil spirit makes the Father very ill. Another priest, Father Bolen (Don Stroud), also tries to help the family in their ordeal.

**25. Amityville II: The Possession.** Orion. US/Mexico. 1982. 100m. C. *Producer:* Ira N. Smith, Stephen R. Greenwald, Dino De Laurentiis *Director:* Damiano Damiani *Writer:* Hans Holzer (book) Tommy Lee Wallace *Cast:* Burt Young, Rutanya Alda, James Olson, Jack Magner, Diane Franklin,

Andrew Prine, Leonardo Cimino, Brent Katz, Erica Katz, Moses Gunn

Same house as in *Amityville Horror* but a different family. The family priest Father Adamski (James Olson) even breaks the law because he feels responsible for the horror. He makes every effort to save the possessed son, who has murdered the family. The house was built on ancient Indian burial grounds. More Amityville films followed.

**26. Anchoress.** International Film Circuit. Belgium/UK. 1993. 106m. B&W. *Producer:* Paul Breuls, Ben Gibson *Director:* Chris Newby *Writer:* Judith Stanley-Smith, Christine Watkins *Cast:* Natalie Morse, Gene Bervoets, Toyah Wilcox, Pete Postlethwaite, Christopher Eccleston, Michael Pas, Brenda Bertin, Annette Badland, Veronica Quilligan, Julie T. Wallace, Francois Beukelaers, Ann Way

In 14th century England, peasant girl Christine Carpenter (Natalie Morse) is so attracted to a statue of the Virgin Mary that the local priest (Christopher Eccleston) ensures that she becomes walled up in the church as an anchoress, a holy woman with responsibility for blessing the villagers. The priest lusts after her. When the priest has her mother tried as being a witch, Christine escapes from her cell. Based on actual letters that were written by such an Anchoress in 1325.

**And There Came a Man** *see* **E venne un uomo**

**27. Andrei Rublyov.** Mosfilm. Soviet Union. 1969. 205m. B&W. *Producer:* Tamara Ogorodnikova *Director:* Andrei Tarkpvsky *Writer:* Andrei Konchalovsky, Andrei Tarkovsky *Cast:* Anatoli Solonitsyn, Ivan Lapikov, Nikolai Grinko, Nikolai Sergeyev, Irma Raush, Nikolai Burlyayev, Yuri Nazarov, Yuri Nikulin

Widely recognized masterpiece tells the story of 15th century Russian monk Andrei Rublyov (Anatoli Solonitsyn), who is considered Russia's greatest creator of religious icons. The film was not seen as the director desired until twenty years after completion. The film in an abridged form wasn't screened in the Soviet Union until 1972. Also known as *Andrei Rublev.*

**28. Angel Baby.** AA. US. 1961. 97m. B&W. *Producer*: Thomas F. Woods *Director*: Paul Wendkos *Writer*: Orin Borsten, Paul Mason, Samuel Roeca, Elsie Oakes Barber (novel) *Cast*: Salome Jens, George Hamilton, Mercedes McCambridge, Joan Blondell, Henry Jones, Burt Reynolds, Roger Clark, Dudley Remus, Victoria Adams, Harry Swoger, Barbara G. Biggart, Davy Bildadeau, Eddie Firestone

Faith healing preacher, Paul Strand (George Hamilton) comes to a small southern town where he meets Jenny (Salome Jens), a mistreated mute. Paul miraculously restores her power of speech and she joins his troop of evangelists. Jenny is persuaded to go on her own billed as Angel Baby, the Preacher of the Ages. She soon finds herself being used in phony healing scam. Soon she is denounced as a fraud and gives up preaching. Paul tries to persuade her to return, but she refuses. Jenny rediscovers her faith when her prayers help a crippled child walk.

**29. Angel in My Pocket.** Universal. US. 1969. 105m. C. *Producer*: Edward J. Montagne *Director*: Alan Rafkin *Writer*: James Fritzell, Everett Greenbaum *Cast*: Andy Griffith, Jerry Van Dyke, Kay Medford, Lee Meriwether, Henry Jones, Edgar Buchanan, Gary Collins, Jack Dodson, Margaret Hamilton, Parker Fennelly, Elena Verdugo, Ruth McDevitt, Richard Van Vleet, Bob Hastings, Jim Boles, Leonard Stone, Steve Franken, Larry D. Mann

Newly ordained Reverend Samuel D. Whitehead (Andy Griffith) and his family move to a small town in Kansas where he has been assigned to his first parish. He must endure numerous complications while trying to win over his congregation. For example, his brother-in-law and a parishioner build a still in the church basement. Also the church has had seven other ministers in the past decade and due to feuding families town progress has stalled. The election of a young lawyer as mayor helps end the feud.

**30. Angel of His Dreams.** Australia. 1912. 54m. B&W. *Producer & Director*: George Marlow *Cast*: Ada Guilford, J. Stanford, H. Twitcham

Tale of a woman with questionable morals, who seduces an innocent young clergyman.

**The Angel Wore Red** *see* **La Sposa bella**

**31. Angels in America.** HBO. (TV). US. 2003. 352m. C. *Producer*: Celia Costas *Director*: Mike Nichols *Writer*: Tony Kushner *Cast*: Meryl Streep, Al Pacino, Emma Thompson, Jeffrey Wright, Mary-Louise Parker, Melissa Wilder, Florence Kastriner, Howard Pinhasik, Ben Shenkman, Justin Kirk, Patrick Wilson, James Cromwell, Brian Markinson, David Zayas, Sterling Brown, Lisa LeGuillou

Meryl Streep plays numerous characters including the rabbi in this tale set in 1985. Prior Walton tells his lover that he is sick and Lou runs away. As Prior get sicker, Lou is torn with guilt. Joe Pitt is Mormon and Republican lawyer who is encouraged to take a job at the Justice Department by Roy Cohn. Both are in the closet, Joe because of religious turmoil and Roy to preserve his power.

**Angels of the Streets** *see* **Les Anges du péché**

**32. Angels with Dirty Faces.** Warner. US. 1938. 97m. B&W. *Producer*: Samuel Bischoff *Director*: Michael Curtiz *Writer*: Rowland Brown, John Wexley, Warren Duff *Cast*: James Cagney, Pat O'Brien, Humphrey Bogart, Ann Sheridan, George Bancroft, Billy Halop, Bobby Jordan, Leo Grocey, Gabriel Dell, Huntz Hall, Bernard Punsly, Joe Downing

Rocky Sullivan (James Cagney) and Jerry Connolly (Pat O'Brien) are hoodlum boyhood buddies. After Rocky is released from prison he is reunited with Jerry now a tough and forceful priest assigned to his home parish. Rocky has returned to start up a criminal operation with gang boss and a crooked lawyer. Father Jerry has started a media campaign against the gang vowing to bring them to justice. Father Jerry is also losing the battle for the minds of the youth while the kids worship Rocky. The gang decides to murder Jerry but Rocky finds out and kills them first. Rocky is caught and sentenced to the electric chair. Jerry tries to convince Rocky to help some young hoodlums before he is executed by acting yellow. During their march down Death Row, Father Jerry pleads with Rocky to act scared. Finally, we hear Rocky crying out for help. It is unclear about Rocky's motive. Father Jerry returns to the boys and answers their questions.

**33. The Angelus.** Ambassador. UK. 1937. 76m. B&W. *Producer*: Julius Hagen *Director*: Thomas Bentley *Writer*: Michael Barringer *Cast*: Anthony Bushell, Nancy O'Neil, Eve Gray, Mary Glynne, Garry Marsh, Zoe Wynn, Richard Cooper, Joyce Evans, Charles Carson, Amy Veness

Sister Angleica (Mary Glynne) goes on leave from her convent to prove her niece, an actress, did not kill producer of the show she had a small role in. Also known as *Who Killed Fen Markham*.

**34. Les Anges du péché.** MGM. France. 1943. 96m. B&W. *Producer:* Roger Richebé *Director:* Robert Bresson *Writer:* Robert Bresson, Raymond Leopold Bruckberger, Jean Giraudoux *Cast:* Renée Faure, Jamy Holt, Sylvie, Mila Parély, Marie-Hélène Dasteé Yolande Laffon, Paula Dehelly, Silvia Monfort, Gilberte Terbois

Rich young Anne-Marie Lamaury (Renée Faure) joins a Dominican convent as a novice. The convent works in rehabilitating female prisoners. Sister Anne-Marie becomes fascinated with Therese (Jamy Holt) and wants to redeem her but Therese claims her innocence. When released Therese shoots the man who committed the crime for which she was jailed, then she joins the convent. She doesn't want to tell her secret while the police search draws closer. She presses so hard for Therese's salvation that Anne-Marie is expelled from the convent. Anne-Marie is tossed out during a rainstorm and realizes her sins of pride and ambition while dying. Also known as *Angels of the Streets*.

**35. Anima.** Hypnotic. US. 2003. 26m. C. *Producer*: Jose C. Mangual *Director & Writer*: Erika Grediaga *Cast*: Claude Soberón, Carol Abney, Dennis Deal, Rick Simon, Katira Santiago, Melodee Spevack, Karen Teliha, Christine Dunn, Jeanne Mount

The film begins in the 16th century. The Catholic Church has expanded throughout the new continent. One hundred years later, Angelica (Claudia Soberón) is forced into God's service against her will due to poverty. She tries to escape into the outside world and as punishment she is confined to her cell. There she is haunted by the spirit of Sister Luciana, who was entombed one hundred years in the convent walls. To free Luciana's trapped soul she must persuade the nuns to leave the convent and pray in the open. However, leaving the cloister is expressly forbidden. She is unable to convince her superiors that this is not another escape attempt.

**36. Anna.** Italian Film Export. Italy/France. 1951. 107m. B&W. *Producer*: Dino De Laurentiis, Carlo Ponti *Director*: Alberto Lattuada *Writer*: Giuseppe Berto, Franco Brusati, Ivo Perilli, Dino Risi, Rodolfo Sonego *Cast*: Silvana Mangano, Gaby Morlay, Raf Vallone, Jacques Dumesnil, Vittorio Gassman, Patrizia Mangano, Natascia Mangano, Piero Lulli, Dina Romano, Rosita Pisano

Anna (Silvana Mangano), a nurse and a nun whose history catches up with her. As a fickle club singer she had to choose between two lovers. Anna chose neither and entered a convent.

**37. Año Mariano.** Aurum Producciones. Spain. 2000. 117m. C. *Producer*: Juanjo Landa *Director*: Fernando Guillén Cuervo *Writer*: Fernando Guillén Cuervo, Karra Elejalde, José Antonio Ortega *Cast*: Karra Elejalde, Fernando Guillén Cuervo, Manuel Manquiña, Gloria Muñoz, Silvia Bel, Fernando Guillén, Juan Viadas, Pepín Tre

Down-and-out salesman Mariano Romero (Karra Elejalde) crashes his car into a marijuana field just as the police arrive to set it on fire. Mariano hallucinates wildly and sees tears of blood coming from a statue of the Virgin Mary. Sister Trini (Gloria Muñoz) hails him as a visionary and when people hear the Virgin spoke to him they leave the church which upsets the priest Don Javier (Juan Viadas). Seeing profit in the situation a small-time crook becomes Mariano's manager and a shrine on the land is built. Also known as *The Year of Maria*.

Anthony of Padua *see* **Antonio di Padova**

**38. Anthracite—cet âge est sans pitié.** Rush Production. France. 1980. 90m. C. *Director & Writer*: Edouard Niermans *Cast*: Bruno Cremer, Jean Bouise, Roland Bertin, Jean-Pol Dubois, Jérôme Zucca, Jean-Pierre Bagot, Pierre Baldini

In a Jesuit school for young boys, a priest attempts to save face in the midst of a loss of funds and post-war changes. The priest finds one boy who seems to share his spirituality. However, having his own personal problems, the boy turns on the priest and joins the other boys in their assault upon him while the school director does nothing. Also known as *This Age Without Pity* and *Cet Age Sans Pitie.*

**39. Antonio di Padova.** Trans Gobal. Italy. 1949. 103m. B&W. *Producer*: Mario Francisci *Director*: Pietro Francisci *Writer*: Raul De Sarro, Fiorenzo Fiorentini, Pietro Francisci, Giorgio Graziosi *Cast*: Aldo Fiorelli, Aldo Fabrizi, Alberto Pomerani, Silvana Pampanini.

Story of Franciscan St. Antony of Padova who preached in France and Italy of the 1200s. This story uses flashbacks and is told through the eyes of a delirious wounded Italian soldier during World War I, as the method to portray the miracles that Franciscan monk Antonio performed. Pope Gregory IX canonized him in 1232. The previous version made in 1931 is considered superior to this one. Also known as *Anthony of Padua.*

**40. Antonio di Padova, il santo dei miracoli.** Italy. 1931. B&W. *Director*: Giulio Antamoro *Cast*: Ruggero Barni, Armando Casini, Elio Cosci, Iris D'Alba, Carlo Pinzauti

The story of Saint Antony of Padova who first entered an Augustinian monastery and then later became a Franciscan friar. He traveled throughout France and Italy preaching. At one point he preaches to the fish when the fishermen refuse to listen.

**41. The Apostle.** October Films. US. 1997. 134m. C. *Producer:* Rob Carliner *Director & Writer:* Robert Duvall *Cast:* Robert Duvall, Billy Bob Thornton, June Carter Cash, Miranda Richardson, Todd Allen, Brother Paul Bagget, John Beasley, Farah Fawcett

Euliss Sonny Dewey (Robert Duvall) is a charismatic Southern Pentecostal preacher struggling with his own demons. His wife Jessie (Farah Fawcett) has a new boyfriend, won't let him see the kids, and tries using church bylaws to take away his church. He responds by hitting her lover with a baseball bat and skips town. He starts a new life in a tiny Louisiana town. He baptizes himself the Apostle E. F. and begins preaching again and helping others.

**42. The Apostle of Vengeance.** Triangle. US. 1916. B&W. *Director*: William S. Hart, Clifford Smith *Writer*: Monte M. Katterjohn *Cast*: William S. Hart, Nona Thomas, Joseph J. Dowling, Fanny Midgley, John Gilbert, Marvel Stafford, Jean Hersholt

A preacher David Hudson (William S. Hart) seeks revenge without the use of a gun.

**43. L'Appel du silence.** Best Film. France. 1936. 75m. B&W. *Producer, Director & Writer*: Léon Poirer *Cast*: Jean Yonnel, Pierre de Guingand, Jacqueline Francell, Jeanne Marie-Laurent, Pierre Juvenet, Auguste Bovério, Fernand Francell, Jean Kolb, Maurice Schutz, St. Ober, Pierre Darteuil

Biographical story of the life of Charles de Foucauld (1856–1916) (Jean Yonnel) who was a monk doing missionary work in the interior of the Hoggar sector of the Sahara. Also known as *The Call.*

**44. Appointment with Danger.** Paramount. US. 1951. 90m. B&W. *Producer*: Robert Fellows *Director*: Lewis Allen *Writer*: Richard Breen, Warren Duff *Cast*: Alan Ladd, Phyllis Calvert, Paul Stewart, Jan Sterling, Jack Webb, Stacy Harris, Harry Morgan, David Wolfe, Dan Riss, Harry Antrim, Geraldine Wall, George J. Lewis

At a hotel in Gary, Indiana one night two men murder a postal inspector. As they are preparing to dump the body they see a nun Sister Augustine (Phyllis Calvert) close by fumbling with her umbrella. To distract her one of the murderers offers to help and she notices the difficulty the other man is having keeping the dead body upright, but they tell her he is drunk. She later asks a motorcycle officer to check on the situation, but he instead chases after a speeding car. Later the body is identified and the police track the nun down to ask for her help in catching the killers. She agrees to work with no-nonsense postal inspector Al Goddard (Alan Ladd), after having initial doubts. They solve the case and Al admits that working with the Sister has made him a better human being.

**45. The Arab.** Paramount. US. 1915. B&W. *Producer & Director*: Cecil B. DeMille *Writer*: Edgar Selwyn, Cecil B. DeMille *Cast*: Edgar Selwyn, Horace B. Carpenter, Milton Brown, William Elmer, Sydney Deane, Gertrude Robinson, J. Parke Jones, Theodore Roberts, Raymond Hatton, Irvin S. Cobb

An old sheik punishes his son Jamil (Edgar Selwyn) for theft by giving his prized horse away. The horse ends up with a Christian missionary, Mary Hilbert (Gertrude Robinson). Jamil meets Mary and they fall in love. Jamil saves Mary and a group of Christians from an attempted Turkish massacre. When his father becomes too ill to rule Jamil gives up his love to be the sheik.

**46. The Arab.** Metro-Goldwyn. US. 1924. B&W. *Director & Writer*: Rex Ingram *Cast*: Ramon Novarro, Alice Terry, Gerald Robertshaw, Max Maxudian, Jean de Limur, Adelqui Migliar, Paul Vermoyal, Alexandresco, Justa Uribe, Paul Franceschi, Giuseppe De Compo

Jamil banished by his father falls in love with the daughter of a Christian missionary. He saves the lives of Christians and his father forgives him.

**47. As Ye Sow.** World Film. US. 1914. B&W. *Director*: Frank Hall Crane *Writer*: Rev. John M. Snyder *Cast*: Alice Brady, Douglas MacLean, Beverly West, John Hines, Edmund Mortimer, George Moss, Charles Dungan, Lydia Knott, W. D. Fischter

A woman marries a no-good drinking man which causes her father to die. After a child is born, he takes money out of the safe and the child and disappears. He leaves the child with his mother. The woman finds herself staying in a village at the home of her husband's brother, a minister. They fall in love and plan to marry. During the cere-mony a ship wrecks on shore and her husband shows up. She returns to her wife duties. Later during a drunken spree her husband and a companion fall to their death.

**Um Asilo muito louco** *see* **O Alienista**
**48. The Assisi Underground.** Cannon Film. US/Italy. 1985. 115m. C. *Producer*: Yoram Globus, Menahem Golan *Director & Writer*: Alexander Ramati *Cast*: Ben Cross, James Mason, Irene Papas, Maximilian Schell, Karlheinz Hackl, Riccardo Cucciolla, Angelo Infanti, Paolo Malco, Tom Felleghy, Delia Boccardo, Roberto Bisacco

Explains the role the Catholic Church and the people of Assisi played in rescuing Italian Jews from the Nazis in 1943. Padre Rufino (Ben Cross) risks his own life to save thousands of refugees from Nazi-occupied Italy.

**49. At Play in the Fields of the Lord.** UI. US. 1991. 189m. C. *Producer*: Saul Zaentz *Director*: Hector Babenco *Writer*: Hector Babenco, Jean-Claude Carriere *Cast*: Tom Berenger, John Lithgow, Daryl Hannah, Aidan Quinn, Tom Waits, Kathy Bates, Stênio Garcia, Nelson Xavier, José Dumont, Niilo Kivirinta,

Martin (Aidan Quinn) and Hazel (Kathy Bates) Quarrier are small-town fundamentalist missionaries sent to the jungles of South America to convert the natives. Martin is a more passionate man having an interest in the native's culture. In contrast, are the Hubens (John Lithgow, Daryl Hannah), also missionaries. Leslie Huben is so arrogant that he treats his wife like a child. The plot also revolves around a part-Indian pilot (Tom Berenger) who delivers goods. He is asked by officials to scare the natives off by dropping a few bombs. His relationship with a missionary's wife brings the flu and devastation to the natives.

**Atonement of Gösta Berling** *see* **Gösta Berlings Saga**
**50. Attack on a Chinese Mission—Bluejackets to the Rescue.** Williamson. UK. 1900. B&W. *Director & Writer*: James Williamson *Cast*: Florence Williamson, Mr. Lipard, Mr. James, Three Acrobats

Boxers break through gates; a missionary is killed as wife waves for help; sailors see the signal; sailors arrive and defeat Boxers.

**51. Attack on a Mission Station.** Mitchell & Kenyon. UK. 1900. B&W.

Missionary barricades house against Boxers and is saved by marines.

**52. Au revoir les infants.** Orion. France. 1988. 103m. C. *Producer, Director & Writer*: Louis Malle *Cast*: Gaspard Manesse, Raphael Fejto, Francine Racette, Stanislas Carré de Malberg, Philippe Morier-Genoud, Francois Berléand, Francois Néget, Peter Fitz, Pascal Rivet, Benoît Henriet

Film is based on the director's life during the German occupation of France in World War II. Julien Quentin (Gaspard Maness) is 12 years old and the smartest boy at a Catholic boarding school until a new student Jean Bonnet (Raphael Fejto) arrives. Jean is a Jew undercover at the school. A brave priest has agreed to hide him at the school. A kitchen employee is discharged and gets revenge by tipping the Gestapo about the hiding of Jews. An agent arrives and asks the Jewish boy to reveal himself. Julien inadvertently glances at Jean and Jean is taken away. Also known as *Goodbye, Children*.

**53. L'auberge rouge.** Cocinor. France. 1951. 98m. B&W/C. *Producer*: Simon Schiffrin *Director*: Claude Autant-Lara *Writer*: Jean Aurenche, Claude Autant-Lara, Pierre Bost, Honoré de Balzac *Cast*: Fernandel, Francoise Rosay, Marie-Claire Olivia, Julien Carette, Grégoire Aslan, Jean-Roger Caussimon, Nane Germon, Didier d'Yd, Lud Germain, Jacques Charon, A. Viala, Robert Berri

A monk (Fernandel) and a group of travelers stay in a lonely inn in the mountains. The host confesses to the monk that he serves poisoned soup to the guests in order to rob them and then he buries them in the backyard. The monk cannot violate the holy secrecy of the confession, but still tries to save the guests' lives. Previously filmed in 1923. Also known as *The Red Inn*.

**Augustine of Hippo** *see* **Agostino d'Ippona**

**54. The Avaricious Monk.** Hepworth. UK. 1912. B&W. *Director*: Warwick Buckland

When a monk refuses an old woman's request for charity, Robin Hood steals his purse and gives it to her. After complaining to King Richard, Robin Hood is sentenced to death and then is later pardoned.

**The Awful Story of the Nun of Monza** *see* **La Monaca di Monza**

**55. A Baby's Shoe.** Biograph. US. 1909. 11m. B&W. *Director & Writer*: D. W. Griffith *Cast*: Florence Lawrence, Owen Moore, Linda Arvidson, George Nichols, Anita Hendrie, Harry Solter, Arthur Johnson

A poor mother abandons her daughter on the doorstep of a family. Before she dies, due to illness, she confesses what she did to a priest. The priest adopts her son. The boy grows up and falls in love with a girl he has saved from danger. The priest discovers that she is the long-lost daughter.

**56. Back from Hell.** Kashmire Pictures. US. 1993. C. *Producer, Director & Writer*: Matt Jaissle *Cast*: Larry DuBois, Shawn Scarbrough, Don Ruem, Chris Heikka, Matt Hundley, Matt Jaissle, William Jaissle

A priest, Father Aaron (Shawn Scarbrough) helps a friend, Jack (Larry DuBois) fight the devil and regain his soul. The friend sold his soul to Satan for Hollywood stardom.

**57. Balarrasa.** Compañía Industrial Film. Spain. 1951. 90m. B&W. *Director*: José Antonio Nieves Conde *Writer*: Vicente Escrivá *Cast*: Fernando Fernán Gómez, María Rosa Slagado, Dina Sten, Luis Prendes, Eduardo Fajardo, Jesús Tordesillas, Maruch Fresno

A Spanish Civil War veteran attempts to be ordained into the priesthood. His nickname is Scapegrace (Fernando Fernán Gómez). After seven years of study and giving up his former life, the rector sends him home to be sure that he wants to give up everything for the priesthood. At home he finds his family involved in the black market and his success in turning his family towards an honest way of life wins him the priesthood. Also known as *Scapegrace*.

**58. The Bamboo Prison.** Columbia. US. 1954. 79m. B&W. *Producer*: Bryan Foy *Director*: Lewis Seiler *Writer*: Edwin Blum, Jack DeWitt *Cast*: Robert Francis, Dianne Foster, Brian Keith, Jerome Courtland, E.G. Marshall, Earle Hyman, Jack Kelly, Richard

Loo, Keye Luke, Murray Matheson, King Donovan, Dick Jones, Pepe Hern, Leo Gordon, Weaver Levy, George Keymas, Denis Martin

In this prisoner of war melodrama, which takes place during the peace treaty negotiation at Panmunjon, Korea, MSgt. John Rand (Robert Francis) appears to be a traitor, but in reality is an American intelligence officer trying to uncover war crimes before the treaty is signed. In another twist in the film, a priest Father Francis Dolan (E.G. Marshall), who is one of the prisoners, turns out to be a fraud dressed in the dead priest's clothes sent to spy on the POWs.

**59. Barbara.** Svensk Filmindustri. Denmark. 1997. 143m. C. *Producer:* Per Holst *Director:* Nils Malmros *Writer:* Jørgen-Frantz Jacobsen *Cast:* Anneke von der Lippe, Lars Simonsen, Trond Høvik, Jesper Christensen, Jens Okking, Helene Egelund, Jytte Kvinesdal, Peter Hesse Overgaard, Ove Pedersen, Peter Reichhardt

Set in 1640, a young vicar falls in love with twice-married to vicars, Barbara. Both husbands are in the grave. They marry and he finds that she is a very liberated woman. While he is away she cannot remain chaste. Filmed entirely in the Faroe Islands and spoken in Old Faroese.

**60. Barry.** Cofranex. France/Switzerland. 1949. 105m. B&W. *Producer:* Sacha Gordine *Director:* Richard Pottier *Writer:* Benne Vigny, Karl Anton *Cast:* Pierre Fresnay, Marc Valbel, Simone Valère, Gérard Landry, Pauline Carton, Yves Deniaud, François Joux, Jean Brochard

In the monastery of St. Bernard, unfortunate travelers are aided by St. Bernard dogs. Barry, the massive St. Bernard who becomes a legend, and his master Theotime (Pierre Fresnay) are the center of the story. An old friend, who also turns out to be the reason why Theotime became a priest, is saved by Barry.

**La Bataille de San Sebastian** *see* **Guns for San Sebastian**

**61. Battle Hymn.** Universal. US. 1957. 108m. C. *Producer:* Ross Hunter *Director:* Douglas Sirk *Writer:* Charles Grayson, Vincent Evans *Cast:* Rock Hudson, Martha Hyer, Dan Duryea, Don DeFore, Anna Kashfi, Jock Mahoney, Alan Hale Jr., Carl Benton Reid, Richard Loo, James Edwards, Phil Ahn

Clergyman Dean Hess (Rock Hudson) gives up his pulpit for pilot wings and goes to Korea with the Air Force. In Korea, he helps care for Korean children left orphans and homeless in the aftermath of war. He also airlifts many orphans to safety. The reason he is so driven is that during World War II, he accidentally bombed a German orphanage. The real Colonel Dean Hess served as an advisor to the film crew.

**62. Battle Stations.** Columbia. US. 1956. 81m. B&W. *Producer:* Bryan Foy *Director:* Lewis Seiler *Writer:* Crane Wilbur, Charles S. Gould *Cast:* John Lund, William Bendix, Richard Boone, Keefe Brasselle, William Leslie, John Craven, Jimmy Lydon, Claude Akins, George O'Hanlon, Eddie Foy III

Father Joe McIntyre (John Lund) is the newly-assigned chaplain aboard a Navy carrier during World War II. The story covers routine life aboard the carrier from the time it leaves a naval station after repairs until it returns for more repairs, after fighting the Japanese. The captain (Richard Boone) believes in the endless training of the crew.

**63. Battleground.** MGM. US. 1949. 118m. B&W. *Producer:* Dore Schary *Director:* William A. Wellman *Writer:* Robert Pirosh *Cast:* Van Johnson, John Hodiak, Ricardo Montalban, Leon Ames, George Murphy, Marshall Thompson, Jerome Courtland, Don Taylor, Bruce Cowling, James Whitmore, Douglas Fowley, Guy Anderson, Jim Arness, Richard Jaeckel

Film deals with the Battle of the Bulge in World War II. It is a close-up of GI Joes as weary warriors. Lutheran chaplain (Leon Ames) tries to help explain why they are fighting. He is as beat up as the rest of the soldiers, especially with frost bite. We get to know the men's backgrounds, see their suffering, and heroism.

**64. The Bay Boy.** Orion Pictures. Canada. 1984. 104m. C. *Producer:* John Kemeny, Denis Heroux *Director & Writer:* Daniel Petrie *Cast:* Liv Ullmann, Kiefer

Sutherland, Mathieu Carriere, Alan Scarfe, Peter Donat, Isabelle Mejias, Lesh Pinsent, Anne McKinnon, Peter Spence, Chris Wiggins, Thomas Peacocke

Setting is small-town life in 1937 Canada. Story centers on the adolescent rites of passage of the son Donald Campbell (Kiefer Sutherland) of hardworking, poor, devoutly Catholic parents. The family wants to see him become a priest. Donald witnesses the murder of an older Jewish couple by a policeman Tom Coldwell (Alan Scarfe). Besides being scared of the killer, he is in love with Coldwell's daughters. A visiting young priest Father Chaisson (Mathieu Carriere) makes tentative homosexual advances to Donald.

**65. The Beachcomber**. Paramount. US. 1938. 86m. B&W. *Producer & Director*: Erich Pommer *Writer*: Bartlett Cormack *Cast*: Charles Laughton, Elsa Lanchester, Tyrone Guthrie, Robert Newton, Eliot Makeham, Dolly Mollinger, D. J. Ward, J. Solomon, Rosita Garcia, Fred Groves, Mah Foo, Ley On, S. Alley

Drunken beachcomber Ginger Ted (Charles Laughton) in the South Seas is reformed by an English missionary Martha Jones (Elsa Lanchester). On the island righteous missionary Dr. Jones (Tyrone Guthrie) and his militant sister want him deported from the island. Ginger Ted "lost it" when his vicar father stopped his marriage with a barmaid. Also known as *Vessel of Wrath*. Another version starring Glynis Johns and Robert Newton was released in 1954.

**66. Becket**. Vitagraph. US. 1910. B&W. *Director*: Charles Kent *Cast*: Maurice Costello, Charles Kent, Hal Reid, William Shea

Henry II and Becket are opponents in a battle for sovereignty between church and state. Also known as *The Martyrdom of Thomas a Becket, Archbishop of Canterbury*

**67. Becket**. Stoll. UK. 1923. B&W. *Director*: George Ridgwell *Writer*: Eliot Stannard, Alfred Lord Tennyson (play) *Cast*: Sir Frank Benson, Gladys Jennings, Mary Clare, A.V. Bramble, Bertram Burleigh, Sydney Paxton, Percy Standing, William Lugg, Sydney Folker, Clive Currie, C. Hargrave Mansell, Alex G. Hunter, Arthur Burne, Bert Daley, Harry J. Worth

Archbishop forces king's mistress to enter convent, and is murdered.

**68. Becket**. Paramount. UK. 1964. 148m. C. *Producer*: Hal Wallis *Director*: Peter Glenville *Writer*: Edward Anhalt *Cast*: Richard Burton, Peter O'Toole, John Gielgud, Donald Wolfit, Martita Hunt, Pamela Brown, Siân Phillips, Paolo Stoppa, Gino Cervi, David Weston, Percy Herbert, Nial MacGinnis, Felix Aylmer, John Phillips

Based on Jean Anouilh's play about King Henry II (Peter O'Toole) and Saint Thomas Beckett (Richard Burton). Writer Anouilh sees a homosexual relationship between the King and Beckett.

**69. Bedevilled**. MGM. US. 1955. 85m. C. *Producer*: Henry Berman *Director*: Mitchell Leisen *Writer*: Jo Eisinger *Cast*: Anne Baxter, Steve Forrest, Simone Renant, Maurice Teynac, Robert Christopher, Ina de la Haye, Joseph Tomelty, Olivier Hussenot, Joean Ozenne, Jacques Hilling, Raymond Bussieres, Victor Francen

Gregory Fitzgerald (Steve Forrest) and Tony Lugacetti (Robert Christopher) are going to Paris to study for the priesthood. Gregory is having doubts about his decision and more scared then when he was a prisoner of war during the Korean War. Gregory becomes involved in a complicated murder mystery. He gives the last rites to a dying woman and later at the seminary looks forward to his religious studies.

**70. Before the Rain.** Gramercy Pictures. Republic of Macedonia/France/UK. 1994. 116m. C. *Producer:* Judy Counihan, Cédomir Kolar, Sam Taylor, Cat Villiers *Director &Writer:* Milcho Manchevski *Cast:* Katrin Cartlidge, Rade Serbedzija, Grégoire Colin, Labina Mitevska, Jay Villiers, Silvija Stojanovska, Phyllida Law, Josif Josifovski, Kiro Ristevski, Petar Mircevski

The film is told in three parts. The opening takes place at a remote Macedonian monastery where a young priest Kiril (Grégoire Colin) finds an Albanian woman hiding in his room. As the monks meet for prayer, Macedonian villagers arrive demanding to search for the woman they say is a killer. Kiril's world is turned upside down. The next part is set in London where a pregnant woman is having an affair with a Macedonian photographer. Next we see the photographer returning home after 16 years to a small half-destroyed village.

**Believe in God** *see* **Creo en Dios**

**71. The Bells of St. Mary.** JMG. UK. 1928. B&W. *Producer*: Arthur Philips *Director*: Herbert "Red" Davis *Writer*: Arrar Jackson *Cast*: Tubby Philips, Barbara Hood, Tom Gibson, Hal Martin, Eric Pavitt, Lena Halliday, Nellie Bowman

New parson converts villagers by fighting local bully.

**72. The Bells of St. Mary's.** RKO. US. 1945. 126m. B&W. *Producer & Director*: Leo McCarey *Writer*: Leo McCarey, Dudley Nichols *Cast*: Bing Crosby, Ingrid Bergman, Henry Travers, William Gargan, Ruth Donnelly, Joan Carroll, Martha Sleeper, Rhys Williams, Richard Tyler, Una O'Connor

Father Charles 'Chuck' O'Malley (Bing Crosby) of *Going My Way* heads a St. Mary's church and Catholic school that is in need of repair. The nuns drove the previous priest into a rest home. The nuns rest their hope on divine intervention while the singing priest convinces an ailing businessman to donate a new building. Sister Mary Benedict (Ingrid Bergman) believes that "We have reason to know more things are wrought by prayer than this world dreams of." Sister Benedict is a tomboy but she also feels that academics are important as well and clashes with Father O'Malley over a number of issues. When Sister Benedict is diagnosed with tuberculosis she is told that she is to be transferred to Arizona because she cannot deal effectively with children. Of course she is tormented but accepts God's will. Father O'Malley comes to his senses and tells her of her illness. The film ends with Sister Benedict praying to understand God's will as she is sent away to recover from tuberculosis. It was reported that Leo McCarey based Bergman's character on his aunt Sister Mary Benedict of the Immaculate Heart Convent in California. Sequel to *Going My Way*. A televised version of the story starring Claudette Colbert, Robert Preston, and Glenda Farrell was broadcast on CBS in 1959.

**73. Benvenuto, Reverendo!** Ente Nazionale Industrie. Italy. 1950. 89m. B&W. *Producer & Director*: Aldo Fabrizi *Writer*: Aldo Fabrizi, Piero Tellini *Cast*: Aldo Fabrizi, Lianella Carell, Giovanni Grasso, Vittorio Duse, Massimo Girotti

A thief puts on priest's clothes to escape angry villagers who had seen him steal from the church's collection box. At the next village, he is mistaken for a priest. There he is asked to settle a farmer's strike and he is given a large sum of money to rebuild the church. Also known as *Welcome Reverend!*

**74. Bernadette.** Cannon Films. Switzerland/France/Luxembourg. 1988. 119m. C. *Director*: Jean Delannoy *Writer*: Robert Arnaut, Jean Delannoy *Cast*: Sydney Penny, Jean-Marc Bory, Michèle Simonnet, Roland Lesaffre, Bernard Dhéran, François Dalou, Stéphane Garcin, Arlette Didier, Malka Ribowska, Beata Tyszkiewicz, Michael Duchaussoy

Film attempts to be entirely historical. The focus is on Bernadette's early life, visions, and the beginning of the Lourdes. It shows Bernadette's use of tobacco, which was prescribed for her asthma.

**75. Bernadette of Lourdes.** Janus Films. France/Italy. 1962. 93m. *Producer*: Georges de La Grandière *Director*: Robert Darène *Writer*: Gilbert Cesbron *Cast*: Danièle Ajoret, Nadine Alari, Robert Arnoux, Blanchette Brunoy, Jean Clarieux, Lise Delamare, Jean-Jacques Delbo, Françoise Engel, Michèle Grellier, Bernard La Jarrige, Renaud Mary

In 1858, while gathering wood in a grotto near Lourdes, Bernadette Soubirous (Danièle Ajoret) sees a lady dressed in white who speaks to her. Each time she returns to the grotto the vision appears. On one visit Bernadette follows the lady's instructions and digs at the ground until a spring bursts forth. The lady claims to be the Immaculate Conception. A sick child is cured when he drinks from the spring and word of this miracle spreads. Bernadette retreats to a convent and becomes Sister Maria Bernadette. Her health fails and she dies on April 16, 1879.

**The Best Intentions** *see* **Den Goda Viljan**

**76. The Better Man**. Famous Players Film Co. US. 1914. B&W. *Director*: William Powers *Writer*: Cyrus Townsend Brady (novel) *Cast*: William Courtleigh Jr., Arthur Hoops, Alice Claire Elliott, Robert Broderick, William R. Randall, Jack Henry, D. Hogan, Morgan Thorpe, Albert S. Howson

The film tells the story of two reverends competing for the affections of Margaret Wharton (Alice Claire Elliott). Reverend Mark Stebbing (William Courtleigh Jr.) is a rough, self-made man and Reverend Lionel Barmore (Arthur Hoops) is a polished aristocrat. Mark volunteers for a poor church and Lionel a rich one. Soon the bishop dies and Mark declares Lionel the better man. Later Mark rushes to rescue Margaret from a shed filled with explosives. She decides to marry Mark even though Lionel is now the Bishop.

**77. The Better Man**. Aywon Film Corp. US. 1922. B&W. *Director*: Wilfred Lucas *Cast*: Rex 'Snowy' Baker, Agnes Vernon, Charles Villiers, Wilfred Lucas

Reverend John Harland (Rex "Snowy" Baker) earns the disapproval of his congregation for his modern methods and he is transferred by his bishop. He vows to protect Muriel Hammond's ranch near his new parish. She sees John as a coward because he does not stand up to Red Jack Braggan. John learns that Red is a cattle thief and rescues Muriel.

**Beware My Brethren** *see* **The Fiend**

**78. Beyond Mombasa**. Columbia. UK. 1956. 90m. C. *Producer*: Tony Owen *Director*: George Marshall *Writer*: Richard English, Gene Levitt, James Eastwood *Cast*: Cornel Wilde, Donna Reed, Leo Genn, Ron Randell, Dan Calvert, Christopher Lee, Dan Jackson, Bartholomew Sketch, Clive Morton

Matt Campbell (Cornel Wilde) arrives in Kenya trying to locate a uranium mine and find out who killed his brother. Joining his safari is missionary Ralph Hoyt (Leo Glenn) and Hoyt's niece Ann Wilson (Donna Reed). The missionary in the party of uranium seekers is leader of native terrorist group and the killer of Campbell's brother.

**79. Big City**. MGM. US. 1948. 103m. B&W. *Producer*: Joe Pasternak *Director*: Norman Taurog *Writer*: Whitfield Cook, Ann Morrison *Cast*: Margaret O'Brien, Robert Preston, Danny Thomas, George Murphy, Karin Booth, Edward Arnold, Jackie 'Butch' Jenkins, Betty Garrett, Lotte Lehmann

Three bachelors in New York City's East Side, cantor David Irwin Feldman (Danny Thomas), Phillip Y. Anderson (Robert Preston) who is a Protestant minister and an Irish American Catholic police officer (George Murphy) adopt an abandoned baby girl named Midge (Margaret O'Brien). The judge rules that the first man to marry will have sole custody of the child. Everything goes well except for a few minor problems until Patrick secretly marries and the other men refuse to give up custody. The judge drops the marriage rule after talking with Midge.

**80. The Big Fisherman**. Buena Vista. US. 1959. 180m. C. *Producer*: Rowland V. Lee *Director*: Frank Borzage *Writer*: Lloyd C. Douglas (novel), Howard Estabrook, Rowland V. Lee *Cast*: Howard Keel, Susan Kohner, John Saxon, Martha Hyer, Herbert Lom, Ray Stricklyn, Marian Seldes, Alexander Scourby, Beulah Bondi, Jay Barney

Story of Simon Peter (Howard Keel), the apostle of Christ called the "fisher of men" and the Rock upon whom the Christian Church was founded. The film deals with his conversion from a fisherman to a believer. He also joins together two lovers from opposite sides of life.

**81. The Big Punch**. Fox. US. 1921. B&W. *Director*: Jack Ford *Writer*: Jack Ford, Jules G. Furthman *Cast*: Buck Jones, Barbara Bedford, George Siegmann, Jack Curtis, Jack McDonald, Al Fremont, Jennie Lee, Edgar Jones, Irene Hunt, Eleanor Gilmore

A young man (Buck Jones) about to enter a seminary is implicated in a crime while trying to help his brother. He is sent to prison. After being released, he converts his outlaw brother and marries a Salvation Army woman.

**82. The Big Tip Off**. AA. US. 1955. 79m. B&W. *Producer*: William F. Broidy *Director*: Frank McDonald *Writer*: Steve Fisher *Cast*: Richard Conte, Constance Smith, Bruce Bennett, Cathy Downs, James Millican, Dick Benedict, Sam Flint, Mary Carroll, Murray Alper, Lela Bliss, G. Pat Collins, George Sanders, Frank Hanley, Harry Guardino, Virginia Carroll, Robert Carraher, Cecil Elliott, Pete Kellett, Tony Rock, Allen Wells, Tony DeMario

A newspaper columnist Johnny Denton (Richard Conte) is taken in by a hoodlum friend Bob (Bruce Bennett), who makes his money by operating a professional fundraising organization for charity drive such as one for St. Anne's Parochial School. Sister Joan (Cathy Downs) is the nun for whom the newspaper columnist convinces his friend to run a legitimate charity event. Sister Joan discovers that Bob is a crook and that he is supplying news tips to Johnny. Sister Joan finally convinces Johnny to tell the police what he knows and to stop Bob.

**83. Biruma no tategoto.** Nikkatsu. Japan. 1956. 116m. B&W. *Producer:* Masayuki Takaki *Director:* Kon Ichikawa *Writer:* Michio Takeyama (novel), Natto Wada *Cast:* Rentaro Mikuni, Shôji Yasui, Jun Hamamura, Taketoshi Naitô, Kô Nishimura, Hiroshi Tsuchikata, Sanpei Mine, Yoshiaki Kato, Sojiro Amano, Yôji Nagahama, Eiji Nakamura, Tatsuya Mihashi, Yûnosuke Itô

A captured gentle Japanese army Private Mizushima (Shôji Yasui), who plays the Burmese harp, is sent by the British to convince one holdout company to surrender. He fails at this and is so revolted by the horror of war that he refuses to return home. He dresses as a monk and stays behind to bury all of the Japanese dead. Re-released in 1967. Also known as *The Harp of Burma* and *The Burmese Harp.*

**84. The Bishop Misbehaves.** Loew's Inc. US. 1935. 86m. B&W. *Producer:* Lawrence Weingarten *Director:* E. A. Dupont *Writer:* Leon Gordon, Frederick Jackson (play) *Cast:* Edmund Gwenn, Maureen O'Sullivan, Lucile Watson, Reginald Owen, Dudley Digges, Norman Foster, Lilian Bond, Melville Cooper, Robert Greig, Charles McNaughton, Etienne Girardot, Ivan Simpson, Lumsden Hare

American Donald Meadows (Norman Foster) helps a young woman, Hester (Maureen O'Sullivan) rob Guy Waller, a man who cheated her father out of a valuable patent. With the help of others the plot goes perfectly until the Bishop of Broadminster (Edmund Gwenn) and his sister accidentally become involved. The Bishop loves reading detective novels so this is exciting to him when they discover the jewels. During one night all is resolved when David and the Bishop convince Waller to give Hester money. Donald and Hester retire from crime and the Bishop burns his detective novels. In Britain the title was changed to *The Bishop's Misadventures* because censors didn't approve of *The Bishop Misbehaves.*

**85. The Bishop of the Ozarks.** FBO. US. 1923. B&W. *Producer:* Milford W. Howard *Director:* Finis Fox *Writer:* Milford W. Howard, Finis Fox *Cast:* Milford W. Howard, Derelys Perdue, Cecil Holland, William Kenton, R.D. MacLean, Mrs. Milo Adams, Rosa Melville, Fred Kelsey, George Reed

Ex-convict Tom Sullivan (Milford W. Howard) changes clothes with a minister Roger Chapman (who is later killed) and continues with the minister's work in the Ozark Mountains and cares for the minister's daughter Margery (Derelys Perdue). Tom earns the respect of his congregation and becomes chaplain of the state prison. The governor pardons Tom after he is exposed. In addition Margery has two suitors—good Dr. Burroughs and evil Dr. Godfrey. After a spiritual séance she chooses Dr. Burroughs.

**86. The Bishop's Bath.** Hepworth. UK. 1912. B&W. *Director & Writer:* Hay Plumb *Cast:* Hay Plumb

Fisherman steals clothes of swimming bishop who then takes those of scouts.

**87. The Bishop's Wife.** RKO. US. 1947. 105m. B&W. *Producer:* Samuel Goldwyn *Director:* Henry Koster *Writer:* Leonardo Bercovici, Robert Sherwood, Robert Nathan (novel) *Cast:* Cary Grant, Loretta Young, David Niven, Monty Woolley, James Gleason, Gladys Cooper, Elsa Lanchester, Sara Haden, Karolyn Grimes, Tito Vuolo, Regis Toomey

Episcopal bishop Henry Brougham (David Niven) is consumed with trying to have a new cathedral built. He prays for help and guidance and soon his prayers are answered with the appearance of an angel named Dudley (Cary Grant). Dudley does help him and everyone else he meets, but not necessarily the way the bishop would prefer. Dudley drives the bishop into feelings of jealousy, remorse, and rediscovery. This film has become a Christmas classic. Remade as *The Preacher's Wife.*

**88. A Bit of Oulde Ireland.** London Cinematograph Co. UK. 1910. B&W.

Betrayed Fenian sheltered by priest, escapes jail, and poses as corpse at wake.

**Bizarre, Bizarre** *see* **Drôle de drame ou L'étrange aventure de Docteur Molyneux**

**89. Black Narcissus.** GFD. UK. 1947. 100m. C. *Producer, Director & Writer:* Michael Powell, Emeric Pressburger *Cast:* Deborah Kerr, Sabu, David Farrar, Flora Robson, Esmond Knight, Jean Simmons, Kathleen Byron, Jenny Laird, Judith Furse, May Hallatt, Shaun Noble, Nancy Roberts, Eddie Whaley Jr.

Five Anglican missionary nuns open a school/hospital in a hill village in the Himalayas. Stern Sister Clodagh (Deborah Kerr) is their leader. The local prince has given them an old palace that once housed his harem. Mr. Dean (David Farrar) is their contact for the Prince. The nuns belong to the Anglican Order of St. Mary, a working order whose vows must be renewed each year. Many of the nuns have their faith shaken by the unsettling environment. They each react very differently but all sense a feeling of strangeness and questioning of their faith. The nuns learn that the Prince has been paying for people to attend their school and hospital. The Prince leaves a beautiful young girl, Kanchi (Jean Simmons) at the convent to keep her safe until marriage. Sister Clodagh persuades the Prince to allow a young Prince (Sabu) to study there. Disaster strikes when a child dies after having been given a bottle of castor oil and the young Prince and Kanchi run away together. Sister Ruth (Kathleen Byron) goes crazy and falls to her death. The film ends with the nuns packing to leave.

**90. Black Noon.** Fenady Associates/ Screen Gems (TV). US. 1971. 74m. C. *Producer & Writer:* Andrew J. Fenady *Director:* Bernard L Kowalski *Cast:* Roy Thinnes, Lyn Loring, Yvette Mimieux, Ray Milland, Henry Silva, Gloria Grahame, William Bryant, Buddy Foster, Hank Worden

In this occult Western about a circuit-riding minister, Reverend John Keyes (Roy Thinnes) and his wife are caught in a web of witchcraft.

**91. Black Robe.** Samuel Goldwyn. Canada/Australia. 1991. 101m. C. *Producer:* Robert Lantos, Sue Milliken, Stéphane Reichel *Director:* Bruce Beresford *Writer:* Brian Moore *Cast:* Lothaire Bluteau, Aden Young, Sandrine Holt, August Schellenberg, Tantoo Cardinal, Billy Two Rivers, Lawrence Bayne, Harrison Liu, Wesley Cote, Frank Wilson, Francois Tassé

Jesuit priest Father Laforgue (Lothaire Bluteau) and a companion are escorted through the wilderness of 17th century Quebec by Huron Indians. They are traveling 1,500 miles west in the dead of winter to a Huron mission. The group endures many conflicting encounters and are captured and tortured by a band of Iroquois. When the priest arrives at the mission he finds the priest dying and the natives decimated by a fever brought by whites.

**Black Widow** *see* **La Viuda negra**

**92. Body and Soul.** Micheaux Film. US. 1925. B&W. *Producer, Director & Writer:* Oscar Micheaux *Cast:* Paul Robeson, Mercedes Gilbert, Julia Theresa Russell, Lawrence Chenault, Marshall Rogers, Lillian Johnson, Madame Robinson, Chester A. Alexander, Walter Cornick

Reverend Isaiah T. Jenkins (Paul Robeson) is a minister who lies, cheats and cons. Jenkins is really an escaped convict posing as a minister. Even with his drinking and questionable associates his followers believe in him. He is true evil behind his righteous façade. A member of the congregation wants her daughter to accept him as a suitor. Jenkin's poor twin brother Syvester also wishes a relationship with the daughter but his evil twin steals her money and she flees. Reverend Jenkins kills, swindles, and takes innocence away from women. The National Board of Review disapproved of an evil clergyman so the conclusion tacks on that it was just a dream.

**93. Bom yeoreum gaeul gyeoul geurigo bom.** Cineclick Asia. South Korea/Germany. 2003. 103m. C. *Producer:* Karl Baumgartner, Seung-jae Lee *Director & Writer:* Ki-duk Kim *Cast:* Yeong-su Oh, Ki-duk Kim, Young-min Kim, Jae-kyeong Seo, Yeo-jin Ha, Jong-ho Kim, Dae-han Ji, Min Choi, Ji-a Park, Min-Young Song, Jung-young Kim

The life of a Buddhist monk from when he was taken in by the floating monastery in the spring to his days as an old man. The film is divided into four sections with a brief final segment. We see him in the spring as a boy monk learning from an old monk. In summer we see him as a young man in love. The seasons reflect innocence, love and evil, enlightenment and rebirth. Also known as *Spring, Summer, Fall, Winter...and Spring.*

**Bonaventure** *see* **Thunder on the Hill**

**94. Boniface VIII.** France. 1911. B&W. *Director:* Geralamo Lo Savio *Cast:* Attilo Fabbri, Dillo Lombardi, Bianca Lorenzoni

Story of the life of Boniface VIII. Also known as *Bonifacio VIII.*

**95. Book of Days.** Stutz Films. US. 1988. B&W/C. *Director & Writer:* Meredith Monk *Cast:* Robert Een, Andrea Goodman, Lenny Harrison, Wayne Hankin, Gregerhansen, Lucas Hoving, Karin Levitas, Rob McBrien, Meredith Monk, Toby Newman

Twentieth century workers discover behind a wall a 14th century community of Christians and Jews threatened by plague. The main character is a young Jewish girl who is a visionary.

**96. Boomerang.** TCF. US. 1947. 88m. B&W. *Producer:* Louis De Rochemont *Director:* Elia Kazan *Writer:* Richard Murphy *Cast:* Dana Andrews, Jane Wyatt, Lee J. Cobb, Cara Williams, Arthur Kennedy, Sam Levene, Taylor Holmes, Robert Keith, Ed Begley, Karl Malden, Barry Kelley, Lewis Leverett, Philip Coolidge

The dramatization of a factual incident taking place in a Connecticut town after a kindly priest is murdered while waiting at a street corner.

**97. Boxed.** Fireproof Films. UK/Ireland. 2002. 80m. C. *Producer:* Lene Bausager, Douglas Graham, Laurence Penn *Director & Writer:* Marion Comer *Cast:* Tom Murphy, Darragh Kelly, Catherine Cusack, Brendan Mackey, Jim Norton, Fanna MacLiam, Gerard Jordan, Joe Gallagher, Robert Patterson, Lloyd Hutchinson

Set in Northern Ireland, the plot concerns a band of IRA terrorists who kidnap an idealistic Catholic priest, Father Brendan (Tom Murphy), so he can hear the final confession of the man they're about to execute. He refuses putting him at odds with Father Morgan (Jim Norton) who does cooperate with the IRA. Soon Father Brendan faces the ultimate test of faith. The film takes place mostly in a single room.

**98. The Boys of St. Vincent.** Alliance. (TV). Canada. 1992. 186m. C. *Producer:* Sam Grana, Claudio Luca, Colin Neale *Director:* John N. Smith *Writer:* Sam Grana, John N. Smith, Des Walsh *Cast:* Henry Czerny, Johnny Morina, Brain Dooley, Philip Dinn, Brian Dodd, Ashley Billard, Greg Thomey, Maurice Podbrey, Sam Grana, Aidan Devine

Brother Peter Lavin (Henry Czerny) is the evil but pathetic superintendent of the orphanage named The Boys of Saint Vincent. Many of the boys suffer physical, emotional, and sexual abuse at the hands of the brothers. Lavin's reign of horror is ended by a janitor, police detective, and a Brother. Followed by *The Boys of St. Vincent: 15 Years Later.*

**99. The Boys of St. Vincent: 15 Years Later.** Canada. 1993. 90m. C. *Producer:* Colin Neale *Director:* John N. Smith *Writer:* Des Walsh, Sam Grana *Cast:* Henry Czerny, Lise Roy, David Hewlett, Timothy Webber, Kristine Demers, Mary Walsh, Sheena Larkin, Pierre Gauthier, Brian Dooley, Michael Chiasson

The boys involved in the events of *The Boys of St. Vincent* testify against the brothers. Peter Lavin (Henry Czerny) is now married with two children and proclaims his innocence. The men must revisit their horrible childhoods. Sequel to *The Boys of St. Vincent.*

**100. Boys Town.** MGM. US. 1938. 93m. B&W. *Producer*: John W. Considine Jr. *Director*: Norman Taurog *Writer*: John Meehan, Dore Schary *Cast*: Spencer Tracy, Mickey Rooney, Henry Hull, Leslie Fenton, Gene Reynolds, Edward Norris, Addison Richards, Minor Watson, Jonathan Hale, Bobs Watson, Martin Spellman, Mickey Rentschler, Frankie Thomas, Jimmy Butler, Sidney Miller, Robert Emmett Keane

Spencer Tracy won an Academy Award for his performance as the tough but socially committed priest, Father Edward J. Flanagan, who created a home for troubled boys near Omaha. Initially, Father Flanagan creates an agency for down and out adults but soon realizes that working with at-risk boys would effect more change. Father Flanagan with the help of a few supporters builds a 'city' for wayward boys called Boys Town.

The main sponsor is a pawnbroker Dave Morris (Henry Hull), who really help makes Boys Town possible. Fundraising and publicity consumes the efforts of Father Flanagan. One day, Flanagan is summoned to the prison to meet with a convict who wants the Father to help his brother Whitey (Mickey Rooney). After a few complications Boys Town is well on its way to becoming a great facility and Father Flanagan turns his dream into a reality. *Boys Town* was one of the top money-making pictures of the year and won two Academy Awards for best actor and original story. Followed by *Men of Boys Town*.

Mickey Rooney played Father Flanagan in a 1995 television movie *Brothers' Destiny* also known as *The Road Home*. The film is about two orphan brothers who travel across the country to reach Boys Town.

**101. Brancaleone alle crociate.** Titanus Distribuzione. Italy/Algeria. 1970. 116m. C. *Producer*: Mario Cecchi Gori *Director*: Mario Monicelli *Writer*: Agenore Incrocci, Furio Scarpelli *Cast:* Adolfo Celi, Sandro Dori, Vittorio Gassman, Beba Loncar, Gigi Proietti, Gianrico Tedeschi, Lino Toffolo, Paolo Villaggio, Stefania Sandrelli

A tale set in the Middle Ages. Brancaleone (Vittorio Gassman) is on quest for the Holy Grail. His followers include a dwarf, a witch, and a masochist who enjoys being kicked. The knight unbeknownst to him becomes involved in the conflict between rival Popes Clement and Gregory who seem to be more interested in their fight than the Crusades. The characters appeared in *L'Armata Brancaleone* (1966).

**102. Branningar.** Hyperion Films. Sweden.

**Father Edward J. Flanagan (Spencer Tracy) provides guidance to Whitey (Mickey Rooney), in *Boys Town* (1938).**

1935. 70m. B&W. *Director:* Ivar Johansson *Writer:* Ivar Johansson, Henning Ohlson, Per Vedin (novel) *Cast:* Ingrid Bergman, Sten Lindgren, Tore Svennberg, Bror Olsson, Carl Ström, Knut Frankman, Weyler Hildebrand, Carin Swensson, Georg Skarstedt, Henning Ohlson

Daniel Nordeman (Sten Lindgren) is forced by his father to become a priest. His first church is a parish in Haelsingland. One stormy night he seduces and rapes a young woman Karin (Ingrid Bergman) when a storm prevents her fisherman father from returning home. Distraught and upset he rushes outside and is hit by lightning. He has lost his memory and is hospitalized. Meanwhile Karin is pregnant and has a child. When David returns he meets Karin and his memory comes back. Also known as *The Surf.*

**103. Breezy Jim.** Triangle. US. 1919. B&W. *Producer:* David Horsley *Director:* Lorimer Johnston *Writer:* J. Francis Dumbar *Cast:* Crane Wilbur, Juanita Hansen

A wealthy New Yorker goes West and meets Breezy Jim (Crane Wilbur), who is traveling with an old miner. When they arrive at their destination of Arizona Jim discovers that an evangelist has stolen the old miner's gold and buried it. The evangelist convinces everyone that Jim is the thief. Jim is jailed, but escapes and saves the New Yorker from the evangelist's pursuit and reveals him to be a wanted ex-convict.

**104. Brides of Christ.** Australian Broadcasting Corporation. (TV-6 episode miniseries). UK/Australia/Ireland. 1991. C. *Producer:* Sue Masters *Director:* Ken Cameron *Writer:* John Alsop, Sue Smith *Cast:* Brenda Fricker, Sandy Gore, Josephine Byrnes, Lisa Hensley, Simon Burke, Melissa Jaffer, Philip Quast, Naomi Watts, Kym Wilson, Russell Crowe, Michael Craig

During the 1960s, six nuns and their students face personal crisis and great change within their Australian convent and girls' school as the Catholic Church enters modern times. Mother Ambrose (Sandy Gore) is the Mother Superior of Santo Spirito when the school hires a male teacher; Sister Agnes (Brenda Fricker) is a conservative

nun; Sister Paul is a devoted nun but leaves the nun for love; Sister Catherine (Josephine Byrnes) welcomes reform; Frances is a student whose parents are divorcing; and Rosemary (Kym Wilson) is a rebellious student.

**105. Bridge of San Luis Rey.** MGM. US. 1929. 60m. B&W. *Producer:* Hunt Stromberg *Director:* Charles Brabin *Writer:* Alice D.G. Miller, Ruth Cummings, Marian Ainslee, Thornton Wilder (novel) *Cast:* Lili Damita, Ernest Torrence, Raquel Torres, Don Alvarado, Henry B. Walthall, Michael Vavitch, Emily Fitzroy, Jane Winton, Gordon Thorpe, Mitchell Lewis

Setting of the film is Lima, Peru in 1714 on the feast day of Saint Louis, patron saint of an ancient bridge. While flocking into the village, the bridge gives way and five people die. Father Juniper (Henry B. Walthall) must face the fear of his questioning parishioners.

**106. The Bridge of San Luis Rey.** UA. US. 1944. 89m. B&W. *Producer:* Benedict Bogeaus *Director:* Rowland V. Lee *Writer:* Thornton Wilder (novel), Howard Estabrook *Cast:* Lynn Bari, Akim Tamiroff, Francis Lederer, Alla Nazimova, Louis Calhern, Blanche Yurka, Donald Woods, Emma Dunn, Barton Hepburn, Joan Lorring, Abner Biberman, Minerva Urecal

Young priest, Brother Juniper (Donald Woods) attempts to clarify why God chose five individuals to die in the collapse of an ancient bridge. Via flashbacks the priest learns about the lives of these five people.

**107. Brigham Young – Frontiersman.** TCF. US. 1940. 114m. B&W. *Producer:* Darryl F. Zanuck *Director:* Henry Hathaway *Writer:* Louis Bromfield, Lamar Trotti *Cast:* Tyrone Power, Linda Darnell, Dean Jagger, Brian Donlevy, Jane Darwell, John Carradine, Mary Astor, Vincent Price, Jean Rogers, Ann E. Todd

In the history of modern Mormons, Brigham Young (Dean Jagger) plays a Saint Paul role. The film tells the true story of Brigham Young, the famous Mormon leader who conquered adversity to transport his followers across the Rocky Mountains to settle in Salt Lake City.

**108. Broken Vows.** (TV). US. 1987. C. *Producer:* Bill Brademan, Edwin Self *Direc-*

*tor*: Jud Taylor *Writer*: Dorothy Salisbury Davis (novel), Ivan Davis *Cast*: Peter Crombie, Jean De Baer, Joseph Drblik, Richard Dumont, Frances Fisher, David Groh, Tommy Lee Jones, Mark Kulik, Anthony La-Guerre, Andrew Nichols, Milo O'Shea, Annette O'Toole, Madeleine Sherwood, Sylvia Short, David Strathairn, M. Emmet Walsh

A priest gives last rites to a man who has been murdered in the slums of New York. He realizes how distant he has been from the problems of the people around him. He then must make a decision of whether to go on as a priest or leave the church for a woman with whom he has fallen in love.

**Brother Andre** *see* **Le Frère André**
**109. Brother Orchid.** Warner. US. 1940. 88m. B&W. *Director*: Lloyd Bacon *Writer*: Earl Baldwin *Cast*: Edward G. Robinson, Ann Southern, Humphrey Bogart, Donald Crisp, Ralph Bellamy, Allen Jenkins, Charles D. Brown, Cecil Kellaway, Morgan Conway, Richard Lane, Paul Guilfoyle, John Ridgely

Little John Sarto (Edward G. Robinson), as head of a gang, gives up his position to Jack Buck (Humphrey Bogart) to see the world. He also leaves behind his girl Flo (Ann Southern). John goes to Europe for a year when he returns broke Jack refuses to let him be leader again. John tries to start a new gang but he is set up and shot. Wounded Little John wanders into a monastery. First, he just sees the monastery as a hideout but gradually is won over by the Brothers' sincerity. He discovers that his old gang is preventing the Brothers from selling their flowers in the city. Little John breaks up the gang and returns to the monastery with a new name of Brother Orchid.

**Brother Sun, Sister Moon** *see* **Fratello sole, sorella luna**

**Brothers' Destiny** *see* **Boys Town**
**110. Bulletproof Monk.** MGM. US. 2003. 103m. C. *Producer*: Charles Roven, Douglas Segal, Terrence Chang, John Woo *Director*: Paul Hunter *Writer*: Ethan Reiff, Cyrus Voris *Cast*: Yun-Fat Chow, Seann William Scott, Jaime King, Karel Roden, Victoria Smurfit, Marcus Jean Pirae, Mako, Roger Yuan

A Monk With No Name (Yun-Fat Chow) is the keeper of a scroll with immense supernatural powers. One of the benefits of holding the scroll is that the aging process stops. Evil forces are always trying to get the scroll for themselves. In a present day North American city, Monk With No Name tries to convince a pickpocket that he is the next rightful carrier of the scroll.

**111. Bunting's Blink.** Browne. UK. 1915. B&W. *Director*: Percy Nash *Cast*: John East

Cleric afflicted with a winking eye lands in jail.

**The Burmese Harp** *see* **Biruma no tategoto**

**112. The Butcher Boy.** Warner. Ireland/US. 1997. 106m. C. *Producer*: Redmond Morris, Stephen Woolley *Director*: Neil Jordan *Writer*: Neil Jordan, Patrick McCabe (novel) *Cast*: Eamonn Owens, Fiona Shaw, Aisling O'Sullivan, Stephen Rea, Alan Boyle, Sinéad O'Connor, Milo O'Shea

Francie (Eamonn Owens) lives with his manic depressed mother and alcoholic father. When his mother commits suicide, Francie sinks deeper into paranoia fixated on a neighbor and his best friend Joe goes off the boarding school. After his father dies he acts more bizarre and has visions of the Virgin Mary. Father Sullivan (Milo O'Shea) makes sexual advances to Francie and holds him when hearing of Francie's visions. The Father dresses Francie in a woman's bonnet like one his mother wore. Francie strikes back by brutally murdering the neighbor and is sent to a mental asylum where he meets an angel.

**113. Byakuya no yojo.** Nikkatsu. Japan. 1958. 88m. C. *Producer*: Masayuki Takaki *Director*: Eisuke Takizawa *Writer*: Toshio Yasumi, Kyoka Izumi *Cast*: Yumeji Tsukioka, Ryoji Hayama, Tadashi Kobayashi, Ichijiro Oya, Jun Hamamura, Akitake Kono

A young Buddhist monk Socho (Ryoji Hayama) seeks shelters in the home of a woman, who transforms men into animals when they succumb to her, and her dwarf husband. Socho finds himself falling in love with her even when he learns of her powers.

She falls in love with him and cannot transform him. Also known as *The Temptress* and *The Temptress and the Monk*.

**114. Bye Bye Braverman.** Warner Bothers/Seven Arts. US. 1968. 84m. C. *Producer & Director*: Sidney Lumet *Writer*: Wallace Markfield (novel), Herbert Sargent *Cast*: George Segal, Jack Warden, Joseph Wiseman, Sorrell Brooke, Jessica Walter, Phyllis Newman, Zohra Lampert, Godfrey Cambridge, Alan King, Graham Jarvis

Sub-plots unfold as a group of four friends, all about 40ish years old, attend the funeral of their friend Braverman. An ambitious rabbi (Alan King) delivers a more entertaining than spiritual eulogy.

**115. El Caballero del dragón.** Salamandra Productions. Spain. 1985. 90m. C. *Producer, Director & Writer*: Fernando Colomo *Cast*: Miguel Bosé, Harvey Keitel, Klaus Kinski, Maria Lomor, Fernando Rey, Julieta Serrano, José Vivó

Taking place in medieval Spain tells the story of an alchemist searching for the fabled philosopher's stone who battles the local bishop. A twist in the story happens when a spaceship arrives leaving an extra-terrestrial, who is mistaken for a dragon. The extra-terrestrial helps the alchemist and marries the count's daughter. The bishop and the count are sent into outer space. Also known as *The Knight of the Dragon* and *Star Knight*.

**The Call** *see* **L'Appel du silence**

**116. The Calling.** Rico Films. US. 2002. 120m. C. *Producer*: Charles Arthur Berg, Damian Chapa, Gregg Edwards *Director & Writer*: Damian Chapa *Cast*: Damian Chapa, Robert Wagner, Faye Dunaway, Brad Dourif, Jill St. John, Nils Allen Stewart, Ricco Chapa, Elyse Mirto, Pattie McLean Stephens, London King, William McNamara

Tells the story of Leroy Jenkins (Damian Chapa) who is called by mysterious forces telling him to become an evangelist. He eventually builds one of the largest ministries in America and becomes a celebrity until his death.

**117. Camila.** GEA. Argentina/Spain. 1984. 105m. C. *Producer*: Lita Stantic *Director*: Maria Luisa Bemberg *Writer*: Beda Do-

campo Feijóo, Juan Bautista Stagnaro, María Luisa Bemberg *Cast*: Susú Pecoraro, Imanol Arias, Héctor Alterio, Elena Tasisto, Mona Maris, Claudio Gallardou

The story takes place five years before Juan Manuel De Rosas was overthrown. Young Catholic socialite Camila (Susú Pecoraro) and Father Ladislao Gutierrez (Imanol Arais) meet and fall in love in Buenos Aires. Plagued by fear, bigotry and prejudice they flee Buenos Aires and travel 500 miles up the Parana River where they settle and live happily for a time. They start a school for the children of nearby settlers. They are discovered by a priest, but are given a chance to escape by the local commander. However after a night of praying they surrender the next morning. Pressed by the Church, society, political enemies their execution is ordered and they are shot. Real-life story occurred in 1847. Camila's story was filmed in 1909 Camila O'Gorman with Blanca Podesta in the title role and directed by Mario Gallo.

**118. Campane a Martello.** Lux. Italy. 1950. 109m. B&W. *Director*: Luigi Zampa *Writer*: Piero Tellini *Cast*: Gina Lollobrigida, Yvonne Sanson, Eduardo De Filippo, Carlo Giustini, Carlo Romano, Clelia Matania, Agostino Salvietti, Ernesto Almirante

Two prostitutes Agostina (Gina Lollobrigida) and Australia (Yvonne Sanson) return to their home town after the departure of American troops from Italy when the war ends. One has been sending her money home thinking that it is being saved for her but due to a misunderstanding the village priest Don Andrea (Eduardo De Filippo) has been using the money to finance an orphanage for illegitimate children. Chaos erupts when she wants her money. English version filmed at the same time and titled *Children of Chance*. Also known as *Children of Chance*.

**119. Canción de cuna.** Generalcine. Argentina. 1941. 86m. B&W. *Director*: Gregorio Martínez Sierra *Writer*: Ramón Gómez Macía, Gregorio Martínez Sierra *Cast*: Catalina Bárcena, Mariá Duval, Nuri Montsé, Pablo Vicuña, María Santos, Miguel Gómez Bao, Gloria Bayardo, Niní Gambier

Sister Joan of the Cross (Catalina

Bárcena) and other sisters at a convent educate an orphan until she is 18 years old when she falls in love with an engineer. This is Gregorio Martinez Sierra's own screen version of his play. Since 1941 there have been other screen versions of the play.

**120. El Capitán de Loyola.** Simpex. Spain. 1948. 100m. B&W. *Producer:* Guillermo Calderón, Pedro Calderón *Director:* José Díaz Morales *Writer:* José Díaz Morales, José María Permán, Francisco Bonmatí de Codecido, Ricardo Toledo, Padre Heredia *Cast:* Rafael Durán, Manuel Luna, María Rosa Jiménez, Maruchi Fresno, Asunción Sancho, Alicia Palacios, Ricardo Acero

Story of the life of St. Ignatius de Loyola (Rafael Durán), founder of the Society of Jesuits. The film sketches his life from his early career as a guard in the Spanish court, his love for the princess who is kept locked up by the mad Queen, and his career as a captain with Spain's forces. He is wounded by the French and during his convalescence he becomes consumed by the life of Christ and the saints. He travels to Montserrat where he lives as a beggar and writes his famous Spiritual Exercises. He then decides to enter the priesthood and while studying at the College of Sainte Barbe at the University of Paris he is ordered whipped with a thorn whip for misleading students. At the last moment he is saved by the rector. Also known as *Loyola, the Soldier Saint.*

**121. Captain Clegg.** UI. UK. 1962. 82m. C. *Producer:* John Temple-Smith *Director:* Peter Graham Scott *Writer:* Anthony Hinds, Russell Thorndike (novel) *Cast:* Peter Cushing, Yvonne Romain, Patrick Allen, Oliver Reed, Michael Ripper, Martin Benson, David Lodge, Daphne Anderson, Derek Francis, Milton Reid

Set in the 18th century the Government suspects smuggling going on so it sends Captain Collier (Patrick Allen) to investigate the village of Dymchurch. Collier discovers that the odd village vicar Dr. Blyss (Peter Cushing) is in fact the "dead" pirate leader. Townspeople are silent about the smuggling because the money is used to help the poor. A vengeful man murders Blyss. Also known as *Night Creatures.*

**122. Capuchin Monks, Rome.** American Mutoscope Co/Kleine Optical Co.UK. 1898. B&W.

No description available.

**123. La Carbonara.** Lion Pictures. Italy. 2000. 100m. C. *Producer:* Cecilia Colonna di Stiggliano, Massimo Ferrero *Director & Writer:* Luigi Magni *Cast:* Lucrecia Lante della Rovere, Nino Manfredi, Valerio Mastandrea, Fabrizio Gifuni, Claudio Amendola

Set in 19th century Italy, innkeeper Cecilia (Lucrecia Lante della Rovere) is known for her carbonara spaghetti and the regular raids at her inn by the police looking for subversives. When her old love Zaccaria (Fabrizion Gifuni) is taken prisoner she seeks help from a liberal cardinal (Nino Manfredi) and through a plan by a handsome young monk Fabrizio (Valerio Mastandrea) Zaccaria is saved.

**124. The Cardinal.** Pathe. UK. 1936. 70m. B&W. *Producer:* Harcourt Templeman *Director:* Sinclair Hill *Writer:* D.B. Wyndham-Lewis *Cast:* Matheson Lang, June Duprez, Eric Portman, Robert Atkins, Henrietta Watson, O.B. Clarence, Douglas Jeffries, F. B. J. Sharp, Wilfred Fletcher, A. Bromley Davenport

Cardinal de Medici (Matheson Lang) fakes madness to force a confession from the general who framed his brother for murder.

**125. The Cardinal.** Columbia. US. 1963. 175m. C. *Producer & Director:* Otto Preminger *Writer:* Robert Dozier, Henry Morton Robinson (novel) *Cast:* Tom Tyron, Romy Schneider, Carol Lynley, Burgess Meredith, John Huston, Dorothy Gish, Maggie McNamara, Bill Hayes, Cameron Prud'Homme, Cecil Kellaway, Bill Hayes, Loring Smith, John Saxon, James Hickman

Traces the career of a parish priest Stephen Fermoyle (Tom Tyron) and his rise to the upper levels of the Roman Catholic Church hierarchy. He starts his journey in 1917 as a newly ordained arrogant priest in Boston. His sister Mona runs away when her marriage to a Jewish man is stopped. Stephen is transferred to a remote parish in order to learn humility. He learns that Mona is pregnant and will die without an abortion.

He denies permission and Mona dies. Upset by this he takes some time off. He decides that the Church is his true vocation and returns. He defends the right of a black priest to have a parish in Georgia. He is then promoted to Bishop. Just before World War II he tries to persuade an Austrian Cardinal to oppose Nazis. As the war begins he is appointed Cardinal.

**Cardinal Messias** *see* **Abuna Messias**

**126. Cardinal Richelieu.** UA. US. 1935. 83m. B&W. *Producer*: Nunnally Johnson, Joseph M. Schenck *Director*: Rowland V. Lee *Writer*: Maude Howell, W. P. Lipscomb, Cameron Rogers *Cast*: George Arliss, Maureen O'Sullivan, Edward Arnold, Cesar Romero, Douglass Dumbrille, Francis Lister, Halliwell Hobbes, Violet Kemble Cooper, Katharine Alexander, Robert Harrigan

In 1630, the feudal lords of France ask the Pope for help in their battle with King Louis XIII's and Cardinal Richelieu (George Arliss) who has prepared an edict to strip them of their lands. The Cardinal's only goal is to make unified France as a great power rather then a grouping of many kingdoms.

**127. Carry On Dick.** Rank. UK. 1974. 91m. C. *Producer*: Peter Rogers *Director*: Gerald Thomas *Writer*: Talbot Rothwell, George Evans, Lawrie Wyman *Cast*: Sid James, Barbara Windsor, Kenneth Williams, Hattie Jacques, Bernard Bresslaw, Joan Sims, Kenneth Connor, Peter Butterworth, Jack Douglas, Patsy Rowlands

Highwayman, Dick Turpin (Sid James) poses as the village vicar to elude Captain Fancy (Kenneth Williams) and others. The captain turns to Reverend Flasher, a minister who lives a double life.

**128. Catholics.** Sidney Glazer Production. (TV). CBS. UK. 1973. 90m. C. *Producer*: Barry Levinson *Director*: Jack Gold *Writer*: Brian Moore *Cast*: Trevor Howard, Martin Sheen, Cyril Cusack, Michael Gambon, Andrew Keir, Godfrey Quigley, Leon Vitali, Seamus Healy, John Kelly, John Franklyn, Patrick Long

In the near future (set in 1999), the Catholic Church has joined with other western religions to dilate much of the original message of religion. A group of Irish monks have started to say mass again in Latin and the world is taking notice. A priest from Rome Father Kinsella (Martin Sheen) is sent to take them to task.

**Caution to the Wind** *see* **Con el culo al aire**

**129. Una Cavalla tutta nuda.** Hubris. Italy. 1972. C. *Director & Writer*: Franco Rossetti *Cast*: Don Backy, Barbara Bouchet, Rita Di Lernia, Renzo Montagnani, Carla Romanelli, Leopoldo Trieste

Two emissaries from a drought-stricken town venture to a neighboring bishop for assistance. Upon arriving at the bishop's palace they no longer remember why they have come and find themselves getting into more difficulty. Sentenced to death, they escape and return home where the drought has now ended.

**Cet âge sans pitie** *see* **Anthracite—cet âge est sans pitié**

**130. Change of Habit.** UI. US. 1969. 93m. C. *Producer*: Joe Connelly *Director*: William Graham *Writer*: James Lee, S. S. Schweitzer, Eric Bercovici, John Joseph, Richard Morris *Cast*: Elvis Presley, Mary Tyler Moore, Barbara McNair, Edward Asner, Leora Dana, Jane Elliot, Robert Emhardt, Regis Toomey, Doro Merande, Ruth McDevitt, Richard Carlson.

A young doctor, John Carpenter (Elvis Presley), practicing in the ghetto, is changed by three medical assistants-speech therapist Sister Michelle (Mary Tyler Moore), Sister Irene (Barbara McNair), and Sister Barabra (Jane Elliot)-who happen to be nuns. John doesn't know his assistants are nuns and falls in love with Sister Michelle. The Sisters make some advancements but also some failures in their quest to change lives. Their Superior Mother Joseph (Leora Dana) demands that they leave the project.

**131. Changing Habits.** A-PixEntertainment Inc. US. 1997. 95m. C. *Producer*: James Dodson *Director*: Lynn Roth *Writer*: Scott Davis Jones *Cast*: Moira Kelly, Taylor Negron, Teri Garr, Eileen Brennan, Shelley Duvall, Dylan Walsh, Jennifer Aspen, Marissa Ribisi, Frances Bay, Anne Haney, Jennifer Youngs, Laurel Moglen, Christopher Lloyd, Bairbre Dowling, Bob Gunton, Annabelle Gurwitch

An aspiring artist Susan Teague (Moira Kelly) with psychological problems moves into a convent where troubled women get cheap lodging in exchange for work. She finds an area in the basement where she paints a mural dealing with all of her problems. Mother Superior (Eileen Brennan) realizes its potential to save the convent. The artist starts a relationship with the owner of an art supply shop where she shop-lifts.

**132. The Chant of Jimmie Blacksmith.** New Yorker Films. Australia. 1978. 120m. C. *Producer, Director & Writer:* Fred Schepisi *Cast:* Tommy Lewis, Freddy Reynolds, Ray Barrett, Jack Thompson, Peter Carroll, Elizabeth Alexander, Angela Punch McGregor, Steve Dodds

Based on the book by Thomas Keneally recounts a true turn-of-the-century incident. Tells the story of a mulatto aborigine Jimmie Blacksmith (Tommy Lewis) who is raised by a Methodist minister. He is torn between his people and his Christian teachings. When he grows up he decides to leave the white family for native life. He gets various jobs where he is exploited and cheated. He has an affair with a white servant girl at the house where he is working and she becomes pregnant. The two marry and the child turns out to not be his, but he accepts it nevertheless. Slowly the family refuses to pay him and after an altercation with the owner there is no food and no pay. When the men of the house are absent he and his uncle go to the house with axes hidden under their coats for protection. When they are refused food it leads to an explosion of all the building tension and they slaughter the wife, two teenage daughters and a school teacher. They are tracked down and eventually killed.

**The Charterhouse of Parme** *see* **La Chartreuse de Parme**

**133. La Chartreuse de Parme.** Superfilm Distributing Corp. France/Italy. 1948. 170m. B&W. *Producer:* André Paulvé *Director:* Christian-Jaque *Writer:* Stendhal (novel), Christian-Jaque, Pierre Jarry, Pierre Véry *Cast:* Gérard Philipe, María Casares, Louis

Salou, Lucien Coëdel, Enrico Glori, Renée Faure, Louis Seigner, Attilio Dottesio, Tullio Carminati, Aldo Silvani, Maria Michi, Claudio Gora, Evelina Paoli, Rudolf H. Neuhaus, Dina Romano

The film depicts Italian court life in the early 1800s. Tells the story a young archbishop Fabrice del Dongo (Gérard Philipe) who falls in love and wants to break his vows to the church. His aunt the Countess of Sanseverina (María Casares) is in love with him and will stop at nothing to further his career. Also known as *The Charterhouse of Parme*.

**134. The Cheater Reformed.** Fox Film Corp. US. 1921. B&W. *Producer:* William Fox *Director:* Scott Dunlap *Writer:* Jules Furthman, Scott Dunlap *Cast:* William Russell, Seena Owen, John Brammall, Sam De Grasse, Ruth King

Reverend Luther McCall (William Russell), accused of once being an embezzler, meets up with his twin brother Lefty, the real embezzler who is evading the law. The Reverend is killed in a train wreck and the twin assumes his identity. In carrying out his ministerial work, he brings about his own conversion and the minister's wife comes to love him.

**135. Les Chiffonniers d'Emmaüs.** Cocinor. France. 1955. 100m. B&W. *Producer:* Ignace Morgenstern *Director:* Robert Darène *Writer:* Boris Simon (novel), René Barjavel, Robert Darène *Cast:* André Reybaz, Gaby Morlay, Bernard La Jarrige, Pierre Mondy, Yves Deniaud, Pierre Trabaud, Madeleine Robinson

The film is based on the career of the religious leader Abbe Pierre (André Reybaz) who works to save homeless people during the cold European winter of 1953. The film concerns the Abbe's efforts to set up a center for the homeless and derelict in France. Also known as *The Ragpickers of Emmaus*.

**136. Child of Darkness, Child of Light.** USA. (TV). US. 1991. 85m. B&W/C. *Producer:* Paul Tucker *Director:* Marina Sargenti *Writer:* James Patterson (novel), Brian Taggert *Cast:* Anthony John Denison, Brad Davis, Paxton Whitehead, Claudette Nevins, Sydney Penny, Kristin Dattilo, Alan Oppenheimer, Eric Christmas, Richard McKenzie, Viveca Lindfors

A Catholic priest, Father O'Carroll (Anthony John Denison) investigates the reports of two immaculate conceptions. One is the child of God and the other is the child of the Devil. He must discover which is which before it is too late.

**137. A Child of God.** Mutual Film Corp. US. 1915. B&W. *Director*: John G. Adolfi *Writer*: Cyrus Townsend Brady *Cast*: Sam de Grasse, Francelia Billington, Richard Cummings

Francis Angel (Francelia Billington), schoolteacher in a western town and Jim MacPherson (Sam de Grasse), a wealthy rancher are attracted to each other. Initially, she refuses his proposal, but develops new respect for him after he saves her from unwanted advances. Her father asks her to come back east where he wants her to marry her former sweetheart Chet. She agrees to marry Chet when she learns that her penniless sister and baby are coming east. The train carrying Jane crashes near Jim's ranch and Jim consents to be the baby's godfather. Parson Perrin (Richard Cummings) baptizes the baby and agrees to bring the baby east. Jim influenced by an evangelist becomes a child of God. He travels east and meets Francis on her wedding day. Chet and Jim fight and Francis accepts Jim's proposal.

**138. Children of Chance.** BL. UK. 1949. 99m. B&W. *Producer*: Ludovico Toeplitz, John Sutro *Director*: Luigi Zampa *Writer*: Piero Tellini, Michael Medwin *Cast*: Patricia Medina, Manning Whiley, Yvonne Mitchell, Barbara Everest, Eliot Makeham, George Woodbridge, Frank Tickle, Eric Pohlmann, Edward Lexy, Carlo Giustini

Two Italian prostitutes return to their village when American troops return home after the war. Unfortunately the village priest has spent one girl's earnings on a home for illegal children. This film was shot at the same time as the Italian version *Campane a Martello*.

**Children of Chance** *see* **Campane a Martello**

**139. Children of the Ghetto.** Fox. US. 1915. B&W. *Producer*: William Fox *Director*: Frank Powell *Writer*: Edward José *Cast*: Wilton Lackaye, Ruby Hoffman, Ethel Kauffman, Frank Andrews, Luis Alberni, Irene Boyle, Victor Benoit, David Bruce, William Hatch, J. Albert Hall

Life in the Jewish section of New York City. Reb Shemuel (Wilton Lackaye), an old rabbi is seen performing some Jewish ceremonies. The story Children of the Ghetto is read by actor Wilton Lackaye. He also portrays Reb Shemuel. In one story Reb Shemuel's son's actions cause his father to shun him. When his son is dying Shemuel hears his son beg for forgiveness before he dies. His beloved daughter Hannah marries David in a civil ceremony and becomes estranged from her father. Years later Shemuel conducts a Passover Seder with Hannah, now widowed, and her two children present.

**140. Chocolat.** Miramax Films. US/UK. 2000. 121m. C. *Producer*: David Brown, Kit Golden, Leslie Holleran *Director*: Lasse Hallstrom *Writer*: Joanne Harris (novel), Robert Nelson Jacobs *Cast*: Juliette Binoche, Lena Olin, Johnny Depp, Judi Dench, Alfred Molina, Peter Stormare, Carrie-Anne Moss, Leslie Caron, John Wood, Hugh O'Conor, Victoire Thivisol, Sally the dog

In this sweet fable, a single mother Vianne (Juliette Binoche) and her daughter (Victoire Thivisol) blow into a small isolated French village and open a chocolate shop. In this film, chocolate is a delicious treat and a metaphor for earthly temptation. Vianne dispenses chocolates as therapy, finding the right candy cure for each person. She disturbs the self-righteous Comte de Reynaud (Alfred Molina) with this edible decadence. He uses his power on the young priest (Hugh O'Conor) to make his crusade against Vianne a religious matter. The wonderful looking chocolates co-star in this film. In the novel the priest character is the enemy of Vianne.

**141. The Chocolate War.** Management Company Entertainment Group. US. 1988. 100m. C. *Producer*: Jonathan Krane *Director*: Keith Gordon *Writer*: Keith Gordon, Robert Cormier (novel) *Cast*: John Glover, Ilan Mitchell-Smith, Wallace Langham, Doug Hutchison, Corey Gunnestad, Brent

David Fraser, Robert Davenport, Jenny Wright, Bud Cort, Adam Baldwin

Jerry Renault (Ilan Mitchell-Smith) is the new boy at a strict Catholic High School. He must endure the sadistic headmaster Brother Leon (John Glover) and the secret society named 'The Vigils.' A chocolate sale for the school's annual fundraising event becomes the focus of the film. Brother Leon is so obsessed with selling more chocolate bars than any other school that he asks 'The Vigils' to strong-arm the sales.

**142. The Chosen.** Analysis Film Releasing Corporation. US. 1981. 108m. C. *Producer*: Edie Landau, Ely A. Landau *Director*: Jeremy Paul Kagan *Writer*: Chaim Potok (novel), Edwin Gordon *Cast*: Maximilian Schell, Rod Steiger, Robby Benson, Barry Miller, Hildy Brooks, Kaethe Fine, Ron Rifkin, Robert John Burke, Lonny Price, Evan Handler, Douglas Warhit, Jeff Marcus

Two Jewish teenagers in 1940's New York become friends after being playground rivals. During a baseball game, Reuven Malter (Barry Miller), a modern Jew, is accidentally hurt by Danny Saunders (Robby Benson) a Hassidic Jew. Danny tries to apologize but it takes time before they feel comfortable with each other. Danny has been raised in a stern rigid environment while Reuven is more worldly and comfortable in the world. Danny's legendary father is a charismatic orthodox Rabbi Reb Sanders (Rod Steiger) must approve of Danny's non-sect friends. The film deals with the boys' friendship and Danny's relationship with his father. The Rabbi has chosen to distance himself emotionally from his son in order to build his character. Danny is fascinated with the world and has a thirst for learning while Reuven is drawn to Danny's world. He is expected to follow in his father's footsteps. Reb allows Danny to enter college with Reuven. With World War II just over, the matter of Israel comes between the families. Reuven's father Professor David Malter and the Rabbi have totally opposite views of Israel. Danny is ordered not to see Reuven. Their friendship is threatened and Danny and his father battle about his future.

**143. Chouchou.** Warner. France. 2003. 105m. C. *Producer*: Christian Fechner *Director*: Merzak Allouache *Writer*: Merzak Allouache, Gad Elmaleh *Cast*: Gad Elmaleh, Alain Chabat, Claude Brasseur, Roschdy Zem, Catherine Frot, Julien Courbey, Arié Elmaleh, Yacine Mesbah, Micheline Presle, Jacques Sereys

Chouchou (Gad Elmaleh) has just arrived in Paris from North Africa and is taken in by a kindly priest Father Leon (Claude Brasseur) who gets him a job with a female psychoanalyst. Father Leon's assistant is Brother Jean (Roschdy Zem) a reformed drug addict and thief, troubled by visions. He really wants to be a woman, so he begins dressing and acting like a woman. After antagonizing one of the doctor's patients he narrowly escapes violence, ends up on a Metro, and gets off in the middle of the red light district where he bumps into his cousin. The two go to a bar where there is a customer named Stanislas who is attracted to Chouchou. Chouchou gets a job as a waitress at the club and Stanislas approaches her, takes her out for dinner and wants to introduce her to his parents.

**144. The Christian.** Vitagraph-Liebler. US. 1914. 96m. B&W. *Producer*: J. Stuart Blackton *Director*: Frederick A. Thomson, Frederick Stanhope *Writer*: Eugene Mullin *Cast*: Earle Williams, Edith Storey, Harry S. Northup, James Morrison, Jane Fearnley, Donald Hall, Edward Kimball, Charles Kent, J. W. Sambrook

When his love Glory Quayle (Edith Storey) becomes an actress on the London stage, John Storm (Earle Williams) enters a monastery. John realizes that this doesn't help him forget Glory so he starts a settlement house in the slums of London. He tries to convince Lord Robert Ure (Harry S. Northup) to marry a poor girl he got pregnant. Instead irate Lord Ure marries another woman. When John exposes the lord, the lord gets revenge by spreading a rumor that John has predicted that the world will end a certain day. Riots break out and John's life is threatened. Glory convinces the crowds of the truth and is reunited with John. Remade in 1915 and in 1923 starring Richard Dix and Mae Busch.

**145. The Christian.** Jury. UK. 1915. B&W. *Director:* George Loane Tucker *Writer:* Hall Caine *Cast:* Derwent Hall Caine, Elizabeth Risdon, Gerald Ames, Mary Dibley, Charles Rock, Bert Wynne, Philip Hewland, Christine Rayner, George Bellamy, Douglas Munro, Frank Stanmore, Gwynne Herbert

Lord's mob kills cleric who sought to save soul of beloved actress.

**146. Christmas Lilies of the Field.** NBC. (TV). US. 1979. 100m. C. *Producer& Director:* Ralph Nelson *Writer:* John McGreevey, Ralph Nelson *Cast:* Billy Dee Williams, Maria Schell, Fay Hauser, Lisa Mann, Hanna Hertelendy, Judith Piquet, Donna Johnston, Bob Hastings, Jean Jenkins, Fred Hart, Sam Di Bello

Homer Smith (Billy Dee Williams) returns to the chapel, which years before he built. The nuns' selfless behaviors motivate Homer to build an orphanage and school for the children. Mother Maria (Maria Schell) motivates him with her faith.

**147. The Christmas Tree.** ABC. (TV). US. 1996. 93m. C. *Producer:* Steven R. McGlothen *Director:* Sally Field *Writer:* Julie Salamon (book), Jill Weber (book), Janet Brownell, Sally Field *Cast:* Julie Harris, Trini Alvarado, Andrew McCarthy, Suzi Hofrichter

A simple tale of a nun, Sister Anthony (Julie Harris), who grew up in a convent with Tree. She has a special friendship with Tree, who at the end of its life becomes the Christmas tree at Rockefeller Center. Richard, the man responsible for choosing the tree every year for Rockefeller Center befriends Sister Anthony. We see both learn to allow love to enter their hearts.

**148. Church and Stage.** Hepworth. UK. 1912. B&W. *Director:* Warwick Buckland *Cast:* Alec Worcester, Gladys Silvani, Marie de Solla

Cleric's wife leaves him to become a dancer and they reunite at church fair.

**149. Cielo sulla palude.** Artisti Associati. Italy. 1949. 111m. B&W. *Producer:* Carlo José Bassoli, Renato Bassoli *Director:* Augusto Genina *Writer:* Suso Cecchi d'Amico, Augusto Genina, Fausto Tozzi *Cast:* Rubi D'Alma, Michele Malaspina, Domenico Viglione Borghese, Inés Orsini, Assunta Radico, Giovanni Martella, Mauro Matteucci, Francesco Tomalillo, María Luisa Landin, Ida Paoloni, Federico Meloni, Jole Savoretti, Giovanni Sestili, Vincenzo Solfiotti

Maria Goretti is a girl who rejects the sexual advances of Alessandro, who shared a home with her family after the death of her father. Because of her refusal to give in to the boy's desires he stabs her to death. Maria was made a saint by the Catholic Church in 1948. In the film, we see the young Maria's joy in life despite a harsh existence and the death of her father. She never loses her spirit of love and forgiveness. Also known as *Heaven Over the Marshes.*

**Cinema Different 3** *see* **Marie et le cure**

**150. Citizen Saint.** Clyde Elliott Attractions. US. 1947. 65m. B&W. *Producer:* Clyde Elliott *Director:* Harold Young *Writer:* Harold Orlob *Cast:* E.V. Dailey, Carla Dare, Jed Prouty, Loraine MacMartin, Walter Butterworth, Robin Morgan, Maurice Cavell, William Harrigan, June Harrison, Lucille Fenton

Semi-documentary story of Mother Cabrini, heralded as the first American to attain sainthood. During the late 1850s Francesca "Cecchina" (Carla Dare) joins a Catholic religious order and is initiated as a novice. When she reaches adulthood she forms the Order of the Missionary Sisters of the Sacred Heart. In America, now known as Mother Cabrini, she is head of the New York State orphanage in New York City. She founded sixty-seven hospitals, numerous orphanages, clinics and schools in the United States and Latin America. During her life she performed three miracles. At the age of 67 she dies of malaria and in 1946 she is canonized in Vatican City.

**Clandestine** *see* **Les Clandestins**

**151. Les Clandestins.** Ciné Sélection. France. 1946. 76m. B&W. *Producer:* Paul Pavaux *Director:*André Chotin *Writer:* André Chotin, Pierre Lestringuez *Cast:* Suzy Carrier, Georges Rollin, Constant Rémy, Samson Fainsilber, André Reybaz, Guillaume de Sax, Howard Vernon

Story of the French underground and Nazi brutality. Wounded resistance leader Laurent (Georges Rollin) attempts to escape the Nazis after a raid on his underground operation. Jewish Dr. Netter (Samson Fainsilber) is caught and tortured for trying to assisting the resistance. A priest (Constant Rémy) tries to help the hostages. Also known as *Clandestine*.

**152. Clérambard**. Cinema V. France. 1969. 94m. C. *Producer:* Alain Poiré, Yves Robert *Director:* Yves Robert *Writer:* Jean-Loup Dabadia, Yves Robert, Marcal Ayme (play) *Cast:* Philippe Noiret, Dany Carrel, Lise Delamare, Gérard Lartiga, Claude Piéplu, Martine Sarcey

An arrogant nobleman, Clerambard (Philippe Noiret), kills cats and dogs and abuses his family by making them work long hours at hand looms. His habits change when one day he is fooled by a farmer into thinking he has seen Saint Francis. But the town priest's recently strangled dog is seen alive and at the end of the film Saint Francis is seen putting a bridle on his horse as he prepares to travel. Everyone in town sees the Saint except for the priest who has forgotten his glasses.

**153. The Cloister and the Hearth.** Hepworth. UK. 1913. B&W. *Director:* Hay Plumb *Cast:* Alec Worcester, Alma Taylor, Hay Plumb, Jamie Darling, Ruby Belasco, Harry Buss

15th century artist turns priest and saves heiress from usurping burgomaster.

**154. The Cloister's Touch.** Biograph. US. 1910. B&W. *Director:* D.W. Griffith *Cast:* Linda Arvidson, Verner Clarges, Arthur Johnson, Marion Leonard, Frank Powell, Mack Sennett, H. B. Walthall, E. Haldeman, Owen Moore

A duke claims the wife of one of his serfs as his bedmate. Being grief-stricken over the loss of her husband and child, she dies. When she is taken away, her husband takes their child and joins a monastery. The duke is so consumed with guilt that he ends up at the same monastery and they meet. The duke promises to raise the child as his own.

**155. Coals of Fire.** Famous Players-Lasky Corp/Paramount. US. 1918. B&W. *Producer:* Thomas H. Ince *Director:* Victor L. Schertzinger *Writer:* R. Cecil Smith *Cast:* Enid Bennett, Fred Niblo, Melbourne MacDowell

The local minister, Reverend Charles Alden (Fred Niblo), is attracted to Nell Bradley (Enid Bennett), whose father owns a bar and who is scorned by the townspeople. One day a salesman buys drinks for a girl with the intention of attacking her. Nell convinces the bartender to rescue the girl. When the minister enters the bar he thinks that Nell is responsible for the girl's condition. He later discovers the truth.

**156. Cold Turkey.** UA. US. 1971. 99m. C. *Producer & Director:* Norman Lear *Writer:* Norman Lear, William Price Fox Jr. *Cast:* Dick Van Dyke, Pippa Scott, Tom Poston, Edward Everett Horton, Bob Elliott, Ray Goulding, Vincent Gardenia, Barnard Hughes, Graham Jarvis, Jean Stapleton, Barbara Cason, Paul Benedict, Bob Newhart

The Valiant Tobacco Company is offering $25,000,000 to any town that can stop smoking for thirty days. Reverend Clayton Brooks (Dick Van Dyke) of the Eagle Rock Community Church in Iowa rallies his town to win that challenge. On the other hand the company's representative Merwin Wren (Bob Newhart) has no intention of paying and will do anything to sabotage the town. The town is frantic in their efforts to stop everyone from smoking.

**157. Come to the Stable.** TCF. US. 1949. 94m. B&W. *Producer:* Samuel G. Engel *Director:* Henry Koster *Writer:* Oscar Millard, Sally Benson *Cast:* Loretta Young, Celeste Holm, Hugh Marlowe, Elsa Lanchester, Thomas Gomez, Dorothy Patrick, Basil Ruysdael, Dooley Wilson, Regis Toomey, Mike Mazurki, Henri Letondal, Walter Baldwin

Two French nuns, Sister Margaret (Loretta Young) and Sister Scholastica (Celeste Holm), travel to the small New England town of Bethlehem to build a hospital for children. Sister Scholastica, a former tennis champion must pick up a racquet to help win a bet, unfortunately she loses. They face many trials in their mission to build the hospital—a pledge made during World War II when Americans gave their lives to save a children's hospital.

**158. Il Compagno Don Camillo.** Cineriz. Italy/France/Germany. 1965. 110m. B&W. *Director:* Luigi Comencini *Writer:* Giovanni Guareschi (novel), Leonardo Benvenuti, Piero de Bernardi *Cast:* Fernandel, Gino Cervi, Leda Gloria, Graziella Granata, Gianni Garko, Marco Tulli, Silla Bettini

This time out Don Camillo (Fernandel), the battling, red belt priest joins forces with his antagonist, Commie Mayor Peppone (Gino Cervi) on an adventure to Russia disguised as a member of the town's Communist council. Also known as *Don Camillo in Moscow.*

**159. Con el culo al aire.** Globe Film. Spain. 1981. 97m. C. *Producer:* Juan Andreu *Director & Writer:* Carles Mira *Cast:* Ovidi Montllor, Eva León, María José Arenos, Juan Monleon, Juan Carlos Senante, Antonio Morant, Rosita Amores, Jorge Segura

Tells the story of Juan, a young man living in a Spanish village. After spending the night with Esperanza, a singer who fronts a group of blind musicians, he is found by his family silent and inert. He is placed in an asylum run by a tyrannical nun (María José Arenos). When Esperanza appears to him in a vision, he causes a riot among the inmates. Seems to be inspired by *One Flew Over the Cuckoo's Nest.* Also known as *Caution to the Wind.*

**160. Confession.** AA UK. 1955. 90m. B&W. *Producer:* Alec Snowden *Director & Writer:* Ken Hughes *Cast:* Sydney Chaplin, Audrey Dalton, John Bentley, Peter Hammond, John Welsh, Jefferson Clifford, Pat McGrath, Robert Raglan, Patrick Allan

American thief Mike (Sydney Chaplin) tries to kill a Catholic priest who may know his secret. The priest has heard the confession of the devout Catholic partner of Mike. Mike kills the man and now goes after the priest, when the police set a trap in the church. Also known as *The Deadliest Sin.*

**161. Le Confessional.** Artificial Eye. Canada/UK/France. 1995. 100m. B&W. *Producer:* Philippe Carcassonne *Director & Writer:* Robert Lepage *Cast* Lothaire Bluteau, Patrick Goyette, Jean-Louis Millette, Kristin Scott Thomas, Ron Burrage, Richard Fréchette, Francois Papineau, Marie Gignac, Normand Daneau, Anne-Marie Cadieux, Suzanne Clément, Lynda Lepage-Beaulieu, Pascal Rollin, Paul Hébert

Takes place in 1952 and 1989. In 1952, a 16 year old pregnant girl who works in a church confesses her guilt to a young priest. In 1989, Pierre Lamontagne (Lothaire Bluteau) returns to Quebec and meets up with his adopted brother, Marc (Patrick Goyette) who has begun to question his identity. The brothers embark on a quest to find their roots which lead back to 1952 and the confession of the 16 year old girl. Film plot coincides with the making of *I Confess.* Also known as *The Confessionnal.*

**162. The Confessional.** Columbia/Warner. UK. 1976. 104m. C. *Producer & Director:* Pete Walker *Writer:* David McGillivray, Pete Walker *Cast:* Anthony Sharp, Susan Penhaligon, Stephanie Beacham, Norman Eshley, Sheila Keith, Hilda Barry, Stewart Bevan, Julia McCarthy, Jon Yule, Mervyn Johns

After taping his female parishioners' confessions, evil Father Xavier Meldrum (Anthony Sharp) then uses the tapes to blackmail them into doing his bidding, etc. When other members of the parish discover his secret he murders them using rosaries and poisoned wafers. His housekeeper grows suspicious of the many deaths. Also known as *House of Mortal Sin.*

**Conflagration** *see* **Enjo**

**163. Il Consiglio d'Egitto.** Keyfilms Roma. 2002. 138m. C. *Producer:* André Farwagi, Amedeo Leticia, Mariella Li Sacchi *Director:* Emidio Greco *Writer:* Emidio Greco, Lorenzo Greco, Leonardo Sciascia (novel) *Cast:* Silvio Orlando, Tommaso Ragno, Renato Carpentieri, Marine Delterme, Giancarlo Giannini, Yann Collette, Antonio Catania, Leopold Trieste, Enzo Vetrano

Costume picture set in 18th century Sicily. In 1782, the Moroccan ambassador to the court of Naples is shipwrecked off Sicilian coast. A priest Don Giuseppe Vella (Silvio Orlando) is asked to interpret and show the ambassador the sights. Don Giuseppe doesn't fully understand Arabic so he makes up what he needs. Don Giuseppe wishes to continue living well even after the ambassador leaves. His chance comes when his patron Monsignor Airoldi (Renato Carpentieri) asks him to examine an old Arabic manuscript. The text isn't anything of real value but Don Giuseppe claims that it is a lost book detailing the history of Sicily and will spend the time necessary to translate it into Italian. Don Giuseppe pretends that the text reveals names of particular families and how they obtain their money. The aristocrats bribe him to get their family names removed from the text. Lawyer Francesco Paola Di Blasi (Tommaso Ragno) plots to turn the country into a republic not unlike what is going on in France. Also known as *The Council of Egypt*.

**164. Conspiracy of Hearts.** Paramount. UK. 1960. 113m. B&W. *Producer:* Betty E. Box *Director:* Ralph Thomas *Writer:* Robert Presnell Jr *Cast:* Lilli Palmer, Sylvia Syms, Yvonne Mitchell, Ronald Lewis, Albert Lieven, Peter Arne, Nora Swinburne, Michael Goodliffe, Megs Jenkins, David Kossoff, Jenny Laird, George Coulouris, Phyllis Neilson-Terry, Rebecca Dignam

In wartime Italy, nuns, especially Mother Katharine (Lilli Palmer), help Jewish children escape from concentration camp. The Italian army officer turns a blind eye to the nun's operation. Unfortunately, when Nazi Colonel Horsten (Albert Lieven) takes over the camp the nuns must face danger to save the children.

**165. Conspiracy of Silence.** Little Wing Films. UK. 2003. 90m. C. *Producer:* Davina Stanley *Director & Writer:* John Deery *Cast:* Jonathan Forbes, Hugh Bonneville, Brenda Fricker, Sean McGinley, Hugh Quarshie, Jason Barry, Olivia Caffrey, Patrick Casey, Catherine Cusack, John Lynch, Jim Norton, James Ellis, Catherine Walker, Patrick Casey, Fintan McKeown

Two incidents within the Irish Catholic Church create chaos and cover ups; the suicide of a parish priest Father Frank Sweeney (Patrick Casey) and the expulsion of a young seminary student Daniel McLaughlin (Jonathan Forbes) from a nearby seminary. Local reporter Dave Foley (Jason Barry) learns that Father Sweeney was HIV positive. Bribery and mysterious threats compound the story.

**166. Constantino il grande.** Embassy Pictures. Italy/Yugoslavia. 1962. 120m. C. *Producer:* Ferdinand Felicioni *Director:* Lionelle De Felice *Writer:* Ennio De Concini, Lionelle De Felice, Diego Fabbri, Ernesto Guida, Fulvio Palmieri, Franco Rossetti, Guglielmo Santangelo *Cast:* Cornel Wilde, Belinda Lee, Massimo Serato, Christine Kaufmann, Elisa Cegani, Tino Carraro, Franco Fantasia

Constantine (Cornel Wilde) made Christianity legal in the Roman Empire. He is regarded as a saint in the Orthodox Church even with his many personal faults. Also known as *Constantine the Great*.

**167. Contestazione generale.** Columbia. Italy. 1970. 125m. C. *Producer:* Mario Cecchi Gori *Director:* Luigi Zampa *Writer:* Silvano Ambrogi, Leonardo Benvenuto, Piero De Bernardi, Alberto Silvestri, Rodolfo Sonego, Franco Verucci, Luigi Zampa *Cast:* Franco Abbiana, Sandro Dori, Vittorio Duse, Enzo Garinei, Paola Gassman, Vittorio Gassman, Enrico Maria, Alberto Sordi, Sergio Tofano, Nino Manfredi, Michel Simon, Marina Vlady, Enrico Maria Salerno

Film consists of three episodes in part *Il Prete*, a downtrodden priest (Alberto Sordi) tries to clear his name when is accused of having an affair with a cashier. His life turns around and he bravely confronts the archbishop and starts making demands. Also known as *Let's Have a Riot*.

**168. The Convert.** Artistic. UK. 1923. B&W. *Producer:* George Redman *Director:* H. Manning Haynes *Writer:* Lydia Hayward *Cast:* Johnny Butt, Bob Vallis, Cynthia Murtagh, Walter Wichelow

Reformed bully slips until preacher fights for fiancée.

**169. The Converts.** Biograph Co. US. 16m. 1910. B&W. *Director:* D. W. Griffith *Cast:* Linda Arvidson, H.B. Walthall, Charles H. West, Mack Sennett, Arthur Johnson, Dell Henderson, George O. Nicholls

An argument about religion leads a man to dress as a priest and preach on the street. Unbeknownst to him, a woman hears his message and repents. He is tormented by his own sermon and discovers the woman. He joins her social mission and begins reaching out to the poor.

**170. Cotton Comes to Harlem.** UA. US. 1970. 97m. C. *Producer*: Samuel Goldwyn, Jr. *Director*: Ossie Davis *Writer*: Chester Himes (novel), Ossie Davis, Arnold Perl *Cast*: Godfrey Cambridge, Raymond St. Jacques, Calvin Lockhart, Judy Pace, Redd Foxx, Emily Yancy, John Anderson, Lou Jacobi, Eugene Roche, J. D. Cannon

Two black cops, Gravedigger Jones (Godfrey Cambridge) and Coffin Ed Johnson (Raymond St. Jacques) are annoyed at the success of the Reverend Deke O'Malley (Calvin Lockhart). The Reverend is selling trips back to Africa to the poor on an installment plan. His truck is hijacked and a bale of cotton stuffed with money is lost in the scam. The ensuing all-out search of Harlem for the bale of cotton involves everyone.

**The Council of Egypt** *see* **Il Consiglio d'Egitto**

**171. Count Three and Pray.** Columbia. US. 1955. 102m. C. *Producer*: Ted Richmond *Director*: George Sherman *Writer*: Herb Meadow *Cast*: Van Heflin, Joanne Woodward, Phil Carey, Raymond Burr, Allison Hayes, Myron Healey, Nancy Kulp, James Griffith, Richard Webb, Katherine Givney, Robert Burton

The post-Civil War South is the setting of this tale of preacher Luke Frago (Van Heflin) who returns home to rebuild the town's church. During his youth he was a hell-raiser who fought for the North but returns a reformed man willing to do whatever it takes to rebuild the church, even against town opposition.

**172. The Courage to Love.** CBS. (TV). Canada/US. 2000. *Producer*: Jean Desormeaux, Stéphane Reichel, Ron Ziskin *Director*: Kari Skogland *Writer*: Heather Hale, Toni Ann Johnson *Cast*: Vanessa L. Williams, Gil Bellows, Karen Williams, Lisa Bronwyn Moore, David LaHaye, Cynda Williams, Stacy Keach, Eddie Bo Smith Jr., Graeme Somerville, Diahann Carroll

Set in 19th century New Orleans this movie tells the heroic story of Henriette Delille (Vanessa L. Williams). Henriette Delille founded the Sisters of the Holy Family.

**173. Courageous Mr. Penn.** Hoffberg Productions. UK. 1943. 78m. B&W. *Producer*: Richard Vernon *Director*: Lance Comfort *Writer*: Anatole de Grunwald *Cast*: Clifford Evans, Deborah Kerr, Dennis Arundell, Aubrey Mallalieu, D.J. Williams, O.B. Clarence, James Harcourt, Charles Carson, Henry Oscar, Max Adrian

Story of William Penn (Clifford Evans) who spearheaded the Quaker movement in England. Ultimately shows Penn leading Quakers to the American colonies and the founding of Pennsylvania. Also known as *Penn of Pennsylvania*.

**174. Cousin Kate.** Vitagraph. US. 1921. B&W. *Producer*: Albert E. Smith *Director*: Mrs. Sidney Drew *Writer*: L. Case Russell *Cast*: Alice Joyce, Gilbert Emery, Beth Martin, Inez Shannon, Leslie Austin, Freddie Verdi, Frances Miller Grant, Henry Hallam

Amy Spencer (Beth Martin) is engaged to artist Heath Desmond (Gilbert Emery). Reverend James Bartlett (Leslie Austin) is also in love with Amy and influences her to break up with the artist. Cousin Kate meets the artist on the train and the two fall in love. During a storm Kate admits that she was only flirting with the Heath. Reverend Bartlett arrives and proposes to Amy and Kate and Heath are reunited.

**175. Cowards.** Jaylo International Films. US. 1970. 88m. C. *Producer, Director& Writer*: Simon Nuchtern *Cast*: John Rose, Susan Sparling, Will Patent, Thomas Murphy, Philip Baker Hall, Alexander Gellman, Edith Briden, Stephen Snow, George Linjeris, Spalding Gray, Kelly Houser, Larry Hunter

Philip Haller (John Rose) opposes the Vietnam War and is trying to decide whether to obtain a deferment, emigrate to Canada or to continue to resist the draft at home. He joins Father Reis (Philip Baker Hall) and an anti-war group in destroying a draft board office, and is arrested and sent to jail.

**Cradle Song** *see* **Canción de cuna**

**176. Creo en Dios.** Clasa-Mohme Inc. Mexico. 1943. 105m. B&W. *Director & Writer*:

Fernando de Fuentes *Cast:* Fernando Soler, Isabela Corona, Miguel Ángel Ferriz, Matilde Palou, Miguel Inclán, Lolita Camarillo

Catholic priest El Padre Bernal (Fernando Soler) is headed for the gallows after being convicted of a murder he did not commit. The real murderer's wife has confessed all to the priest but he cannot tell because of the confessional oath, even to save his life. The real murderer stole the Father's clothing and killed a pawnbroker. Before committing suicide the murderer signs a confession and his wife races to save the priest. Also known as *Believe in God.*

**The Crime of Father Amaro** *see* **El Crimen del Padre Amaro**

**177. Crime on the Hill.** Wardour. UK. 1933. 69m. B&W. *Director:* Bernard Vorhaus *Writer:* Michael Hankinson, Vera Allinson, E.M. Delafield, Bernard Vorhaus *Cast:* Sally Blane, Nigel Playfair, Lewis Casson, Anthony Bushell, Phyllis Dare, Judy Kelly, George Merritt, Reginald Purdell, Gus McNaughton, Hal Gordon, Jimmy Godden, Hay Petrie, Kenneth Kove

Vicar Michael Gray (Lewis Casson) proves convicted man did not poison fiancé's rich uncle.

**178. El Crimen del Padre Amaro.** Columbia. Spain/Argentino/France/Mexico. 2002. 118m. C. *Producer:* Alfredo Ripstein, Daniel Birman Ripstein *Director:* Carlos Carrera *Writer:* Vicente Leñero *Cast:* Gael García Bernal, Sancho Gracia, Ana Claudia Talancón, Angélica Aragón, Ernesto Gómez Cruz, Luisa Huertas, Damián Alcázar, Gastón Melo, Pedro Armendáriz Jr., Roger Nevares, Andrés Montiel

Follows the title character, a young priest (Gael García Bernal) anointed by the higher-ups into the provincial hinterlands where he is to fatten his resume before frying bigger fish in Rome. In Los Reyes, Padre Amaro quickly learns that his superior, Father Benito (Sancho Gracia) is in cahoots with local drug lords to finance the building of a clinic. Father Amalio (Damián Alcázar) is aiding the guerillas. Father Benito is sleeping with restaurateur Sanjuanera (Angélica Aragón). Soon her daughter Amelia (Ana

After initial resistance, Amelia (Ana Claudia Talancón) and young Father Amaro (Gael Garcia Bernal) enter into an affair, in *El Crimen del Padre Amaro* (2002).

Claudia Talancón) becomes taken with Father Amaro. Amelia's old boyfriend is a journalist trying to oppose the corruption of the Church. The Church is so powerful that the story is retracted. After initial resistance, Amelia and Father Amaro enter into an affair and Amelia finds herself pregnant. Father Amaro's crime is not the violation of celibacy but the choice of ambition over morality.

The film created much controversy upon its release and many groups called for a boycott of the film. It went on to become the highest-grossing Mexican film in its native country. Based on the 1875 novel by Portuguese author Jose Maria Eca de Queiroz. Also known as *The Crime of Father Amaro*.

**179. Crimes and Misdemeanors.** Orion. US. 1989. 107m. C. *Producer*: Robert Greenhut *Director & Writer*: Woody Allen *Cast*: Jerry Orbach, Bill Bernstein, Martin Landau, Claire Bloom, Stephanie Roth, Gregg Edelman, George J. Manos, Anjelica Huston, Woody Allen, Jenny Nichols, Joanna Gleason, Alan Alda, Sam Waterston, Mia Farrow

A woman who has had an affair with an ophthalmologist Judah Rosenthal (Martin Landau) threatens to ruin his life if he doesn't marry her. He contemplates murder which is suggested by his brother Jack. Compassionate Rabbi Ben (Sam Waterston) is a spiritual advisor and extremely positive husband and father. Meanwhile documentary filmmaker Clifford Stern (Woody Allen) must make a film about his brother-in-law Lester (Alan Alda), who he despises.

**180. The Criminal Path.** State Rights, Inc. US. 1914. B&W. *Director & Writer*: Will S. Davis *Cast*: Stuart Holmes, Edith Hallor, H. Jeffries, Charles Travis, Jack Hopkins, Phillip Scoville, Will S. Davis, Flora Naso

Mary Jepson (Edith Hallor) is arrested and sentenced to four years in prison for a crime she didn't commit. When she is released starvation tempts her to steal a purse, but music coming from a nearby church stops her. Reverend John Horton (Jack Hopkins) takes her to the hospital and then finds her a job with his sister, soon the Reverend

and Mary fall in love. The minister's brother-in-law makes unwanted advances toward Mary and when he turns up dead she is accused of the murder. The real killer finally confesses to the crime.

**181. Crooks in Cloisters.** Warner-Pathe. UK. 1963. 97m. C. *Producer*: Gordon L.T. Scott *Director*: Jeremy Summers *Writer*: Mike Watts, T.J. Morrison *Cast*: Ronald Fraser, Barbara Windsor, Grégoire Aslan, Bernard Cribbins, Davy Kaye, Wilfrid Brambell, Melvyn Hayes, Joseph O'Conor, Corin Redgrave, Francesca Annis, Patricia Laffan

Walt (Ronald Fraser) and his gang of forgers take over a deserted monastery on a remote island while on the lam from police. They pose as monks and soon start enjoying the simple life and are almost reformed by country life. They are caught when one of the fake monks makes big bets at the dog races.

**182. Cross and the Switchblade.** Gateway Films. US. 1970. 106m. C. *Producer*: Dick Ross *Director*: Don Murray *Writer*: David Wilkerson (book), John Sherrill (book), Elizabeth Sherrill (book), Don Murray, James Bonnet *Cast*: Pat Boone, Erik Estrada, Jackie Giroux, Jo-Ann Robinson, Dino DeFilippi, Don Blakely, Gil Frazier, Don Lamond, Sam Capuano, Stew Silver

Reverend David Wilkerson (Pat Boone), a country preacher from Pennsylvania, travels to New York City to help a group of teenage gang members on trial for the murder of a young boy. Wilkerson's persuasive preaching starts to make a difference in the lives of the troubled youths.

**Cross Country** *see* **Kros Contri**

**183. Cross Currents.** B&D/ Paramount British. UK. 1935. 66m. B&W. *Producer*: Anthony Havelock-Allan *Director*: Adrian Brunel *Writer*: Adrian Brunel, Pelham Leigh Amann, Gerald Elliott (novel) *Cast*: Ian Colin, Marjorie Hume, Evelyn Foster, Frank Birch, Aubrey Mallalieu, Kate Saxon, Aubrey Dexter, Bryan Powley, Sally Gray

Village vicar, Reverend Eustace Hickling (Frank Birch), is suspected of killing rival for widow.

**184. Cry, the Beloved Country.** UA. UK. 1951. 103m. *Producer*: Zoltan Korda,

Alan Paton *Director*: Zoltan Korda *Writer*: Alan Paton *Cast*: Canada Lee, Charles Carson, Sidney Poitier, Joyce Carey, Geoffrey Keen, Michael Goodliffe, Edric Connor, Charles McRae, Lionel Ngakane, Vivien Clinton

The film studies the conditions of a submerged native population ruled by the whites in South Africa. A native country preacher Stephen Kumalo (Canada Lee) travels to Johannesburg to find a missing sister and a wayward son. He finds them both in the crime-ridden slums of the city. In Johannesburg, Reverend Msimangy (Sidney Poitier) helps Stephen Kumalo. Kumalo's son has been involved in a robbery and has killed a white man, who happens to be the son of a rich farmer living in the area where the preacher has his church.

**185. Cry the Beloved Country.** Miramax Films. South Africa/US. 1995. 106m. C. *Producer*: Anant Singh, Harry Alan Towers *Director*: Darrell Roodt *Writer*: Ronald Harwood, Joshua Sinclair, Alan Paton (novel) *Cast*: James Earl Jones, Tsholofelo Wechoemang, Richard Harris, Charles Dutton, Dolly Rathebe, Ramalao Makhene, Jack Robinson, Jennifer Steyn

Zulu Anglican minister Stephen Kumalo (James Earl Jones) never loses faith in God even when tested. His son in a failed robbery attempt, murders a white man who has been working against apartheid in South Africa. The last shot of the film has Kumalo, after the hanging of his son and his own reconciliation with the murdered man's father, kneeling in prayer on a mountainside.

**The Crypt** *see* **Hearts of Humanity**
**The Cup** *see* **Phörpa**
**186. El Cura gaucho.** Pampa Films. Argentina. 1941. 82m. B&W. *Director*: Lucas Demare *Writer*: Hugo MacDougall, Miguel Mileo *Cast*: Enrique Muñio, Aída Alberti, Eloy Álvarez, Homero Cárpena, Salvador Lotito, Mecha López, Marino Seré, José Casamayor, Horacio Priani, Héctor Torres, Graciliano Batista, Jose de Angelis

Veteran priest Father Brochero (Enrique Muñio) starts a church in a small mountain village. He fights for the respect of his apathetic flock by helping to stop a plague and a landowner from driving the villagers from their farms. This is based on a true story and filmed in the Sierras de Cordoba where the priest actually lived. Also known as *The Gaucho Priest.*

**187. A Curate's Love Story.** Hepworth. UK. 1912. B&W. *Director*: Lewin Fitzhamon *Cast*: Hay Plumb, Chrissie White, Douglas Munro, Rachel de Solla

Squire's daughter nurses madman and is saved by cleric she rejected.

**188. The Curate's New Year Gifts.** Clarendon. UK. 1910. B&W. *Director*: Percy Stow

Cleric's young brother changes labels on presents.

**189. Le Curé de village.** France Film. Canada. 1949. 89m. B&W. *Producer*: Paul L'Anglais *Director*: Paul Gury *Writer*: Robert Choquette *Cast*: Ovila Légaré, Lise Roy, Denis Drouin, Paul Guèvremont, Camille Ducharme, Eugène Daigneault, Jeanne Quintal, Blanche Gauthier, Juliette Huot

Story revolves around the village priest Le Curé (Ovila Légaré) who is the religious leader, counselor, and final authority of the village. One of his charges is a motherless girl, who was entrusted to him by her dying grandfather. Because of her parentage the girl is not seen as marriage material for the son of a leading family. Her father turns up after serving a prison sentence. Le Curé steps in and helps resolve this situation.

**Da san yuan** *see* **Tristar**
**Da un paese lontano** *see* **From a Far Country**
**190. Dablova past.** Salisbury Films. Czechoslovakia. 1961. 85m. B&W. *Director*: Frantisek Vlácil *Writer*: Alfred Technik (novel), Frantisek A. Dvorák, Milos Václav Kratochvil *Cast*: Vitezslav Vejrazka, Miroslav Machácek, Cestmír H. Randa, Vlastimil Hasek, Vit Olmer, Karla Chadimová, Frantisek Kovárík, Bedrich Karen

Takes place during a drought in 16th century Czechoslovakia. A fanatical priest who is a member of the Inquisition, Prokus (Miroslav Machácek), suspects that the miller has sold his soul to the devil after the miller locates an underground spring. Also known as *The Devil's Trap.*

**191. Damien.** PBS. (TV) US. 1978. 90m. *Cast*: Terence Knapp

Father Damien de Veuster, the Roman Catholic priest, comes to the Hawaiian Islands in the late 1800's to work with lepers. He dies himself a leper after serving the mission for sixteen years. One-man television drama first presented as a stage play at the University of Hawaii in 1976. The Hawaii Public Television production was broadcast nationally on PBS in 1978 and again on *American Playhouse* in 1986.

**Damien the Leper Priest** *see* **Father Damien: The Leper Priest**

**192. Dancing at Lughnasa.** Sony. Ireland/UK/US. 1999. 96m. C. *Producer*: Noel Pearson *Director*: Pat O'Connor *Writer*: Frank McGuinness, Brian Friel (play) *Cast*: Meryl Streep, Michael Gambon, Catherine McCormack, Rhys Ifans, Sophie Thompson, Kathy Burke, Brid Brennan

On the family farm in 1936, five unmarried sisters struggle to maintain their independence. Kate Munday (Meryl Streep) teaches in the parish school. Christina (Catherine McCormack), the most beautiful sister, has a love child. One day their brother Father Jack Mundy (Michael Gambon) returns from Uganda after nearly 20 years as a missionary priest in a leper colony. Father Jack arrives home a shattered man who confuses his own faith with African religion.

**193. The Dancing Girl.** Cricks & Martin. UK. 1912. B&W. *Director*: Edwin J. Collins *Cast*: Una Tristram

Rejected lover becomes priest and saves rival's life.

**194. Dandy Dick.** BIP. UK. 1935. 62m. B&W. *Producer*: Walter C. Mycroft *Director*: William Beaudine *Writer*: Frank Miller, William Beaudine, Clifford Grey, Will Hay *Cast*: Will Hay, Nancy Burne, Esmond Knight, Davy Burnaby, Mignon O'Doherty, Syd Crossley, Robert Nainby, Hal Gordon, Jimmy Godden, John Singer, Wally Patch, Moore Marriott, Kathleen Harrison

Vicar Reverend Richard Jedd (Will Hay) trying to raise money for a new church steeple is falsely accused of drugging a racehorse. Reverend Judd is not a gambler but he is forced to bet the church money on a horse named Dandy Dick. His daughter falls in love with the horse's part-owner.

**195. The Dangerous Lives of Altar Boys.** ThinkFilm. US. 2002. 104m. C. *Producer*: Jodie Foster, Meg LeFauve, Jay Shapiro *Director*: Peter Care *Writer*: Michael Petroni, Chris Fuhrman (novel), Jeff Stockwell *Cast*: Jodie Foster, Kieran Culkin, Jena Malone, Emile Hirsch, Vincent D'Onofrio, Jake Richardson, Tyler Long, Arthur Bridgers

Coming of age story follows a group of Catholic school boys in the 1970's who battle the strict rules of wicked peg-legged Sister Assumpta (Jodie Foster). The film centers on two friends Francis Doyle and Tim Sullivan. The glue of their friendship is the collaboration on action-adventure comic book in which their hero battles school officials like Sister Assumpta. Chain smoking and soccer loving Father Casey (Vincent D'Onofrio) knows what the boys are up to but is also wary of Sister Assumpta. He is more amused than appalled by the confiscated comic book

**196. Dangerous Paths.** Arrow Co. US. 1921. B&W. *Producer*: Ben Wilson *Director*: Duke Worne *Writer*: Joseph W. Girard *Cast*: Ben Wilson, Neva Gerber, Edith Stayart, Joseph W. Girard, Henry Van Sickle

Reverend John Emerson (Ben Wilson) is in love with a young girl, Ruth (Neva Gerber) whose father wants her to marry a rich man. They argue and she leaves home and goes to the city. Now penniless, a prostitute helps her and she becomes a housekeeper. One evening as they are walking on the street the police arrest them. The rich man gets her out of jail and then wants a sexual reward. She refuses and he spreads rumors about her. When the minister hears of her problems, he rescues her while beating up the rich man. During a sermon the minister exposes the truth and they marry.

**Dark Habits** *see* **Entre tinieblas**
**Dark Hideout** *see* **Entre tinieblas**
**197. Dark Waters.** York Home Video. UK/Italy/Russia. 1994. 94m. C. *Director*: Mariano Baino *Writer*: Andy Bark *Cast*: Valeri Bassel, Mariya Kapnist, Louise Salter, Venera Simmons, Pavel Sokolov

After her father dies, Elizabeth (Louise Salter) travels to a primitive island to find out why her father was sending money to a convent. Previously she was tortured by horrible visions. On the island she finds an evil order of nuns led by Mother Superior (Mariya Kapnist).

**198. Daughter of Darkness.** Paramount. UK. 1948. 91m. *Producer*: Victor Hanbury *Director*: Lance Comfort *Writer*: Max Catto *Cast*: Anne Crawford, Maxwell Reed, Siobhan McKenna, Grant Tyler, Honor Blackman, Barry Morse, George Thorpe, Denis Gordon, Liam Redmond, Arthur Hambling, David Greene

Takes place in an Irish village where Emma Baudine (Siobhan McKenna) works for the village priest Father Corcoran (Liam Redmond). Men find her irresistible, and the women insist that the priest get rid of her. The film follows a series of sordid adventures with several lovers murdered by Emma who no one suspects.

**199. Daughters of Destiny.** Cinédis. France/Italy. 1954. 94m. B&W. *Producer*: Henry Deutschmeister *Director*: Christian-Jaque, Jean Delannoy, Marcello Pagliero *Writer*: Sergio Amidei, André-Paul Antoine, Jean Aurenche, Pierre Bost, Jean Ferry, Henri Jeanson, Horace McCoy, Vladimir Pozner, Gian Luigi Rondi *Cast*: Michèle Morgan, Daniel Ivernel, Andrée Clément, Michel Piccoli, Robert Dalban, Dora Doll, Gil Delamare, Jacques Fabbri, Gérard Buhr, Albert Michel, Katherine Kath, Claudette Colbert, Eleonora Rossi Drago, Mirko Ellis, Martine Carol, Raf Vallone, Paolo Stoppa, Nyta Dover, Nerio Bernardi, Mario Carotenuto, Giuseppe Porelli, Aldo Silvani

Three tales of three famous women of history: Elizabeth I, Lysistrata, and the abandonment of Joan of Arc by her king and soldiers. Also known as *Destinees*.

**200. David.** Kino International. Germany. 1979. 125m.C. *Producer*: Joachim von Vietinghoff *Director*: Peter Lilienthal *Writer*: Jurek Becker, Ulla Zieman, Peter Lilienthal, Joel Konig (novel) *Cast*: Walter Taub, Irena Vrkljan, Eva Mattes, Mario Fischel, Dominique Horwitz

Based on a true story of an orthodox Rabbi Singer (Walter Taub) and his close family trying to survive Nazi persecutions. David (Mario Fischel) his son does everything to escape and eventually gets to Israel. Even after Rabbi Singer's temple is burned down by Nazis, he isn't convinced of the danger. When he realizes the danger he and his wife try to escape.

**Day of Wrath** *see* **Vredens Dag**
**Days of St. Patrick** *see* **In the Days of St. Patrick**

**201. Dead Man Walking.** Gramercy Pictures. US. 1995. 122m. C. *Producer:* Jon Kilik, Tim Robbins, Rudd Simmons *Director:* Tim Robbins *Writer*: Tim Robbins, Helen Prejean (book) *Cast*: Susan Sarandon, Sean Penn, Robert Prosky, Raymond J. Barry, R. Lee Ermey, Celia Weston, Lois Smith, Scott Wilson, Roberta Maxwell, Margo Martindale

Sister Helen Prejean (Susan Sarandon) is asked to be a pen pal of prison inmate Matthew Poncelet (Sean Penn) who was convicted of rape and murder. She travels to the Louisiana State Prison to meet Poncelet. She is repelled by him but yet she's determined to help him. Plot explores her role as a spiritual advisor to this condemned man and the victim's family. Film based on the book by Sister Helen, C.S. J., who works with death-row inmates and their victims' families.

**The Deadliest Sin** *see* **Confession**
**Death in the Vatican** *see* **Morte in Vaticano**
**Death, Where Is Your Victory?** *see* **Mort, où est ta victoire?**

**202. Il Decamerone.** UA. Italy/France/Germany. 1971. 112m. C. *Producer*: Alberto Grimaldi *Director*: Pier Paolo Pasolini *Writer:* Pier Paolo Pasolini, Giovanni Boccaccio (novel) *Cast*: Franco Citti, Ninetto Davoli, Angela Luce, Pier Paolo Pasolini, Silvana Mangano, Jovan Jovanovic, Vincenzo Amato, Giuseppe Zigaina

Retelling of nine selected tales from Boccaccio. One part tells the stories of Andreuccio of Perugia (Ninetto Davoli), the abbess caught in bed with a priest.

**203. Le Défroqué.** Gaumont. France. 1954. 107m. B&W. *Producer:* Alain Poiré,

Sister Helen Prejean (Susan Sarandon) meets her pen pal, death-row prison inmate Matthew Poncelet (Sean Penn), who was convicted of rape and murder, in *Dead Man Walking* (1995).

Roger Ribadeau-Dumas *Director*: Léo Joannon *Writer*: Léo Joannon, Denys de La Patellière *Cast*: Pierre Fresnay, Pierre Trabaud, Nicole Stéphane, Marcelle Géniat, Léo Joannon, René Blancard, Abel Jacquin, Guy Decomble

A defrocked priest Maurice (Pierre Fresnay) finds pleasure in mocking and finding fault with the church. In an army prison camp he gives absolution to a dying priest but a young man, Gérard (Pierre Trabaud), mistakenly takes it as an indication that he still cares. The young man is now convinced of his own vocation. He becomes a priest and attempts to get Maurice back to the church. Maurice feels as if he has finally cleansed himself when Gérard appears. In a fit of rage and agony, Maurice kills Gérard and then turns himself in wearing the dead man's robe. Also known as *The Unfrocked One*.

**The Demise of Father Mouret** *see* **La Faute de l'Abbé Mouret**

**204. Le Désert de Pigalle.** Cinedis. Italy/France. 1958. 105m. B&W. *Producer*:

Michel Safra, Serge Silberman *Director*: Léo Joannon *Writer*: Hervé Bromberger, Jacques Robert, Jacques Sigurd, Serge Groussard, Leo Joannon *Cast*: Pierre Trabaud, Annie Girardot, Pierre Jolivet, Léo Joannon, Claire Guibert, Nelly Vignon, Monique Vita

A priest, Father Janin (Pierre Trabaud) attempts to salvage the souls of prostitutes in the underworld of Pigalle. The young priest is fighting white slavers with the help of a prostitute, Josy (Annie Girardot). The slavers are caught, Josy is killed, and the priest is hospitalized. Also known as *The Desert of Pigalle*.

**The Deserter** *see* **Il Disertore**

**Destinées** *see* **Daughters of Destiny**

**205. Les Destinées sentimentales.** Pathé. France/Switzerland. 2000. 180m. C. *Producer*: Bruno Pésery *Director*: Olivier Assayas *Writer*: Olivier Assayas, Jacques Fieschi, Jacques Chardonne (novel) *Cast*: Emmanuelle Béart, Charles Berling, Isabelle Huppert, Olivier Perrier, Dominique Reymond, André Marcon, Alexandra London, Julie Depardieu, Louis-Do de Lencquesaing

In Barbazac in 1900, a young Protestant cleric, Jean Barnery (Charles Berling) divorces his wife Nathalie (Isabelle Huppert) when he learns of her infidelity and soon he falls in love with Pauline (Emmanuelle Béart), daughter of a rich parishioner. Jean is also heir to a porcelain factory. In order to ease his guilt about the divorce, Jean gives his wealth to his ex-wife and daughter. Pauline visits Jean, who has fallen on hard times and is bedridden with tuberculosis. Jean and Pauline marry and move to Switzerland. Soon his family needs his help to run the business. He accepts the responsibility but Pauline doesn't agree. This decision and the Great War change him and his relationship with Pauline. He is sent to the front lines and Pauline becomes a nurse. After the war, he works to increase productivity of the factory. His daughter is rebellious but she takes holy orders. Also known as *Les Destinées*.

**206. The Devil at 4 O'Clock.** Columbia. US. 1961. 126m. C. *Producer*: Fred Kohlmar, Mervyn LeRoy *Director*: Mervyn LeRoy. *Writer*: Liam O'Brien, Max Catto *Cast*: Spencer Tracy, Frank Sinatra, Kerwin Mathews, Jean-Pierre Aumont, Grégoire Aslan, Alexander Scourby, Barbara Luna, Cathy Lewis, Bernie Hamilton, Martin Brandt, Lou Merrill

A tiny volcanic island is the setting of this tale of redemption. A seaplane arrives with three convicts and a replacement young Father Joseph Perreau (Kevin Mathews) for the elderly and bad-tempered hard-drinking Father Matthew Doonan (Spencer Tracy), who seems to have lost faith in God. The natives think Doonan is crazy because of his devotion to the mountain-top hospital he has built for children with leprosy. When the volcano erupts Doonan convinces the three convicts to help him rescue the children by offering them paroles. One convict Harry (Frank Sinatra) during the trek falls in love with Camille and are married by Doonan. The children are saved but the three convicts and Doonan die.

**207. The Devil Is a Woman.** TCF. UK/ Italy. 1975. 105m. C. *Producer*: Anis Nohra *Director*: Damiano Damiani *Writer*: Damiano Damiani, Audrey Nohra, Fabrizio Onofri *Cast*: Glenda Jackson, Claudio Cassinelli, Lisa Harrow, Adolfo Celi, Arnoldo Foá, Francisco Rabal, Rolf Tasna, Duilio Del Prete, Gabriele Lavia

Sister Geraldine (Glenda Jackson) is the strange head of a religious convent/hostel. She is obsessed with cleansing the souls of the guests such as a Polish priest, a writer, and a murderous widow. The convent is more like a psycho ward than a religious institution. The writer uncovers the secrets while writing a priest's memoirs. Also known as *Il Sorriso del grande tentatore* and *The Tempter*.

**208. The Devil Never Sleeps.** TCF. UK/US. 1962. 125m. C. *Producer & Director*: Leo McCarey *Writer*: Leo McCarey, Claude Binyon, Pearl Buck (novel) *Cast*: William Holden, Clifton Webb, France Nuyen, Weaver Lee, Athene Seyler, Martin Benson, Edith Sharpe, Robert Lee, Marie Yang, Andy Ho

Father O'Banion (William Holden) arrives at a mission in China accompanied by a young native girl. He has been sent to relieve the older and weaker Father Bovard (Clifton Webb). Communist soldiers seize the mission as a command post and their leader rapes the young girl. The Communist colonel reforms and realizes his evil ways and the four flee to the border. Also known as *Satan Never Sleeps*.

**209. The Devils.** Warner. UK. 1971. 111m. C. *Producer*: Ken Russell, Robert Solo *Director*: Ken Russell *Writer*: Aldous Huxley (novel), Ken Russell, John Whiting *Cast*: Vanessa Redgrave, Oliver Reed, Dudley Sutton, Max Adrian, Gemma Jones, Murray Melvin, Michael Gothard, Georgina Hale, Brian Murphy, Christopher Logue, John Woodvine

Cardinal Richelieu (Christopher Logue) and other power-hungry groups seek to take control of pre-renaissance France. First, they must destroy Father Grandier (Oliver Reed), who runs the fortified town that stops their plans. They set him up as warlock in control of a devil-possessed nunnery, where the mother superior Sister Jeanne (Vanessa Redgrave) is sexually obsessed by him. A mad-witch hunter is sent to gather evidence. Also known as *The Devils of Loudon.*

**210. The Devil's Disciple.** UA. UK. 1959. 83m. B&W. *Producer:* Harold Hecht *Director:* Guy Hamilton *Writer:* John Dighton, Roland Kibbee, George Bernard Shaw (play) *Cast:* Burt Lancaster, Kirk Douglas, Laurence Olivier, Janette Scott, Eva LeGallienne, Harry Andrews, Basil Sydney, George Rose, Neil McCallum, David Horne, Mervyn Johns, Erik Chitty

Reverend Anthony Anderson (Burt Lancaster) is a peace-loving parson who ends up a firebrand rebel captain during the American Revolution after witnesses many disturbing events. One incident is the public hanging of a man and that the body remains hanging, until the dead man's son Dirk Dungeon (Kirk Douglas), a scamp who ends up a virtuous hero, cuts the body down one night and brings it to the pastor. Dirk is willing to take the place of the reverend and be sent to the gallows. Reverend Anderson saves the day for the rebels and Dirk. A neighboring parson is portrayed as a coward and a loyalist.

**The Devils of Loudon** *see* **The Devils**

**211. The Devil's Party.** Universal. US. 1938. 65m. B&W. *Producer:* Edmund Grainger *Director:* Ray McCarey *Writer:* Roy Chanslor, Borden Chase (novel) *Cast:* Victor McLaglen, William Gargan, Paul Kelly, Beatrice Roberts, Frank Jenks, John Gallaudet, Samuel S. Hinds, Joe Downing, Arthur Hoyt, David Oliver

Four children growing up on the sidewalks on New York City agree to meet yearly to confirm their friendship. One boy is sidetracked when he is sent to reform school. He grows up to become gambler Marty Malone (Victor McLaglen). Jerry Donovan (Paul Kelly) is now a priest and Mike O'Mara (William Gargan) and Joe O'Mara (John Gallaudet) are policeman brothers. Marty is involved murder of a man with a gambling debt. During the investigation Joe is killed. Father Jerry is instrumental in bringing justice.

**212. The Devil's Playground.** EMC. Australia. 1976. 107m. C. *Producer, Director& Writer:* Fred Schepisi *Cast:* Arthur Dignam, Nick Tate, Simon Burke, Charles McCallum, John Frawley, Jonathan Hardy, Gerry Duggan, Peter Cox, John Diedrich, Thomas Keneally, Sheila Florance, Alan Cinis

The film concentrates on the emotional sexual seething amidst young boys at a Roman Catholic boarding school. Of course the Brothers run a chaste and sterile environment.

**The Devil's Trap** *see* **Dablova past**

**213. Dharmaga tongjoguro kan kkadalgun.** Milestone Film & Video. South Korea. 1989. 137m. C. *Director & Writer:* Yong-Kyun Bae *Cast:* Hae-Jin Huang, Su-Myong Ko, Pan-Yong Yi, Won-Sop Sin

The story is about three people living in a remote Buddhist monastery near Mount Chonan. There is Hyegok (Pan-Yong Yi), the old master; Kibong (Won-Sop Sin), a young man who has left his family to seek enlightenment; and Haejin (Hae-Jin Huang), an orphan brought to the monastery to be raised as a monk. The film is told in flashbacks and mainly about Kibong, such as how he came to the monastery. Hyegok is seen as a teacher, protector, and father figure. Also known as *Why Did Bodhi-Dharma Leave for the East?*

**214. Diary of a City Priest.** Heartland Film. US. 2001. 77m. C. *Producer:* Ed Givnish, Eugene Martin, Lisa Rosenstein, Cate Wilson *Director:* Eugene Martin *Writer:* Eugene Martin, Father John McNamee (book) *Cast:* David Morse, John Ryan, Phillip Goodwin, Ana Reeder, Robert Sella, Judy Bauerlein, Marylouise Burke, J. D. Jackson

Father John McNamee (David Morse) is faced with a tough job at his church in rough area of Philadelphia. The film covers a year in his life where he faces spiritual and physical demands. The director Eugene Martin happen to have been baptized as a baby over 30 years ago by Father McNamee. The Father hopes the film portrays his church as a place that reaches beyond its geographic and denominational borders.

**Diary of a Country Priest** *see* **Journal d'un curé de campagne**

**215. Dieu a besoin des hommes.** TCF. France. 1950. 100m. B&W. *Producer:* Paul

Graetz, Louis Wipf *Director:* Jean Delannoy *Writer:* Jean Aurenche, Pierre Bost *Cast:* Pierre Fresnay, Madeleine Robinson, Daniel Gélin, André Clément, Jean Brochard, Sylvie

The only church on a barren island is left without a priest. The residents demand the person in charge Thomas (Pierre Fresnay) offer some sort of service. He is forced into doing rituals he has no right to do. He goes to the Bishop and begs for a priest with no luck. He decides to give a mass for his mother. The Church and police interfere but he performs a shipboard burial. He then sends the worshippers to the real mass. Also known as *God Needs Men.*

**216. The Disappearance of Aimee.** NBC. (TV). US. 1976. 120m. C. *Producer:* Paul Leaf *Director:* Anthony Harvey *Writer:* John McGreevey *Cast:* Faye Dunaway, Bette Davis, James Sloyan, James Woods, John Lehne, Lelia Goldoni, Severn Darden, William Jordan, Sandy Ward, Barry Brown, Irby Smith, Hartley Silver

A dramatization of the unexplained six-week disappearance of evangelist Sister Aimee Semple McPhearson (Faye Dunaway) in 1926. Was she kidnapped and taken to Mexico or had she planned a clandestine meeting with a married man?

**217. The Disciple.** Triangle. US. 1915. B&W. *Producer:* Thomas H. Ince *Director:* William S. Hart *Writer:* Thomas H. Ince, S. Barret McCormick *Cast:* William S. Hart, Dorothy Dalton, Thelma Salter, Robert McKim, Charles K. French, Jean Hersholt

Jim Houston (William S. Hart), the "Shootin Iron Parson," and his wife Mary arrive to reform the town of Barren Gulch. Mary is seduced by the local gambling hall owner, Doc Hardy (Robert McKim). After this betrayal Jim leaves the ministry and takes his daughter to live in the mountains. When his daughter falls ill the only person he can call upon, who is actually a doctor, is Doc Hardy. His wife comes to her senses and wishes to return to her husband. Jim is just about to kill Hardy when he beholds a vision on a hilltop and spares Hardy's life.

**218. Il Disertore.** Istituto Luce/SACIS. Italy. 1983. 92m. C. *Director:* Giuliana Berlinguer *Writer:* Giuseppe Dessi (novel), Giu-liana Berlinguer, Massimo Felisatti *Cast:* Irene Papas, Omero Antonutti, Mattia Sbragia

The film takes place in a remote Sardinian village in 1922. The town fathers are collecting money for a war memorial. Only Mariangela (Irene Papas), who lost two sons in the war, gives 15 years of her savings for the cause. Father Cosi (Omero Antonutti) is opposed to the monument because he sees it as burying the truth rather that remembering the sacrifices it took. In a series of flashbacks we learn the truth about the death of Mariangela's younger son. He actually deserted after killing his captain and returned home very ill. His mother nursed him in secret and Father Cosi knew of this. The boy dies, asking not to be turned over to authorities. Father Cosi is torn between the boy and his duty as a priest and citizen to give up the boy. After the dedication of the monument the miners and the fascists clash. Mariangela and Father Cosi see her son's grave as a symbol of protest. Also known as *The Deserter.*

**219. The Disputation.** (TV). UK. 1986. C. *Producer:* Jenny Reeks *Director:* Geoffrey Sax *Writer:* Hyam Maccoby *Cast:* Alan Dobie, Bernard Hepton, Christopher Lee, Helen Lindsay, Bob Peck, Toyah Willcox

At the request of the Catholic establishment, the King of Aragon (Christopher Lee) sets up a public debate (disputation) between the leader of the local Jewish community and a Jewish convert who is now a brilliant clergyman.

**220. Distant Trumpet.** Apex. UK. 1952. 63m. B&W. *Producer:* Harold Richmond, Derek Elphinstone *Director:* Terence Fisher *Writer:* Derek Elphinstone *Cast:* Derek Bond, Jean Patterson, Derek Elphinstone, Anne Brooke, Grace Gavin, Keith Pyott

Society doctor David Anthony (Derek Bond) reluctantly changes places with his ill and very idealist missionary brother Richard Anthony (Derek Elphinstone).

**221. The Divine Enforcer.** Prism. US. 1991. 90m. C. *Producer:* Scott Pfeiffer *Director:* Robert Rundle *Writer:* Robert Rundle, Tanya York *Cast:* Jim Brown, Jan-Michael Vincent, Carrie Chambers, Erik Estrada,

Michael M. Foley, Adam Karpel, Judy Landers, Fred Mancuso, Don Stroud

A mysterious priest comes to town and stays with two priests (Erik Estrada and Jan-Michael Vincent). Soon the new guy in town is cleaning up the neighborhood and then he meets the vampire serial killer Otis (Don Stroud) in the confessional. What's a priest to do? Also a female psychic enters the picture.

**The Doctor and the Healer** *see* **Il Medico e lo stregone**

**222. Dr. Brian Pellie Escapes from Prison.** Clarendon. UK. 1912. B&W. *Director*: Wilfred Noy

Crook poses as chaplain and escapes by car and is chased by cycling wardens.

**Dr. Schweitzer** *see* **Il Est minuit Docteur Schweitzer**

**223. Dr. Syn.** GFD. UK. 1937. 78m. B&W. *Producer*: Michael Balcon, Edward Black *Director*: Roy William Neill *Writer*: Michael Hogan, Roger Burford, Russell Thorndike (novel) *Cast*: George Arliss, John Loder, Margaret Lockwood, Roy Emerton, Graham Moffatt, Frederick Burtwell, George Merritt, Athole Stewart, Wally Patch, Meinhart Maur, Muriel George, Wilson Coleman

Revenue agent unmasks vicar Doctor Syn (George Arliss) as the dead pirate Captain Clegg, leader of a gang of smugglers.

**224. Dr. Syn, Alias the Scarecrow.** Buena Vista. UK. 1962. C. *Producer*: Walt Disney, Bill Anderson *Director*: James Neilson *Writer*: Russell Thorndike (novel), Robert Westerby *Cast*: Patrick McGoohan, George Cole, Tony Britton, Michael Hordern, Geoffrey Keen, Patrick Wymark, Eric Pohlmann, Eric Flynn, Jill Cuzon, Sean Scully, Kay Walsh

Dr. Christopher Syn (Patrick McGoohan) is a country minister who leads a rebel band against the King's naval press gangs. Press gangs roam the country beating young men into unconsciousness in order to enslave them in the Royal British Navy. Dr Syn is a mild-mannered minister by day and the Scarecrow by night. Also known as *The Scarecrow of Romney Marsh.*

**The Dog's Night Song** *see* **A Kutya éji dala**

**225. Don Bosco.** DuWorld Pictures. Italy. 1935. B&W. *Director*: Goffredo Alessandrini *Writer*: Goffredo Alessandrini, R. Ugucione, Aldo Vergano *Cast*: Gian Paolo Rosmino, Maria Staffi, Ferdinando Mayer, Roberto Pasetti

Film biography of Giovanni (John) Bosco who became the founder of the Salesain teaching order which ministered to homeless boys.

**226. Don Bosco.** Radiotelevisiones Italiana. Italy. 1988. 108m. C. *Producer*: Alfio Sugaroni *Director*: Leandro Castellani *Writer*: Silvano Buzzo, Ennio De Concini *Cast*: Ben Gazzara, Patsy Kensit, Karl Zinny, Laurent Terzieff, Piera Degli Esposti, Philippe Leroy, Raymond Pellegrin, Edmund Purdom

A television movie about St. John Bosco (Ben Gazzara), popular saint of Turin. He overcomes great obstacles to help homeless children find a better life.

**Don Camillo** *see* **Le Petit monde de Don Camillo**

**227. Don Camillo e i giovani d'oggi.** Cineriz. Italy/France. 1972. 111m. C. *Producer*: Luigi Rovere *Director*: Mario Camerini *Writer*: Giovanni Guareschi (novel), Lucio De Caro, Adriano Baracco, Leonardo Benvenuti, Mario Camerini, Piero De Bernardi *Cast*: Gastone Moschin, Lionel Stander, Carole André, Paolo Giusti, Daniele Dublino, Dolores Palumbo, Elvira Tonelli, Luciano Bartoli

Mayor Peppone (Lionel Stander) might lose the elections. Don Camillo (Gastone Moschin) makes sure the mayor's son straighten out. Don Camillo's niece leads Peppone to think that she is pregnant by his son. Don Camillo faces the challenge of modernity. First he is sent a help young curate with a mandate to bring Vatican II to his parish. Second he gets a visit from his niece, a flower child. Mayor Peppone must deal with his rebellious son. Also known as *Don Camillo et les contestataires.*

**228. Don Camillo e l'onorevole Peppone.** Cinedis. Italy/France. 1955. 100m. B&W. *Director*: Carmine Gallone *Writer*: René Barjavel, Leonardo Benvenuti, Giovanni Guareschi, Agenore Incrocci, Furio Scarpelli *Cast*: Fernandel, Gino Cervi,

Claude Sylvain, Gaston Rey, Leda Gloria, Umberto Spadaro, Memmo Carotenuto, Manuel Gary, Guido Celano, Marco Tulli, Giovanni Onorato, Carlo Duse, Luigi Tosi, Gustavo De Nardo, Stefano Alberici

Don Camillo (Fernandel) and Mayor Peppone (Gino Cervi) battle again. Third in the series about cleric Don Camillo (Fernandel) and Mayor Peppone (Gino Cervi) who battle for village honors. Don Camillo helps the mayor pass an exam and then blackmails the mayor into approving a church project. Also known as *Don Camillo's Last Round*.

**Don Camillo et les contestataires** *see* **Don Camillo e i giovani d'oggi**.

**Don Camillo in Moscow** *see* **Il Compagno Don Camillo**

**229. Don Camillo monsignore ma non troppo.** Italy/France. 1961. 115m. B&W. *Director*: Carmine Gallone *Writer*: Giovanni Guareschi (novel), René Barjavel, Leonardo Benvenuti, Piero De Bernardi *Cast*: Fernandel, Gino Cervi, Gina Rovere, Leda Gloria, Alexandre Rignault, Valeria Ciangottini, Saro Urzi, Armando Bandini, Karl Zoff, Emma Gramatica, Paul-Emile Deiber

Don Camillo (Fernandel) is now a bishop and Peppone (Gino Cervi) is now a senator. Their rivalry is ignited when Don Camillo learns that Peppone is promoting the building of an apartment complex on the site of an old church. Also known as *Don Camillo: Monsignor*.

**Don Camillo's Last Round** *see* **Don Camillo e l'onorevole Peppone**

**230. Don't Cry It's Only Thunder.** Sanrio. US. 1982. 108m. C. *Producer*: Walt deFaria *Director*: Peter Werner *Writer*: Paul Hensler *Cast*: Dennis Christopher, Susan Saint James, Lisa Lu, Tu Thuy, Mai Thi Lien, Truong Minh Hai, Robert Englund, James Whitmore Jr., Roger Aaron Brown

Drug-dealing medic Brian Anderson (Dennis Christopher) during the Vietnam War is blackmailed by Army doctor Katherine Cross (Susan Saint James) into helping a group of orphans and two nuns Sister Marie (Lisa Lu) and Sister Hoa (Thu Thuy).

**231. Dorotej.** Yugoslavia. 1981. 98m. C. *Director*: Zdravko Velimirovic *Writer*: Dobrilo Nenadic, Borislav Mihajlovic-

Mihiz, Zdravko Velimirovic *Cast*: Gojko Santic, Gorica Popovic, Velimir Bata Zivojinovic, Darko Damevski, Meto Jovanovski, Jordanco Cevrevski

Set in the year 1308, tells the story of a monk Dorotej (Gojko Santic) who has scientific knowledge of herbs and can cure some illnesses. One day he wanders to the monastery of the Holy Virgin to cure the sick abbot. He is asked to stay, but a hopeful successor to the now cured abbot is angry and tries to discredit him. The news of his abilities spreads and an injured warlord sends for him. He cures him and attracts the attention of the lady of the castle. She falls in love with him. He gives into her love when he is expelled from the monastery after the ill abbot dies. A nobleman who also has eyes for the lady kills them both.

**232. A Dream for Christmas.** ABC. (TV). US. 1973. 120m. C. *Producer*: Walter Coblenz *Director*: Ralph Senensky *Writer*: John McGreevey, Max Hodge *Cast*: Hari Rhodes, Beah Richards, Lynn Hamilton, George Spell, Marlin Adams, Robert DoQui, Ta-Ronce Allen, Joel Fluellen, Juanita Moore, Bebe Redcross, Clarence Muse, Dorothy Meyer

A pilot for a proposed television series involves a southern minister, Reverend Will Douglas (Hari Rhodes), and his family assigned to a poor parish in California. The congregation is drifting away and the church is scheduled for demolition.

**233. Drôle de drame ou L'étrange aventure de Docteur Molyneux.** Lenauer International Films. France. 1937. 84m. B&W. *Producer*: Corniglion Molinier *Director*: Marcel Carné *Writer*: J. Storer Clouston (novel), Jacques Prévert *Cast*: Louis Jouvet, Francoise Rosay, Michel Simon, Jean Louis Barrault, Nadine Vogel, Pierre Alcover, Henri Guisol, Jeanne Lory, Marcel Duhamel

Story about a bourgeoisie family whose head makes his living writing crime stories. The Vicar of Bedford (Louis Jouvet), a cousin of the family, invites himself for a weekend. The family's servants have walked out of their jobs and Mme. Molyneux turns cook. To explain her absence her husband says she is visiting friends. However, to create mischief or perhaps revenge the vicar spreads a rumor that Molyneux has killed his wife. Scotland Yard becomes involved. Also known as *Bizarre, Bizarre*.

**Dust of Empire** *see* **Hon vong phu**

**234. E venne un uomo.** Paramount. UK/Italy. 1965. 90m. C. *Producer*: Vincenzo Labella, Harry Saltzman *Director*: Ermanno Olmi *Writer*: Ermanno Olmi, Vincenzo Labella *Cast*: Rod Steiger, Adolfo Ceil, Rita Bertocchi, Pietro Germi, Antonio Bertocchi, Fabrizio Rossi, Alberto Rossi, Giovanni Rossi, Alfonso Orlando, Antonio Ruttigni, Giorgo Fortnato

Biographical telling of the life of Pope John XXIII. Also known as *And There Came a Man*.

**235. Edge of Doom.** RKO. US. 1950. 99m. B&W. *Producer*: Samuel Goldwyn *Director*: Mark Robson (Charles Vidor-opening and closing scenes) *Writer*: Leo Brady (novel) Philip Yordan, Ben Hecht (prologue and epilogue) *Cast*: Dana Andrews, Farley Granger, Joan Evans, Robert Keith, Paul Stewart, Mala Powers, Adele Jergens, Harold Vermilyea, John Ridgely, Douglas Fowley

Hoping to persuade a disillusioned parishioner to reconsider his decision to leave the church, a parish priest Father Thomas Roth (Dana Andrews) tells him the story of Martin Lynn (Farley Granger) a boy who found his faith after rejecting it and turning to crime. Martin is a poor man who wants to give his mother the funeral she deserves. First he goes to the parish priest to make arrangements. The priest is unsympathetic and Martin kills the Father with a crucifix in a fit of rage. While running away, Martin is arrested as a suspect in a robbery. Father Roth has Martin released from jail. Martin continues to make arrangements for a funeral and suffers guilt for the killing. Finally so tormented by guilt he confesses.

**236. Edges of the Lord.** Miramax Films. US/Poland. 2001. 95m. C. *Producer*: Zev Braun, Philip Krupp *Director & Writer*: Yurek Bogayevicz *Cast*: Haley Joel Osment, Willem Dafoe, Liam Hess, Richard Banel, Olaf Lubaszenko, Malgorzata Foremniak, Andrzej Grabowski

A view of the Nazi invasion of Poland from a child's perspective. A Jewish child Romek (Haley Joel Osment) is torn from his parents in Krakow and brought out of the city in a gunnysack. A peasant boards the blond, blue-eyed boy and passes him off as a nephew. The tormented and wise parish priest (Willem Dafoe) coaches the boy in Catholic catechism while respecting his Jewish heritage.

**237. The Eighteenth Angel.** Rysher Entertainment. US. 1998. 95m. C. *Producer*: Douglas Curtis, William Hart *Director*: William Bindley *Writer*: David Seltzer *Cast*: Christopher McDonald, Rachael Leigh Cook, Stanley Tucci, Wendy Crewson, Maximilian Schell, Cosimo Fusco, Venantino Venantini, Ted Rusoff, Federico Pacifici, John Crowther

Crazed satanic priest Father Simeon (Maximilian Schell) is in charge of the Etruscan order of monks. They believe that Satan is coming and the monks are conducting genetic experiment on children's bodies preparing for Satan's rebirth. They need 18 children to fulfill the prophecy and they already have 17. A genetic scientist Norah Stanton (Wendy Crewson) interviews Father Simeon to discuss his controversial experiments. She happens to bring along her 13-year-old daughter Lucy (Rachel Leigh Cook). Norah soon throws herself off a church tower. Her husband Hugh (Christopher McDonald) and Lucy end up in trouble in Rome, where Lucy is starting a modeling career. Those monks really want Lucy.

**238. Elmer Gantry.** UA. US. 1960. 146m. C. *Producer*: Bernard Smith *Director & Writer*: Richard Brooks, Sinclair Lewis (novel) *Cast*: Burt Lancaster, Jean Simmons, Arthur Kennedy, Dean Jagger, Shirley Jones, Patti Page, Edward Andrews, John McIntire, Hugh Marlowe, Joe Maross, Philip Ober, Barry Kelley, Wendell Holmes, Dayton Lummis

Elmer Gantry (Burt Lancaster), a leering lecher of a salesman, teams up with evangelist Sister Sharon Falconer (Jean Simmons) to sell religion in 1920s America. Sister Falconer is a devout preacher of the gospel and works out of a traveling tent ministry. With Gantry's help she is able to build

During a tent revival, Elmer Gantry (Burt Lancaster) preaches to a lost soul, in *Elmer Gantry* (1960).

her tabernacle. Gantry and his ambitions are in jeopardy when he is put into a compromising situation and photographs are taken. "You're all sinners...You'll all burn in hell!"

The Embezzled Heaven *see* Der Veruntreute Himmel

**239. Encrucijada para una monja.**

Universal. Italy/Spain. 1967. 100m. C. *Producer:* José María Reyzabal *Director:* Julio Buchs *Writer:* Federico De Urrutia, Manuel Sebares, Victor Auz, José Luis Hernández Marcos, Julio Buchs *Cast:* Rosanna Schiaffino, John Richardson, Mara Cruz, Ángel Picazo, Paloma Valdés, Lili Muráti,

Lex Monson, Margot Cottens, Andrés Mejuto, Wilhem P. Elie

A struggle for power follows the Congo's independence from Belgium in 1960 and impacts a group of nuns at a Belgian Roman Catholic mission. The nuns cannot leave without receiving orders from the Bishop. Sister Maria (Rosanna Schiaffino) is raped in the woods and the mother superior is killed. After being saved by a group of white mercenaries, Sister Maria returns to Brussels where she discovers that she is pregnant from the rape. She decides to keep the child and leave the religious order, but refuses to marry her childhood sweetheart because she is already married to Christ. Also known as *A Nun at the Crossroads*.

**End of a Priest** *see* **Faráruv Konec**

**240. End of the World.** The Irwin Yablans Co. US. 1977. 88m. C. *Producer*: Charles Band *Director*: John Hayes *Writer*: Frank Ray Perilli *Cast*: Kirk Scott, Sue Lyon, Christopher Lee, Liz Ross, Dean Jagger, Lew Ayres, Macdonald Carey, Simmy Bow, John Hayes, Roscoe Born

Father Pergado (Christopher Lee) goes on a spiritual retreat after witnessing a man's death in a bizarre accident. While on his retreat he encounters his alien double that is after world conquest.

**241. Enemies: A Love Story.** TCF. US. 1989. 119m. C. *Producer & Director*: Paul Mazursky *Writer*: Isaac Bashevis Singer (novel), Roger L. Simon, Paul Mazursky *Cast*: Ron Silver, Anjelica Huston, Lena Olin, Margaret Sophie Stein, Alan King, Judith Malina, Rita Karin, Phil Leeds, Elya Baskin, Paul Mazursky

In 1949 New York City, a Holocaust survivor Herman Broder (Ron Silver) who is a ghostwriter for a rabbi (Alan King), is involved with three women-his wife, his mistress, and his first wife thought to have died in a concentration camp. The rabbi is a hustler, a schemer who is winning to do anything to get ahead.

**242. The English Rose.** Whincup. UK. 1920. B&W. *Producer*: John Robyns *Director*: Fred Paul *Writer*: Paul Rooff, Robert Buchanan (play), George Sims (play) *Cast*: Fred Paul, Humberston Wright, Sydney Folker,

Mary Morton, Jock Raymond, Amy Brandon Thomas, George Turner, Clifford Desborough

Priest Father Michael (Fred Paul) learns truth of murder but is unable to save framed man.

**243. Enjo.** Daiei. Japan. 1958. 99m. B&W. *Producer*: Masaichi Nagata *Director*: Kon Ichikawa *Writer*: Yukio Mishima (novel), Keiji Hasebe, Kon Ichikawa, Natto Wada *Cast*: Raizô Ichikawa, Tatsuya Nakadai, Ganjiro Nakamura, Yoichi Funaki, Tamao Nakamura, Jun Hamamura, Tanie Kitabayashi, Michiyo Aratama, Kinzo Shin, Yôko Uraji

Based on a true story in 1950. Corruption and commercialization around a young novice Buddhist priest (Raizô Ichikawa) becomes too much and he burns down a temple, originally built by Shogun Yoshimitsu (1358–1409). Also known as *Conflagration* and *Flame of Torment*.

**244. Entertaining Angels: The Dorothy Day Story.** Paulist Pictures. US. 1996. 112m. C. *Producer*: Ellwood Kieser *Director*: Michael Ray Rhodes *Writer*: John Wells *Cast*: Moira Kelly, Martin Sheen, Lenny von Dohlen, Melinda Dillon, Paul Lieber, Heather Graham, Boyd Kestner, James Lancaster, Geoffrey Blake, Brian Keith

The founder of the Catholic Worker, Dorothy Day (Moira Kelly) is not a saint yet but the Paulist Fathers are involved with promoting her. As a social activist of the 1920's and 1930's she fought social injustices wherever she saw them. Entertaining Angels refers to the practice of treating all guests as if they were visiting angels.

**245. Entre tinieblas.** Cinevista. Spain. 1983. 114m. C. *Producer*: Luis Calvo *Director & Writer*: Pedro Almódovar *Cast*: Cristina Sánchez Pascual, Julieta Serrano, Marisa Paredes, Carmen Maura, Mary Carrillo, Lina Canalejas, Manuel Zarzo, Chus Lampreave, Berta Riaza

Nightclub singer Yolanda decides to hide at a convent when her boyfriend dies of an overdose of heroin. She goes to the convent because she had met two of nuns previously when they asked for an autograph. The nuns and the convent's priest are weird but devout. They call themselves the humble redeemers and each has a degrading nickname such as Sister Manure, Sister Snake, and Sister Sin. One nun writes pulp fiction under a pseudonym, another keeps a pet tiger, another is a drug addict, and one that is into self-mortification. The convent is low on money so one nun blackmails a wealthy widow into continuing her contribution. Plus a new Mother Superior is coming. Also known as *Dark Hideout* and *Dark Habits*.

**246. Epsteins Nacht.** Media Cooperation One. Germany/Austria/Switzerland. 2002. 86m. C *Producer:* Andreas Bareiß *Director:* Urs Egger Writer: Jens Urban *Cast:* Mario Adorf, Otto Tausig, Bruno Ganz, Günter Lamprecht, Annie Giradot, Nina Hoss

One of three childhood friends, Jochen Epstein (Mario Adorf), who all survived a World War II concentration camp at Birkenau becomes convinced that a parish priest Father Groll (Günter Lamprecht) is really Geisser, an SS officer from Birkenau. His other friends, Karl Rose (Otto Tausig) and Adam Rose (Bruno Ganz) aren't sure whether he is right because it has been many years and Geisser's name was on a list of the dead. The priest is confronted by the friends. Is Father Groll guilty or innocent? The story begins ten years later after Jochen Epstein has been released from prison. Also known as *Epstein's Night.*

**247. Esthappan.** General Pictures. India. 1979. 94m. C. *Director:* Govindan Aravindan *Writer:* Govindan Aravindan, Isaac Thomas Kottukapally *Cast:* Rajan Kakkanadan, Krishnapuram Leela, Sudharma, Shobhana

Esthappan (Rajan Kakkanadan) is a mystic and Christ-like fisherman in a coastal village south of Bombay. Miracles abound wherever he goes, such as walking on water, healing the sick, and changing stones into food. Also known as *Stephen.*

**248. The Eternal Jew.** Jewish Talking Picture Co. US. 1933. 63m. B&W. *Producer:* Abraham Leff, Joseph Seiden *Director:* George Roland *Writer:* Abraham Armband *Cast:* Louis Leibele Waldman, Celina Breene,

Rubin Wendorf, Morris B. Samuylow, Barney Schechtman, Bernard Holtzman

A rabbi and his assistant tell the biblical story of Abraham to a group of children.

**249. The Eternal Magdalene.** Goldwyn. US. 1919. B&W. *Producer:* Samuel Goldwyn *Director:* Arthur Hopkins *Writer:* Robert McLaughlin (play) *Cast:* Charles Dalton, Margaret Marsh, Charles Trowbridge, Donald Gallaher, Maude Cooling, Vernon Steele, Maxine Elliot

A rural banker Elijah Bradshaw (Charles Dalton), with an obsession to reform, wants to bring a famous evangelist to town for $30,000. When he thinks that his daughter is seeing one of his clerks, he kicks her out of the house. Later he dreams of a horrible life for her and awakens eager to forgive. We learn that she and the clerk were secretly married. Elijah immediately cancels the evangelist's visit.

**Eternal Secret** *see* **Az Örök Titok**

**250. Evangeline.** UA. US. 1929. 87m. B&W. *Producer & Director:* Edwin Carewe *Writer:* Finis Fox *Cast:* Dolores del Rio, Roland Drew, Alec B. Francis, Donald Reed, Paul McAllister, James Marcus, George Marion, Bobby Mack, Louis Payne, Lee Shumway

An Arcadian woman Evangeline (Dolores del Rio) struggles in the world searching for her lost love and sadly by becoming a Sister of Mercy. She finds him dying during an epidemic in Philadelphia. She too dies and they are buried together. Based on the poem by Henry Wadsworth Longfellow. Other versions of the story have been filmed.

**251. The Evangelist.** General Film. US. 1915. B&W. *Director:* Barry O'Neil *Writer:* Henry Arthur Jones (play), Clay Greene *Cast:* Gladys Hanson, Walter Law, Ferdinand Tidmarsh, George Soule Spencer, Jack Standing, George Clarke, Peter Lang, Arthur Matthews, Bartley McCullum, Richard Wangermann, Eleanor Dunn, Betty Brice, Ruth Bryan

When Christabel Nuneham's husband neglects her for his work she is drawn by the attentions of a young officer. After staying with him overnight to bid him farewell she is involved in an automobile accident. Celebrated evangelist Sylvanus Rebbings (George Soule Spencer) rescues the injured Christabel. Although he is loved by the townspeople, the clergy dislike him because of his radical views. Rebbings also prevents the suicide of a poor shop girl. When the young officer returns home Christabel meets him to end their affair, but her husband catches them and threatens divorce. Rebbings convinces him to reconcile for the sake of their daughter.

**252. Everything You Always Wanted to Know About Sex But Were Afraid to Ask.** UA. US. 1972. 87m. B&W/C. *Producer:* Charles H. Joffe *Director & Writer:* Woody Allen, David Reuben (novel) *Cast:* Woody Allen, John Carradine, Lou Jacobi, Louise Lasser, Anthony Quayle, Tony Randall, Lynn Redgrave, Burt Reynolds, Gene Wilder, Jack Barry, Baruch Lumet

Seven stories based on sections of the book. One sketch called "What's Your Perversion?" where old Rabbi Baumel is allowed to act out his fantasy-tied to a chair, whipped by a beautiful blonde, and watches his wife eat pork.

**253. The Exorcist.** Warner. US. 1973. 122m. C. *Producer&Writer:* William Peter Blatty *Director:* William Friedkin *Cast:* Ellen Burstyn, Max von Sydow, Lee J. Cobb, Kitty Winn, Jack MacGowran, Linda Blair, Jason Miller

Something is wrong with the 14-year-old Regan (Linda Blair) daughter of actress Chris MacNeil (Ellen Burstyn). Young Jesuit priest psychiatrist Father Karras (Jason Miller) fails to unearth the hidden psychological problem of the child and becomes convinced she happens to be possessed by the devil. Father Karras calls in exorcist Father Merrin (Max von Sydow). Both the priest and the girl suffer horrors before the exorcism cures her. Sequels are *Exorcist II: The Heretic* (1977) and *Exorcist III* (1990).

**254. La Faille.** First Run Features. France/Spain/Belgium/Netherlands. 1998. 112m. C. *Producer & Director:* Marion Hänsel *Writer:* Damon Galgut (novel), Marion Hänsel *Cast:* John Lynch, Oscar Petersen, Sylvia Esau, Jody Abrahams, Serge-Henri Valcke, Jonathan Phillips

A gay pastor in rural South Africa is accidentally murdered by a hitchhiker (John Lynch) after a sexual incident. The drifter buries the body in an old quarry. He then assumes the pastor's identity and takes over his new job as pastor in a rural community. His identity is threatened when thieves discover his secret. Also known as *The Quarry*.

**255. Faith for Gold.** Mission Film Society. US. 1930. B&W.

Alice Burg rejects her rich family to become a nun, a decision which upsets her brother Joseph an aspiring pianist. When Alice donates her part of the family money, Joseph denounces her and forbids mentioning the church. Fifteen years later Joseph is apparently lost at sea and his wife and son Johnny pray for his safety. Joseph returns but is still against God. Father Thomas, a friend of Johnny, tries to help but can't break Joseph's feelings. When Johnny is hurt, Alice comes to help and Joseph's wife asks for a divorce. However through the intervention of Father Thomas the couple reconciles and Joseph realizes his mistake of giving up faith for gold.

**256. The Faith Healer.** Hepworth. UK. 1911. B&W. *Director:* Bert Haldane

Faith healer cures sick child when doctor gives up hope.

**257. The Family Nobody Wanted.** ABC. (TV). US. 1975. 90m. C. *Producer:* William Kayden *Director:* Ralph Senensky *Writer:* Suzanne Clauser, Helen Doss (book) *Cast:* Shirley Jones, James Olson, Katherine Helmond, Woodrow Parfrey, Beeson Carroll, Claudia Bryar, Ann Doran, C. Lindsay Workman, Willie Aames, Ernest Esparza III, Dawn Biglay, Guillermo San Juan, Jina Tanner, Tina Toyota, Haig Movsesian, Tim Kimber, Sherry Lynn Kapahu, Michael and Robert Stadnik, Knar Keshishian

Tells the true story of a minister Carl Doss (James Olson) and his wife Helen (Shirley Jones) who assemble a family of twelve racially mixed children, who nobody else wanted.

**258. Fanny and Alexander.** Embassy Pictures. Sweden/France/Germany. 1982. 188m. C. *Producer:* Jörn Donner, Daniel Toscan du Plantier *Director & Writer:* Ingmar Bergman *Cast*: Ewa Fröling, Bertil Guve, Pernilla Allwin, Gunn Wållgren, Allan Edwall, Jarl Kulle, Börje Ahlstedt, Mona Malm, Christina Schollin, Jan Malmsjö, Erland Josephson, Anna Bergman, Stina Ekblad, Harriet Andersson, Gunnar Björnstrand, Lena Olin

The film opens in 1907 with the Ekdahl family celebrating Christmas. The story revolves around Oscar (Allan Edwall), an actor, and his wife Emilie (Ewa Fröling) and their two children Fanny (Pernilla Allwin) and Alexander (Bertil Guve). After Oscar dies suddenly, Emilie marries Bishop Edvard Vergerus (Jan Malmsjö), a stern and humorless puritan. He forces Emilie and the children to leave all their possessions and friend behind and live in a house with bars on the windows, like a prison. At the Vergerus' family, black clothing is the rule and the Bishop has a black cat. Her family comes to the rescue.

**259. Faráruv Konec.** Grove Press. Czechoslovakia. 1969. 98m. B&W. *Director*: Evald Schorm *Writer*: Evald Schorm, Josef Skvorecky *Cast*: Pavel Bosek, Jana Brejchová, Vlastimil Brodský, Gueye Cheick, Vladimir Jedenáctik, Václav Kotva, Maria Landova, Pavel Landovský, Jan Libícek, Jirí Lír, Josefa Pechlatová, Eva Repiková, Martin Ruzek, Helena Ruzicková, Jaroslav Satoranský, Zdena Skvorecka, Vladimir Valenta

A verger, who dresses as a priest, is invited by one of the villagers to assume the position of pastor at a vacant church. An atheist teacher tries to embarrass him in various ways because the people are confessing to him and preferring him to the teacher. The false priest is crucified by the people who demand too much of him, the police, and the cardinal. Also known as *End of a Priest*.

**260. Father Brown.** Columbia. UK. 1954. 91m. B&W. *Producer*: Paul Finder Moss *Director*: Robert Hamer *Writer*: Thelma Schnee, Robert Hamer, G. K. Chesteron (stories) *Cast*: Alec Guinness, Joan Greenwood, Peter Finch, Cecil Parker, Bernard Lee, Sid James, Gerard Oury, Ernest Thesiger, Ernest Clark, Everley Gregg, Austin Trevor, Marne Maitland, Eugene

Deckers, Jim Gérald, Noel Howlett, John Salew, John Horsley

Catholic priest, Father Brown (Alec Guinness), decides to transport a priceless cross himself from London to Rome, against the wishes of the Bishop (Cecil Parker). Father Brown is outsmarted by an international thief (Peter Finch) and looses the cross. Father Brown returns disgraced but is determined to save the sacred cross from the thief as well as the thief's soul. Father Brown learns some tricks from his flock.

**Father Damien** *see* **Molokai: The Story of Father Damien**

**261. Father Damien: The Leper Priest.** USA Video (TV). US. 1980. 95m. C. *Director*: Steve Gethers *Cast*: Roger Bowen, Alan Chappuis, William Daniels, Mike Farrell, Ken Howard, Wilfrid Hyde-White, Sydney Lassick, Logan Ramsey, David Ogden Stiers

Story of the Belgian missionary Joseph Damien de Beuster (1840–89) (Ken Howard) in Hawaii, who offered a place for lepers. Also known as *Damien: The Leper Priest*.

**The Father Kino Story** *see* **Padre on Horseback**

**262. Father O'Flynn.** Regal Films. UK. 1919. B&W. *Director:* Geoffrey Malins, Tom Watts *Writer*: Tom Watts *Cast*: Ethel Douglas, Reginald Fox, Ralph Foster, Eileen Bellamy, Little Rex, Tom Coventry

Father O'Flynn (Ralph Foster) solves the mystery of who killed the evil landowner. An innocent man is blamed when another farmer shoots the landowner who had seduced his daughter.

**263. Father O'Flynn.** Hoffberg. UK. 1935. 82m. B&W. *Producer*: Wifred Noy *Director*: Wilfred Noy, Walter Tennyson *Writer*: Frank Miller *Cast*: Thomas Burke, Jean Adrienne, Robert Chisholm, Henry Oscar, Ralph Truman, Denis O'Neil, Dorothy Vernon, Johnnie Schofield

Allegedly based on a famous song of the same name. This is the story of the romance of Macushia (Jean Adrienne) and a local boy Nigel (Robert Chisholm), her wayward father's attempt to take her away from her sweetheart, and of Father O'Flynn (Thomas Burke), who has looked after her since childhood.

**Father Sergius** *see* **Otete Sergiy**

**264. Father Tom.** Playgoers Pictures. US. 1921. B&W. *Director*: John B. O'Brien *Writer*: Rodney Hickok, Carl Krusada *Cast*: Tom Wise, James Hill, May Kitson, Myra Brooks, Ray Allen, Harry Boler, Alexander Clark, James Wallace, Nancy Deaver

Father Tom (Tom Wise) helps Bob, who is distressed by his mother's infatuation for a man he distrusts, and assists Margie, an orphan girl, with a horse. Bob and Margie enter the horse in a race to win money for the church mortgage. The horse is stolen but Father Tom finds it in time for the big race.

**The Fault of Abbot Mouret** *see* **La Faute de l'Abbé Mouret**

**Faustina** *see* **Faustyna**

**265. Faustyna.** Poland. 1995. 73m. C. *Director*: Jerzy Lukaszewicz *Writer*: Maria Nowakowska-Majcher *Cast*: Dorota Segda, Danuta Szaflarska, Agnieszka Czekanska, Stanislawa Celinska, Miroslawa Dubrawska, Anna Milewska, Teresa Budzisz-Krzyzanowska, Zofia Rysiówna, Krzysztof Wakulinski, Piotr Pawlowski, Janusz Michalowski

Sister Faustina Kowalska (Dorota Segda) was a Polish mystic from the early 20th century who later became a saint. She has visions of Jesus, in which she is instructed to have an image painted. Also known as *Faustina*.

**266. La Faute de l'Abbé Mouret.** Valoria. Italy/France. 1970. 100m. C. *Producer*: Vèra Belmont *Director*: Georges Franju *Writer*: Émile Zola (novel), Jean Ferry, Georges Franju *Cast*: Francis Huster, Gillian Hills, Margo Lion, André Lacombe, Lucien Barjon, Fausto Tozzi, Tino Carraro, Silvie Feit

A young, dedicated priest Serge Mouret (Francis Huster) has an attack while praying before the statue of the Virgin and his uncle takes him to the game warden's old castle to recuperate. He develops amnesia and meets the girl who is taking care of him and the two of them develop a romantic relationship. He is nursed back to health by Albine, the niece (Gillian Hills) of the outspoken atheist Jeanbernat (Fausto Tozzi). When he regains his memory he tries to efface his sins and assumes more kinship with the suffering of

Jesus. The girl dies and Serge buries her in consecrated ground. The film ends with the young priest looking at the Virgin Mary and seeing the young girl's face. Previously filmed in 1937. Also known as *The Fault of Abbott Mouret* and *The Demise of Father Mouret.*

**Fear No Evil** *see* **Il Sole di Montecassino**

**267. The Fiend.** Cinerama. UK. 1971. 87m. C. *Producer & Director*: Robert Hartford-Davis *Writer*: Brian Comport *Cast*: Ann Todd, Patrick Magee, Tony Beckley, Madeleine Hinde, Percy Herbert, Suzanna Leigh, David Lodge, Ronald Allen, Maxine Barrie, Jeannette Wild, Diana Chappell, Suzanna East

Birdy (Ann Todd), a religious fanatic, and her son are under the influence of a religious cult. Her son kills prostitutes to save their souls. Birdy has given her home and life over to the Brethren, an evangelical movement led by The Minister (Patrick Magee). Also known as *Beware My Brethren.*

**268. Fighting Father Dunne.** RKO. US. 1948. 93m. B&W. *Producer*: Phil L. Ryan *Director*: Ted Tetzlaff *Writer*: Martin Rackin, Frank Davis *Cast*: Pat O'Brien, Darryl Hickman, Charles Kemper, Una O'Connor, Arthur Shields, Harry Shannon, Joe Sawyer, Anna Q. Nilsson, Donn Gift, Myrna Dell, Ruth Donnelly, Jim Nolan

Story recalls how Father Peter J. Dunne (Pat O'Brien) became the patron saint of newsboys everywhere. He works with newsboy in early 20th century St. Louis. Father Dunne is inspired to better the lives of these poor boys.

**269. The Fighting Parson.** Jury. UK. 1912. B&W. *Director*: George Gray, Bert Haldane *Writer*: George Gray, Chris Davis *Cast*: George Gray

Disowned heir takes blame for brother's illegitimate child, joins the church, and fights slum bully.

**270. The Fighting Parson.** Allied Pictures. US. 1933. 66m. B&W. *Producer*: M. H. Hoffman Jr. *Director & Writer*: Harry L. Fraser *Cast*: Hoot Gibson, Marceline Day, Skeeter Bill Robbins, Ethel Wales, Stanley Blystone, Robert Frazer, Charles King, Phil Dunham, Jules Cowles

While running away from the law Steve Bentley (Hoot Gibson) and his sidekick Arizona Joe (Skeeter Bill Robbins) find the clothing and papers of a preacher. Steve disguises himself as the parson and assumes his identity. He is forced to stop the hanging of outlaw Mike (Charles King) because he knows that he is not the real parson.

**271. The Fighting 69th**. Warner. US. 1940. 90m. B&W. *Producer:* Hal B. Wallis, Jack L. Warner *Director:* William Keighley *Writer:* Norman Reilly Raine, Fred Niblo Jr., Dean Franklin *Cast:* James Cagney, Pat O'Brien, George Brent, Jeffrey Lynn, Alan Hale, Frank McHugh, Dennis Morgan, Dick Foran, William Lundigan, Guinn Williams, John Litel, Henry O'Neill, Sammy Cohen, Harvey Stephens, Charles Trowbridge, William Hopper, Tom Dugan, Frank Wilcox

Tells the story of arrogant Jerry Plunkett (James Cagney) and Father Francis Duffy (Pat O'Brien), members of the fighting 69th New York regiment, and their time overseas during World War I. Chaplain Father Francis Duffy works hard to try and reform Jerry. Father Duffy is there to take care of the souls of the men. Father Duffy prayers to God just before the troops go overseas. The soldiers respect the Father and gladly attend his services. Father Duffy is right there at the front lines being a hero. When Jerry causes the death of some of the troops, he is branded a coward and court-martialed and sentenced to death. His prison is hit and he is able to escape with help from Father Duffy. He sees Father Duffy with the wounded soldiers and finds the faith and courage to fight. Jerry rushes to the front lines and becomes a hero. He is fatally wounded during the attack and receives the last rites from Father Duffy. Father Duffy was a real person and a statute of him can be seen in New York City.

**Une Fille nommée Madeleine** *see* **Maddalena**

**272. The Final Conflict**. TCF. UK/US. 1981. 108m. C. *Producer:* Harvey Bernhard *Director:* Graham Baker *Writer:* Andrew Birkin *Cast:* Sam Neill, Rossano Brazzi, Don Gordon, Lisa Harrow, Barnaby Holm, Mason Adams, Robert Arden, Tommy Duggan, Leueen Willoughby, Louis Mahoney,

Marc Boyle, Richard Oldfield, Milos Kirek, Tony Vogel

The reborn antichrist Damien Thorn (Sam Neil) is now a man and has become an ambassador. His only obstacle to taking over the world is the baby to be born when three stars conjoin. Monks led by DeCarlo (Rossano Brazzi) are using sacred daggers in an attempt to kill Damien before the special baby is born. The monks are not very inept in killing. Last film in the *Omen* trilogy. Also known as *Omen III: The Final Conflict*.

**273. The Final Judgment**. Concorde. US. 1992. 90m. C. *Producer:* Mike Elliott *Director:* Louis Morneau *Writer:* Kirk Honeycutt *Cast:* Brad Dourif, David Ledingham, Maria Ford, Simone Allen, Isaac Hayes, Orson Bean, Karen Black, Bert Williams, Howard Shangraw, Michael James McDonald

Father Tyrone (Brad Dourif) is the main suspect in the brutal murder of a young stripper. He tries to solve the case by himself by plunging into the world of strip clubs and pornography.

**274. The Finger of Justice**. Arrow Film. US. 1918. 35m. B&W. *Producer:* Reverend Paul Smith *Director:* Louis William Chaudet *Writer:* Grace Marbury Sanderson *Cast:* Crane Wilbur, Harry Barrows, Jane O'Rourke, Mae Gaston, Leota Lorraine, Beulah Booker, Velma Whitman, Jean Hathaway, John Oaker, Jack Lott

Minister Noel Delaney (Crane Wilbur) is aided by his sweetheart Mary in his fight against a system of corruption. A thug, Flip, lures the political boss' daughter into an underworld resort unaware of her true identity. The father fights Flip over this. Noel and Mary eventually clean up the system.

**275. The Fireball**. TCF. US. 1950. 84m. B&W. *Producer:* Bert Friedlob *Director:* Tay Garnett *Writer:* Tay Garnett, Horace McCoy *Cast:* Mickey Rooney, Pat O'Brien, Beverly Tyler, James Brown, Marilyn Monroe, Ralph Dumke, Bert Begley, Milburn Stone, Sam Flint, John Hedloe

The story of an orphan boy (Mickey Rooney) who runs away from the orphanage run by Father O'Hara (Pat O'Brien). The boy becomes a roller skating champion, gets polio and then fights his way back.

**276. Fires of Innocence**. Butcher. UK. 1922. B&W. *Producer:* Frank Spring *Director & Writer:* Sidney Morgan *Cast:* Joan Morgan, Marie Illington, Madge Tree, Neil Emerald, Bobby Andrews, Arthur Lennard

The film's theme is the social battle between the vicar and the wealthy of the village. The vicar becomes the center of scandal when he calls upon a widow of the village. The bishop demands an explanation and finds him innocent. The gossips turn to other issues around town such as the vicar's son having stolen jewelry.

**277. The First Legion**. UA. US. 1951. 86m. B&W. *Producer & Director:* Douglas Sirk *Writer:* Emmet Lavery *Cast:* Charles Boyer, William Demarest, Lyle Bettiger, Barbara Rush, Leo G. Carroll, Walter Hampden, Wesley Addy, Taylor Holmes, H. B. Warner, George Zucco, John McGuire, Clifford Brooke, Dorothy Adams, Molly Lamont, Queenie Smith, Jacqueline deWitt, Bill Edwards

The film is based on a Broadway play by the same name about life in a Jesuit seminary. Early stages of the film profile the different characters within the seminary. A crisis develops when bedridden Father Jose Sierra (H. B. Warner) suddenly regains the use of his leg. Everyone calls it a miracle and attributes it Joseph Martin, a Jesuit and founder of the seminary. This miracle attracts the attention many pilgrims and people is search of healing. Father Marc Arnoux (Charles Boyer), an ex-criminal attorney, gets the town doctor Peter Morell (Lyle Bettger) to admit that he caused his patient to walk using the power of suggestion after hearing his confession. A real miracle occurs when wheelchair bound Terry Gilmartin (Barbara Rush) prays so hard at the chapel that she is able to takes several steps.

**278. Five Gates to Hell**. TCF. US. 1959. 98m. B&W. *Producer, Director & Writer:* James Clavell *Cast:* Dolores Michaels, Patricia Owens, Neville Brand, Ken Scott, Nobu McCarthy, Nancy Kulp, Shirley Knight, Irish McCalla, Linda Wong

Two Red Cross doctors, seven nurses, and a nun are abducted by guerillas in French Indochina (later Vietnam) in the 1950s. Their lives are spared if they save a dying warlord but when he dies they attempt to escape. The nun is raped and murdered during their containment.

**Flame of Torment** *see* **Enjo**

**279. Flame over Vietnam**. Producers Releasing Organization. Spain/Germany. 1967. 88m. B&W. *Producer:* Sidney W. Pink *Director:* Joe Lacy (pseudonym for José María Elorrieta) *Writer:* Rafael J. Salvia, Joe Lacy, John Hart *Cast:* Elena Barrios, José Nietos, Manolo Morán, Nicolás D. Perchicot, Rosita Palomar, Félix Defauce, María Martín, Vicente P. Ávila

The story takes place during the French-Indochina War. Gunrunner Lazlo (José Nietos) is wounded and is nursed back to health by Sister Paula (Elena Barrios). Fleeing enemy forces Sister Paula and a group of orphaned children encounter Lazlo, who takes them to a railway depot. The children are forbidden to leave and Sister Paula refuses to abandon them and accompanies them to a concentration camp. Lazlo bribes a guard and arranges for their release. Lazlo is killed by a sniper's bullet as he rescues a girl left behind in the confusion.

**Flames of Paradise** *see* **Myrkrahöfðinginn**

**280. The Flapper and the Curates**. Regal. UK. 1912. B&W. *Director & Writer:* Lewin Fitzhamon *Cast:* Constance Somers-Clarke

Man poses as missionary to win dean's niece.

**281. The Flower of Faith**. International Film. US. 1916. B&W. *Director:* Burton L. King *Writer:* Charles T. and Frank Dazey *Cast:* Jane Grey, Frank Mills, Albert Travernier, Percy Helton, Mary B. Stuart, William Reynolds

A traveling evangelist, his daughter and son travel to a small community. Ruth, the evangelist's daughter (Jane Grey), tries to convert an unbeliever in the community. Tom, the son (Percy Helton) is entrusted with some church funds, but loses it in a card game and then robs a local store in order to cover up his gambling. While trying to escape he is shot and staggers to the house of the unbeliever, Lee (Frank Mills) who gets his sister. Searching for the thief the posse is led to Lee's house where Tom is concealed so they think they have caught Ruth and Lee in an illicit affair. Just when Lee is about to be lynched a bolt of lightening strikes down the limb of the tree and Tom confesses. Lee becomes a believer again.

**The Flowers of St. Francis** *see* **Francesco, giullare di Dio**

**282. Folly to Be Wise.** Fine Arts. UK. 1953. 91m. B&W. *Producer:* Sidney Gilliat *Director:* Frank Launder *Writer:* James Bridie, John Dighton, Frank Launder *Cast:* Alastair Sim, Elizabeth Allan, Roland Culver, Colin Gordon, Martita Hunt, Janet Brown, Peter Martyn, Miles Malleson, Edward Chapman, Cyril Chamberlain, Michael Ripper, Robin Bailey

A newly-arrived army chaplain Captain Paris (Alastair Sim) is in charge of camp entertainment. Everyone is willing to give their idea of what soldiers will like.

**283. Footloose.** Paramount. US. 1984. 107m. C. *Producer:* Lewis J. Rachmil, Craig Zadan *Director:* Herbert Ross *Writer:* Dean Pitchford *Cast:* Kevin Bacon, Lori Singer, John Lithgow, Dianne Wiest, Chris Penn, Sarah Jessica Parker, John Laughlin, Elizabeth Gorcey, Frances Lee McCain, Jim Youngs

Teenager Ren McCormack (Kevin Bacon) moves from Chicago to a small town where rock music and dancing are illegal. The ordinance came about after the death of a kid driving home from a dance. Bible citing Baptist Reverend Shaw Moore (John Lithgow) is responsible for keeping dancing illegal and morals in-check. Ren falls in love with the minister's daughter Ariel Moore (Lori Singer) and fights to allow dancing at the prom.

**284. For Heaven's Sake.** Paramount. US. 1926. 58m. B&W. *Director:* Sam Taylor *Writer:* John Grey, Ted Wilde, Clyde Bruckman *Cast:* Harold Lloyd, Jobyna Ralston, Noah Young, Jim Mason, Paul Weigel

J. Harold Manners (Harold Lloyd), a debonair young millionaire, accidentally starts a fire at an evangelist's coffee stand and gives him a thousand dollars for the damages. The evangelist uses the money to open a mission in the name of the donor. On his way to protest this honor he runs into the evangelist's daughter, Hope (Jobyna Ralston). Harold's friends abduct him to prevent his marriage to Hope, but his inebriated friends rescue him and they race back to the mission where Hope and Harold are married.

**285. For the Defense.** Paramount. US. 1916. B&W. *Director:* Frank Reicher *Writer:* Hector Turnbull, Margaret Turnbull *Cast:* Fannie Ward, Jack Dean, Paul Byron, Horace B. Carpenter, Camille Astor, James Neill, Gertrude Kellar

In New York, novice Fidele Roget (Fannie Ward) is captured by a white slaver. During her escape she witnesses a murder and meets Jim Webster (Jack Dean), whom she dissuades from committing suicide, and he agrees to help her get to Canada. Jim is arrested for the murder that his butler committed. Fidele realizes this is the murder she witnessed and poses as a maid in the Webster household and tricks the butler into a confession. She leaves her Order and ends up marrying Jim.

**286. For the Empire.** Gaumont. UK. 1914. B&W. *Director:* Harold Shaw *Cast:* Douglas Munro, George Bellamy, Charles Rock, Christine Rayner, Wyndham Guise, Frank Stanmore

Pacifist vicar fights back after Germans occupy his house.

**287. For the Love of Mike.** TCF. US. 1960. 87m. C. *Producer:* Robert B. Radnitz, George Sherman *Director:* George Sherman *Writer:* D. D. Beauchamp *Cast:* Richard Basehart, Stuart Erwin, Arthur Shields, Armando Silvestre, Elsa Cárdenas, Michael Steckler, Rex Allen, Danny Bravo

A young Native American orphan Michael (Danny Bravo) trains a horse for an important race with the hope of winning enough money to build a shrine for the village. His friends include young Father Phelan (Richard Basehart) and Father Walsh (Arthur Shields). Also known as *None but the Brave.*

**Forbidden** *see* **Proibito**

**288. Forever Young.** TCF. UK. 1983. 84m. B&W/C. *Producer:* Chris Griffin *Director:* David Drury *Writer:* Ray Connolly *Cast:* James Aubrey, Nicholas Gecks, Alec Mc-Cowen, Karen Archer, Joseph Wright, Liam Holt, Jane Forster, Jason Carter, Oona Kirsch

In Great Britain, Jimmy and Mike dreamed of being rock stars but went their separate ways. Mike (Nicholas Gecks) became an idealistic priest and Jimmy (James Aubrey) a cynical teacher. The two unexpectedly meet again 20 years later and their initial joy at seeing each other changes to discovery that what they share are frustrated musical dreams, sadness and resentment. Also is a subplot about a young boy who idolizes the priest and learns about betrayal.

**The Forgiven Sinner** *see* **Léon Morin, Prêtre**

**The Forgotten Light** *see* **Zapomenuté světlo**

**289. Francesco.** Hemdale Film. Italy/Germany. 1989. 150m. C. *Producer:* Roberta Cadringher *Director:* Lilian Cavani *Writer:* Lilana Cavani, Roberta Mazzoni, Hermann Hesse (novel) *Cast:* Mickey Rourke, Helena Bonham Carter, Mario Adorf, Peter Berling, Paolo Bonacelli, Nikolaus Dutsch, Edward Farrelly, Stanko Molnar, Hanns Zischler, Domiziano Arcangeli, Fabio Bussotti

Docudrama about the life of Saint Francis of Assisi told in flashback. The film follows a series of episodes in the saint's life. Saint Clare (Helena Bonham Carter) is the inspiration for his humanitarian life. In 2002, an Italian television show about Francesco starring Raoul Bova was shown.

**290. Francesco d'Assisi.** Clodio. Italy. 1966. 134m. B&W. *Director:* Liliana Cavani *Writer:* Liliana Cavani, Tullio Pinelli *Cast:* Lou Castel, Marco Bellocchio, Kenneth Belton, Ricardo Bernardini, Mimo Billi, Giuseppe Campodifiori, Gerig Domain, Gérard Herter, John Karlsen, Franco Marchesi, Giancarlo Sbragia, Gianni Turillazzi

The life of Saint Francis of Assisi retold from the sixties point of view. Also known as *Francis of Assisi*.

**291. Francesco, giullare di Dio.** Joseph Burstyn Inc. Italy. 1950. 75m. B&W. *Producer:* Angelo Rizzoli *Director:* Roberto Rossellini *Writer:* Federico Fellini, Father Antonio Lisandrini, Father Felix Morión *Cast:* Aldo Fabrizi, Brother Nazario Gerardi, Arabella Lemaitre

The re-telling of the story of St. Francis with sketches of different events concentrating on the daily lives of monks and not necessarily on the life of St. Francis. Most of the actors in the film were non-professionals and Franciscan friars. Also known as *The Flowers of St. Francis, Francis, God's Fool* and *Francis, God's Jester*.

**Francis, God's Fool** *see* **Francesco, giullare di Dio**

**Francis, God's Jester** *see* **Francesco, giullare di Dio**

**292. Francis of Assisi.** TCF. US. 1961. 105m. C. *Producer:* Plato Skouras *Director:*

**Francis Bernardone of Assisi (Bradford Dillman) is a fighting young adventurer first and later the religious man and lover of animals; *Francis of Assisi* (1961).**

Michael Curtiz *Writer*: James Forsyth, Jack W. Thomas, Eugene Vale, Louis De Wohl (novel) *Cast*: Bradford Dillman, Dolores Hart, Stuart Whitman, Cecil Kellaway, Eduard Franz, Athene Seyler, Finlay Currie, Mervyn Johns, Russell Napier, John Welsh, Harold Goldblatt, Edith Sharpe, Pedro Armendáriz, Jack Lambert

Francis Bernardone (Bradford Dillman) is a fighting young adventurer first and later becomes the religious man known as Saint Francis. In battle he hears God's voice telling him to go home and later God tells him to rebuild a church near Assisi. He forms the Franciscan religious order and receives the blessing of the Pope. Clare (Dolores Hart) is so moved by his preaching that she becomes a nun. The Pope requests Francis to travel to the Holy Land. Upon his return he is disheartened that the Brothers have given up on their vow of poverty. With blindness setting in Saint Francis goes to a cave and is tended by Clare. He prays and receives the stigmata. On his deathbed his old repentant friend arrives as well as admirers.

**Francis of Assisi** *see* **Francesco d'Assisi**

**293. Le Franciscain de Bourges.** Gaumont. France. 1968. 110m. C. *Director*: Claude Autant-Lara *Writer*: Marc Toledano (novel), Jean Aurenche, Pierre Bost *Cast*: Hardy Kruger, Jean-Pierre Dora, Claude Vernior, Reinhard Kolldehoff, Suzanne Flon, Jean Desailly, Christian Barbier

Based on the real-life incident about a Franciscain monk Albert (Hardy Kruger) who was a medical orderly at a resistance prison in occupied France. He is content in just trying to patch up the victims of Nazi torture and tries to help them escape while not endangering his fellow countrymen. The main theme is his involvement with two brothers in the Nazi prisons. The picture is based on the book of one of these men. Also known as *Franciscan of Bourges.*

**Franciscan of Bourges** *see* **Le Franciscain de Bourges**

**294. Frate Francesco.** Integrity Film. Italy. 1927. 85m. B&W. *Director*: Giulio Antamoro *Writer*: Aldo De Benedetti, Carlo Zangarini *Cast*: Romuald Joubé, Alberto Pasquali, Alfredo Robert, Franz Sala

Tells the story of the young Francis (Alberto Pasquali) who leaves his life as a soldier and libertine to live a simple life of poverty. He establishes a religious order and devotes his life to the poor. Also known as *The Passion of St. Francis.*

**Frate Julianus** *see* **Julianus barát**

**295. Frate Sole.** Tespi Films. Italy. 1918. B&W. *Director*: Mario Corsi *Cast*: Rina Calabria, Silvia Malinverni, Lucienne Myosa, Umberto Palmarini, Bruno Emanuel Palmi, Filippo Ricci

Depicts the story of Francis visiting a leper colony, comforting the poor of Assisi and dying displaying the stigmata. Also known as *San Francesco d'Assisi.*

**296. Fratello sole, sorella luna.** Paramount. Italy/UK. 1972. 135m. C. *Producer*: Dyson Lovell, Luciano Perugia *Director*: Franco Zeffirelli *Writer*: Suso Cecchi d'Amico, Kenneth Ross, Lina Wertmüller, Franco Zeffirelli *Cast*: Graham Faulkner, Judi Bowker, Leigh Lawson, Kenneth Cranham, Lee Montague, Valentina Cortese, Alec Guinness, Michael Feast, Nicholas Willat, Peter Firth, John Sharp, Adolfo Celi

Life Story of St. Francis Assisi (Graham Faulkner) and St. Clare (Judi Bowker) told from a youth oriented point of view. Songs throughout the film performed by Donovan. Also known as *Brother Sun, Sister Moon.*

**297. Free to Love.** US. 1925. 49m. *Producer*: B. F. Schulberg *Director*: Frank O'-Connor *Writer*: Adele Buffington *Cast*: Clara Bow, Donald Keith, Raymond McKee, Hallam Cooley, Charles Hill Mailes

The main character is a preacher James Crawford (Donald Keith) who runs the Settlement house where ex-convicts go for religion. The minister is described as being straitlaced, mechanical, inanimate who seems shackled to convention. Other characters include an unscrupulous master of crooks, a crippled crook and a woman Marie Anthony (Clara Bow) who has been sent away to prison, although she is innocent.

**298. Le Frère André.** Les Productions de la Montagne. Canada. 1987. C. *Producer*:

Pierre Valcour *Director:* Jean-Claude La-brecque *Writer:* Guy Dufresne *Cast:* Marc Legault, Sylvie Ferlatte, Roger Baulu, André Cailloux, René Caron, Raymond Cloutier, Roger Garceau, Roland Lepage, Guy Provost, Gilles Renaud

The story of the life of Brother André (Marc Legault), a little brother of Montreal who was an idol to French Canadians because of his faith in God and Saint Joseph. He is associated with miracles and the building of the Saint Joseph's Basilica in Montreal. Also known as *Brother Andre.*

**Friar Julianus** *see* **Julianus barát**
**Friday the Rabbi Slept Late** *see* **Lanigan's Rabbi**
**299. The Frisco Kid.** Warner. US. 1979. 122m. C. *Producer:* Mace Neufeld *Director:* Robert Aldrich *Writer:* Michael Elias, Frank Shaw *Cast:* Gene Wilder, Harrison Ford, Ramon Bieri, Val Bisoglio, George Di-Centro, Leo Fuchs, Penny Peyser, William Smith, Jack Somack, Beege Barkett, Shay Duffin

Rabbi Avram Belinsky (Gene Wilder),

a newly ordained Polish Yeshiva rabbi, teams up with cowboy Tommy (Harrison Ford) for a westward journey to a leaderless 1850's San Francisco congregation where he is to be their first rabbi. His attempts to conform to Jewish doctrine in the old west form the basis of this film. He wins people over with his sweetness and innocence.

**300. From a Far Country.** NBC. (TV). UK/Italy/Poland. 1981. 140m. C. *Producer:* Giacomo Pezzali *Director:* Krzysztof Zanussi *Writer:* Andrzej Kijowski, Jan Jósef Szczepanski, David Butler, Vincenzo Labello, Krzysztof Zanussi *Cast:* Sam Neill, Christopher Cazenove, Lisa Harrow, Maurice Denham, Cezary Morawski, Warren Clarke, Jonathan Blake, Kathleen Byron, John Franklyn-Robbins, Carol Gillie, Philip Latham, Emma Relph, John Welsh, Susan Dutton, Rupert Frazer, Daniel Olbrychski

Life of the Archbishop of Krakow who became the first non-Italian Pope, Pope Paul II. The film attempts to cover from 1930's to his election of the Pope. Also known as *Da un paese lontano* and *Z dalekiego Kraju.*

Rabbi Avram Belinsky (Gene Wilder), a newly ordained Polish Yeshiva rabbi, teams up with cowboy Tommy (Harrison Ford) on their westward journey, in *The Frisco Kid* (1979).

**301. The Fugitive.** RKO. Mexico/US. 1947. 104m. B&W. *Producer:* Merian Cooper, John Ford *Director:* John Ford *Writer:* Graham Greene (novel), Dudley Nichols *Cast:* Henry Fonda, Dolores del Rio, Pedro Armendáriz, Ward Bond, Leo Carrillo, J. Carrol Naish, Robert Armstrong, John Qualen, Fortunio Bonanova

Story of a revolutionary priest in Central America. A nameless priest (Henry Fonda) becomes a fugitive when the government renounces Christianity and wants all religious figures dead. He heroically stays behind to serve his flock even when it means his own execution. The priest is given directions to Puerto Grande, where he could board a ship and sail to freedom in America. A man claims that he will help but in reality is a police informer. Based on Graham Greene's *The Power and the Glory*. Also known as *El Fugitivo*. The film was not a commercial success but it is said that John Ford feels that this was his only perfect film.

**302. Fugitive from Sonora.** Republic. US. 1943. 57m. B&W. *Director:* Howard Bretherton *Writer:* Norman Hall *Cast:* Don 'Red' Barry, Wally Vernon, Lynn Merrick, Harry Cording, Ethan Laidlaw, Pierce Lyden, Gary Bruce, Kenne Duncan, Tommy Coats, Frank McCarroll

Twin brothers (Don 'Red' Barry), one a preacher and the other a killer, meet after being separated for many years. The preacher travels throughout the Old West bringing religion to the lawless towns. He is helped by the niece of a gang leader and finally by his repentant brother, who gives his life for his preacher brother.

**El Fugitivo** *see* **The Fugitive**

**303. Full Confession.** RKO. US. 1939. 73m. B&W. *Producer:* Robert Sisk *Director:* John Farrow *Writer:* Jerome Cady *Cast:* Victor McLaglen, Sally Eilers, Joseph Calleia, Barry Fritzgerald, Elisabeth Risdon, Pamela Blake, Malcolm 'Bud' McTaggart, John Bleifer, William Haade, George Humbert

Catholic priest Father Loma (Joseph Calleia) hears the confession of a dying man McGinnis (Victor McLaglen). McGinnis confesses to a murder that someone else, Michael O'Keefe (Barry Fitzgerald), was convicted of and is awaiting death. Father Loma gives a transfusion to the dying McGinnis and saves his life. Father Loma convinces McGinnis to step forward and confess to save the innocent man from the electric chair.

**304. Fuori dal mondo.** Entertech Releasing Corp. Italy. 1999. 100m. C. *Producer:* Lionello Cerri *Director:* Giuseppe Piccioni *Writer:* Giuseppe Piccioni, Gualtiero Rosella, Lucia Maria Zei *Cast:* Margherita Buy, Silvio Orlando, Carolina Freschi, Maria Cristina Minerva, Sonia Gessner, Alessandro Di Natale, Riccardo De Torrebruna, Stefano Abbati, Fabio Sartor, Giuliana Lojodice, Marina Massironi

Owner of a dry-cleaning business Ernesto (Silvio Orlando) and a novice nun, Sister Caterina (Margherita Buy), team up to care for an abandoned baby. The sister finds the baby in a park, gives it to the authorities, and tracks the baby to Ernesto. He thinks that he may be the father. They soon become friends and help each other face life and the world. Sister Caterina is questioning her vocation and possibly leaving the Order. Also known as *Not of this World*.

**305. Gabriel.** Belgium. 1999. 11m. C. *Producer:* Geert Bert *Director:* Renaat Coppens *Writer:* Siska Lemans *Cast:* Kai Walgraven, Magdalena Przybylek, Greta Van Langhendonck, Nand Buyl

Gabriel is an eight-year-old boy who lives in a convent with twenty nuns. He thinks he is an angel and is anxious to grow wings and fly. He collects feathers from the geese on the convent grounds. Sylvia, a young nun who befriends Gabriel, may be in on his secret.

**306. Galileo.** Seven Keys. UK. 1975. 145m. C. *Producer:* Ely Landau *Director:* Joseph Losey *Writer:* Bertolt Brecht (play), Joseph Losey, Barbara Bray *Cast:* Topol, Colin Blakely, Georgia Brown, Edward Fox, John Gielgud, Margaret Leighton, Clive Revill, Tom Conti. Michael Lonsdale, Richard O'Callaghan, Mary Larkin, Judy Parfitt, Patrick Magee

Galileo's scientific beliefs bring him into conflict with the Catholic Church. By threatening him with torture, the Church forces him to recant his views and he is sentenced to house arrest.

**307. Galileo's Battle for the Heavens.** Channel Four. UK. 2002. 114m. C. *Producer:* David Axelrod *Director:* Peter Jones *Writer:* David Axelrod, Dava Sobel (book) *Cast:* Simon Callow, Laura Nardi, John Fraser, Alexa Jargo, Liev Shreiber

Deals with Galileo's fight and trial about his controversial theory that the earth revolves around the sun. We learn of the story from letters written by his illegitimate daughter Maria Celeste a cloistered nun. Made into an episode of NOVA the television series.

**308. Galloping Gallagher.** FBO. US. 1924. 55m. B&W. *Producer:* Harry Joe Brown *Director:* Albert Rogell *Writer:* Marion Jackson *Cast:* Fred Thomson, Hazel Keener, Frank Hagney, Nelson McDowell, N. E. Hendrix, Andy Morris, Silver King the horse

Newly elected sheriff Bill Gallagher (Fred Thomson) captures a gang with the help of his horse. He also rescues a lady minister, Evelyn Churchill (Hazel Keener) and finds love. Fred Thompson was a Presbyterian minister in real life. Also known as *The Sheriff of Tombstone.*

**309. A Gamble in Souls.** Triangle. US. 1916. B&W. *Producer:* Thomas H. Ince *Director:* Walter Edwards *Writer:* Lanier Bartlett *Cast:* William Desmond, Dorothy Dalton, P. Dempsey Tabler, Charles K. French, Jack Vosburgh

Evangelist Arthur Worden (William Desmond) runs a mission on San Francisco's Barbary Coast. He is met with scornful laughter when he asks a chorus girl Freda Maxey (Dorothy Dalton) to attend services. He meets her again aboard a ship. There is a shipwreck and the two of them end up on an isolated island where love blossoms.

**310. The Garden of Allah.** MGM. US. 1927. 96m. B&W. *Director:* Rex Ingram *Writer:* Robert Hichens (novel), Willis Goldbeck *Cast:* Alice Terry, Ivan Petrovich, Marcel Vibert, H.H. Wright, Madame Pâquerette, Armand Dutertre, Ben Sadour, Gerald Fielding, Michael Powell, Rehba Ben Salah, Claude Fielding

By taking the vow of silence, constant prayer, and chastity Father Adrien (Ivan Petrovich) gains entrance to the Trappist Monastery of Notre Dame d'Afrique in Algeria. While clearing a tree from the monastery wall he accidentally knocks a girl unconscious. Upon reviving her he embraces her. Drawn by the beauty of the girl and the outside world he renounces his vows and escapes into the desert. On his journey he meets Domini Enfilden (Alice Terry) and saves her from a Bedouin riot and they marry. He confesses to breaking his vows and returns to the monastery to do penance. Previously made in 1916 starring Helen Ware and Tom Santschi.

**311. The Garden of Allah.** UA. US. 1936. 79m. C. *Producer:* David O. Selznick *Director:* Richard Boleslawski *Writer:* Robert Hichens (novel), W.P. Lipscomb, Lynn Riggs *Cast:* Marlene Dietrich, Charles Boyer, Basil Rathbone, C. Aubrey Smith, Joseph Schildkraut, John Carradine, Alan Marshal, Lucile Watson, Henry Brandon, Tilly Losch

After the death of her invalid father, Domini Enfilden (Marlene Dietrich) returns to Le Couvent de Ste. Cecile and the Mother Superior tells her to find herself in the solitude of the Sahara Desert. Brother Antoine (Charles Boyer), the only Brother who knows the secret formula for a famous liquor, leaves his monastery. Domini and the Brother meet on a train. Later he introduces himself as Boris Androvsky. They fall in love and he keeps his secret. A stranger exposes the true identity of Boris and about the liquor. Boris feels that he must return and make up for what he has done. He promises to return to Domini but at the gates of the monastery they embrace for the last time. There was some apprehension concerning the public reaction about the release of this film by studio executives. Clergymen were asked their opinions and it was decided that some people will be upset but the story was acceptable.

**312. The Garden of Redemption.** Showtime. (TV). US. 1997. 95m. C. *Producer:* Marianne Moloney *Director:* Thomas Michael Donnelly *Writer:* Anthony DiFranco (short story), Thomas Michael Donnelly *Cast:* Marta Amaro, Anthony LaPaglia, Joao

Arouca, Embeth Davidtz, Rui Pedro Cardoso, Dan Hedaya, Manuel Castro e Silva, Peter Firth, Brad Cherry, Jorge Sanz

In Nazi occupied Italy, a priest Don Paolo Montale (Anthony LaPaglia) questions his religious beliefs upon seeing his countrymen murdered. He also becomes attracted to a female resistance fighter. Does he remain a pacifist or join in the fight?

**313. Gates to Paradise.** Jointex. UK/Yugoslavia. 1968. 89m. *Producer:* Sam Waynberg *Director:* Andrzej Wajda *Writer:* Jerzy Andrzejewski (novel), Donald Kravanth *Cast:* Lionel Stander, Ferdy Mayne, Matthieu Carrière, Pauline Challoner, John Fordyce, Jenny Agutter

A 13th century monk (Lionel Stander) accompanies children on crusade from France to Jerusalem. It is hope that their innocence will defeat the infidels. During the journey, some of the children confess to him that belief is not driving them to the Holy Land but attraction to their female leader. He confesses that a lecherous Count Ludovic told him to make the journey. He realizes this crusade must stop. He is trampled by the marching children as they go towards certain death. Based on true early 13th century crusades that young people attempted to make to the Holy Lands. The journeys ended in disaster with some children being sold into slavery.

**The Gaucho Priest** *see* **El Cura gaucho**

**314. Gente così.** Artista Associati. Italy. 1949. 90m. B&W. *Producer:* Giorgio Venturini *Director:* Fernando Cerchio *Writer:* Giovanni Guareschi *Cast:* Vivi Gioi, Adriano Rimoldi, Camillo Pilotto, Renato De Carmine, Marisa Mari, Saro Urzì

In a small mountain village, a parish priest Don Candido (Camillo Pilotto) and the mayor/barber Mayor Giusà (Saro Urzì) watch over the village. Giàn (Adriano Rimoldi), a young smuggler, falls in love with schoolteacher Theresa (Vivi Gioi), a communist. Do to some misunderstanding they are separated when she becomes pregnant and leaves. She wants him to have his freedom. They come together but unfortunately Giàn is shot and while he lies dying Don

Candido marries the couple. Film was released in 1954 in the United States under the title of *Mistress of the Mountains.*

**315. Un Giorno nella vita.** Orbis Films. Italy. 1946. B&W. *Producer:* Salvo D'Angelo *Director:* Alessandro Blasetti *Writer:* Alessandro Blasetti, Mario Chiari, Diego Fabbri, Anton Giulio Majano, Cesare Zavattini *Cast:* Enzo Biliotti, Elisa Cegani, Ada Colangeli, Ada Dondini, Arnoldo Foà, Massimo Girotti, Flavia Grande, Mariella Lotti, Dante Maggio, Secondo Maronetto

Some Italian partisans take refuge in a convent to escape German raids. Initially the nuns reject the partisans but after seeing the wounded, the nuns accept them. When the partisans leave the Germans take revenge on the convent.

**316. Giovanna d'Arco.** Savoia. Italy. 1913. B&W. *Director:* Nino Oxilia *Cast:* Arturo Garzes, Maria Jacobini, Alberto Nepoti

The director adds two special touches to the tale of Joan of Arc. One is that she is accompanied by Bertrand, her companion. Secondly, in her final captivity, the Earl of Stafford attempts to stab Joan, and her confessor tries to get her to declare her guilt. At the end he is begging for her pardon. Also known as *Joan of Arc.*

**317. Giovanna d'Arco al rogo.** Produzione Cinematografiche. France/Italy. 1954. 80m. C. *Producer:* Giorgio Criscuolo, Franco Francese *Director:* Roberto Rossellini *Writer:* Paul Claudel, Roberto Rossellini *Cast:* Ingrid Bergman, Tullio Carminati, Giacinto Prantelli, Augusto Romani, Plinio Clabassi, Saturno Meletti

While being burned at the stake Joan of Arc (Ingrid Bergman) and a priest Fra Domenico (Tullio Carminati) reviews the events of her life that have led up to this horrible end. This was Bergman's second film as Joan of Arc. Also known as *Joan at the Stake.*

**318. Girlfriends.** Warner. US. 1978. 86m. C. *Producer & Director:* Claudia Weill *Writer:* Vicki Polon *Cast:* Melanie Mayron, Eli Wallach, Anita Skinner, Bob Balaban, Christopher Guest, Gina Rojak, Amy Wright, Viveca Lindfors, Mike Kellin, Russell Horton

A young photographer, Susan (Melanie

Mayron), faces loneliness when her best friend suddenly marries. She struggles with her own personal and work relationships. Rabbi Gold (Eli Wallach), for whom she sometimes photographs Bar Mitzvahs and weddings, acts as her advisor.

**319. Girls in Prison.** AI. US. 1956. 87m. B&W. *Producer:* Alex Gordon *Director:* Edward Cahn *Writer:* Lou Rusoff *Cast:* Richard Denning, Joan Taylor, Adele Jergens, Helen Gilbert, Lance Fuller, Jane Darwell, Raymond Hatton, Phyllis Coates, Diana Darrin, Mae Marsh, Laurie Mitchell, Diane Richards, Luana Walters, Riza Royce

Prisoner Anne Carlson (Joan Taylor) claims she is innocent of the crime. The prison chaplain Reverend Fuller (Richard Denning) believes in her and tries to help. Her cellmates think that she does know where the $38,000 from the bank robbery is hidden. They conspire to break out and get the money. Meanwhile, Paul Anderson (Lance Fuller) in on the robbery is after the money too. They all meet at Anne's home when an earthquake allows them to escape from prison. Reverend Fuller (ex-star college boxing champ) must use his fists against the bad guy.

**320. Giv Gud en Chance om Søndagen.** Athena Film. Denmark. 1970. 94m. B&W. *Producer:* Leif Feilberg *Director:* Henrik Stangerup *Writer:* Jørgen Stegelmann, Henrik Stangerup *Cast:* Ulf Pilgaard, Ove Sprogøe, Lotte Tarp, Vibeke Reumert, Ole Storm, Rachel Bæklund, Erik Nørgaard, Ebbe Kløvedal Reich, Erik Halskov-Jensen

Young vicar Reverend Niels Riesing (Ulf Pilgaard) loses his entire congregation to a journeying faith healer. A fellow vicar encourages him to make religion part of today's world. Near the end he breaks into the church very drunk with former divinity students and preaches from the pulpit. Also known as *Give God A Chance On A Sunday.*

**Give God a Chance on a Sunday** *see* **Giv Gud en Chance om Søndagen**

**321. Glory of Faith.** French Film Exchange. France. 1936. 70m. B&W. *Director:* Georges Pallu *Cast:* Gabriel Farguette, Jacqueline Francell, Alice Tissot, Raymond Galle, Jean Dax, Germaine Sablon

Seamstress Marie-Therese (Jacqueline Francell) befriends the son of wealthy parents in the house where she works. There is an attempted kidnapping of the youth plus a life-threatening illness for the child. With Marie-Therese's prayers and motivated by her belief in St. Theresa, he is cured of his illness. Underlying this plot is the story of Saint Theresa – The Little Flower. Her story is told through flashbacks. Also known as *St. Theresa, The Little Flower.*

**322. Go Ask Alice.** ABC. (TV). US. 1973. 74m. C. *Producer:* Gerald I. Isenberg *Director:* John Korty *Writer:* Ellen M. Violett, Beatrice Sparks (novel) *Cast:* Jamie Smith-Jackson, William Shatner, Ruth Roman, Wendell Burton, Julie Adams, Andy Griffith, Ayn Ruymen, Mimi Saffian, Jennifer Edwards, Daniel Michael Mann, Michael Morgan, Jeanne Avery, Frederick Herrick, Robert Carradine, Gary Marsh

A drama based on the diary of a teenage girl (Jamie Smith-Jackson) caught in the world of drug addiction. We *see* her enter the world of prostitution. A priest (Andy Griffith) tries to help her family.

**323. Go Down Death.** Sack Amusement Enterprises. US. 1944. 56m. B&W. *Producer:* Alfred Sack *Director:* Spencer Williams *Writer:* Sam Elljay, Spencer Williams *Cast:* Myra D. Hemmings, Samuel H. James, Eddye L. Houston, Spencer Williams, Amos Droughan, Walter McMillion, Irene Campbell, Charlie Washington, Helen Butler, Dolly Jones

An underworld leader Big Jim Bottom plans to frame Reverend Jasper Jones in a sex scandal. The minister's reputation is in question as he wavers between heaven and hell. Aunt Caroline learns of the plot but she is struck down by Big Jim. During her funeral the Reverend gives his Go Down, Death sermon. Big Jim is tortured by grief and dies. Based on a poem by James Weldon Johnson.

**324. Go Straight.** Universal Film. US. 1921. B&W. *Director:* William Worthington *Writer:* George Hively *Cast:* Frank Mayo, Cora Drew, Harry Carter, Lillian Rich, George F. Marion, Lassie Young, Charles Brinley

In a backwoods community in Kentucky a young minister, Keith Rollins (Frank Mayo), finds that lawlessness and politics are against him and threaten his position with his congregation. His only supporters are his housekeeper and Hope (Lillian Rich), the daughter of a crooked evangelist. Keith is called away and held by thugs so he will miss a town meeting. Hope and Buck help him escape and make it to the meeting.

**325. God Is My Partner.** TCF. US. 1957. 82m. B&W. *Producer:* Sam Hersh *Director:* William F. Claxton *Writer:* Charles Francis Royal *Cast:* Walter Brennan, John Hoyt, Marion Ross, Jesse White, Nelson Leigh, Charles Lane, Ellen Corby, Paul Cavanagh, Nancy Kulp, John Harmon

Dr. Charles Grayson (Walter Brennan), a successful elderly surgeon, is brought to trial by two nephews on a charge that he is incompetent to handle his money. He testifies that he gave $50,000 to his church because without his belief he would have never become such a great surgeon. Grayson's granddaughter happens to be an attorney and wins the case thanks to the testimonies of his grateful patients.

**God Needs Men** *see* **Dieu a besoin des hommes**

**326. Den Goda Viljan.** Channel 4. Sweden. 1992. 181m. C. *Producer:* Ingrid Dahlberg *Director:* Billie August *Writer:* Ingmar Bergman *Cast:* Samuel Fröler, Pernilla August, Max von Sydow, Ghita Norby, Lennart Hjulström, Mona Malm, Lena Endre, Keve Hjelm

Set in early 1900s Sweden. Against parental objections, an emotionally neutral Lutheran pastor Henrik Bergman (Samuel Fröler) marries a vivacious nurse. Their marriage is a troubled one. Bergman's parents served as the basis of this autobiographical screenplay. Swedish title is *The Best Intentions.*

**327. God's Good Man.** Stoll. UK. 1919. B&W. *Director:* Maurice Elvey *Writer:* Kate Gurney *Cast:* Basil Gill, Peggy Carlisle, Barry Bernard, Hugh Dabernon-Stoke, Teddy Arundell, Julian Henry, Temple Bell, Kate Gurney

Heiress Maryilla Vancourt (Peggy Carlisle) weds poor parson Reverend John Walden (Basil Gill) after discharged agent hurts her during hunt.

**328. Going My Way.** Paramount. US. 1944. 130m B&W. *Producer & Director:* Leo McCarey *Writer:* Frank Butler, Frank Cavett *Cast:* Bing Crosby, Risē Stevens, Barry Fitzgerald, Frank McHugh, Gene Lockhart, William Frawley, James Brown, Jean Heather, Porter Hall

Father Charles 'Chuck' O'Malley (Bing Crosby) is a regular guy who had a girlfriend before becoming a priest. We first see him seeking directions in black clericals and a straw hat. He helps old crusty Father Fitzgibbon (Barry Fitzgerald) reunite with his aged mother from Ireland and raises money to rebuild the church, located in a poor section of NYC, when it burns down. All tasks completed with seemingly little effort and quite a few songs.

Father Chuck represents the model of the ideal priest who has no desire for money, power or sex and who provides comfort to all. Father Chuck's gift is to see everyone's need and in magical "priestliness" provides for it. This film and its sequel *The Bells of St. Mary's* were huge box office hits. This film won seven Academy Awards, including best picture. The film received a certificate of approval from PCA.

**329. The Golden Lily.** Gaumont/Kleine Optical. France. 1910. B&W.

A poor street musician turns to a Catholic Church for comfort. He starts to play his violin at the altar and prays. The Virgin Mary appears and gives him a golden lily. He takes it to a goldsmith in hopes of selling it. The gunsmith thinks he is a thief and he is arrested. He tries to explain his story but no one believes him. Finally, they allow him back in the church and the miracle is repeated.

**330. Der Golem wie er in die Walt Kam.** UFA. Germany. 1920. 91m. B&W. *Producer:* Paul Davidson *Director:* Paul Wegener, Carl Boese *Writer:* Wegener, Henrik Galeen *Cast:* Paul Wegener, Albert Steinrück, Ernst Deutsch, Lydia Salmonova, Hans Stürm, Otto Gebühr, Lothar Muthel

Jewish folk legend set in medieval Prague about a rabbi. Rabbi Lowe (Albert

Steinrück) creates a monster Golem out of clay. The monster then falls in love with the rabbi's daughter. The monster brings fear and is finally destroyed by an innocent child, when he offers the child an apple and his Star of David is removed. Previously filmed in 1915 and again in 1936. Also known as *The Golem: How He Came Into the World.*

**331. Golpes a mi puerta.** International Film Circuit. Venezuela/Argentina/Cuba. 1994. 105m. C. *Producer & Director:* Alejandro Saderman *Writer:* Juan Carlos Gené, Alejandro Saderman *Cast:* Verónica Oddó, Elba Escobar, Juan Carlos Gené, José Antonio Rodríguez, Ana Castell, Mirta Ibarra, Frank Spano, Eduardo Gil, Dimas González, Rogelio Eliaín

In an unnamed South American country two brave nuns Ana (Verónica Oddó) and Ursula (Elba Escobar) provide refuge to a rebel soldier who suddenly appeared at their home. The mayor of the town is suspicious of them but does nothing because they are nuns and he doesn't want any trouble with the Church. The military cares nothing about that and soon captures and shoots the rebel. The nuns are now in great danger. Also known as *Knocks at My Door.*

**332. Gone to Earth.** BL. UK. 1950. 110m. C. *Producer, Director & Writer:* Michael Powell, Emeric Pressburger *Cast:* Jennifer Jones, David Farrar, Cyril Cusack, Esmond Knight, Sybil Thorndike, Hugh Griffith, Edward Chapman, Beatrice Varley, George Cole, Frances Clare, Valentine Dunn, Richmond Nairne

A father wants his animal-loving and free spirit daughter Hazel (Jennifer Jones) to marry the first man that proposes to her. The first proposal is from the local parson Edward Marston (Cyril Cusack). After the wedding she runs away with another man, the fox-hunting evil squire, but is brought back home by her husband. Later she dies trying to save her pet fox from a hunt. Edited version released under the title *The Wild Heart.*

**333. Good Against Evil.** ABC. (TV). US. 1977. 90m. *Director:* Paul Wendkos *Writer:* Jimmy Sangster *Cast:* Dack Rambo, Elyssa Davalos, Richard Lynch, Dan O'Herlihy, John Harkins, Jenny O'Hara, Leila

Goldoni, Peggy McCay, Peter Brandon, Kim Cattrall, Natasha Ryan, Richard Sanders, Lillian Adams, Erica Yohn, Richard Stahl, Sandy Ward, Isaac Goz

An exorcism with a priest Father Kemschler (Dan O'Herlihy) is required when a young couple is beset by evil forces.

**334. A Good Story.** American Mutoscope Co. UK. 1897. B&W.

One priest tells a funny story to another priest while having coffee after their meal in this reproduction of a painting.

**335. A Good Story.** G.A.S. Films. UK. 1901. B&W. *Director:* G. A. Smith

Monk tells fellow brother a naughty story.

**336. The Good Vicar.** Royal Film Exchange. 1909. B&W.

No description is available.

**Goodbye, Children** *see* **Au revoir les enfants**

**337. GOSPA.** The Penland Co. Croatia/Canada/US. 1995. C. *Director:* Jakov Sedlar *Writer:* Ivan Aralica, Paul Gronseth, Barry Morrow *Cast:* Martin Sheen, Michael York, Morgan Fairchild, Pal Guilfoyle, George Coe, Ray Girardin, Frank Finlay, Tony Zazula, William Hootkins, Angelo Santiago, Mustafa Nadarevic, Zlatko Crnkovic

GOSPA means Our Lady in Croatian. Film about a reportedly true event in Medjugorje, where six children believed they saw the Virgin Mary in 1981. A parish priest Father Jozo Zovko (Martin Sheen) struggles to defend the six children. Millions flock to see the Virgin Mary causing the government great concern. When the Father delivers a controversial sermon, the government imprisons and tortures him.

**338. The Gospel According to Vic.** Skouras Pictures. UK. 1985. 92m.C. *Producer:* Michael Relph *Director & Writer:* Charles Gormley *Cast:* Tom Conti, Helen Mirren, David Hayman, Brain Pettifer, Jennifer Black, Ewen Bremner, Tom Busby

A Catholic school named after Blessed Edith Semple in Scotland is devoted to finding two more miracles that would promote Semple to sainthood. Non-believer Scottish teacher Mathews (Tom Conti) is involved in a possible miracle. Also known as *Heavenly Pursuits*.

**339. Gösta Berlings Saga.** Svinsk Filmindustri. Sweden. 1924. 183m. B&W. *Director*: Mauritz Stiller *Writer*: Selma Lagerlof (novel), Ragnar Hyltén-Cavallius, Mauritz Stiller *Cast*: Greta Garbo, Lars Hanson, Gerda Lundeqvist, Otto Elg-Lundberg

Minister Gösta Berling (Lars Hanson) loses his position because he drinks too much and has a rebellious attitude. Gösta meets married Countess Elizabeth Dohna (Greta Garbo) and they soon fall in love. With her love he redeems himself. Also known as *Atonement of Gösta Berling*.

**340. Gostanza da libbiano.** Italy. 2000. 93m. B&W. *Producer*: Giovanni Carratori *Director*: Paolo Benvenuti *Writer*: Stefano Bacci, Giovanni Benvenuti, Mario Cereghino *Cast*: Lucia Poli, Valentino Davanzati, Renzo Cerrato, Paolo Spaziani, Lele Biagi, Nadia Capocchini, Teresa Soldaini

Based on original trial records of the eponymous, 60-year-old Tuscan nun Gostanza (Lucia Poli) accused of witchcraft in 1594.

**341. The Governor's Daughter.** Kalem. US. 1909. B&W. *Writer:* James Montaque Munroe

During the Colonial period a clergyman falls in love with the daughter of the Governor of Virginia. He becomes a spy against the British and disguises himself as a woman. When he is discovered his ex-love hides him in her house. When he is found, there is a struggle and the British officer is knocked unconscious. The clergyman puts on the uniform and orders the soldiers to leave and then makes his escape.

**342. Grand Canary.** Fox. US. 1934. 78m. B&W. *Producer:* Jesse L. Lasky *Director:* Irving Cummings *Writer:* Ernest Pascal, A. J. Cronin (novel) *Cast:* Warner Baxter, H. B. Warner, Madge Evans, Marjorie Rambeau, Juliette Compton, Zita Johnson, Gilbert Emery

A female medical missionary tries to reform a derelict alcoholic jungle doctor journeying to the Canary Islands. When the boat docks, yellow fever is prevalent. The doctor regains his skills and saves the victims.

**343. La Grande aurora.** Superfilm. Italy. 1946. 90m. B&W. *Director*: Giuseppe Maria Scotese *Writer*: Cesare Zavattini *Cast*: Pierino Gamba, Rossano Brazzi, Renée Faure, Giovanni Gransso, Michele Riccardini, Yvonne Samson, Fausto Guerzoni, Loris Gizzi, Guglielmo Sinaz, Pierino Gamba

The main plot is about the conflict between the talents of young Gamba (Italy's nine-year-old musical prodigy) and his materialistic grandfather. The child is secretly aided by a priest Don Terenzio (Michele Riccardini) who organizes an orchestra for him to conduct at an open-air concert. In the end the grandfather accepts the child's musical career. His parents, after being separated, are happily reunited and the child achieves success as a symphony orchestra conductor. Also known as *The Great Dawn*.

**The Great Dawn** *see* **La Grande aurora**

**344. The Greatest Gift.** NBC. (TV). US. 1974. 100m. C. *Producer*: Dean Hargrove *Director*: Boris Sagal *Writer*: Abby Mann *Cast*: Glenn Ford, Julie Harris, Lance Kerwin, Harris Yulin, Charles Tyner, Dabbs Greer, Cari Anne Warder, Albert Smith, Furman Walters, Leslie Thorsen, Elsie Travis, Ken Renard, J. Don Furguson, Burt Douglas

Set in a small southern town in 1940, tells the story of Reverend Holvak (Glenn Ford) who struggles to provide for his family. He also has to deal with a dwindling congregation, restless church deacons and a bullying sheriff.

**345. The Greatest Wish in the World.** International Exclusives. UK. 1918. B&W. *Director:* Maurice Elvey *Writer:* Bannister Merwin *Cast:* Bransby Williams, Odette Goimbault, Edward Combermere, Ada King, Douglas Munro, Gwynne Herbert, Teddy Arundell, Jean Alwyn, Will Corrie

Waif adopted by priest is seduced, has a baby, and becomes a nun.

**346. The Green Pastures.** Warner. US. 1936. 93m. B&W. *Director*: Marc Connelly, William Keighley *Writer*: Sheridan Gibney, Marc Connelly *Cast*: Rex Ingram, Oscar Polk, Eddie Anderson, Frank Wilson, George Reed, Abraham Gleaves, Myrtle Anderson, Al Stokes, Edna M. Harris, James Fuller

One Sunday afternoon in the Louisiana delta a black preacher, Mr. Deshee (George Reed), tells bible stories to his Sunday school class. Based on a play "The Green Pastures" by Marc Connelly and suggested by the book Ol' Man Adam An' His Chillun by Roark Bradford. The play won the 1930 Pulitzer Prize and ran on Broadway for five years.

**347. Guaglio.** Lux. Italy. 1948. 88m. *Producer*: Gigi Martello, Carlo Ponti *Director*: Luigi Comencini *Writer*: Luigi Comencini, Suso Cecchi D'Amico *Cast*: Adolfo Celi, Tina Pica, Mario Russo, Luigi Demastro, Antonio Cirelli, Carlo Della Posta, G. F. Mattia, Carlo Barbieri, Clemente De Michele

Inspired by Father Flanagan's "Boys' Town." The central character is a young missionary Don Pietro (Adolfo Celi). His suitcase is stolen by a group of juvenile delinquents. He decides to abandon a trip to Africa in order to set up an Italian counterpart to Boys' Town. With the help of one youngster the priest manages to rehabilitate the boys and win public support for his plan. The 30 boys are played by themselves. Also known as *Hey, Boy*.

**348. Guilty of Treason.** Eagle-Lion. US. 1950. 86m. B&W. *Producer*: Jack Wrather, Robert Golden *Director*: Felix Feist *Writer*: Emmet Lavery *Cast*: Charles Bickford, Paul Kelly, Bonita Granville, Richard Derr, Berry Kroeger, Elizabeth Risdon, Roland Winters, John Banner, Alfred Linder

Based on a chapter of the Overseas Press Club report "As We See Russia," film depicts the circumstances of the trial and conviction of Cardinal Mindszenty (Charles Bickford) in Hungary from 1949–50. The film begins from his early conflict with the Hungarian Communist regime to his imprisonment. His confession is obtained with the use of torture, hypnosis and drugs. A parallel plot concerns a romance between a Hungarian girl and a Russian colonel.

**349. The Gun and the Pulpit.** ABC. (TV). US. 1974. 90m. C. *Producer*: Paul Maslansky *Director*: Daniel Petrie *Writer*: William Bowers *Cast*: Marjoe Gortner, Slim Pickens, David Huddleston, Geoffrey Lewis, Estelle Parsons, Pamela Sue Martin, Jeff Corey, Karl Swenson, Jon Lorimer, Robert Phillips, Larry Ward, Joan Goodfellow

A fugitive gunfighter discovers the body of a minister who has been killed in an ambush He disguises himself as the minister and defends townspeople from a crooked land baron.

**350. Gun Gospel.** First National. US. 1927. 60m. B&W. *Producer*: Charles R. Rogers *Director*: Harry Joe Brown *Writer*: Marion Jackson *Cast*: Ken Maynard, Bob Fleming, Romaine Fielding, Virginia Brown Faire, J. P. McGowan, Jerry Madden, Noah Young, William Dyer, Slim Whitaker, Tarzan the horse

Granger Hume (Ken Maynard) discovers at a masquerade ball that Bill Brogan (J. P. McGowan) seeks his capture because of a grudge against Dad Walker (Bob Fleming). In a confrontation with Brogan, Walker is killed, but before dying he makes Hume promise not to avenge his death. While he is disguised as a parson, Hume overhears Brogan's plot to raid neighboring ranches and warns the people. In self-defense he kills Brogan and is hailed as a hero.

**351. Guns for San Sebastian.** MGM. France/Mexico/Italy. 1968. 111m. C. *Producer*: Jacques Bar *Director*: Henri Verneuil *Writer*: William Barby Faherty (novel), James R. Webb *Cast*: Anthony Quinn, Anjanette Comer, Charles Bronson, Sam Jaffe, Silvia Pinal, Jorge Martinez de Hoyos, Jaime Fernández, Rosa Furman, Jorge Russek, Leon Askin, José Chávez, Ivan Desny, Fernand Gravey, Pedro Armendáriz Jr.

During in the 18th century Mexico, rebel bandit Leon Alastray (Anthony Quinn) seeks sanctuary in a church to escape from government troops. Father Joseph (Sam Jaffe) hides him and they travel together. Father Joseph dies early on thus paving the way for Alastray to assume his identity as a priest in Mexico. At a village, the people ask him to stay and be their spiritual leader. He helps them build a dam and obtain weapons. The village is besieged but with Alastray they defeat the invaders. Villager Kinita (Anjanette Comer) knows Alastray is not a priest, but asks him to say mass. When troops arrive with a new priest, the villagers help Alastray and Kinita escape. Also known as *La Bataille de San Sebastian*.

**352. Guy Fawkes.** Stoll. UK. 1923. B&W. *Director:* Maurice Elvey *Writer:* Alicia Ramsey, Harrison Ainsworth (novel) *Cast:* Matheson Lang, Nina Vanna, Hugh Buckler, Shayle Gardner, Lionel d'Aragon, Jerrold Robertshaw, Edward O'Neill, Robert English, Dallas Cairns, Pino Conti

Papistshire Dutchman plots to blow up parliament in revenge for anti-catholic decree.

**353. Guyana: Cult of the Damned.** Universal. Mexico/Spain/Panama. 1979. 90m. C. *Producer & Director:* René Cardona Jr. *Writer:* Carlos Valdemar, René Cardona Jr. *Cast:* Stuart Whitman, Gene Barry, John Ireland, Joseph Cotton, Bradford Dillman, Jennifer Ashley, Yvonne De Carlo, Tony Yound

Low budget drama based on the Jonestown massacre. The film's disclaimer is that the story is true, but the names have been changed. Reverend James Johnson (Stuart Whitman) hands out the lethal doses of poison from his church in Guyana to his followers. Also known as *Guyana, el crimen del siglo*.

**354. Ha-Hesder.** Kino International. Israel. 2000. 102m. C. *Producer:* David Mandil, Eyal Shiray *Director & Writer:* Joseph Cedar *Cast:* Aki Avni, Tinkerbell, Idan Alterman, Assi Dayan, Abrahm Celektar, Amnon Volf, Shimon Mimran, Uri Klauzner, Samuel Calderon

In a remote West Bank settlement, beloved and revered Rabbi Meltzer (Asi Dayan) is the leader of a yeshiva. His yeshiva is getting its own military company headed by Menachem (Aki Avni). The outside world warily eyes the rabbi, fearful of what may happen. The rabbi wants his rebellious daughter Michal (Tinkerbell) to marry sickly Pini (Edan Alterman) but she is attracted to Menachem. Unfortunately, when Menachem will not disobey the rabbi she leaves the settlement. Upset Pini and others plot to destroy the Dome of the Rock, the mosque on the Old City site, holy to both Jews and Moslems. The same Temple Mount that the

rabbi wanted redeemed for Israel. Also known as *Time of Favor*.

**355. Hallelujah.** MGM. US. 1929. 109m. B&W. *Producer & Director:* King Vidor *Writer:* Wanda Tuchock *Cast:* Daniel L. Haynes, Nina May McKinney, William Fountaine, Harry Gray, Fannie Belle DeKnight, Everett McGarrity, Victoria Spivey, Dixie Jubilee Singers

Zeke (Daniel L. Haynes), a Southern cotton picker, accidentally kills his favorite brother. He becomes extremely remorseful and full of agony. When Zeke receives forgiveness, he is redeemed and turns into the brimstone and fire preacher Brother Zekiel. Even though Zeke is now a preacher he still has human desires and wishes to fulfill those needs. It is an all-African American cast.

**356. Hand in Hand.** Columbia. UK. 1960. 78m. B&W. *Producer:* Helen Winston *Director:* Philip Leacock *Writer:* Diana Morgan *Cast:* Loretta Parry, Philip Needs, John Gregson, Sybil Thorndike, Finlay Currie, Derek Sydney, Miriam Karlin, Arnold Diamond, Kathleen Byron, Barry Keegan, Martin Lawrence, Babara Hicks, Denis Gilmore, Peter Pike, Susan Reid, Eric Francis, Stratford Johns, Donald Tandy, Madge Ryan

Two children, one a Roman Catholic and one a Jew, are very good friends and become blood brothers. Older children tell Michael that Jews killed Jesus which threatens their friendship. To show confidence in their friendship they visit each other's church. When Rachel almost drowns in a boating accident and thinking she has died, Michael rushes to Father Timothy for help who stresses that God loves everyone. Rachel is fine and the children talk to Rabbi Benjamin. Michael realizes that both religions are good and their friendship is confirmed. Also known as *The Star and the Cross*.

**The Harp of Burma** *see* **Biruma no tategoto**

**357. Harvest Is Rich.** Distribuidora Cinematografica. Spain. 1948. 142m. B&W. *Director:* José Luis Sáenz de Heredia *Writer:* Vincente Escrivá, José Rodulfo Boeta *Cast:* Fernando Fernán-Gómez, Sarita Montiel, Enrique Guitart, Rafael Romero Marchent, Antonio Almorós

Young missionary Father Santiago (Fernando Fernán-Gómez) takes charge of a Catholic mission in Madras, India. There is rivalry with the Protestant pastor, trickery and other dangers that the Father faces. Also known as *La Mies Es Mucha*.

**358. Hawaii.** UA. US. 1966. 189m. C. *Producer*: Walter Mirisch *Director*: George Roy Hill *Writer*: James A. Michener (novel), Dalton Trumbo, Daniel Taradash *Cast*: Julie Andrews, Max von Sydow, Richard Harris, Carroll O'Connor, Elizabeth Cole, Diane Sherry, Heather Menzies, Torin Thatcher, Gene Hackman, John Cullum, Lou Antonio, Michael Constantine

Film concerns the commercial-religious development of Hawaii during the period 1820–1841. The New England Protestant fire and brimstome Puritan heritage is brought to Hawaii by missionaries such as Abner Hale (Max von Sydow). He comes as a young and over-zealous Protestant missionary with a new bride Jerusha (Julie Andrews).The natives are seen as happy and loving pagans who enjoy life. Reverend John Whipple (Gene Hackman) is also a doctor, Reverend Abraham Hewlett (Lou Antonio) is expelled, and there is Reverend Immanuel Quigley (John Cullum), all are also there to do God's work. Many acts of cruelty are done in the name of God.

**Hawks and Sparrows** *see* **Uccellacci e uccellini**

**359. Häxan.** Sweden. 1922. 87m. B&W. *Director & Writer*: Benjamin Christensen *Cast*: Maren Pedersen, Clara Pontoppidan, Elith Pio, Oscar Stribolt, Tora Teje, John Andersen

Documentary style film of the history of witchcraft. In one scene a young man lies sick while a priest performs a test for any signs of witchcraft. He determines that the patient is under a spell of a witch. An old female beggar as well as the man's wife stands accused. The old woman is tortured and confesses while implicating others. They are condemned to the stake. The priest lusts for the wife and submits to flagellation. The wife is accused of bewitching the priest and is executed. Also known as *Witchcraft*.

**360. Hearts of Humanity.** AP&D. UK. 1936. B&W. *Producer & Director*: John Baxter *Writer*: Herbert Ayres *Cast*: Bransby Williams, Wilfrid Walter, Cathleen Nesbitt, Pamela Randall, Eric Portman, Hay Petrie, J. Fisher White, Fred Duprez

Village cleric, Reverend John Maitland (Wilfrid Walter), fleeing gossip helps drunkards and catches gang. He is upset that his parishioners are more interested in looking into his past than worshipping in church. Also known as *The Crypt*.

**361. Heaven Help Us.** TriStar. US. 1985. 104m. C. *Producer*: Mark Carliner, Kenneth Utt, Dan Wigutow *Director*: Michael Dinner *Writer*: Charles Purpura *Cast*: Donald Sutherland, John Heard, Andrew McCarthy, Mary Stuart Masterson, Kevin Dillon, Malcolm Danare, Jennifer Dundas, Kate Reid, Wallace Shawn, Jay Patterson, George Anders

Sixteen-year-old Michael Dunn (Andrew McCarthy) is the new boy at St. Basil's Catholic School for boys in Brooklyn during the sixties. Brother Thadeus (Donald Sutherland) is headmaster of the school where all the teachers are members of the same religious order. While Brother Thadeus is a strict disciplinarian, he also includes other values as well. He believes in suspending rather than expelling students and protecting students from sadistic staff. He transfers Brother Constance (Jay Patterson) from the school when he oversteps his authority. Dunn and his fellow misfits clash with the repressive priest staff and faculty. School bully Rooney (Kevin Dillon) intimidates him and others into performing numerous pranks such as disrupting confession which leads to punishment.

**362. Heaven Knows, Mr. Allison.** TCF. US. 1957. 108m. C. *Producer*: Buddy Adler, Eugene Frenke *Director*: John Huston *Writer*: John Huston, John Lee Mahin, Charles Shaw (novel) *Cast*: Deborah Kerr, Robert Mitchum

Shipwrecked and marooned on a small Pacific island during World War II, a marine corporal Mr. Allison (Robert Mitchum) meets a nun, Sister Angela (Deborah Kerr), also stranded on the island when a missionary is killed. They are hiding in a cave from a Japanese task force. The marine falls in love probably for the first time in his life with Sister Angela.

**Heaven Over the Marshes** *see* **Cielo sulla palude**

**363. Heaven With a Gun.** MGM. US. 1969. 101m. C. *Producer:* Frank King, Maurice King *Director:* Lee H. Katzin *Writer:* Richard Carr *Cast:* Glenn Ford, Carolyn Jones, Barbara Hershey, John Anderson, David Carradine, J. D. Cannon, Noah Beery Jr., Harry Townes, William Bryant

Jim Killian (Glenn Ford), who is a gunslinger turned preacher, arrives in Vinagaroon, Arizona around 1870 to open his first church. He becomes involved in the hanging of an Indian sheepherder by a cattleman. Killian gets the sheepherders and cattlemen together for a preaching session and is exposed as an ex-con by his former cellmate. There is constant conflict between the sheepherders and the cattlemen and the brutal death of one of their sons sets off complications.

**Heavenly Pursuits** *see* **The Gospel According to Vic**

**364. Heavens Above!** Janus. UK. 1963. 105m. B&W. *Producer:* Roy Boulting, John Boulting *Director:* John Boulting *Writer:* John Boulting, Frank Harvey *Cast:* Peter Sellers, Cecil Parker, Isabel Jeans, Ian Carmichael, Bernard Miles, Brock Peters, Eric Sykes, Irene Handl, Miriam Karlin, Joan Miller, Miles Malleson, Eric Barker.

Reverend John Smallwood (Peter Sellers) a prison chaplain is mistakenly appointed to an upper-crust prosperous English village ruled by the Despard family, makers of Tranquilax. The villagers think they are getting another Reverend Smallwood. He causes quite a bit of trouble from having the rich work on weird charities to great unemployment. The townspeople, now out of work, riot. Smallwood escapes and is re-assigned to a parish on a remote island. On the island, a taunting astronaut "eggs" him on so much that Smallwood takes his place in the rocket and becomes known as "Bishop of outer space."

**365. Held to Answer.** Metro. US. 1923.

67m. B&W. *Director:* Harold Shaw *Writer:* Winifred Dunn, Peter Clark MacFarlane *Cast:* House Peters, Grace Carlyle, John St. Polis, Lydia Knott, Evelyn Brent, James Morrison, Bull Montana, Gale Henry, Thomas Guise, William Robert Daly, Charles West, Charles Hill Mailes

Actor becomes a minister, John Hampstead (House Peters), and is accused of theft by his jealous ex-girlfriend, who wants him to return to the stage. The church wants him to resign and the father of the real criminal is supporting his resignation. John knows the identity of the real criminal but can't tell because he knows via a confession. At the last minute the boy confesses and the minister is cleared.

**366. Hell-to-Pay Austin.** Triangle. US. 1916. B&W. *Director:* Paul Powell *Writer:* Mary H. O'Connor *Cast:* Wilfred Lucas, Bessie Love, Ralph Lewis, Mary Alden, Eugene Pallette, James O'Shea, Clyde Hopkins, Marie Wilkinson, Allen Sears, William H. Brown, Tom Wilson

Briar Rose (Bessie Love) is taken in by a drinking, fighting woodsman Hell-to-Pay Austin (Wilfred Lucas), when her minister father dies due to alcoholism. The girl falls in with the wrong crowd and Austin takes her away from the bad influences.

**367. Hellfire.** Republic Pictures. US. 1949. 90m. C. *Producer:* William J. O'Sullivan, Bill Elliott *Director:* R. G. Springsteen *Writer:* Dorrell McGowan, Stuart E. McGowan *Cast:* Bill Elliott, Marie Windsor, Forrest Tucker, Jim Davis, H. B. Warner, Paul Fix, Grant Withers, Emory Parnell, Esther Howard, Jody Gilbert, Louis Faust, Harry Woods, Denver Pyle

Gambler Zeb Smith (Bill Elliott) becomes a preacher when a minister takes a bullet meant for him. He vows to build the church that the minister wanted. Zeb tries to convince female outlaw Doll Brown (Marie Windsor) to turn herself in and the reward money used for the church.

**368. Hell's Hinges.** Triangle. US. 1916. 64m. B&W. *Producer:* Thomas Ince *Director:* Charles Swickard *Writer:* C. Gardner Sullivan *Cast:* William S. Hart, Clara Williams, Jack Standing, Alfred Hollingsworth, Robert

McKim, J. Frank Burke, Louise Glaum, John Gilbert, Jean Hersholt, Robert Kortman, Leo Willis

Reverend Robert Henley (Jack Standing) and his sister Faith (Clara Williams) arrive in Hell's Hinges. Soon saloon owner Silk Miller (Alfred Hollingsworth) senses that his evil ways may be threatened. He hires Blaze Tracy (William S. Hart) to get rid of the Reverend and his sister. Blaze falls in love with Faith and changes his ways.

**369. Her Children.** London Film. UK. 1914. B&W. *Director:* Harold M. Shaw *Writer:* Bannister Merwin *Cast:* Lilian Logan, Arthur Holmes-Gore, George Bellamy

Vicar reforms widow after finding her neglected children locked in church.

**370. Her Life in London.** DFSA. UK. 1915. B&W. *Director:* R. Harley West *Writer:* Arthur Shirley *Cast:* Alesia Leon, Fred Morgan, Nina Lynn

Detective's daughter poses as soldier to help cleric save vicar's daughter from blind crook's gang.

**Hey, Boy** *see* **Guaglio**

**371. The Hidden Scar.** World Film. US. 1916. B&W. *Director:* Barry O'Neil *Writer:* Mrs. Owen Bronson, Frances Marion *Cast:* Ethel Clayton, Holbrook Blinn, Irving Cummings, Montagu Love, Madge Evans, Edward Kimball, Eugenie Woodward

Unbeknownst to him minister Dale Overton (Irving Cummings) marries a woman Janet Hall (Ethel Clayton) with a past, she had an illegitimate child. He preaches about charity and forgiveness but when his wife's past is discovered he is unable to forgive her. A friend points out his hypocrisy. The minister forgives and takes back his wife.

**372. Hildegard of Bingen.** BBC. UK. 1994. C. *Director:* James Runcie *Writer:* James Runcie, Nigel Williams *Cast:* Michael Byrne, Robert Gwilym, Edward Jewesbury, Amanda Root, Patricia Routledge, Janet Suzman, Peter Vaughan

Hildegard of Bingen (Patricia Routledge) starts her own community for religious women after rebelling against church law. St. Hildegard (1098–1179) was known for her visions and also for being a physi-

cian, naturalist, poet, and musician. She has never been officially canonized but she is referred to as St. Hildegard.

**373. Hiroku onnadera.** Daiei International. Japan. 1969. 79m. B&W. *Director:* Tokuzo Tanaka *Writer:* Shozaburo Asai *Cast:* Michiyo Yasuda, Shigako Shimegi, Sanae Nakahara, Michiko Hasegawa, Naomi Kobayashi, Yasuyo Matsumura

Taking place in the late 18th century tells the story of Shigetsuin (Shigako Shimegi), who is made mother superior of a convent as punishment for her misdeeds. Oharu (Michiyo Yasuda) pretends to join the convent to investigate her brother's mysterious disappearance and discovers that Shigetsuin is luring young men to her and murdering them after sexually satisfying herself. In the end, Shigetsuin sets fire to the temple and ends up dying herself. Also known as *Secrets of a Women's Temple.*

**374. His People.** Universal. US. 1925. 93m. B&W. *Director:* Edward Sloman *Writer:* Isadore Bernstein *Cast:* Rudolph Schildkraut, Rosa Rosanova, George Lewis, Bobby Gordon, Arthur Lubin, Albert Bushaland, Blanche Mehaffey, Jean Johnson, Kate Price, Virginia Brown Faire, Nat Car, Bertram Marburgh, Edgar Kennedy, Charles Sullivan, Sidney Franklin

This film tells the story of Rabbi David Cominsky (Rudolph Schildkraut) and his two sons living in New York's Lower East Side. The rabbi favors Morris (Arthur Lubin), the older son who wants to be a lawyer over the Sammy (George Lewis), the younger son who sells papers to put his older brother through college. When the rabbi learns that Sammy has become a prizefighter he drives him out of the house. Meanwhile the rabbi pawns his overcoat to buy Morris a dress suit, which he throws in the trash and becomes engaged to his bosses daughter. After recovering from a severe cold the rabbi attends the engagement party and Morris refuses to acknowledge him. Sammy, having won the lightweight championship denounces Morris and drags him home where Morris realizes his sins and asks and receives forgiveness. The rabbi acknowledges his gratitude to Sammy.

**375. Hitler's Children.** RKO. US.

1943. 82m. B&W. *Producer:* Edward A. Golden *Director:* Edward Dmytryk *Writer:* Emmet Lavery, Gregor Ziemer (novel) *Cast:* Tim Holt, Bonita Granville, Kent Smith, Otto Kruger, H. B. Warner, Lloyd Corrigan, Erford Gage, Hans Conried, Gavin Muir, Nancy Gates

Lieutenant Karl Bruner (Tim Holt) rises from Hitler's youth program to Gestapo army officer. He cannot forget the girl Anna Muller (Bonita Granville) he once loved during childhood. The Bishop's (H. B. Warner) church service is broken up by Gestapo agents searching for the girl who has been hiding at the church.

**376. Hoi Duiong Mau Da Cam.** Vietnam. 1984. 90m. C. *Director:* Nguyen Ngoc Trung *Writer:* Nguyen Dinh Chinh *Cast:* Thé Anh, Hoang Cuc, Hong Puc, Le Cung Bac

A former captain in the South Vietnamese Air Force is now a Buddhist monk. An old comrade shows up and attempts to blackmail him into plotting against the Socialist government. After arguing, the monk breaks down and tells him about secret American flights which sprayed agent orange and napalm over the land to defoliate the forests. His friend realizes that the spraying indirectly caused the death of his wife who committed suicide after giving birth to a deformed baby. The monk's confession helps clear his conscience. Also known as *Orange-Colored Bells.*

**377. The Holly and the Ivy.** BL. UK. 1952. 83m. B&W. *Producer:* Anatole de Grunwald *Director:* George More O'Ferrall *Writer:* Anatole de Grunwald, Wynyard Browne *Cast:* Ralph Richardson, Celia Johnson, Margaret Leighton, Denholm Elliott, Hugh Williams, John Gregson, Margaret Halstan, Maureen Delaney, William Hartnell, Robert Flemyng, Roland Culver

Widowed Reverend Martin Gregory (Ralph Richardson) learns the truth about the lives and loves of his daughters during a family reunion at Christmas. His son Mick (Denholm Elliott) confronts his father with the bitter truth of how his being a parson has created a wall between him and the family.

**378. A Home of Our Own.** CBS. (TV).

US. 1975. 120m. C. *Producer:* Fred Baum *Director:* Robert Day *Writer:* Blanche Hanalis *Cast:* Jason Miller, Pancho Córdova, Enrique Novi, Pedro Armendáriz Jr., Richard Angarola, Carmen Zapata, Farnesio de Bernal, Rosario Álvarez, Nancy Rodman

The film is based on the work of Father William Wasson (Jason Miller), founder and director of a home for orphaned children in Mexico. He takes a particular interest in a boy named Julio, who has lost his parents. Julio succeeds and becomes a doctor. One day his wife and daughter are killed and he visits Father Wasson.

**379. Hon vong phu.** Prodis. France/Vietnam. 1983. 103m. C. *Director:* Lâm Lê *Writer:* Henry Colomer *Cast:* Dominique Sanda, Jean-Francois Stévenin, Thang-Long, Yann Roussel, Anne Canovas, Lan Hoang, Myriam Mézières

In the 1950s a missionary nun (Dominique Sanda) and a French sergeant are hiding out from the advancing enemy in Vietnam. A small Vietnamese boy is entrusted with passing on a written message which he is to give to the wife of a resistance fighter. She is supposed to live in a certain Villa, but the boy sees her boarding a boat bound for France. Meanwhile the missionary and the sergeant die from sniper bullets. The message passes from hand to hand and turns up in Paris at a Vietnamese reunion. Twenty years later it is laid to rest. Also known as *Dust of Empire* and *Poussière d'empire.*

**380. The Hoodlum Priest.** UA. US. 1961. 101m. B&W. *Producer:* Don Murray, Walter Wood *Director:* Irvin Kershner *Writer:* Don Murray, Joseph Landon *Cast:* Don Murray, Larry Gates, Keir Dullea, Cindi Wood, Logan Ramsey, Don Joslyn, Sam Capuano, Vince O'Brien, Al Mack, Lou Martini, Norman McKay, Joseph Cusanelli

The true story of Reverend Charles Dismas Clark (Don Murray), a Jesuit priest who worked with former convicts in St. Louis and ministered to street gangs. His mission centers on Billy Lee Jackson (Keir Dullea) a tormented ex-con who gets into crimes which are not of his alone.

**381. Hounds of Notre Dame.** Pan-

Canadian Film. Canada. 1980. 96m. C. *Producer:* Fil Fraser *Director:* Zale Dalen *Writer:* Ken Mitchell *Cast:* Thomas Peacocke, Frances Hyland, Barry Morse, David Ferry, Lawrence Reese, Lenore Zann, Phil Ridley, Dale Heibein, Paul Bougie, Rob MacLean, Bill Sorenson, Bill Morton

This film is a tribute to Father Athol Murray (Thomas Peacocke) who founded the College of Notre Dame in Saskatchewan, Canada. Murray is seen as a hard drinking and traditional priest.

**House of Mortal Sin** *see* **The Confessional**

**382. Household Saints.** Fine Line Features. US. 1993. 124m. C. *Producer:* Richard Guay, Peter Newman *Director:* Nancy Savoca *Writer:* Nancy Savoca, Richard Guay, Francine Prose (novel) *Cast:* Tracey Ullman, Vincent D'Onofrio, Lili Taylor, Judith Malina, Michael Rispoli, Victor Argo, Michael Imperioli, Rachael Bella, Illena Douglas

One hot summer night butcher Joseph Santangelo (Vincent D'Onofrio) wins Catherine Falconetti (Tracey Ullman) in a card game. Joseph becomes determined to marry Catherine. Both families have their problems and the marriage takes place. Joseph's mother Carmela (Judith Malina) is a devout woman but also a witch. The couple has a baby named Teresa (Lili Taylor). As a child, Teresa is concerned that the pope hasn't released the secret of the Fatima. When Teresa becomes a teenager, she yearns to join a convent and become a nun after winning a copy of St. Therese's Story of a Soul. Her parents make every effort to stop this type of thinking. Teresa experiences a vision while she irons her boyfriend's shirt.

**383. How Green Was My Valley.** TCF. US. 1941. 118m. B&W. *Producer:* Darryl F. Zanuck *Director:* John Ford *Writer:* Philip Dunne, Richard Llewellyn (novel) *Cast:* Walter Pidgeon, Maureen O'Hara, Donald Crisp, Anna Lee, Roddy McDowall, John Loder, Sara Allgood, Barry Fitzgerald, Patric Knowles, Arthur Shields, The Welsh Singers, Ann Todd, Morton Lowry

Told through the eyes of Huw Morgan (Roddy McDowall) as he recounts the story of his family the Morgans, a mining clan. Minister Mr. Gruffydd (Walter Pidgeon) tries to help the lives of this Welsh coal-mining community and inspires Huw with a thirst for knowledge. The residents have stereotypes of clergy as stiff and views that align them with the owners of the mine. During a party the townspeople hide their drinking when the new minister arrives, however he surprises them by taking a drink. They realize this is not your typical minister when he thinks that they should form a labor union. Angharad (Maureen O'Hara) is the minister's unrequited love. She marries the mine owner's son. In 1975, the BBC presented a six-hour television version starring Stanley Baker.

**384. The Hypocrites.** Paramount. US. 1915. 49m. B&W. *Director & Writer:* Lois Weber *Cast:* Courtenay Foote, Herbert Standing, Margaret Edwards, Myrtle Stedman, Adele Farrington, Dixie Carr

Gabriel (Courtenay Foote), a pastor, denounces hypocrisy and scolds a choir singer for reading a newspaper in church. In the paper he notices a painting of truth as a naked woman and he falls asleep. He dreams of a difficult path to righteousness. The next day he is found dead in the church, newspaper on the minister's lap, a sin on the Sabbath.

**I Am with You** *see* **Jag är med eder…**
**I Believe** *see* **The Man Without a Soul**

**385. I Can't…I Can't.** AIP. Ireland. 1969. 99m. C. *Producer:* Philip N. Krasne *Director:* Piers Haggard *Writer:* Lee Dunne, Piers Haggard *Cast:* Tessa Wyatt, Dennis Waterman, Alexandra Bastedo, Eddie Byrne, Martin Dempsey, Patrick Laffan, Marie O'-Donnell

Mady (Tessa Wyatt) is about to get married but she is terrified about becoming pregnant, especially since her mother dies after being pregnant for the eighth time. She is unable to consummate the marriage because of her fear of pregnancy. She is caught between religion which rejects birth control and desire. Her religious upbringing and counseling prevent her from seeing a doctor. Her priest adds to her fear with fire and brimstone chats. Also known as *Wedding Night*.

**386. I Confess.** Warner. US. 1952.

95m. B&W. *Producer & Director:* Alfred Hitchcock *Writer:* George Tabori, William Archibald *Cast:* Montgomery Clift, Anne Baxter, Karl Malden, Brian Aherne, O. E. Hasse, Dolly Haas, Roger Dann, Dolly Haas, Charles Andre, Judson Pratt

In Quebec, a lawyer is robbed and killed by Keller, the lay caretaker of a local church. Returning to the church altar that night he confesses to young Father Michael Logan (Montgomery Clift). Logan's ex-girlfriend happens to have been blackmailed by the murdered lawyer over her affair with the priest prior to his ordination. The evidence points towards Father Logan. Bound by his priestly commitment and not wanting to draw in his ex-girlfriend, he maintains his silence during the trial. He is acquitted because of reasonable doubt. People still view him as guilty but at the end of the film, Keller's wife turns against her husband and after a chase, Keller confesses to the murder.

**387. I Don't Want to Be Born.** AIP. UK. 1975. 95m. C. *Producer:* Norma Corney *Director:* Peter Sasdy *Writer:* Stanley Price *Cast:* Joan Collins, Eileen Atkins, Ralph Bates, Donald Pleasence, Caroline Munro, Hilary Mason, John Steiner, Janet Key, George Claydon

Lucy Carlesi (Joan Collins) gives birth to a very abnormal baby who seems larger than normal and then the nursemaid mysteriously dies. Lucy and her Italian husband Gino (Ralph Bates) turn to his nun sister Sister Alabana (Eileen Atkins) after the doctors have no answers.

**388. I Heard the Owl Call My Name.** CBS. (TV). US. 1973. 90m. C. *Producer& Director:* Daryl Duke *Writer:* Gerald Di Pego *Cast:* Tom Courtenay, Dean Jagger, Paul Stanley, Marianne Jones, George Clutesi, Keith Pepper, Margaret Atleo

Father Mark Brian (Tom Courtenay), a young American priest, finds that his schooling has not prepared him for his mission work in a remote Canadian Indian village in British Columbia.

**I, the Worst of All** *see* **Yo, la peor de todas**

**389. I'd Climb the Highest Mountain.** TCF. US. 1951. 88m. C. *Producer:* Lamar Trotti *Director:* Henry King *Writer:* Corra Harris (novel), Lamar Trotti *Cast:* Susan Hayward, William Lundigan, Rory Calhoun, Barbara Bates, Gene Lockhart, Lynn Bari, Ruth Donnelly, Kathleen Lockhart, Alexander Knox, Jean Inness, Frank Tweddell, Jerry Vandiver, Richard Wilson, Thomas Syfan, Kay and Fay Fogg

The plot is strung together with a series of episodes in the life of a very human Methodist minister William Asbury Thompson (William Lundigan) and his city-bred bride Mary (Susan Hayward). His first assignment for the church is in the red-clay hills of northern Georgia. The episodes are told through the eyes of his bride. One project by Thompson is to bring Christmas to the children of this poor community. After three years of building trust and respect, Reverend Thompson sadly accepts his mandatory reassignment.

**I'll Find You Again** *see* **Ti ritrovera**

**390. Il Est minuit, Docteur Schweitzer.** Cocinor. France. 1952. 110m. B&W. *Producer:* Louis Brunet *Director:* André Haguet *Writer:* Gilbert Cesbron (play), André Haguet, André Legrand *Cast:* Pierre Fresnay, Raymond Rouleau, Jeanne Moreau, André Valmy, Jean Debucourt

The film depicts the period when Dr. Albert Schweitzer (Pierre Fresnay) is a pastor in Alsace. He has just finished his medical training and has decided to dedicate himself to the suffering of the natives. Also known as *It is Midnight, Dr Schweitzer* and *Dr. Schweitzer.*

**391. Immoral Charge.** Eros. UK. 1959. 87m. B&W. *Producer:* Mickey Delamar *Director:* Terence Young *Writer:* Guy Elmes, Mickey Delamar, Philip King (play) *Cast:* Anthony Quayle, Sarah Churchill, Andrew Ray, Irene Browne, Percy Herbert, Noel Howard, Wensley Pithey, Leigh Madison, Judith Furse, Jean Cadell

Ex-army chaplain Howard Phillips (Anthony Quayle) now a vicar in a small English town develops programs for youth activities to deal with a serious juvenile delinquency problem facing the town. The old vicar's daughter Hester Peters (Sarah Churchill) respects him and falls in love with him.

One irresponsible boy Larry Thompson (Andrew Ray), who has gotten a girl pregnant, and a young girl falsely accuse the vicar of making sexual advances. Howard's mother steps in and the truth comes out. Also known as *Serious Charge.*

**392. In God We Trust.** UI. US. 1980. 97m. C. *Producer:* George Shapiro, Howard West *Director:* Marty Feldman *Writer:* Marty Feldman, Chris Allen *Cast:* Marty Feldman, Peter Boyle, Louise Lasser, Richard Pryor, Andy Kaufman, Wilfrid Hyde-White, Severn Darden

A monk Brother Ambrose (Marty Feldman) sets out into the world to raise money to keep his monastery in business. He ends up on Hollywood Boulevard. The main object of his search is a television evangelist Armageddon T. Thunderbird (Andy Kaufman).

**393. In the Days of Saint Patrick.** Janion. Ireland/UK. 1920. 80m. B&W. *Producer & Director:* Norman Whitton *Writer:* Mr. McGuinness *Cast:* Ira Allen, Vernon Whitten, Alice Cardinall, Dermont McCarthy, J. B. Carrickford, George Brame, Ernest Matthewson, George Griffin, Maude Hume, Mary Murnane, Herbert Mayne, Eddie Lawless, O'Carroll Reynolds, Jack McDermott

The tale of Saint Patrick (Ira Allen) who was brought to Ireland as a prisoner by pirates. Patrick escapes and returns home to France and enters a monastery. Later he goes to Rome. After he becomes a Bishop, Pope Celestine sends him back to Ireland as a missionary. He succeeds in converting Ireland to Christianity. Original subtitles were in Irish. Also known as *Days of St. Patrick* and *Aimsir Padraig.*

**In the Pope's Eye** *see* **Il Pap'occhio**

**394. In This House of Brede.** CBS. (TV). US. 1975. 105m. C. *Producer & Director:* George Schaefer *Writer:* Rumer Godden (novel), James Costigan *Cast:* Diana Rigg, Judi Bowker, Gwen Watford, Pamela Brown, Denis Quilley, Nicholas Clay, Gladys Spencer, Julia Blalock, Frances Rowe, Charlotte Mitchell, Peter Sproule, Margaret Heery, Elizabeth Bradley, Dervla Molloy, Ann Rye, Catherine Willmer, Valerie Lush

Widow Dame Phillipa (Diana Rigg)

gives up a successful business career and the man who loves her to become a cloistered Benedictine nun at Stanbrook Abbey.

**395. The Inn of the Sixth Happiness.** TCF. US. 1958. 158m. C. *Producer:* Buddy Adler *Director:* Mark Robson *Writer:* Isobel Lennart, Alan Burgess (novel) *Cast:* Ingrid Bergman, Curt Jürgens, Robert Donat, Ronald Squire, Athene Seyler, Noel Hood, Richard Wattis, Joan Young, Moultrie Kelsall, Peter Chong, Michael David, Edith Sharpe

The film is based on a novel, which was based on the true story of a rejected missionary English servant girl Gladys Aylward (Ingrid Bergman) who becomes a missionary by saving the money to send herself to China anyway. She works with an elderly missionary (Athene Seyler). The Mandarin (Robert Donat) befriends her. She almost has a romance with Chinese army officer Captain Lin Nan (Curt Jürgens). Gladys guides a group of 100 children over the mountain to safety from a Japanese attack.

**396. Interno d'un convento.** Parafrance. Italy. 1977. 95m. C. *Director & Writer:* Walerian Borowczyk *Cast:* Ligia Branice, Marina Pierro, Gabriella Giacobbe, Loredano Martínez, Mario Maranzana, Howard Ross, Rodolfo Dal Pra

Loosely based on Stendhal's *Promenade in Rome.* Examines an early 19th century convent with an outbreak of sexuality among the young nuns. The handsome priest confessor encourages strict enforcement of the rules. Also known as *Within a Cloister.*

**397. The Iron Stair.** Lakeshore. UK. 1920. B&W. *Director & Writer:* F. Martin Thornton *Cast:* Reginald Fox, Madge Stuart, Frank Petley, H. Agar Lyons, J. Edwards Barber

Man (Reginald Fox) poses as clerical twin to cash forged checks but later takes cleric's place when he escapes from jail.

**398. It Is for England.** P&C. UK. 1916. B&W. *Producer, Director & Writer:* Lawrence Cowen *Cast:* Helene Gingold, Percy Moran, Marguerite Shelley, Gilbert Esmond, Sir Gilbert Parker, Sir William Bull, Sir Kintoch-Cooke, Arthur Collins, Willie Clarkson

Reincarnated saint unmasks baronet as German spy.

**It Is Midnight Dr. Schweitzer** *see* **Il Est minuit Docteur Schweitzer**

**399. Ítélet.** Mokép. Hungary/Czechoslovakia/Romania. 1970. 91m. B&W. *Producer:* Tibor Dimény *Director:* Ferenc Kósa *Writer:* Sándor Csoóri, Ferenc Kósa *Cast:* Ferenc Bessenyei, János Koltai, Tamás Major, George Motoi, Stefan Török, Sára Kiss

During the 16th century the Turks threatened Europe and the Pope asked for a crusade. A Hungarian Cardinal puts Gyorgy Dozsa (Ferenc Bessenyei) in charge of an army of serfs from Eastern Europe. Instead of attacking the Turks he fights the Cardinal. His army is defeated and it is hoped that this will wipe out his fame. He is tortured but refuses to renounce his actions. Also known as *Judgment.*

**400. It's a Wonderful Life.** RKO. US. 1946. 129m. B&W. *Producer & Director:* Frank Capra *Writer:* Francis Goodrich, Albert Hackett, Frank Capra, Jo Swerling *Cast:* James Stewart, Donna Reed, Henry Travers, Thomas Mitchell, Lionel Barrymore, Samuel S. Hinds, Frank Faylen, Gloria Grahame, H. B. Warner, Ellen Corby, Sheldon Leonard, Beulah Bondi, Ward Bond, Frank Albertson, Todd Karns, Mary Treen, Charles Halton, Karolyn Grimes

Classic Christmas story of George Bailey (James Stewart), a frustrated small business man, who is saved from suicide with the help of an angel. Young George Bailey prevents Mr. Gower (H. B. Warner), the pharmacist, from accidentally giving a patient poison instead of the correct prescription. With the aid of a would-be angel, we see what would have happened to Mr. Gower and the others if George had never lived. Even though it does not have a religious figure except an angel this film demonstrates how one person can make a difference in people's lives. One of the American Film Institute's 100 greatest American movies.

**401. The Ivory Hand.** Clarendon. UK. 1915. B&W. *Director:* Wilfred Noy

Tale of Chinese priest's vengeance on man who stole jeweled hand of sacred idol.

**402. Jag är med eder…** Svensk. Sweden.

1948. 94m. *Director:* Gösta Stevens *Writer:* Gösta Stevens, Rune Lindström *Cast:* Victor Sjöström, Rune Lindstrom, Carin Cederström, Nils Dahlgren, Äke Fridell, Carl Ström

Story dealing with Swedish missionaries in Africa. Most of the picture was shot in Africa. Also known as *I Am With You.*

**James' Journey to Jerusalem** *see* **Massa'ot James Be'eretz Hakodesh.**

**Jan Amos' Peregrination** *see* **Putování Jana Amose**

**403. Janani.** Badarudeen. India. 1998. 97m. *Producer & Director:* Thankamaniamma Rajeevnath *Writer:* Zachariah, Thankamaniamma Rajeevnath *Cast:* Latiff, Kavitha, Rosline, Santhakumari, Rukmimi

Story about seven retired nuns living in a convent in the remote mountains of India. During Christmas mass they discover an abandoned baby in their chapel. Although the nuns intend to send him to an orphanage, return him to his natural parents or adopt him to a couple, through circumstances they end up keeping him.

**404. Jane Eyre.** W.W. Hodkinson. US. 1921. B&W. *Producer & Director:* Hugo Ballin *Writer:* Hugo Ballin, Charlotte Bronte (novel) *Cast:* Norman Trevor, Mabel Ballin, Crauford Kent, Emily Fitzroy, John Webb Dillon, Louis Grisel, Stephen Carr, Vernie Atherton, Elizabeth Aeriens, Harlan Knight, Helen Miles, Julia Hurley, Sadie Mullen, June Ellen Terry, Florence Flagler, Bertha Kent, Marie Schaefer

Tale about an orphan girl, Jane (Mabel Ballin) who is taken into the home of Mr. Fairfax Rochester (Norman Trevor) for a companion to his young ward Adele. Clergyman St. John Rivers (Crauford Kent) falls in love with Jane. Some other film productions do not have the clergyman involvement. Jane and Rochester are united at the end after great turmoil.

**405. Jaws of Satan.** MGM. US. 1981. 92m. C. *Producer:* Bill Wilson *Director:* Bob Claver *Writer:* Gerry Holland *Cast:* Fritz Weaver, Gretchen Corbett, Jon Korkes, Norman Lloyd, Diana Douglas, Bob Hannah, Nancy Priddy, Christina Applegate, John McCurry, Jack Gordon

Dr. Maggie Sheridan (Gretchen Corbett), a local doctor, a university herpetologist Dr. Paul Hendricks (Jon Korkes), and a cursed priest Father Tom Farrow (Fritz Weaver) hunt for a large cobra, which happens to be Satan. The priest's family was cursed by a Druid priest for prosecuting his people. Also known as *King Cobra*.

**406. Jeanne d'Arc.** Star Films. France. 1897. B&W. *Director:* Georges Méliès *Cast:* Mlle. Calviere, Georges Méliès, Madame Méliès

Tells the story of Joan's success in driving English troops from France and her later capture and trial, ending with Joan being burned at the stake.

**407. Jeanne d'Arc.** S. Lubin. France. 1899. 10m. B&W. *Director & Writer:* Georges Méliès *Cast:* Bleuette Bernon, Georges Méliès, Jeanne d'Alcy

Early telling of the Joan of Arc story.

**408. Jeanne d'Arc.** France. 1909. B&W. *Director:* Albert Capellani *Cast:* Leontine Massart

The film was released to coincide with the beatification of Joan in 1909. Tells the story of Joan of Arc from her visions to her death at the burning stake.

**409. Jeanne la Pucelle**

**Part 1. Les batailles.** Pierre Grise Productions. France. 1994. 160m. C. *Producer:* Martine Marignac, Maurice Tinchant *Director:* Jacques Rivette *Writer:* Pascal Bonitzer, Christine Laurent, Jacques Rivette *Cast:* Sandrine Bonnaire, Marcel Bozonnet, André Marcon, Jean-Louis Richard, Didier Sauvegrain, Jean-Pierre Becker, Bruno Wolkowitch, Jean-Marie Richier, Baptiste Roussillon, Bernadette Giraud

Describes her early life, her visions, and first battles. She tries to convince a captain to escort her to the Dauphin. It ends with her first battle at Orleans. Script relies on court transactions and eyewitness accounts. Also known as *Joan the Maid 1. The Battles*.

**Part 2. Les prisons.** Pierre Grise Productions. France. 1994. 176m. C. *Producer:* Martine Marignac *Director:* Jacques Rivette *Writer:* Pascal Bonitzer, Christine Laurent, Jacques Rivette *Cast:* Sandrine Bonnaire, Marcel Bozonnet, André Marcon, Jean-Louis Richard, Didier Sauvegrain, Jean-

Pierre Lorit, Bruno Wolkowitch, Patrick Le Mauff, Romain Lagarde, Florence Darel

Details her series of victories, captured, imprisonment, and trial. Joan faces two judges and stands accused of sorcery, impurity, wearing men's clothing, and refusal to submit to English rule. She is condemned as a heretic and burned at the stake.

The New Yorker (November 15th, 1999) called this the most historically accurate version of the story of Joan of Arc. Also known as *Joan the Maid Part2 The Prisons*.

**410. Jericó.** Det Danske. Venezuela. 1990. 90m. C. *Director & Writer:* Luis Alberto Lamata *Cast:* Wilfredo Cisneros, Cosme Cortázar, Doris Díaz, Amilcar Marcano, Alexander Milic, Reggie Nalder, Luis Pardi, Francis Rueda, Yajaira Salazar

In early 16th century a priest Santiago (Cosme Cortázar) joins Spanish conquerors in order to bring Christianity to the natives. The natives kill everyone but the priest. He attempts to continue to convert them but he slowly becomes one of them. Then the Spaniards return.

**411. Jerusalem.** First Look Pictures. Sweden/Denmark/Norway/Finland/Iceland. 1996. 168m. C. *Producer:* Ingrid Dahlberg, Marko Röhr *Director:* Bille August *Writer:* Selma Lagerlöf (novel), Bille August, Charlotte Lesche, Klas Östergren *Cast:* Maria Bonnevie, Ulf Friberg, Pernilla August, Lena Endre, Sven-Bertil Taube, Reine Brynolfsson, Jan Mybrand, Max von Sydow, Olympia Dukakis, Björn Granath, Viveka Seldahl

Gertrud (Maria Bonnevie) and Ingmar (Ulf Friberg) are in love. While Ingmar is away for the winter, Gertrud becomes a follower of a new Christian belief. The new priest wants his followers to immigrate with him to Palestine. Ingmar's sister decides to follow him and sells the family home. In order to save the home, Ingmar marries the daughter of the man who bought it. With Ingmar married, Gertrud follows the others to Palestine. Ingmar finds himself still in love with Gertrud and eventually follows her.

**412. Jésus de Montréal.** Orion Classics. Canada/France. 1989. 120m. C. *Producer:* Roger Frappier, Pierre Glendron, Monique Létourneau *Director & Writer:*

Denys Arcand *Cast*: Lothaire Bluteau, Catherine Wilkening, Johanne-Marie Tremblay, Rémy Girard, Robert Lepage, Gilles Pelletier, Yves Jacques, Cédric Noel, Pauline Martin, Véronique Le Flaguais

The pastor of the Shrine of St. Joseph brings a young actor to modernize the church's production of the *Passion Play*. The new director, playing the role of Jesus, researches modern biblical scholarship, reinterprets the story and invites a group of unorthodox friends (a fashion model, a pornographic film maker, a science film producer) to join the production. During the story they confront the evils of the modern city and the main actor "becomes" Jesus in his real life. The Catholic Church begins to oppose the production.

**413. The Jew's Christmas.** Universal Film Manufacturing. US. 1913. B&W. *Director*: Phillips Smalley, Lois Weber *Writer*: Lois Weber *Cast*: Phillips Smalley, Lois Weber, Lule Warrenton, Ella Hall

This film is the earliest portrayal of a rabbi in American films. When Rabbi Isaacs's daughter marries a gentile, he disowns her. At the climax of the movie the Rabbi sells his prayer book so that his daughter's impoverished family can buy a Christmas tree.

**Joan at the Stake** *see* **Giovanna d'Arco al rogo**

**Joan of Arc** *see* **Giovanna d'Arco**

**414. Joan of Arc.** Edison. US. 1895. B&W. *Director*: Alfred Clark

First attempt at the filming of Joan of Arc story.

**415. Joan of Arc.** Éclair. 1914. B&W. Story of Joan of Arc told in 5 parts.

**416. Joan of Arc.** RKO. US. 1948. 145m. C. *Producer*: Walter Wanger *Director*: Victor Fleming *Writer*: Maxwell Anderson, Andrew Solt *Cast*: Ingrid Bergman, Francis L. Sullivan, J. Carrol Naish, Ward Bond, Shepperd Strudwick, Gene Lockhart, John Emery, Leif Erickson, Cecil Kellaway, Jose Ferrer

Story of the peasant girl Joan of Arc (Ingrid Bergman) who leads the Dauphin's forces to victory over the English armies in France. She is betrayed and tried as a witch and finally burned at the stake.

**417. Joan of Arc.** CBS. (TV) Canada. 1999. 140m. *Director*: Christian Duguay *Writer*: Michael Alexander Miller, Ronald Parker *Cast*: Leelee Sobieski, Jacqueline Bisset, Powers Boothe, Neil Patrick Harris, Maury Chaykin, Olympia Dukakis, Jonathan Hyde, Robert Loggia, Shirley MacLaine, Peter O'Toole, Maximilian Schell, Peter Strauss

Joan of Arc hears voices and she begins her mission to save France from the English.

**418. The Joan of Arc of Loos.** Australia. 1916. 55m. B&W. *Director*: George Willoughby *Writer*: Herbert Ford *Cast*: Jane King, Jean Robertson, Clive Farnham, Beatrice Esmond, Arthur Greenaway, Austin Milroy, Harry Halley, Winter Hall, Irve Hayman, Arthur Spence, Fred Knowles

Early telling of the story.

**419. Joan of Paris.** RKO. US. 1942. 91m. B&W. *Producer*: David Hempstead *Director*: Robert Stevenson *Writer*: Charles Bennett, Ellis St. Joseph *Cast*: Michèle Morgan, Paul Henreid, Thomas Mitchell, Laird Cregar, May Robson, Alexander Granach, Alan Ladd, Jack Briggs, James Monks, Richard Fraser

During World War II, five RAF pilots are shot down over France. The pilots steal civilian clothes and overpower a German soldier and take his wallet. The men split up and agree to meet in a cathedral in Paris. Meanwhile, the Germans learn of the pilots and realize that they have taken marked money. The leader of the pilots, Paul (Paul Henreid) is originally from France who had escaped to England. He enters a confessional to see his boyhood priest Father Antoine (Thomas Mitchell) to ask for his help. Joan (Michèle Morgan) meets Paul and ends up helping him and they fall in love. Meanwhile, the Gestapo is hot on the trail of the pilots and the pilots are almost captured. In the end, Joan sacrifices herself in order to save Paul. As she bravely faces the firing squad Paul and the others fly back to England.

**420. Joan of Plattsburg.** Goldwyn. US. 1918. B&W. *Director*: George Loane Tucker, William Humphrey *Writer*: George Loane Tucker, Porter Emerson Browne *Cast*: Mabel

Peasant girl Joan of Arc (Ingrid Bergman) leads the Dauphin's forces to victory over the English armies in France, in *Joan of Arc* (1948).

Normand, Robert Elliott, William Fredericks, Joseph Smiley, Edward Elkas, John Webb

Joan (Mabel Normand) is an orphan living in an asylum near a World War I training camp when a soldier gives her a copy of the Joan of Arc story. When she hears voices plotting against the government she thinks that they are from another world. She tells what she hears to Captain Lain (Robert Elliott) but he doesn't believe her.

Soon the truth about the voices which are really German spies is exposed and Joan helps capture the spies. Joan also wins the hand of the captain.

**Joan of the Angels** *see* **Matka Joanna od aniolów**

**Joan the Maid** *see* **Jeanne la Pucelle**

**421. Joan the Woman.** Paramount. US. 1916. 138m. B&W. *Producer & Director:* Cecil B. DeMille *Writer:* Jeanie Macpherson

*Cast:* Geraldine Farrar, Raymond Hatton, Hobart Bosworth, Theodore Roberts, Wallace Reid, Charles Clary, James Neill, Tully Marshall, Lawrence Peyton, Horace B. Carpenter, Lillian Leighton, Marjorie Daw, Stephen Gray, Ernest Joy, John Oaker, Hugo B. Kotch, William Conklin, Walter Long, William Elmer, Emilius Jorgensen, Cleo Ridgely, Donald Crisp

With opera singer Geraldine Farrar as Joan. A British soldier, on the verge of a suicide mission during World War I, discovers part of a sword he imagines to be Joan of Arc's. In flashback, he is a reincarnation of an English soldier who fell in love with Joan and unwittingly contributes to her undoing. At the end of the film the modern day soldier dies on his suicide mission. Film was made before the outcome of World War I was certain.

**422. John Wesley.** UK. 1954. 77m. C. *Director:* Norman Walker *Writer:* Lawrence Barrett *Cast:* Leonard Sachs, Gerard Lohan, Neil Heayes, Keith Pyott, Curigwen Lewis, Derek Aylward, John Witty, Patrick Barton, John Slater, Philip Leaver

This semi-documentary film is about the birth of the Methodist movement in 18th century England and the life of John Wesley (Leonard Sachs), churchman, educator and evangelist. Five hundred churches contributed toward the $200,000 production cost and received first run privileges.

**423. Johnny Nobody.** Columbia. UK. 1961. 88m. *Producer:* John R. Sloan *Director:* Nigel Patrick *Writer:* Patrick Kirwan *Cast:* Nigel Patrick, Yvonne Mitchell, Aldo Ray, William Bendix, Cyril Cusack, Bernie Winters, Niall MacGinnis, Noel Purcell, Eddie Byrne, John Welsh, Michael Brennan

Father Carey (Nigel Patrick) proves that stranger-amnesiac Johnny Nobody (Aldo Ray) was not divinely impelled to shoot drunken author James Ronald Mulcahy (William Bendix) in an Irish village. Since the shooting took place in his village, Father Carey decides to solve the mystery while Johnny Nobody waits for his trial. The film had a belated release in the US.

**424. Jolly Monks.** Lubin. France. 1903. B&W.

Two monks sit at a table drinking beer and smoking their pipes. One has told a funny story. After exchanging snuff boxes, one monk uses so much that he sneezes and rolls on the floor.

**425. The Jolly Monks of Malabar.** American Mutoscope/Biograph Co. US. 1906. B&W.

No description available.

**426. Joshua.** Crusader. US. 2002. 90m. C. *Producer:* Howard Baldwin, Paul Pompian, Karen Elise Baldwin *Director:* Jon Purdy *Writer:* Keith Giglio, Brad Mirman *Cast:* Tony Goldwyn, F. Murray Abraham, Kurt Fuller, Stacy Edwards, Colleen Camp, Giancarlo Giannini, Kevin Scott Greer, Jordan Allen

A mysterious man Joshua (Tony Goldwyn) arrives in a small Midwestern town in the late 19th century. He starts a carpenter shop and after bad weather nearly destroys the town's African-American church he offers to repair the church. Joshua convinces others to help rebuild the church including Father Pat (Kurt Fuller) of the Catholic Church. His goodness and charm attracts the attention of Father Tardon (F. Murray Abraham). The Father asks Joshua to carve a new statue of Saint Peter for their church. Soon the Father and others become suspicious of Joshua. Is he the Second Coming? Joshua makes a trip to the Vatican to speak with the Pope (Giancarlo Giannini).

**427. Journal d'un curé de campagne.** Brandon Films. France. 1951. 110m. B&W. *Producer:* Lèon Carré, Robert Sussfeld *Director:* Robert Bresson *Writer:* Georges Bernanos (novel), Robert Bresson *Cast:* Claude Laydu, Léon Arvel, Antoine Balpêtré, Jean Danet, Jeanne Étiévant, André Guibert, Bernard Hubrenne

A young sick Priest of Ambricourt (Claude Laydu) arrives in his first parish, a village in the north of France, and is unable to resolve the problems of the hostile village. He is assailed by self-doubt and dies of stomach cancer whispering "all is grace." The narrative mainly takes the form of a journal kept by the young priest during the last year of his life. He records his spiritual struggle over his failed efforts. The locals attribute his

Young Priest of Ambricourt (Claude Laydu) discusses his spiritual struggle with an older neighboring priest, in *Journa d'un curé de campagne* (1951; also known as *Diary of a Country Priest*).

stomach ailment to drunkenness. On his deathbed he expresses an abiding faith. As French critic Andre Bazin has written, "Probably for the first time the cinema gives us a film in which the only genuine incidents are those of the life of the spirit. It also offers us a new dramatic form that is specifically religious or better still, specifically, a phenomenology of salvation and grace." Also known as *Diary of a Country Priest*.

**428. Journey into Light.** TCF. 1951. 87m. B&W. *Producer*: Joseph Bernhard, Ansom Bond *Director*: Stuart Heisler *Writer*: Stephanie Nordli, Irving Shulman, Ansom Bond *Cast*: Sterling Hayden, Viveca Lindfors, Thomas Mitchell, Ludwig Donath, H. B. Warner, Jane Darwell, John Berkes, Peggy Webber, Paul Guilfoyle, Charles Evans, Marion Martin, Everett Glass, Raymond Bond

The story of conservative minister John Burrows (Sterling Hayden), who preaches in a small New York town, loses his faith and then regains it. Pastor Burrows goes crazy when his alcoholic wife commits suicide. One of the reasons for her action was the self-righteous attitude of the church leaders. John loses his faith in God, resigns

and heads west ending up in skid row where he takes a job as a janitor in a mission. Soon he falls in love with the blind daughter of the mission leader. When she is accidentally hurt he takes to the pulpit and regains his faith. They marry and he agrees to stay at the mission and preach. Also known as *Skid Road*.

**429. The Jovial Monks No. 1.** Williamson. UK. 1899. B&W. *Director*: James Williamson *Cast*: D. Philippe

Monk tricks fellow brother into drinking bad wine.

**430. The Jovial Monks No. 2—Tit for Tat.** Williamson. UK. 1899. B&W. *Director*: James Williamson *Cast*: D. Philippe

Monk tricks fellow brother into drinking bad wine.

**431. The Jovial Monks in the Refectory.** R.W. Paul. UK. 1898. B&W.

Novice gets drunk while tolling bell.

**432. Judge Not.** Jury. UK. 1920. B&W. *Director*: Einar J. Bruun *Writer*: Holger Madsen *Cast*: Fay Compton, Fred Groves, Chappell Dossett, Eric Barclay, Frank Stanmore, Mary Brough, Henry Vibart, George Bellamy, Wallace Bosco, Christine Silver

Street missionary seeks lost daughter after shooting wife on suspicion of adultery.

**Judgment** *see* **Ítélet**

**433. Judgment.** HBO. (TV). US. 1990. 90m. C. *Producer*: Rob Hershman, Dan Wigutow *Director & Writer*: Tom Topor *Cast*: Keith Carradine, Blythe Danner, Jack Warden, David Strathairn, Michael Faustino, Bob Gunton, Mitch Ryan, Robert Joy, Steve Hofvendahl, Mary Joy

True story of priest in Louisiana Father Frank Aubert (David Strathairn) accused of molesting young parishioners. Also tells the story of the family of one of the victims caught between love for their son and loyalty to their Church. The church tries to cover up the whole affair and the Father is in complete denial of the evil he has done by being a pedophile.

**434. The Juggler of Our Lady.** TCF. US. 1957. 9m. C. *Director:* Al Kouzel, Gene Deitch *Cast:* (the voice of) Boris Karloff

This is an animated film based on a 12th century folktale. The main character, Candlebert, joins a monastery when he has little success making money, and tries to follow the example of the monks, who do work in honor of the Virgin Mary. Since his only skill is juggling, he dedicates his juggling to the Virgin Mary.

**435. Julianus barát.** Inter-Cene. (TV). Hungary/Italy. 1991. *Producer&Writer:* Gábor Koltay, György Lendvai *Director:* Gábor Koltay *Cast:* Hirtling Istvan, Nino Manfredi, Franco Nero, Raf Vallone, Tibi Antal

A young Hungarian peasant joins a monastery, but soon leaves when he discovers that the monks live in luxury. He petitions the king to begin a pilgrimage to find the origins of the Magyar people, who were originally a nomadic group. After he is denied royal sanction he travels to Italy and obtains the king's permission. Julianus and other monks encounter persecution on their journey. Also known as *Frate Julianus* and *Friar Julianus.*

**436. Der Junge Mönch.** Germany. 1978. 84m. C. *Producer, Director & Writer:* Herbert Achternbusch *Cast*: Heinz Josef Braun, Branko Samarovski, Karolina Herbig, Herbert Achternbusch, Barbara Gass

A simple country boy, who is a new-born Christ, wants to redeem someone and seeks converts. He follows his vision to Rome where he works his way from a monk up to becoming Pope whose God is the Easter Bunny. Also known as *The Young Monk.*

**437. Kadosh.** Kino International. France/Israel. 1999. 110m. C. *Producer*: Amos Gitai, Michel Propper *Director*: Amos Gitai *Writer*: Eliette Abecassis, Amos Gitai *Cast*: Yael Abecassis, Yoram Hattab, Meital Barda, Uri Klauzner, Yussuf Abu-Warda, Leah Koenig, Sami Hori, Rivka Michaeli, Samuel Calderon, Shireen Kadivar, Amos Gitai

In Jerusalem's Orthodox Mea Shearim quarter, Rivka (Yael Abecassis) is happily married to Meir (Yoram Hattab), but they remain childless. The yeshiva's rabbi, who happens to be Meir's father, wants him to divorce Rivka saying "a barren woman is no woman." Meanwhile Rivka's sister, Malka (Meital Barda), is in love with Yakov (Sami Hori) who is shunned by the yeshiva. The rabbi arranges Malka's marriage to Yossef (Uri Klauzner). The sisters must try to find their way within this patriarchal world.

**Keepers of the Night** *see* **Nachtwache**

**438. Keeping the Faith.** Buena Vista. US. 2000. 128m. C. *Producer:* Stuart Blumberg, Hawk Koch, Edward Norton *Director:* Edward Norton *Writer:* Stuart Blumberg *Cast:* Ben Stiller, Edward Norton, Jenna Elfman, Anne Bancroft, Eli Wallach, Ron Rifkin, Milos Forman, Holland Taylor, Lisa Edelstein, Rena Sofer, Ken Leung

The friendship of Rabbi Jake Schram (Ben Stiller) and Father Brian Finn (Edward Norton) is thrown into chaos with the arrival of their old childhood friend Anna Riley (Jenna Elfman). Both men find themselves in love with this beauty. Unfortunately Father Finn has his vow of celibacy and Rabbi Schram's family and synagogue would not accept a non-Jewish wife. In fact, Jakes' temple members are setting him up with their daughters. Both young and vital clergymen are portrayed in positive light and offer very up-to-date methods in recruiting new worshippers. Jake is seen as a model of the modern rabbi and Father Brian as a modern priest. An elder rabbi and a priest offer valuable advice and support to the younger Jake and Brian.

**The Key to Paradise** *see* **Nøeglen til Paradis**

**439. The Keys of the Kingdom.** TCF. US. 1944. 137m. B&W. *Producer*: Joseph L. Mankiewicz *Director*: John M. Stahl *Writer*: A. J. Cronin (novel), Joseph L. Mankiewicz, Nunnally Johnson *Cast*: Gregory Peck, Thomas Mitchell, Vincent Price, Ross Stradner, Roddy McDowall, Edmund Gwenn, Cedric Hardwicke, Peggy Ann Garner, Anne Revere, James Gleason

Monsignor Sleeth (Cedric Hardwicke) travels to replace the aging priest missionary Father Francis Chisholm (Gregory Peck). As the monsignor reads the priest's journals, the story of the priest's life is told in flashback. The story begins with the priest's unrequited love in youth and later of his unselfish devotion to his mission over half a century of his life. The action begins in Scotland, then to China and back to the land of his birth.

**440. Kid Monk Baroni.** Realart. US. 1952. 79m. B&W. *Producer*: Jack Broder *Director*: Harold Schuster *Writer*: Aben Kandel *Cast*: Richard Rober, Bruce Cabot, Allene Roberts, Mona Knox, Leonard Nimoy, Jack Larson, Budd Jaxon, Archer MacDonald, Kathleen Freeman, Joseph Mell, Paul Maxey, Stuart Randall, Chad Mallory, Maurice Cass, William Cabanne

Nicknamed Monk because of his disfigured face, Paul Baroni (Leonard Nimoy) is leader of a street gang until Father Callahan (Richard Rober) takes him under his wing and gets him interested in boxing. The efforts of Father Callahan to reform the gangs are working well, until one night Monk accidentally hits the priest. He leaves the neighborhood and becomes a pro fighter. He has plastic surgery on his face and leaves Emily (Allene Roberts), his church girlfriend and takes up with golddigger June Travers (Mona Knox). To protect his new face he becomes a defensive boxer and is defeated. He returns to the church to lead its athletic program and gets back together with Emily.

**441. King.** NBC. (TV-Miniseries). US. 1978. 300m. C. *Producer*: Paul Maslansky *Director & Writer*: Abby Mann *Cast*: Paul Winfield, Cicely Tyson, Tony Bennett, Roscoe Lee Browne, Lonny Chapman, Ossie Davis, Cliff De Young, Al Freeman Jr., Clu Gulager, Steven Hill, William Jordan, Warren Kemmerling, Lincoln Kilpatrick, Kenneth McMillan, Howard Rollins Jr., David Spielberg, Dolph Sweet, Dick Anthony Williams, Julian Bond, Ramsey Clark, Roger Robinson, Frances Foster, Ernie Lee Banks, Art Evans, Yolanda King, Patrick Hines, Roy Jenson

Based on the career of Martin Luther King, Jr. (Paul Winfield) from his days as a Southern Baptist minister in the South in the 1950's to his assassination in 1968 Memphis.

**King Cobra** *see* **Jaws of Satan**

**442. The Knight and the Friar.** Majestic. UK. 1912. B&W.

Friar Tuck interrupts a knight, Sir Tristram, while he is serenading his beloved Lady Alice and summons the girl's father. The knight later ambushes the Friar and steals his robe. When Lady Alice comes for confession Tristram forces the friar to marry them.

**The Knight of the Dragon** *see* **El Caballero del dragon**

**Knocks at My Door** *see* **Golpes a mi puerta**

**443. Ein Komischer heiliger.** Munic Films. Germany. 1979. 83m. C. *Producer*: Michael Fengler, Hans Kaden *Director & Writer*: Klaus Lemke *Cast*: Wolfgang Fierek, Cleo Kretschmer, Luitpold Roever, Peter Emmer, Horatius Häberle, Arno Mathes, Ingo Fischer

A young naïve clergyman (Wolfgang Fierek) is determined to save souls in the bad part of Munich but no one is convinced by him. Only B-Girl Baby (Cleo Kretschmer), a fortune telling curse dispensing woman, likes him. They fall in love and leave town together after trouble with the police. Also known as *Some Kind of Saint.*

**444. Kros Contri.** Yugoslavia Film. Yugoslavia. 1969. 89m. C. *Director & Writer*: Mladomir 'Purisa' Djordjevic *Cast*: Milena Dravic, Mircela Vujicic, Ljuba Tadic, Neda Americ, Nikola-Kole Angelovski

Story is about a priest who is training a young girl for a cross country event in the upcoming Olympics. Also known as *Cross country*.

**445. Kundun.** Buena Vista. US. 1997. 128m. C. *Producer*: Barbara De Fina *Director*: Martin Scorsese *Writer*: Melissa Mathison *Cast*: Tenzin Thuthob Tsarong, Gyurme Tethong, Tulku Jamyang Kunga Tenzin, Tenzin Yeshi Paichang, Tencho Gyalpo, Tsewang Migyur Khangsar, Geshi Yeshi Gyatso, Sonam Phuntsok, Lobsang Samten, Gyatso Lukhang, Jigme Tsarong, Tenzin Trinley, Robert Lin

In 1937, a two-year-old child living in a remote area of Tibet is identified as the reincarnation of the Dalai Lama. The Dalai Lama is referred to as Kundun which means "The Presence." The film follows his life into adulthood. At four he is brought to Lhasa and schooled as a monk and as head of state; at 14 the Chinese invade Tibet, and finally in 1959 he flees to India.

**446. Kutya éji dala.** Mokép. Hungary. 1983. 139m. C. *Producer & Director*: Gábor Bódy *Writer*: Sandor Erdelyl, Gábor Bódy, Vilmos Csaplár (story) *Cast*: Gábor Bódy, Attila Grandpierre, András Fekete, János Derzsi, Marietta Méhes, Gabriella Seres

A priest (Gábor Bódy), who is eventually revealed to be a phony, arrives in a small village, where he meets and helps some of the various villagers. For example, he befriends a wheelchair bound former Communist Party Chief, and helps a woman with tuberculosis confess. Other characters include an astronomer who sings with a punk group, and an erratic army officer and his wife. Also known as *The Dog's Night Song*.

**447. Ladies They Talk About.** Warner. US. 1933. 69m. B&W. *Producer*: Raymond Griffith *Director*: Howard Bretherton, William Keighley *Writer*: Brown Holmes, William McGrath, Sidney Sutherland, Dorothy Mackaye (play), Carlton Miles (play) *Cast*: Barbara Stanwyck, Preston Foster, Lyle Talbot, Dorothy Burgess, Lillian Roth, Maude Eburne, Ruth Donnelly, Harold Huber, Robert McWade, Robert Warwick

A radio evangelist, David Slade (Preston Foster), recognizes Nan Taylor (Barbara Stanwyck), who has been arrested for playing a decoy in a bank robbery, as a former classmate whose father was the town deacon. The district attorney agrees to parole her to Slade's care. When she confesses that she was actually guilty of the crime Slade withdraws his support and she is sent to prison. When Nan learns that the members of her gang have been arrested she uses Slade to help with their escape plans. She slips a letter into his pocket which falls into the hands of the police and their escape fails. Believing that Slade betrayed her she hunts him down, after she is released from prison, with the intention of killing him. She shoots him and is instantly remorseful. When the police arrive Slade tells them that they are getting married.

**The Lady of Monza** *see* **La Monaca di Monza**

**448. Lanigan's Rabbi.** NBC. (TV). US. 1976. 120m. C. *Producer*: Robert C. Thompson, Roderick Paul *Director*: Lou Antonio *Writer*: Harry Kemelman (novel), Don M. Mankiewicz, Gordon Cotler *Cast*: Art Carney, Stuart Margolin, Janis Paige, Janet Margolin, Lorraine Gary, Robert Reed, Andrew Robinson, Jim Antonio, David Sheiner, Barbara Carney, Robert Doyle, William Wheatley, Steffan Zacharias, Barbara Flicker

A mystery-comedy about Rabbi David Small (Stuart Margolin) and an Irish Catholic police chief Paul Lanigan (Art Carney) who team up to solve the murder of a housekeeper whose body was discovered on the front steps of the synagogue. This was the pilot film to the series which aired during the 1976–77 season. Also known as *Friday the Rabbi Slept Late*.

**449. The Last Flight of Noah's Ark.** Buena Vista. US. 1980. 97m. C. *Producer*: Ron Miller *Director*: Charles Jarrot *Writer*: Steven W. Carabatsos, Sandy Glass, George Arthur Bloom *Cast*: Elliott Gould, Geneviève Bujold, Ricky Schroder, Tammy Lauren, Vincent Gardenia, John Fujioka, Yuki Shimoda, John P. Ryan, Dana Elcar

Missionary Bernadette Lafleur (Geneviève Bujold) convinces a scruffy pilot Noah Dugan (Elliott Gould) to fly his run down plane to airlift animals to a needy island in the South Pacific. Two children sneak aboard to make sure the animals are alright. Enroute the plane crashes on a remote island inhabited by two Japanese soldiers who don't realize that World War II is over. They all unite and become a team in order to get off the island. They manage to convert the airplane into a sailboat. The gruff pilot wants to leave the animals behind but the children throw a tantrum and the animals are taken aboard.

**450. Last Rites.** MGM. US. 1988. 103m. C. *Producer*: Donald P. Bellisario, Patrick McCormick *Director & Writer*: Donald P. Bellisario *Cast*: Tom Berenger, Daphne Zuniga, Chick Vennera, Anne Twomey, Dane Clark, Paul Dooley, Vassili Lambrinos, Adrian Paul, Deborah Pratt, Tony DiBenedetto

Because of his blood ties to the Mafia, a New York priest Father Michael Pace (Tom Berenger) uses the Church to protect the mistress Angela (Daphne Zuniga) of a murdered Mafia Don, after meeting in the confessional. Betrayals and twists permeate the plot.

**451. Law and Disorder.** BL. UK. 1958. 76m. B&W. *Producer*: Paul Soskin *Director*: Charles Crichton *Writer*: T. E. B. Clarke, Patrick Campbell, Vivienne Knight *Cast*: Michael Redgrave, Robert Morley, Elizabeth Sellars, Ronald Squire, George Coulouris, Joan Hickson, Lionel Jeffries, Jeremy Burnham, Harold Goodwin, Meredith Edwards, Brenda Bruce, David Hutcheson, Michael Trubshawe, Irene Handl, John Warwick

Habitual crook Percy Brand (Michael Redgrave) poses as a cleric tries to prevent his son, a judge's marshal, from learning the truth. His friends rally around him to help deceive his son.

**452. The Lawton Story.** Hallmark Productions, Inc. US. 1949. 111m. C. *Producer*: Kroger Babb, J. S. Jossey *Director*: William Beaudine, Harold Daniels *Writer*: Scott Darling *Cast*: Ginger Prince, Forrest Taylor, Millard Coody, Ferris Taylor, Gwynne Shipman, Darlene Bridges, Maude Eburne, Willa Pearl Curtis, Raymond Largay

Taking place in Lawton, Oklahoma, the main plot involves Reverend Mark Wallock (Forrest Taylor) who is planning the annual Easter pageant while the community expresses concern over his deteriorating health. When his sister arrives for an extended stay she is determined to reunite the Reverend with his estranged brother, the town banker. When the Reverend collapses, one Sunday after church services, the doctor orders bed rest. After viewing the pageant the banker brother recognizing his brother's inspiring work decides to return home and reconcile.

**453. Leap of Faith.** Paramount. US. 1992. 108m. C. *Producer*: Michael Manheim, David Picker *Director*: Richard Pearce *Writer*: Janus Crone *Cast*: Steve Martin, Debra Winger, Lolita Davidovich, Liam Neeson, Lukas Haas, Meal Loaf, Philip Seymour Hoffman, M.C. Gainey, La Chanze, Delores Hall

Fake and cynical faith healer Jonas Nightengale (Steve Martin) and his caravan travel the country putting on their religious revival show. When one of their truck breaks down, they end up stranded in a small town. While in town things begin to fall apart, Jonas attempts to seduce a waitress Marva (Lolita Davidovich) and his assistant Jane (Debra Winger) falls in love with the local sheriff Will (Liam Neeson). The sheriff really wants to expose the fraud. Marva's crippled brother Boyd (Luke Haas) becomes involved with the story. Marva and Boyd have been fooled by other faith healers.

**454. Lease of Life.** GFD. UK. 1954. 94m. C. *Producer*: Jack Rix *Director*: Charles Frend *Writer*: Eric Ambler *Cast*: Robert Donat, Kay Walsh, Denholm Elliott, Adrienne Corri, Walter Fitzgerald, Reginald Beckwith, Vida Hope, Cyril Raymond, Jean Anderson, Mark Daly, Russell Waters, Richard Wattis, Beckett Bould, Frank Atkinson, Frederick Piper, John Salew

Country village vicar, Reverend William Thorne (Robert Donat), learns he only has one year to live, even with this knowledge he finds real happiness and gives a controversial sermon. His one dilemma is the problem of raising money for his daughter's tuition to music school. His wife gives into temptation and steals some money for the tuition.

**455. The Leather Saint.** Paramount. US. 1956. 86m. B&W. *Producer:* Norman Retchin *Director:* Alvin Ganzer *Writer:* Norman Retchin, Alvin Ganzer *Cast:* Paul Douglas, John Derek, Jody Lawrence, Cesar Romero, Richard Shannon, Ernest Truex, Ricky Vera, Thomas Browne Henry, Lou Nova

Father Gil Allen (John Derek), a young Episcopalian priest, sheds his clergy robes for boxing gloves every Saturday night to raise money for medical equipment, such as an iron lung and a swimming pool, for a group of children who are polio victims. His manager Gus (Paul Douglas) does not suspect his real profession. He explains his winnings as donations from a friend in the leather business.

**456. The Left Hand of God.** TCF. US. 1955. 87m. C. *Producer:* Buddy Adler *Director:* Edward Dmytryk *Writer:* Alfred Hayes, William Barrett (novel) *Cast:* Humphrey Bogart, Gene Tierney, Lee J. Cobb, Agnes Moorehouse, E. G. Marshall, Jean Porter, Carl Benton Reid, Victor Sen Yung, Philip Ahn, Richard Cutting, Benson Fong

An American flier Joe Carmody (Humphrey Bogart) impersonates a priest Father John O'Shea at a Catholic mission to escape a Chinese warlord. At the missionary hospital, he meets a nurse Anne Scott (Gene Tierney) searching for her husband lost in war and believed dead, and a doctor who fears for the safety of the mission's staff. Joe wrestles with the problem of how not to perform expected priestly duties. He saves the village by winning a dice game with the warlord Mieh Yang (Lee J. Cobb). Anne feels attracted to Father O'Shea and feels relieved when she learns that he is not a priest. Newly arrived Father Cornelius (Carl Benton Reid) learns of the story and is impressed by what Joe has accomplished. Joe is asked to continue impersonating a priest and travel to Sinkiang, where his punishment will be decided.

**457. The Legend of Provence.** Mutual Film Corp. US. 1913. B&W. *Cast:* Maude Fealy, James Cruze, Lila Chester, Carey Hastings

Sister Angela (Maude Fealy) as a baby was left at the convent gate and reared by the sisters. One day while tending to the wounds of Sir Henry (James Cruze) she falls in love with him and renounces her vows to become his wife. When she leaves, the statue of the Virgin Mary assumes the form of Sister Angela and continues her work. Sir Henry's drunkenness and adultery force her to return to the convent where she is transformed back into Sister Angela and the statue reappears in its old niche. At the end, Sister Angela dies and ascends into heaven.

**458. Léon Morin, Prêtre.** Lux Films. France/Italy. 1961. 130m. B&W. *Producer:* Georges de Beauregard, Carlo Ponti *Director:* Jean-Pierre Melville *Writer:* Beatrice Beck (novel), Jean-Pierre Melville *Cast:* Jean-Paul Belmondo, Emmanuelle Riva, Irène Tunc, Nicole Mirel, Gisèle Grimm, Marco Behar, Monique Bertho, Monique Hennessy

A young sexually frustrated widow Barny (Emmanuelle Riva), who is a communist militant, lives with her little girl in a small French town, during the Occupation. One day she enters a church and randomly chooses a priest Léon Morin (Jean-Paul Belmondo) and begins to criticize the Catholic religion. The priest happens to be young handsome and very clever. Slowly she realizes his moral strength. The film was shortened by 22 minutes for its American release due to the censorship climate of 1961. Also known as *The Forgiven Sinner* and *Leon Morin, Priest.*

**Leon Morin, Priest** *see* **Léon Morin, Prêtre**

**Let's Have a Riot** *see* **Contestazione generale**

**459. Liam.** Lions Gate. UK/Germany/France. 2000. 90m. C. *Producer:* Colin McKeown, Martin Tempia *Director:* Stephen Frears *Writer:* Jimmy McGovern *Cast:* Ian Hart, Claire Hackett, Anthony Borrows, David Hart, Megan Burns, Anne Reid, Russell Dixon, Julia Deakin, Andrew Sehofield, Bernadette Shortt

Told from the point of view of a 7-year-old boy Liam (Anthony Borrows), the film depicts the trials and tribulations of a working-class Catholic family during tight financial times. At Catholic school, his teacher,

Mrs. Abernathy (Anne Reid) and Father Ryan (Russell Dixon) prepare him for his first communion. The priest and the teacher continually drum into the kids how filthy their souls will become if they sin and the horrors of hell. His father (Ian Hart) is unable to get work after the shipyard closes. Growing very bitter he turns to fascism which ultimately leads to violence.

**460. Life and Miracles of Blessed Mother Cabrini.** Clyde Elliott. Italy. 1946. 70m. B&W. *Director*: Auerlio Battistoni *Cast*: La Cheduzzi, Mila Lanza, Luigi Badniati, Gennaro Quaranta

Biographical semi-documentary film of the life of Mother Cabrini (La Cheduzzi). The picture traces the nun's career showing the events that the Catholic Church deems miracles and that led to her canonization. The film also shows her influence of the social development of Chicago and New York.

**461. A Life for a Life.** Warwick Trading Co. UK. 1906. B&W. *Director:* Charles Raymond

Cleric helps husband escape from country after husband avenges wife's death.

**The Life of a Nun** *see* **Nonnen fra Asminderod**

**462. The Life of Charles Peace.** Haggar & Sons. UK. 1905. B&W. *Director:* William Haggar *Cast:* Walter Haggar, Violet Haggar, Henry Haggar, Lilian Haggar

Fugitive burglar, Charles Peace (Walter Haggar) poses as a parson, is caught, tries to escape from train but is caught and hanged.

**463. The Life of St. Patrick.** Photo-Historic Film Company. US. 1912. B&W. *Director:* J. Theobald Walsh

Previously a slave, Patrick arrives back in Ireland and banishes all the reptiles. He converts all the Irish to Christianity and dies surrounded by angels.

**Life Starts Now** *see* **Nu Börjar Livet**

**464. The Light of Happiness.** Metro. 1916. B&W. *Director & Writer:* John H. Collins *Cast:* Viola Dana, George Melville, Lorraine Frost, Harry Linson, Edward Earle, Jack Busby, Mona Kingsley, Robert Walker

The premise is based on the ninth commandment "Thou Shall Not Bear False Witness Against Thy Neighbor." Social outcast Tangletop (Viola Dana), because of her drunk of a father, is used by Emmett Dwight (Jack Busby) to deceive his wealthy blind ward Lowell Van Order (Edward Earle). Tangletop goes along with the plan until she meets Reverend Clyde Harmon (Robert Walker). Under his influence, she confesses the plot to Lowell. Lowell gets his true love and Tangletop marries Clyde.

**465. The Lilac Sunbonnet.** Butcher. UK. 1922. B&W. *Producer:* Frank Spring *Director & Writer:* Sidney Morgan *Cast:* Joan Morgan, Warwick Ward, Pauline Peters, Arthur Lennard, Lewis Dayton, Forrester Harvey, Charles Levey, A. Harding Steerman, Nell Emerald

Girl wins cleric's approval by revealing she is daughter by runaway marriage.

**466. Lilies of the Field.** UA. US. 1963. 94m. B&W. *Producer & Director*: Ralph Nelson *Writer:* James Poe, William Barrett (novel) *Cast:* Sidney Poitier, Lilla Skala, Lisa Mann, Isa Crino, Francesca Jarvis, Pamela Branch, Stanley Adams, Dan Frazer, Ralph Nelson

A black ex-GI Homer Smith (Sidney Poitier) becomes a handyman to five East German refugee nuns in Arizona. Mother Superior Maria (Lilia Skala) is intent on having him build a chapel on the site. Finally he gives into her request and agrees to help build the chapel while teaching the nuns English. He must secure another job to help pay for supplies. When the materials are gone, Homer leaves. He returns a few weeks later ready to build again. The townspeople feel guilty and join to help finish the chapel before the Bishop arrives. At the end, Homer leaves without a word.

**467. The Lion's Den.** Metro. US. 1919. B&W. *Director & Writer:* George D. Baker *Cast:* Bert Lytell, Alice Lake, Joseph Kilgour, Edward Connelly, Augustus Phillips, Howard Crampton, Seymour Ross, Alice Newland, Mother Anderson

Reverend Sam Webster (Bert Lytell) admonishes his parishioners for their failure to support a boys club. So he goes out to hustle for money in order to build the club, which leads to all sorts of complications. The vestrymen have decided to relieve him of his parish. At the last second, he rescues his enemy from a fire and wins the hand of the girl he loves.

**468. Lise et André.** Les Films á Un Dollar. France. 2000. 87m. C. *Producer*: Tom Dercourt *Director & Writer*: Denis Dercourt *Cast*: Isabelle Candelier, Michel Duchaussoy, Aissa Maiga, Augustin Bartholomé, Héléne Surgère, Jean-Christophe Bouvet

A call girl and a reluctant priest set off together on a pilgrimage from Paris to the site of a miracle. After her son is hit by a car and fallen into a coma Lise (Isabelle Candelier) enlists Father André (Michel Duchaussoy) to accompany her on a pilgrimage. Their destination is a field where the Virgin appeared to starving children at the turn of the century and threw grains of wheat which immediately grew.

**469. Little Church Around the Corner.** Warner. US. 1923. 55m. B&W. *Director*: William Seiter *Writer*: Olga Printzlau *Cast*: Kenneth Harlan, Claire Windsor, Hobart Bosworth, Walter Long, Pauline Starke, Alec Francis, Margaret Seddon, George Cooper, Winter Hall, Cyril Chadwick

Set in a mining town tells the story of an orphaned boy David Graham (Kenneth Harlan) who is sent to divinity school. Upon his return there is a mining accident and he leads the search for survivors. When a vengeance-seeking mob confronts the mine owner Morton (Hobart Bosworth) and his daughter, the minister diffuses the situation by performing a miracle in which a dumb girl speaks.

**470. The Little Door into The World.** Astra-National. UK. 1923. B&W. *Producer, Director & Writer*: George Dewhurst *Cast*: Lawford Davidson, Nancy Beard, Olaf Hytten, Peggy Patterson, Victor Tandy, Arthur Mayhew, Bob Williamson

Nun saves dancer from squire by luring him, then revealing she is his illegal daughter.

**471. The Little Flower Girl and the Fighting Parson.** Walter Tyler. UK. 1908. B&W.

Cleric thrashes drunkard and adopts his stepdaughter.

**472. Little Flower of Jesus.** Sunray. France. 1939. 67m. B&W. *Director*: Georges Chaperot *Cast*: Simone Bourday, Suzanne Christy, André Marnay, Jane Dolys, Nicolas Mallkov, Colette Dubois, Lionel Salem

Chronicles the life of Saint Therese of Lisieux. The cast is comprised mostly of amateur actors. Also known as *Saint Therese of Lisieux*.

**473. A Little Hero.** Walturdaw. UK. 1908. B&W.

Drunkard kills his wife by poisoning her port and dies after robbing and setting fire to house of cleric who adopted his son.

**474. The Little Minister.** Jury. UK. 1915. B&W. *Director*: Percy Nash *Writer*: J. M. Barrie *Cast*: Joan Ritz, Gregory Scott, Henry Vibart, Fay Davis, Dame May Whitty, Douglas Payne, Frank Tennant, John East, Brian Daly, Douglas Cox, Alfred Wilmore

Lord's fiancée poses as gypsy and falls in love with new minister Reverend Gavin Dishart (Gregory Scott). Other versions have been filmed.

**475. The Little Minister.** RKO. US. 1934. 110m. B&W. *Producer*: Pandro S. Berman *Director*: Richard Wallace *Writer*: Sarah Mason, Jane Murfin, Victor Heerman, J. M. Barrie (play) *Cast*: Katharine Hepburn, John Beal, Alan Hale, Donald Crisp, Lumsden Hare, Andy Clyde, Beryl Mercer, Billy Watson, Dorothy Stickney, Mary Gordon, Frank Conroy, Eily Malyon, Reginald Denny, Leonard Carey, Herbert Bunston

The film takes place in rural 1840's Scotland. Reverend Gavin Dishart (John Beal) arrives in Thrum's Auld Licht to become the new "little minister" of the church. He meets Babbie (Katharine Hepburn), a young gypsy girl who is more than she seems. The two must overcome her secret, the villagers' fears of her, and Gavin's devotion to his mother's sensibilities before they can declare their love.

**The Little Nuns** *see* Le Monachine

**476. The Little Samaritan.** Art Drama. US. 1917. B&W. *Director*: Joseph Levering *Writer*: Reverend Clarence J. Harris *Cast*: Marian Swayne, Carl Gerard, Lucile Dorrington, Sam Robinson, Bernard Niemeyer, Charles MacDonald, Mrs. Allen Walker, Olive Corbett

Lindy Gray (Marian Swayne) an orphan ward of her grandmother is treated poorly by others. The evil squire wishes to foreclose on her grandmother's house. A new minister (Carl Gerard) arrives and there is a taking of the church collection money. Lindy is suspected of the theft but faithful friend Noah takes the blame and is jailed. The minister uncovers the truth and clears Lindy and Noah. The real thief is the son of the village snob. The minister finds love with Lindy.

**477. The Little Welsh Girl.** Jury. UK. 1920. B&W. *Director:* Fred Paul *Cast:* Christine Silver, Humberston Wright, Booth Conway, Adelaide Grace, Daphne Grey, Robert Michaelis, Dorothy Ardley

Expelled priest is accused of killing servant girl, who fled from his attack.

**The Little World of Don Camillo** *see* **Le Petit monde de Don Camillo**

**478. The Littlest Outlaw.** Buena Vista. US. 1955. 75m. C. *Producer:* Larry Lansburgh *Director:* Roberto Gavaldón *Writer:* Bill Walsh *Cast:* Pedro Armendáriz, Joseph Calleia, Rodolfo Acosta, Andrés Velázquez, Pepe Ortiz, Laila Maley, Gilberto Gonzáles, José Torvay

A little stable boy Pablito (Andrés Velázquez) attempts to save the life of the general's horse by running away after it has been ordered killed. The general wants the horse destroyed only because it will not take a certain jump during a meet. The reason it will not jump is due to an evil trainer. Padre (Joseph Calleia), in who's the church the boy takes refuge with the horse, is very compassionate and helpful about the situation.

**479. La Loca de la casa.** Mier y Brooks. Mexico. 1950. 104m. B&W. *Producer:* Juan Bustillo Oro, Gonzalo Elvira *Director:* Juan Bustillo Oro *Writer:* Juan Bustillo Oro, Gonzalo Elvira, Benito Pérez Galdós *Cast:* Pedro Armendáriz, Susana Freyre, Julio Villarreal, Luis Beristáin, Beatriz Aguirre

A strong willed convent novice is being returned home by the Mother Superior to make sure of her choice between the world and the veil. Also known as *Madcap of the House*.

**480. The Longest Hundred Miles.** NBC. (TV). US. 1967. 100m. C. *Producer:* Jack Leewood *Director:* Don Weis *Writer:* Winston Miller *Cast:* Doug McClure, Katharine Ross, Ricardo Montalban, Ronald Remy, Helen Thompson, Berting Labra

The story is set in the Philippines during the Japanese invasion. American GI Steve Bennett (Doug McClure), an army nurse Laura (Katharine Ross), a local priest Father Sanchez (Ricardo Montalban) and a busload of native children are fleeing the enemy in a rundown bus.

**The Longing** *see* **Das Verlangen**

**481. The Lost Chord.** Clarendon. UK. 1917. B&W. *Director:* Wilfred Noy *Writer:* Reuben Gillmer *Cast:* Barbara Conrad, Malcolm Keen, Concordia Merrill, Dorothy Bellew, Mary Ford, H. Manning Haynes

Musician loves married woman who later becomes nun when her brute of a husband dies during a duel; later he loves her daughter.

**482. Lost in the Stars.** American Film Theatre. US. 1974. 97m. C. *Producer:* Ely A. Landau *Director:* Daniel Mann *Writer:* Maxwell Anderson (play), Alan Paton (novel) Alfred Hayes *Cast:* Brock Peters, Melba Moore, Raymond St. Jacques, Clifton Davis, Paul Rogers, Paula Kelly, Alan Weeks, Paulene Myers, John Williams, Ivor Barry

Dramatic musical based on Alan Paton's novel *Cry of the Beloved Country*. Brock Peters portrays the South African minister Stephen Kumalo devastated by his son's actions.

**483. Lourdes.** Rai Fiction. (TV). Italy/France/Luxembourg. 180m. C. *Producer:* Luca Bernabei, Roberta Cadringher, Monica Paolini *Director:* Lodovico Gasparini *Writer:* Alessandra Caneva, Mario Falcone, Alessandro Jachia, Vittorio Messori, Francesco Scardamaglia *Cast:* Alessandro Gassman, Angèle Osinsky, Florence Darel, Roger Souza, Sydne Rome, Helmut Griem, Gunther Maria Halmer, Andréa Ferréol, Umberto Orsini

Another version of the story of Bernadette (Angèle Osinsky) and the Lourdes. When the Virgin Mary appears to her in a cavern near Lourdes, no one believes her.

The authorities keep it quiet but to no avail. The Empress Eugenie requests water for her sickly son and finally all are convinced of this miracle. Doctor Henri Guillaumet (Alessandro Gassman) is bringing his tuberculosis-ailing fiancée Claire (Florence Darel) to a sanatorium when he meets Bernadette and the healing water. Although Claire is cured he still believes Bernadette to be a liar. Slowly he realizes the truth.

**Loyola, the Soldier Saint** *see* **El Capitán de Loyola**

**484. Luther.** Reformation Films. Germany. 1927. 90m. B&W. *Director:* Hans Kyser *Cast:* Eugene Klöpfer, Karl Elzer, Jakob Tiedtke, Hans Carl Mueller, Elsa Wagner, Bruno Kastner

Biographical film about Martin Luther, the German religious leader and founder of the Lutheran Church. Other versions of the story have been filmed.

**485. Luther.** American Film. UK/Canada. 1973. 112m. C. *Producer:* Ely Landau *Director:* Guy Green *Writer:* Edward Anhalt, John Osborne (play) *Cast:* Stacy Keach, Patrick Magee, Hugh Griffith, Robert Stephens, Alan Badel, Julian Glover, Judi Dench, Leonard Rossiter, Maurice Denham, Peter Cellier, Thomas Heathcote, Malcolm Stoddard, Bruce Carstairs

The life of Martin Luther (Stacy Keach) whose ideas lead to charge of heresy in the Catholic Church.

**486. Luther.** R.S. Entertainment Inc. Germany. 2003. 113m. C. *Producer:* Dennis A. Clauss, Brigitte Rochow *Director:* Eric Till *Writer:* Camille Thomasson, Bart Gavigan *Cast:* Joseph Fiennes, Alfred Molina, Bruno Ganz, Jonathan Firth, Peter Ustinov, Claire Cox, Uwe Ochsenknecht, Benjamin Sadler, Jochen Horst, Torben Liebrecht, Mathieu Carriére

The biography of Martin Luther (Joseph Fiennes), the 16th century Augustinian monk, who led the Christian Reformation.

**487. Luther Is Dead.** PAN-Film. Germany. 1984. 60m. C. *Director & Writer:* Frank Burckner *Cast:* Ingeborg Drewitz, Hermann Treusch, Ulrich Kuhlmann, Wolfgang Bathke, Gerhard Friedrich, Eberhard Wechselberg

Five actors interpret key moments in the life of Martin Luther; as monk, reformer, fugitive, political force in the Peasants' War, and prophet on the occasion of the 500th anniversary of Martin Luther's birth in1483. Also known as *Luther Ist Tot.*

**Lynx** *see* **Rys**

**The Mad Adventures of Rabbi Jacob** *see* **Les Adventures de Rabbi Jacob**

**Madcap of the House** *see* **La Loca de la casa**

**488. Das Mädchen Johanna.** UfA. Germany. 1935. 87m. B&W. *Producer:* Bruno Duday *Director:* Gustav Ucicky *Writer:* Gerhard Menzel *Cast:* Willy Birgel, René Deltgen, Heinrich George, Gustaf Gründgens, Veit Harlan, Theodor Loos, Erich Ponto, Angela Salloker, Aribert Wäscher

This is Nazi film propaganda loosely based on the story of Joan of Arc (Angela Salloker).

**489. Maddalena.** IFE. Italy/France. 1953. 90m. C. *Producer:* Giuseppe Bordogni *Director:* Augusto Genina *Writer:* Augusto Genina, Alessandro De Stefani, Giorgio Prosperi, Pierre Bost *Cast:* Märta Torén, Gino Cervi, Charles Vanel, Jacques Sernas, Folco Lulli, Angiola Faranda

In a small village in the mountains of Italy, the town leader Giovanni Lamberti (Charles Vanel) thinks the town priest Don Vincenzo (Gino Cervi) has overshadowed him and plots to show up the priest. An annual village event is the Good Friday pageant where a local beauty plays the Virgin Mary. Lamberti sneaks in a prostitute Maddalena (Märta Torén) for the role. The priest picks her for the role and soon she is associated with a miracle. She confesses all to the priest but is convinced to return to the festival. A bitter Lamberti tells the crowd of Maddalena's true identity and an angry mob stone her to death. Also known as *Une fille nommée Madeleine.*

**490. Madeline.** Tristar. US/France. 88m. 1998. C. *Producer:* Saul Cooper, Allyn Stewart, Pancho Kohner *Director:* Daisy von Scherler Mayer *Writer:* Mark Levin, Jennifer Flackett, Malia Scotch Marmo *Cast:* Frances McDormand, Nigel Hawthorne, Hatty Jones, Kristian de la Osa, Stéphane Audran,

Chantal Neuwirth, Ben Daniels, Julien Maurel, Clare Thomas, Bianca Strohmann, Alix Ponchon, Jessica Mason, Christina Mangani, Alice Lavaud, Emilie Jessula, Pilar Garrard, Morgane Farcat, Eloise Eonnet

Based on Ludwig Bemelman's books about a spunky redheaded nine-year-old named Madeline. Miss Clavel (Frances McDormand) is the nun and headmistress of the Parisian school for girls that Madeline attends. Madeline befriends a young boy and has some adventures. Miss Clavel is kind and beloved by the girls. Trouble erupts when Lord Covington decides to sell the school.

**491. Madness of Youth.** Fox Film Corp. US. 1923. B&W with Color Sequences *Producer:* William Fox *Director:* Jerome Storm *Writer:* Joseph Franklin Poland *Cast:* John Gilbert, Billie Dove, Donald Hatswell, George K. Arthur, Wilton Taylor, Ruth Boyd, Luke Lucas, Julanne Johnston

The story of the final adventure of a young crook whose desires include robbing the rich. He assumes the role of an evangelist to protect himself from suspicion. He falls in love with the daughter of the man he is planning to rob and finds himself a convert of his own preaching.

**492. Madonna of the Streets.** First National. US. 1924. 87m. B&W. *Producer & Director:* Edwin Carewe *Writer:* Frank Griffin, William Babington Maxwell (novel) *Cast:* Alla Nazimova, Milton Sills, Claude Gillingwater, Courtenay Foote, Tom Kennedy, John T. Murray, Vivien Oakland, Harold Goodwin, Rosa Gore, Maybeth Carr, Herbert Prior

John Morton (Milton Sills) is a pastor preaching on the street when he meets a girl. He eventually falls in love with her and they marry. She becomes enraged when he decides to donate his fortune to charitable works. When he finds out that she had been his uncle's mistress he drives her away, and then searches for her for months. She appears at the mission he built for fallen women and the doctors predict that she will die. The prayers of her husband are apparently answered and she returns from the dead. There is also a 1930 version of the film.

**Madre Teresa** *see* **Mother Teresa of Calcutta**

**493. Madron.** Four Star Excelsior Releasing Co. Israel. 1970. 90m. C. *Producer:* Emanuel Henigman, Rick Weaver *Director:* Jerry Hopper *Writer:* Edward Chappell, Leo McMahon *Cast:* Richard Boone, Leslie Caron, Gabi Amrani, Chaim Banai, Paul Smith, Aharon Ipalé, Ya'ackov Banai, Sami Shmueli, Mosko Alkalai, Avraham Pelta, Willy Gafni

A band of Apaches massacres a wagon train of French Canadian nuns bound for Santa Fe. The sole survivor, Sister Mary (Leslie Caron), buries the dead and eventually meets gunslinger Madron (Richard Boone). The two of them set off for a journey across the desert. After a gun battle with outlaws, Sister Mary befriends the survivor Angel and the three now head across the desert. To confuse pursuers Angel rides off alone. Madron makes love to Sister Mary after a close escape from Apaches. Sister Mary removes her coif and asks to be called Antoinette. When Madron learns that Angel has been captured by the Apaches, he tells Antoinette to continue onto Santa Fe. Madron shoots Angel to end his agony of being skinned alive. He kills most of the Apaches himself before dying from a gunshot wound. Sister Mary continues on her journey.

**494. Magdalene.** France. 1989. 113m. C. *Producer:* Ernst R. von Theumer Jr., *Director & Writer:* Monica Teuber *Cast:* Steve Bond, Nastassia Kinski, David Warner, Gunter Meisner, Cyrus Elias, Katharina Böhm, Ferdy Mayne, Franco Nero, Anthony Quayle, William Carr Hickey, Janet Agren, Max Tidof, Karina Szulc, Ralf Weikinger, Ulrich Günther, Armin Kraft, Christoph von Goetz, Francesca Ferre

Father Joseph Mohr (Steve Bond), a newly appointed priest in a town near Salzburg befriends the beautiful prostitute Magdalene (Nastassia Kinski). His views are perceived as radical and his superiors are looking for anyway to get rid of him. They see an opportunity with his relationship with Magdalene.

**495. The Magdalene Sisters.** Miramax Films. UK/Ireland. 2002. 119m. C. *Producer:*

Frances Higson *Director & Writer:* Peter Mullan *Cast:* Nora-Jane Noone, Geraldine McEwan, Anne-Marie Duff, Dorothy Duffy, Eileen Walsh, Mary Murray, Britta Smith, Frances Healy, Eithne McGuinness, Phyllis MacMahon, Daniel Costello

The film is based on the true story of Irish women given into the custody of the Madgalene Sisters Asylum to correct their "sinful" behavior. The wayward women are kept as slaves working in the laundries under strict and sadistic supervision of the nuns. This story centers on three of the young Irish women held in their evil grasp of the Sisters. Rose is disowned by her parents after giving birth out of wedlock, Margaret is raped by a cousin, and Bernadette did nothing more than flirt. Sister Bridget (Geraldine McEwan) the asylum head has strict rules. The girls are flogged and the nuns allow a priest to force sex upon them. The goal of the girls is to escape from the horrors. The Vatican was outraged by this film.

**496. Major Barbara.** UA. UK. 1941. 121m. B&W. *Producer & Director:* Gabriel Pascal *Writer:* Anatole de Grunwald, George Bernard Shaw (play) *Cast:* Wendy Hiller, Rex Harrison, Robert Morley, Robert Newton, Sybil Thorndike, Emlyn Williams, Marie Lohr, Penelope Dudley-Ward, Walter Hudd, David Tree, Deborah Kerr

A young and idealistic woman Barbara Undershaft (Wendy Hiller) rejects the family business of armaments and joins the Salvation Army. She is saving souls in the Limehouse slums when she becomes disillusioned when the Salvation Army accepts a large sum of money from her father and a rich distiller. The father tries to prove that he does more for the poor than the Salvation Army.

**497. The Maldonado Miracle.** Showtime. (TV). US. 2003. 99m. C. *Producer:* Susan Aronson, Don Schain, Eve Silverman *Director:* Salma Hayek *Writer:* Paul Cooper, Theodore Taylor (novel) *Cast:* Peter Fonda, Mare Winningham, Christina Cabot, Bill Sage, Eddy Martin, Dan Merket, Rubén Blades

Father Russell (Peter Fonda), who is ministering to a dying small California town, questions his ability to help his parishioners. A young "illegal" boy Jose Maldonado (Eddy Martin) slips into town one night bleeding and stumbles into the local church and spends the night on the scaffolding above the crucifix. In the morning he leaves the church and a parishioner runs out of the church claiming the miracle of the bleeding statue. The town is inundated with pilgrims, fanatics and reporters. The miracle becomes a symbol of hope for the townsfolk and the lost boy gives the demoralized priest something to care about.

**498. Malia.** Lupa Film. Italy. 1945. 98m. B&W. *Producer & Director:* Giuseppe Amato *Writer:* Luigi Capuana (play), Renato Castellani, Giuseppe Amato *Cast:* Rossano Brazzi, María Denis, Anna Proclemer, Roldano Lupi, Gino Cervi, Virginia Balestrieri, Nando Tamberlani, Adriana de Roberto, Giovanna Scotto

The main theme of the film is of a village priest Don Alfonso (Gino Cervi) who stamps out witchcraft, mysticism and voodooism among the natives. Instead of following up with other acts of religious faith the film turns to an involved romance. A newly-married groom falls in love with his wife's sister. The priest acts as arbiter to bring the two sisters back together. Released in the US in 1952.

**499. Man Afraid.** UI. US. 1957. 84m. B&W. *Producer:* Gordon Kay *Director:* Harry Keller *Writer:* Herb Meadow *Cast:* George Nader, Phyillis Thaxter, Tim Hovey, Eduard Franz, Harold J. Stone, Judson Pratt, Reta Shaw, Butch Bernard, Mabel Albertson, Martin Milner

The story depicts the consequences that follow after a preacher Reverend David Collins (George Nader) kills a delinquent teenage burglar. The dead teenager's father Carl Simmons (Eduard Franz) plots revenge for the killing of his son. Reverend David Collins converts the grieving father while he asks for forgiveness from Carl Simmons.

**500. A Man Called Peter.** TCF. US. 1955. 119m. C. *Producer:* Samuel G. Engel *Director:* Henry Koster *Writer:* Catherine Marshall (novel), Eleanore Griffin *Cast:* Richard Todd, Jean Peters, Marjorie Rambeau, Jill Esmond, Les Tremayne, Robert Burton,

Gladys Hurlbut, Richard Garrick, Gloria Gordon, Billy Chapin

While returning home from school in Scotland one night Peter Marshall (Richard Todd) thinks he hears a voice and nearly falls into a quarry. Convinced that it was God's voice he tells his mother that God is sending him to America to become a minister. After three years of working double shifts he saves enough to buy passage to America. Once in America he works a number of odd jobs until God leads him to the Columbia Theological Seminary where he graduates and is offered two positions. He eventually ends up at a church in Atlanta where he encounters an indifferent congregation and his future wife who God has chosen for him. He continues to preach around the country until he becomes chaplain to the United States Senate. Peter Marshall preached an upbeat and hopeful message of religion.

**501. A Man for All Seasons.** Columbia. UK. 1966. 120m. C. *Producer & Director*: Fred Zinnemann *Writer*: Robert Bolt *Cast*: Paul Scofield, Wendy Hiller, Leo McKern, Robert Shaw, Orson Welles, Susannah York, Nigel Davenport, John Hurt, Corin Redgrave, Colin Blakely, Yootha Joyce

Story based on the 16th century politico-religious situation between adulterous King Henry VIII (Robert Shaw) and Catholic Sir Thomas More (Paul Scofield). Thomas More is willing to make sacrifices if he can do so with a clear conscience. More's opposition to King Henry VIII's break with the Catholic Church led to his execution. The story has been filmed many times. In 1964, there was a television and also in 1988, a television version starring Charleton Heston aired.

**502. The Man Without a Body.** Budd Rogers. US/UK. 1957. 80m. B&W. *Producer*: Guido Coen *Director*: W. Lee Wilder, Charles Saunders *Writer*: William Groter *Cast*: Robert Hutton, George Coulouris, Julia Arnall, Nadja Regin, Sheldon Lawrence, Michael Golden, Peter Copley, Kim Parker

A doctor revives Nostradamus', the prophet, head and attaches it to the body of an American tycoon with a brain tumor.

**503. The Man Without a Soul.** Jury. UK. 1916. B&W. *Director*: George Loane Tucker *Writer*: Kenelm Foss *Cast*: Milton Rosmer, Edna Flugrath, Barbara Everest, Edward O'Neill, Charles Rock, Frank Stanmore, Janet Ross, Hubert Willis, Kenelm Foss

Mission worker, adopted son of a preacher and the scientist who does not believe clash in the slums. During his work on developing a formula to produce life, an explosion occurs. The scientist dreams that the mission worker loses his soul when the scientist revives his dead body. The scientist realizes that the soul is important and that now he believes. Also known as *I Believe*.

**504. Manhã Submersa.** Filmes Lusomundo. Portugal. 1980. 127m. C. *Producer&Director*: Lauro António *Writer*: Vergilio Ferreira (novel), Lauro António *Cast*: Eunice Muñoz, Vergilio Ferreira, Canto e Castro, Jacinto Ramos, Carlos Wallenstein, Joaquim Manuel Dias, Miguel Franco, Maria Olguim

Tells the story of a poor boy from a small village who is chosen by a patroness to study at a seminary for the priesthood. He has little desire for the vocation and does not wish to leave his family but he has no choice. At the seminary, he befriends another boy and they predict that they would leave the seminary in one year. A letter he has written to his mother about his homesickness is intercepted and he talks with the rector. After this talk he decides to stay. On a break home he is introduced to the life of a priest in the village. He returns to the seminary and observes incidents of sexuality. When his friend dies, he recalls the prediction. During his next visit home he intentionally injuries his hand and doesn't return to the seminary. The film was banned and censored by the government. Based on a novel by Vergilio Ferreira, who had spent time in a seminary. Also known as *Morning Mist*.

**505. El Mar.** Gémini Films. Spain. 2000. 107m. C. *Producer*: Paulo Branco, Luís Ferrando, Augustín Villalonga *Director*: Augustín Villalonga *Writer*: Antonio Aloy, Blai Bonet (novel), Biel Mesquida, Augustín Villalonga *Cast*: Roger Casamajor, Bruno Bergonzini, Antónia Torrens, Hernán González, Juli Mira, Simón Andreu, Ángela Molina,

Nilo Mur, Tony Miquel Vanrell, Victoria Verger, Sergi Moreno

In a small Spanish village during the Civil War in 1936, children witness the execution of leftists. In an act of revenge, a boy whose father was among the victims kills the son of the leading executioner and then commits suicide. Ten years later, three who survived the incident are reunited in a sanitarium for tuberculosis patients. Manuel (Bruno Bergonzini) has become obsessed by religion, Andreu (Roger Casamajor) appears to love the ladies but has a secret, and Francisca (Antónia Torrens) is now a nun who works at the sanitarium. The tormented characters meet in a bloody finale. Also known as *The Sea.*

**Marcelino Bread and Wine** *see* **Marcelino pan y vino**

**506. Marcelino pan y vino.** Chamartín. Spain/Italy. 1955. 90m. B&W. *Director:* Ladislao Vajda *Writer:* José María Sánchez Silva, Ladislao Vajda *Cast:* Pablito Calvo, Rafael Rivelles, Antonio Vico, Juan Calvo, José Marco Davó, Joaquín Roa, Fernando Rey, José Nieto

Story about an abandoned baby brought up by monks. When the boy turns six, the evil town mayor solicits signatures in order to revoke the charter of the monastery. The boy causes a miracle, which brings the townspeople together and saves the monastery. The boy offers a piece of bread to a figure of Jesus Christ and it takes the bread and eats it. Also known as *Marcelino Bread and Wine* and *The Miracle of Marcelino.*

**507. Marie et le curé.** Argos. France. 1970. 35m. *Director & Writer:* Diourka Madveczky *Cast:* Bernadette Lafont, Jean-Claude Castelli

Short film loosely based on a real story of an obsessed priest (Jean-Claude Castelli) from a small village church who kills a woman he had impregnated, tears out the fetus, baptizes it, and then kills it. This was one of three parts from a film called *Cinema Different 3.*

**508. Mariette in Ecstasy.** Savoy Pictures. US. 1996. *Producer:* Frank Price *Director:* John Bailey *Writer:* Ron Hansen *Cast:* Alex Appel, Nancy Beatty, Rutger Hauer,

John Mahoney, Mary McDonnell, Geraldine O'Rawe, Cara Pifko, Eva Marie Saint

Mariette (Geraldine O'Rawe) is a teenager who is determined to be a nun. Her sister, Celine (Mary McDonnell), who happens to be the Mother Superior of the convent, warns Mariette of hard times. Mariette hears Jesus whisper "I will reveal myself to you." The chaplain Father Henri (Rutger Hauer) warns her that it might be Satan. Celine becomes ill and dies. After Celine's death, Mariette bears the stigmata and goes into trances. The other nuns become spiteful and do not appreciate the attention she is getting. There is an investigation into the stigmata. When villagers hear of her visions, they flock to the convent hoping to be cured.

**The Mark of the Hawk** *see* **The Accused**

**509. The Market of Vain Desire.** Triangle. US. 1916. B&W. *Director:* Reginald Barker *Writer:* C. Gardner Sullivan *Cast:* H. B. Warner, Clara Williams, Charles Miller, Gertrude Claire, Leona Hutton

Mrs. Badgley (Gertrude Claire) arranges for her daughter Helen (Clara Williams) to marry Count Bernard d'Montaigne (Charles Miller). She asks Reverend John Armstrong (H. B. Warner) to announce the engagement during services. John knows that Helen is not in love with the Count so he pays a prostitute to attend church services also. During the service he proclaims that women who marry for money are just like prostitutes. The Count breaks off the engagement and beats up John. When Helen hears the news she rushes to John.

**510. Martin Luther.** Louis de Rochemont Associates. US/Germany. 1953. 105m. B&W. *Producer:* Lothar Wolff *Director:* Irving Pichel *Writer:* Allan Sloane, Lothar Wolff, Jaroslaw Pelikan, Theodore G. Tappert *Cast:* Niall MacGinnis, John Ruddock, Pierre Lefevre, Guy Verney, Alastair Hunter, David Horne, Fred Johnson, Philip Leaver, Leonard White

Tells the story Martin Luther who founded the Lutheran church. In 1505, German law student Martin Luther gives away his possessions and becomes an Augustinian monk. Soon he begins speaking out against many of the trappings of the church. Over the years Martin's teaching spreads, prompting many priests and nuns to leave their own religious communities. Martin marries a former nun and stays an outlaw.

**511. The Martyrdom of Philip Strong.** Paramount. US. 1916. B&W. *Director*: Richard Ridgely *Writer*: Francis Neilson, Everett McNeil, Charles Sheldon (novel) *Cast*: Robert Conness, Mabel Trunnelle, Janet Dawley, Bigelow Cooper, Helen Strickland, Frank Lyon, William Wadsworth, Herbert Prior, Olive Wright, Edith Wright, Brad Sutton

The pastor of a rich church Reverend Philip Strong (Robert Conness) has a wife and daughter, a wealthy father-in-law, and ambition. When a poor wanderer shows up at the door Phillip gives up everything to minister to the poor. His wife leaves him and takes their daughter. He improves the life of the poor so much that local millionaires decide to discredit him. They spread rumors of his dealings with a former prostitute. The truth comes out and his wife decides to return to Phillip but it is too late as he dies from worry.

**The Martyrdom of St. Sébastian** *see* **Le Martyre de Saint Sébastien**

**512. The Martyrdom of Thomas a Becket.** Clarendon. UK. 1908. B&W. *Director*: Percy Stow *Writer*: Langford Reed

King Henry II has the archbishop of Canterbury Thomas Becket murdered and then repents.

**The Martyrdom of Thomas a Becket, Archbishop of Canterbury** *see* **Becket**

**513. Le Martyre de Saint Sébastien.** UNITEL Film. (TV). Germany. 1984. 82m. C. *Producer*: Hans-Gunther Herbertz *Director*: Petr Weigl *Writer*: Gabriele D'Annunzio (play) *Cast*: Michael Biehn, Nicholas Clay, Franco Citti, Urs Althaus, Pietro Speciale, Jan Gabriel, Ivan Varga, Fabio Caretti, Jana Hlavácová, Michael Gulyás

Retells the story of Saint Sébastian (Michael Biehn), who was a chief in the Roman army, and converted to Christianity. His devotion to Christ drives him to reject the Emperor's love. Angry, the Emperor or-

ders Sébastian to be shot with arrows. Also known as *The Martyrdom of St. Sébastian.*

**The Marvelous Life of Joan of Arc** *see* **La Merveilleuse vie de Jeanne d'Arc**

**514. Mary the Fishergirl.** Cosmo. UK. 1914. B&W. *Producer*: Harry Lorraine *Director*: Sidney Northcote *Writer*: Harold Brett *Cast*: Harry Lorraine

Vicar saves fiancée from drowning after fight with jealous girl.

**515. M\*A\*S\*H.** TCF. US. 1970. 116m. C. *Producer*: Ingo Preminger *Director*: Robert Altman *Writer*: Ring Lardner Jr., Richard Hooker (novel) *Cast*: Sally Kellerman, Donald Sutherland, Elliot Gould, Robert Duvall, Tom Skerritt, Jo Ann Pflug, Rene Auberjonois, Roger Bowen, Gary Burghoff, Fred Williamson, John Schuck, Bud Cort

A black comedy about the antics of surgeons and nurses in a Mobile Army Surgical Hospital during the Korean conflict. A suicidal sex-starved dentist, Margaret "Hot Lips" Houlihan (Sally Kellerman) the nurse, surgeons Hawkeye (Donald Sutherland), Trapper John (Elliot Gould), Father John Patrick 'Dago Red' Mulcahy (Rene Auberjonois) and Frank Burns (Robert Duvall) are some of the memorable characters. Sincere but bumbling Father Dago doesn't seem to know what to do with his immoral flock. A big football game and a desire to play golf are elements. One of the American Film Institute's 100 greatest American movies. The long-running television series *M\*A\*S\*H* was based on the film.

**516. Mass Appeal.** MCA/Universal. US. 1984. 99m. C. *Producer*: Lawrence Turman, David Foster *Director*: Glenn Jordan *Writer*: Bill C. Davis *Cast*: Jack Lemmon, Zeljko Ivanek, Charles Durning, Louise Latham, Alice Hirson, Helene Heigh, Sharee Gregory, James Ray

Confrontations between a crafty, compromising, and very popular priest Father Tim Farley (Jack Lemmon) and fiery zealous seminary student Mark Dolson (Zeljko Ivanek) who is to be his deacon. Their stormy relationship causes Father Farley to examine his own beliefs. Father Farley admits to Mark that he badly needs the popularity he now has. Monsignor Thomas Burke

(Charles Durning) who runs the seminary wants Mark expelled and when he learns that Mark has tried physical love with both women and men he seizes the opportunity..

**The Mass Is Ended** *see* **La Messa è finita**

**Massacre in Rome** *see* **Rappresaglia**

**517. Massa'ot James Be'eretz Hakodesh.** Zeitgeist. Israel. 2003. 87m. C. *Producer:* Amir Harel *Director:* Ra'anan Alexandrowicz *Writer:* Ra'anan Alexandrowicz, Sami Duenias *Cast:* Siyabonga Melongisi Shibe, Arieh Elias, Salim Dau, Sandra Schonwald, Hugh Masebenza, Florence Bloch

James (Siyabonga Melongisi Shibe), the son of a Zulu preacher, is sent on a pilgrimage from his African village to see the Holy sites of Jerusalem on behalf of devout Christians back home. Upon his arrival in Tel Aviv, a cynical immigration officer doesn't believe his story and throws him in jail. James is bailed out by a smooth operator, who exploits illegal aliens as cheap labor. James joins the illicit labor market. He attends a Black Christian church where the preacher welcomes him. James is planning to take over as preacher for his village back home. Soon James' decision to make money dealing in the illegal labor market nets him lots of money. When the preacher realizes that James now has money, the preacher has his and the congregation's hands out. James comes to his senses and returns to his village in Africa. Also known as *James' Journey to Jerusalem.*

**518. The Masterpiece.** Gaumont. 1909. B&W.

A monk is torn between being an artist or the cloistered life. One of his paintings catch the attention of visitors to the galleries of the monastery. They want to meet the painter of the masterpiece. The Abbott is so upset that he makes the monk paint out his signature. According to the Abbott, joy must come from creating for the Master. The film ends with the monk crying at the altar seeking strength.

**519. Mat Mariya.** Sovexport. Russia. 1983. 94m. C. *Director:* Sergei Kolosov *Writer:* Sergei Kolosov, Yelena Mikulina

*Cast:* Ljudmila Kasatkina, Aleksandr Timoshkin, Veronika Polonskaya, Leonid Markov, Igor Gorbachyov, Yevgeniya Khanayeva

Tells the story of the real life pre-revolutionary poetess Elisaveta Jurevna Kuzmina Karavaeva. Living in exile drives her to leave her poet-husband and becomes a nun. During World War II she is an organizer in France of other Russian exiles and is wanted by the Germans. Having taken on the identity of a mother of three women she wants to save she willingly goes to her death in the Ravensbruk concentration camp. Also known as *Mother Mary.*

**520. Matka Joanna od aniolów.** Telepix Corp. Poland. 1961. 105m. B&W. *Director:* Jerzy Kawalerowicz *Writer:* Tadeusz Konwicki, Jerzy Kawalerowicz *Cast:* Lucyna Winnicka, Mieczyslaw Voit, Anna Ciepielewska, Maria Chwalibóg, Kazimierz Fabisiak, Stanislaw Jasiukiewicz, Zygmunt Zintel, Franciszek Pieczka, Jerzy Kaczmarek, Jaroslaw Kuszewski, Lech Wojciechowski, Marian Nosek, Jerzy Walden, Marian Nowak, Zygmunt Malawski, Stanislaw Szymczyk

Mother Joan of the Angels (Lucyna Winnicka), the Mother Superior of a convent of Ursuline nuns in 17th century Poland, is said to be possessed by demons. After four priests fail to exorcise the demons, a fifth priest, Father Jozef Suryn (Mieczyslaw Voit) takes on the task to restore Mother Joan to her saintliness. After failing himself, he turns to a rabbi who tells him he may only be combating human nature. As Father Jozef finds himself more and more drawn to Joan, he slays two stable grooms in a desperate attempt to save her. Also known as *Joan of the Angels.*

**521. Il Medico e lo stregone.** Cineriz. Italy/France. 1958. 102m. B&W. *Producer:* Guido Giambartolomei *Director:* Mario Monicelli *Writer:* Mario Monicelli, Ennio De Concini, Agenore Incrocci, Furio Scarpelli, Luigi Emmanuele *Cast:* Vittorio De Sica, Marcello Mastroianni, Gabriella Pallotti, Lorella De Luca, Marisa Merlini

Doctor Francesco Marchetti (Marcello Mastroianni) arrives at a "backward" village to set up a medical practice. First he must deal with a faith healer Antonio Locoratolo (Vittorio De Sica) who has all the patients in the town. The physician wins in the end. Also known as *The Doctor and the Healer.*

**522. Meet Simon Cherry.** Exclusive. UK. 1950. 67m. B&W. *Producer:* Anthony Hinds *Director:* Godfrey Grayson *Writer:* Gale Pedrick, Godfrey Grayson, A. R. Rawlinson *Cast:* Zena Marshall, John Bailey, Hugh Moxey, Anthony Forwood, Ernest Butcher, Jeannette Tregarthen, Courtney Hope, Arthur Lovegrove

Vacationing Reverend Simon Cherry (Hugh Moxey) proves an invalid and rich woman died of heart failure and was not murdered.

**523. Melissa of the Hills.** Mutual. US. 1917. B&W. *Director:* James Kirkwood *Writer:* Maibelle Heikes Justice *Cast:* Mary Miles Minter, Spottiswoode Aitken, Allan Forrest, George Periolat, Perry Banks, Harry Clark, Frank Thompson, John Gough, Gertrude Le Brandt, Emma Kluge, Anne Schaefer

Drama about Melissa (Mary Miles Minter), the daughter of a self-styled evangelist Jethro Stark (Spottiswoode Aitken), living in the Tennessee hills. She writes to a society lady who has offered to give clothes to a deserving girl. When the lady and her husband visit Melissa, her husband recognizes Jethro as a fugitive wanted for murder. Jethro is killed trying to stop a fight between feuding families and his innocence is confirmed.

**524. Men of Boys Town.** MGM. US. 1941. 106m. B&W. *Producer:* John Considine Jr. *Director:* Norman Taurog *Writer:* James Kevin McGuinness *Cast:* Spencer Tracy, Mickey Rooney, Bobs Watson, Larry Nunn, Darryl Hickman, Henry O'Neill, Mary Nash, Lee J. Cobb, Sidney Miller, Addison Richards, Lloyd Corrigan, George Lessey, Robert Emmett Keane, Arthur Hohl, Bem Welden, Anne Revere

Sequel to *Boys Town.* Father Edward J. "Eddie" Flanagan (Spencer Tracy) is back at Boys Town. The story focuses attention on the kindly and understanding Father and his charges. The Father brings Ted Martley (Larry Nunn), a crippled boy who is bitter and never laughs to Boys Town. He had his back broken by a guard at a reformatory. He never told the true story of how a guard was killed. Ted doesn't respond to anyone until Whitey (Mickey Rooney) gives him a dog "Beau Hunk." The dog belongs to the Maitlands, members of the parole board. The Maitlands are persuaded to let the dog remain with Ted. The dog brings the child so much happiness until the dog is accidentally killed and buried on the grounds. Then things go wrong at Boys Town. After an operation, Ted is able to walk to the dog's grave. At the conclusion all problems at Boys Town are resolved. It was reported that the sequel was made after donations to the real Boys Town dropped because people thought that Boys Town no longer had financial problems.

**525. Men Without Souls.** Columbia. US. 1940. 62m. B&W. *Producer:* Wallace MacDonald *Director:* Nick Grinde *Writer:* Robert Hardy Andrews, Joseph Carole, Harvey Gates *Cast:* John Litel, Barton MacLane, Rochelle Hudson, Glenn Ford, Don Beddoe, Cy Kendall, Eddie Laughton, Dick Curtis, Richard Fiske, Walter Soderling

Johnny Adams (Glen Ford) commits a crime in order to get himself sentenced to prison so he can get revenge on the brutal guard whose mistreatment killed his father. The prison chaplain Reverend Thomas Storm (John Litel) rescues Johnny after a group of convicts murder the guard and attempt a jail break.

**526. La Merveilleuse vie de Jeanne d'Arc.** Production Natan. France. 1929. 125m. B&W. *Director:* Marco de Gastyne *Cast:* Jean Debucourt, Pierre Denols, Simone Genevois, Philippe Hériat, Férnand Mailly, Choura Milena, Georges Paulais

The story of Joan of Arc (Simone Genevois). Also known as *The Marvelous Life of Joan of Arc* and *Saint Joan the Maid.*

**527. La Messa è finità.** SACIS. Italy. 1988. 94m. C. *Director:* Nanni Moretti *Writer:* Nanni Moretti, Sandro Petraglia *Cast:* Nanni Moretti, Ferruccio De Ceresa, Marco Messeri, Enrica Maria Modugno, Dario Cantarelli, Giovanni Buttafava, Luisa De Santis, Pietro De Vico, Eugenio Masciari, Vicenzo Salemme

A priest is transferred from an island parish to his hometown near Rome. His new assignment is a small church in of repairs on the outskirts of town. He is now able to visit his parents and sisters, all of whom he loves. He is also able to see his pre-priest friends. One friend is hyper-religious, another one is a terrorist on trial, and so on. Also he discovers that his church has lost parishioners because the previous priest got married and lives across the road from the church. He is a sincere priest but he feels that there are parts of life that organized religion cannot touch. At the end he leaves his now-restored church for one in Tierra del Fuego. One thing missing from this film is carnal temptation – he is good-looking too. He confides to a friar that people confess sexual sins but never real sins. Also known as *The Mass is Ended*.

**528. The Messenger: The Story of Joan of Arc.** Sony. France. 1999. 148m. C. *Producer*: Patrice Ledoux *Director*: Luc Besson *Writer*: Luc Besson, Andrew Birkin *Cast*: Milla Jovovich, John Malkovich, Faye Dunaway, Dustin Hoffman, Pascal Gregory, Vincent Cassel, Tchéky Karyo, Richard Ridings, Desmond Harrington, Jane Valentine, Timothy West

The classic story of the 15th century devoutly religious French girl (Milla Jovovich) who became a liberating hero to her country during the Hundred Years' War by leading an army against the English. It is believed that Joan's visions were God's way of telling her to save France. She was betrayed and burned at the stake.

**529. Messenger of Peace.** Astor Pictures. US. 1950. 87m. B&W. *Producer*: Roland D. Reed *Director*: Frank Strayer *Writer*: Glenn Tryon *Cast*: John Beal, Peggy Stewart, William Bakewell, Paul Guilfoyle, Fred Essler, Ray Bennett, Maude Prickett, Al Bridge, Elizabeth Kerr, William Gould, Edythe Elliott

The story told via flashbacks follows a seminary student from graduation to his retirement, Pastor Armin Ritter (John Beal), demonstrates the usefulness and service to the community the pastor provides.

**530. Michael Angel.** HBO. US. 1998. C.

*Producer*: Igor Barkagan *Director & Writer*: William Gove *Cast*: Dennis Hopper, Richard Grieco, Ivonne Coll, Efrain Figueroa, Michael Cole, Frank Medrano, Johanna Quintero

In San Juan, an agnostic Jesuit priest Michael Killan (Richard Grieco) aids the police in investigating two gristly murders. His brother was the first victim. Because the murderer used the victims' blood to paint the walls by the bodies, the police conclude that they are looking for an abstract-expressionist painter. All fingers point to an aging local artist.

**531. The Midnight Flower.** Aywon Film Corp. US. 1923. B&W. *Producer*: Nathan Hirsch *Director*: Captain Leslie T. Peacock *Cast*: Gaston Glass, Vola Vale

At midnight each evening Myra (Vola Vale), called "Midnight Flower," does a dance atop a table in a local gambling den. A young Spaniard, who is in love with Myra, holds up the most profitable table and gives the money to Myra. She is caught trying to escape and is sent to prison where she meets and falls in love with a young evangelist. When she is released from prison she joins him in his missionary work. At the end it is revealed that she was kidnapped as an infant and is really the daughter of a wealthy family.

**532. The Midnight Story.** UI. US. 1957. 89m. B&W. *Producer*: Robert Arthur *Director*: Joseph Pevney *Writer*: Edwin Blum, John Robinson *Cast*: Tony Curtis, Marisa Pavan, Gilbert Roland, Jay C. Flippen, Argentina Brunetti, Ted de Corsia, Richard Monda, Kathleen Freeman, Herb Vigran, Peggy Maley, John Cliff

In San Francisco, the police investigate the murder of a beloved priest Father Thomasino. Cop Joe Martini (Tony Curtis) becomes so obsessed with the murder that he goes undercover to find the murderer.

**La Mies es mucha** *see* **Harvest Is Rich**

**533. Miffo.** Sonet Film. Sweden. 2003. 105m. C. *Producer*: Susanne Lundqvist, Daniel Lind Lagerlöf *Director*: Daniel Lind Lagerlöf *Writer*: Malin Lind Lagerlöf *Cast*: Jonas Karlsson, Livia Millhagen, Ingvar Hirdwall, Iso Aouifia, Fyr Thorvald Strömberg, Liv Mjones, Kajsa Ernst

Film is about the romance between a stiff, upper-class minister Tobias (Jonas Karlsson) and a wheelchair bound working girl Carola (Livia Millhagen). They meet when he leaves his large church to preach in a small community.

**534. Miguelin.** Paramount. Spain. 1964. 66m. B&W. *Director:* Horacio Valcárcel *Writer:* Joaquín Aguirre Bellver *Cast:* Luis María Hidalgo, Luis Domínguez Luna, Alberto Domarco, Rufino Inglés, José Luis Blanco, Francisco José Huetos, Rosa Fúster

A serious minded boy (Luis María Hidalgo) sells his mule and leaves the money in the poor box at the church. The money is to go for the poor. The village priest observes this unselfish act. The priest and other boys get the boy's mule back in time for the blessing of the animals.

**535. Milagros de San Martín de Porres.** Mexico. 1959. B&W. *Director:* Rafael Baledón *Cast:* Lorena Velázquez, Roberto Cañedo, Rosa de Castilla, Andrés Soler, Dagoberto Rodríguez, René Cardoná, Rebeca Iturbide, Emma Roldán, María Alejandra

Relates the story of St. Martin de Porres, who was born at Lima, Peru in 1579. He died on November 3, 1639 and was canonized on May 6, 1962. At fifteen he became a lay brother at the Dominican monastery at Lima where he spent his whole life. Since it was not possible for him to travel to a foreign mission to earn the palm of martyrdom he subjected himself to severe penances. In turn, God endows him with many graces and gifts.

**536. Milarepa.** Lotar. Italy. 1974. 108m. C. *Director:* Liliana Cavani *Writer:* Liliana Cavani, Italo Moscati *Cast:* Lajos Balázsovits, Paolo Bonacelli, Marisa Fabbri, Marcella Michelangeli, George Wang

After being sent back in time, a recovering patient from a car accident tells a doctor about the 11th century Tibetan monk Milarepa (an important figure in Tibetan history).

**537. The Milky Way.** Universal Marion. France/Germany/Italy. 1969. 105m. C. *Producer:* Serge Silberman *Director:* Luis Buñuel *Writer:* Luis Buñuel, Jean-Claude Carrière *Cast:* Laurent Terzieff, Paul Frankeur, Delphine Seyrig, Bernard Verley, Georges Marchal, Jean Piat, Jean-Claude Carrière, Julien Guiomar, Michel Piccoli

Surrealistic film about two pilgrims traveling from Paris to visit the tomb of John De Compostello in Spain. One man sees it as a good begging opportunity and the other man questions God. They encounter Jesus, God, biblical characters, and other people on their journey. In one segment a priest and a policeman discuss the meaning of communion and whether the wafers and wine are symbols or the actually Christ's body and blood. The priest turns out to be an escaped asylum inmate, an ex-priest who could not deal with contradiction. Requires special knowledge to appreciate this film. Also known as *La Via Lattea* and *La Voie lactèe.*

**The Miracle** *see* **Il Miracolo**

**538. The Miracle.** Warner. US. 1959. 121m. C. *Producer:* Henry Blanke *Director:* Irving Rapper *Writer:* Karl Vollmöller (play), Frank Butler, Jean Fouverol *Cast:* Carroll Baker, Roger Moore, Walter Slezak, Vittorio Gassman, Katina Paxinou, Dennis King, Gustavo Rojo, Isobel Elsom, Carlos Rivas

The statue of the Virgin Mary comes to life and takes the place of a young nun Teresa (Carroll Baker) who leaves the convent in Spain to go out into the world and possibly see the wounded soldier that she loves.

**539. Miracle at Moreaux.** Wonder Works. (TV). US. 1986. 58m. C. *Producer:* Janice Platt *Director:* Paul Shapiro *Writer:* Jeffrey Cohen, Paul Shapiro *Cast:* Loretta Swit, Geneviéve Appleton, Milan Cheylov, Simon Craig, Thomas Hellman, Robert Joy, Robert Kosoy, Bonfield Marcoux, Marsha Moreau, Carla Napier

In December 1943, three Jewish children flee Nazi occupied France and find refuge in a Catholic school run by Sister Gabrielle (Loretta Swit). At first the other children are frightened but soon they risk their own live to devise a plan for the Jewish children to reach freedom.

**540. The Miracle Man.** Paramount. US. 1932. 85m. B&W. *Director:* Norman Z.

McLeod *Writer:* George M. Cohan (play), Robert Hobart Davis (novel), Frank L. Pickard (novel), Waldemar Young *Cast:* Sylvia Sidney, Chester Morris, Robert Coogan, John Wray, Ned Sparks, Hobart Bosworth, Lloyd Hughes, Virginia Bruce, Boris Karloff, Irving Pichel, Frank Darien, Florine McKinney

A gang from San Francisco moves their operation to a small town. Their leader John Madison (Chester Morris) decides to start a new con game by exploiting a local faith healer. He is going to fake healings and make some money. The healer happens to be the real thing. Instead of getting rich, the gang builds a new chapel. Remake of 1919 silent film.

**The Miracle of Marcelino** *see* **Marcelino pan y vino**

**541. The Miracle of Our Lady of Fatima.** Warner. US. 1952. 102m. C. *Producer:* Bryan Foy *Director:* John Brahm *Writer:* Crane Wilbur, James O'Hanlon *Cast:* Gilbert Roland, Angela Clarke, Frank Silvera, Jay Novello, Richard Hale, Norman Rice, Frances Morris, Carl Millitaire, Susan Whitney, Sherry Jackson, Sammy Ogg

Visions of the Virgin Mary which took place at Fatima in Portugal in 1917. A beautiful lady appears to three peasant children. The lady asks them to return to the spot over the next six months. People start believing when the word of the vision gets out. The police state government becomes involved because religious visions are punishable by law. The crowds grow larger and larger. The lady only appears to the children and gives them warning of an upcoming war. Finally the lady presents a promised miracle for the crowd – sun appears to falls, the earth is dry after heavy rains, and many of the sick are healed. Skeptics become believers. Two of the visionaries died very young, and have since been beatified.

**542. Miracle of Saint Therese.** Ellis Films Inc. France. 1952. 115m. B&W. *Producer:* Paul de Saint-André *Director:* André Haguet *Writer:* André Haguet, André Legrand *Cast:* Francois Darbon, Jean Debucourt, France Descaut, Albert Dinan, Denis d'Inès, Suzanne Flon, Catherine Fonteney, Marcelle Géniat, Jeanne Herviale, Jean Meyer, Martine Sarcey, Valentine Tessier, Jean Yonnel, Hélène Delval

Depicts the story of Saint Therese. Also known as *Trial at the Vatican* and *Proces au Vatican.*

**543. The Miracle of the Bells.** RKO. US. 1948. 120m. B&W. *Producer:* Jesse L. Lasky, Walter MacEwen *Director:* Irving Pichel *Writer:* Ben Hecht, Quentin Reynolds, Russell Janney (novel) *Cast:* Fred MacMurray, Alida Valli, Frank Sinatra, Lee J. Cobb, Harold Vermilyea, Charles Meredith, Jim Nolan, Veronica Pataky, Philip Ahn, Frank Ferguson, Frank Wilcox

A Hollywood press agent Bill Dunnigan (Fred MacMurray) returns the body of his friend, actress Olga Treskovna (Alida Valli), to her home in Coaltown, Pennsylvania. While arranging Olga's funeral Bill tells her story to Father Paul (Frank Sinatra), the priest of Coaltown's St. Michael's church. Olga wanted to be buried at the church. Just before her death, Olga was playing the role of Joan of Arc in a film. During the filming she grows ill from tuberculosis developed as a child while living around coal dust. Olga continues and a day after the filming ended she dies. It is decided to shelf the film because she was an unknown actress. Bill's idea is to have all the churches in town ring their bells at the same time. Bill's plan is not working out until two statutes move to face Olga's casket. Father Paul realizes that they moved due to their weight and the crowd but Bill convinces him to explain the movement as divine intervention. The film is going to be released and a hospital in Olga's name will be built.

**544. The Miracle Woman.** Columbia. US. 1931. 90m. B&W. *Producer:* Harry Cohn *Director:* Frank Capra *Writer:* Jo Swerling *Cast:* Barbara Stanwyck, David Manners, Sam Hardy, Beryl Mercer, Russell Hopton, Charles Middleton, Eddie Boland, Thelma Hill, Aileen Carlyle, Al Stewart, Harry Todd

When her father, an elderly minister, dies Florence Fallon (Barbara Stanwyck) becomes Sister Fallon, leader of the Temple of Happiness where she performs fake miracles. With the help of con man Bob Hornsby

(Sam Hardy), her evangelism becomes a very profitable scam. She falls in love with a blind man John Carson (David Manners) and she decides to tell her followers the truth. She is confessing to her followers when a fire is accidentally set. She asks the congregation to sing and she guides them to safety. She becomes a Salvation Army worker and is reunited with John.

**545. Il Miracolo.** CEIAD. Italy. 1948. 37m. B&W. *Producer & Director*: Roberto Rossellini *Writer*: Roberto Rossellini, Tullio Pineill *Cast*: Anna Magnani, Frederico Fellini

A mentally unbalanced shepherdess (Anna Magnani) is given drink and seduced by a bearded vagabond she thinks is Saint Joseph. She believes she will be giving birth to the Savior. The villagers mock and torment her. She escapes to a hilltop church and experiences religious ecstasy while giving birth. The film caused controversy and many groups attempted to censor the film. In 1950, this short was combined with two other short films to become *Ways of Love* a feature length film. Also known as *The Miracle*.

**546. Miraklet.** Rembrandt. Sweden. 1913. B&W. *Director*: Victor Sjöström *Writer*: Sven Elvestad, Martin Jörgensen, Émile Zola *Cast*: Carl Borin, John Ekman, Clara Pontoppidan, Jenny Tschernichin-Larsson, Carlo Wieth

A scheming lecherous priest attempts to win the love of a girl engaged to a friend. He persuades the man's father to will his money to the church and for his son to join the order. The girl falls very ill and is taken to a healing sacred spring. She is cured when she sees her love. All of his deceptions are uncovered and he is banished and cursed. Also known a *Within the Gates*.

**547. Les Misérables.** TCF. US. 1952. 105m. B&W. *Producer*: Fred Kohlmar *Director*: Lewis Milestone *Writer*: Victor Hugo (novel), Richard Murphy *Cast*: Michael Rennie, Debra Paget, Robert Newton, Edmund Gwenn, Sylvia Sidney, Cameron Mitchell, Elsa Lanchester, James Robertson Justice, Joseph Wiseman, Rhys Williams, Florence Bates, Merry Anders, John Rogers, Charles Keane

The story is told in three parts. The first episode is when Jean Valjean (Michael Rennie) is sentenced to ten years as a galley slave for stealing a loaf of bread. In the second part Valjean is released and becomes a pottery owner. He gets his first lesson in humanity from a kindly bishop (Edmund Gwenn). During this time he aids a dying woman and takes in her daughter. He even becomes mayor of the village, only to have it all taken away when he refuses to allow a halfwit to be falsely accused of being Valjean. Many versions of this story have been filmed. It was first filmed in 1919 and again in 1927, 1935, and 1936. Also even today versions of the story are being filmed.

**548. The Mission.** Warner. UK. 1986. 126m. C. *Producer*: Fernando Ghia, David Puttnam *Director*: Roland Joffé *Writer*: Robert Bolt *Cast*: Robert De Niro, Jeremy Irons, Ray McAnally, Aidan Quinn, Cherie Lunghi, Ronald Pickup, Chuck Low, Liam Neeson, Bercelio Moya, Sigifredo Ismare, Daniel Berrigan

The film depicts conflict within a Jesuit mission of San Carlos in remote mountains of Paraguay during the mid-eighteenth century. The Vatican has sent Cardinal Altamirano (Ray McAnally) to determine whether to continue the mission. His decision not to continue maintaining the mission leads to disastrous results. The natives, the Guarani Indians, are pawns for slave traders and a Vatican willing to sacrifice them to avoid pressure on the church. The missionaries renounce their vows to stay with the natives. The mission leader, saintly Father Gabriel (Jeremy Irons) dies celebrating mass with the natives when mercenaries attack. Father Mendoza (Robert DeNiro), a former slave trader who repented and converted, violently tries to help but all is in vain. Daniel Berrigan, a radical Jesuit priest advised and acted in the film.

**Mission to Glory** *see* **Padre on Horseback**

**549. Missionary.** Columbia. UK. 1982. 90m. C. *Producer:* Michael Palin, Neville C. Thompson *Director:* Richard Loncraine *Writer:* Michael Palin *Cast:* Michael Palin, Maggie Smith, Trevor Howard, Denholm

Elliott, Michael Hordern, Phoebe Nicholls, Graham Crowden, David Suchet, Tricia George, Valerie Whittington, Timothy Spall

After 10 years of missionary work in Africa, Reverend Charles Fortescue (Michael Palin) is given a new assignment. He is to minister to the fallen ladies of the East End of London. His fiancée Deborah Fitzbanks (Phoebe Nicholls) is troubled by it and soon he is seduced by the girls. In addition, Lady Isabel Ames (Maggie Smith) will not fund the mission unless he beds her.

**550. Un Missionnaire.** UCEP. France. 1955. 98m. C. *Producer, Director & Writer:* Maurice Cloche *Cast:* Charles Vanel, Yves Massard, Albert Préjean, Jacques Berthier, Marie-France Planeze, René Blancard

Young missionary priest is very excited about being sent to Africa and facing adventures. He is disappointed to learn he will primarily be a parish priest. Also known as *A Missionary.*

**551. Mist in the Valley.** Hepworth. UK. 1923. B&W. *Director:* Cecil M. Hepworth *Writer:* George Dewhurst, Dorin Craig (novel) *Cast:* Alma Taylor, G. H. Mulcaster, James Carew, Esme Hubbard, John McAndrews, Gwynne Herbert, Maud Cressall, Charles Vane, Douglas Munro, Lionel d'Aragon, Bertram Terry, Fred Rains

Ex-nun (Alma Taylor) weds amnesia victim and is framed for killing usurping uncle who posed as father.

**552. Mr. Brown Comes Down the Hill.** MRA. UK. 1965. 88m. B&W. *Producer & Director:* Henry Cass *Writer:* Henry Cass, Howard Koch (play) *Cast:* Eric Flynn, Mark Heath, Lillias Walker, John Richmond, Richard Warner, Bryan Coleman, Alan White, Donald Simpson

A black man, a prostitute and a bishop find faith through a strange preacher Mr. Brown (Eric Flynn) who is killed by betrayers.

**Mistress of the Mountains** *see* **Gente così**

**553. La Moglie del prête.** Warner. Italy/France. 1971. 103m. C. *Producer:* Carlo Ponti *Director:* Dino Risi *Writer:* Ruggero Maccari, Dino Risi, Bernardino Zapponi *Cast:* Sophia Loren, Marcello Mastroianni,

Venantino Venantini, Gino Cavalieri, Giuseppe Maffioli, Pippo Starnazza

After discovering her boyfriend is married, a young lady Valeria Billi (Sophie Loren) attempts suicide, but pauses to phone a help line. In the hospital she meets the priest Don Mario Carlesi (Marcello Mastroianni) who took the call. She tries to seduce him and he succumbs to her charms. Their major problem however is his holy vow of celibacy. Also known as *The Priest's Wife.*

**554. Le Moine et la sorcière.** European Classics. France. 1987. 97m. C. *Producer:* Paméla Berger, Annie Leibovici, George Reinhart *Director:* Suzanne Schiffman *Writer:* Paméla Berger, Suzanne Schiffman *Cast:* Christine Boisson, Jean Carmet, Tchéky Karyo, Raoul Billerey, Catherine Frot, Féodor Atkine, Maria de Medeiros, Gilette Barbier

A Dominican friar in search of heretics arrives in a small village where a faith healer immediately attracts his attention. Upon following her into the woods he discovers that the villagers worship a dog saint who sacrificed his life to save a young child. The friar accuses the faith healer of sorcery and condemns her to death. When a mute girl arrives in the village she turns out to be the friar's daughter conceived when he raped a woman years earlier. In the end the faith healer is set free and the friar learns some valuable lessons. The film is based on the writings of a 13th century friar Etienne de Bourbon who described the cult and the greyhound as a saint. Also known as *The Sorceress.*

**555. Molokai: The Story of Father Damien.** Unapix. Belgium/Netherlands/Australia. 1999. 122m. C. *Producer:* Grietje Lammertyn, Tarsicius Vanhuysse *Director:* Paul Cox *Writer:* John Briley, Hilde Eynikel (book) *Cast:* Peter O'Toole, Kris Kristofferson, David Wenham, Derek Jacobi, Alice Krige, Leo McKern, Sam Neill, Tom Wilkinson

This drama explores the life of Father Damien (David Wenham), a priest and missionary devoted to God and the exiled lepers in Hawaii. When he arrives in the late 1800s, the lepers have no running water, little food, and poor housing. Also known as *Father Damien.*

**556. La Monaca di Monza.** Tower Productions. Italy. 1969. 105m. C. *Producer:* Silvio Clementelli *Director:* Eriprando Visconti *Writer:* Mario Mazzucchelli (novel), Eriprando Visconti, Giampiero Bona, Edward Bond *Cast:* Anne Heywood, Antonio Sabato, Carla Gravina, Tino Carraro, Luigi Pistilli, Margarita Lozano, Anna Maria Alegiani, Giovanna Galletti, Caterina Boratto, Michel Bardinet, Laura Belli, Pier Paolo Capponi, Francesco Carnelutti, Giulio Donnini, Hardy Krüger

In Italy, early in the 17th century, nobleman Gian Paolo Osio (Antonio Sabato) seeks refuge with Father Arrigon (Hardy Krüger) after killing a Spanish soldier. Osio is immediately attracted to Virginia de Leyva (Anne Heywood), prioress of the Convent of Santa Margherita at Monza, and attempts to rape her. Eventually she succumbs to her passions and joins him in passionate lovemaking. Guilty she has Osio arrested and then arranges for his escape after bearing his child. Church authorities begin to investigate the murder of a nun who had witnessed the lovemaking. Virginia is found guilty of having sexual relations and of being an accomplice in murder and is sentenced to be walled up in a prison cell for life. *The Awful Story of the Nun of Monza, The Nun of Monza,* and *The Lady of Monza.*

**557. Le Monache di Sant'Arcangelo.** MPI. Italy/France. 1973. 100m. C. *Producer:* Tonino Cervi *Director:* Domenico Paolella *Writer:* Tonino Cervi, Domenico Paolella *Cast:* Anne Heywood, Luc Merenda, Ornella Muti, Martine Brochard, Muriel Catalá, Claudia Gravy, Maria Cumani Quasimodo, Pier Paolo Capponi, Claudio Gora, Duilio Del Prete

During the 16th century, a nun pretends to be helping the Mother Superior deal with an illness but she is really trying to kill her in order to become the Mother Superior. The Cardinal senses something is wrong and brings the guilty to trial. Also known as *The Nun and the Devil* and *Sisters of Satan.*

**558. Le Monachine.** Embassy Pictures. 1965. 100m. B&W. *Producer:* Ferruccio Bru-

sarosco *Director:* Luciano Salce *Writer:* Franco Castellano, Giuseppe Moccia *Cast:* Catherine Spaak, Sylva Koscina, Amedeo Nazzari, Didi Perego, Umberto D'Orsi, Sandro Bruni, Annie Gorassini, Alberto Bonucci, Lando Buzzanca

Sister Celeste (Catherine Spaak) and Mother Rachele (Didi Perego) travel to Rome to convince the authorities to change the airplanes' route which passes directly over their convent/school. As the jet planes pass over the convent the sound wave vibrations are destroying the convent's ancient fresco of Saint Domitilla and disturbing the children in the school. Also known as *The Little Nuns.*

**559. The Monk in the Monastery Wine Cellars.** G.A.S. Films. UK. 1902. B&W. *Director:* G.A. Smith

Monk gets drunk.

**560. Monkeys, Go Home!** Buena Vista. US. 1967. 101m. C. *Producer:* Walt Disney *Director:* Andrew V. McLaglen *Writer:* G.K. Wilkinson (novel), Maurice Tombragel *Cast:* Maurice Chevalier, Dean Jones, Yvette Mimieux, Bernard Woringer, Clément Harai, Yvonne Constant, Marcel Hillaire, Jules Munshin, Alan Carney, Maurice Marsac, Darleen Carr

Hank Dussard (Dean Jones) is heir to a rundown French olive farm and decides to use four chimpanzees as labor. The village priest Father Sylvain (Maurice Chevalier), who is also a village leader, offers much needed advice to Hank. The chimps are former members of an air force team so they are quick to learn. The village farm laborers are very upset about the chimps. To add to Hank's problems, his new chimp is a male and the four others are females.

**561. The Monks.** R.W. Paul. UK. 1898. B&W.

A monk smokes a cigar and accidentally burns his sleeping friend.

**562. The Monk's Mother.** Kleine Optical Co. France. 1909. B&W.

No description available.

**563. Monk's Vengeance.** Society Italian Cines. 1907. B&W.

No description is available.

**564. Monsieur Vincent.** Lopert Pictures. France. 1947. 111m. B&W. *Producer:*

Viscount George de la Grandiere *Director:* Maurice Cloche *Writer:* Jean Anouilh, Jean Bernard-Luc, Maurice Cloche *Cast:* Pierre Fresnay, Yvonne Gaudeau, Jean Carmet, Lise Delamare, Jean Debucourt, Gabrielle Dorziat, Pierre Dux, Germaine Dermoz, Aimé Clariond, Yvonne Claudie, Georges Vitray, Marcel Pérès

The life and achievements of St. Vincent de Paul. He was a poor French boy born in 1576 and lived in France until captured by Algerian pirates and made a slave. After being freed he becomes a priest. Father Vincent de Paul (Pierre Fresnay) struggles to bring peace among the people during the Black Death in Europe. He ministers to the poor in all states of life. In today's terms he would be considered a social worker. Film won a special Oscar as the best foreign film.

**565. Monsignor.** TCF. US. 1982. 121m. C. *Producer:* David Niven Jr., Frank Yablans *Director:* Frank Perry *Writer:* Jack-Alain Léger (novel), Wendell Mayes, Abraham Polonsky *Cast:* Christopher Reeve, Geneviève Bujold, Fernando Rey, Jason Miller, Joseph Cortese, Adolfo Celi, Leonardo Cimino, Tomas Milian, Robert Prosky, Joe Pantoliano, Milena Vukotic

After World War II, an ambitious priest Father Flaherty (Christopher Reeve) seduces a novice nun Clara (Geneviève Bujold) and leads the Vatican down the wrong financial path. During the war, he served as a military chaplain in Europe and gunned down many Nazis. The Vatican gives him control over their weak financial situation. He arranges a deal with the Mafia, who ultimately steal the funds. Father Flaherty finally does some soul searching and tries to do right.

**566. Monsignor Quixote.** PBS. (TV). UK. 1985. C. *Producer:* Christopher Neame *Director:* Rodney Bennett *Writer:* Graham Greene (novel), Christopher Neame *Cast:* Alec Guinness, Leo McKern, Ian Richardson, Grahm Crowden, Maurice Denham, Philip Stone, Rosalie Crutchley, Valentine Pelka, Don Fellows, Gareth Kirkland, Clive Merrison,

This is a modern adaptation of the Don Quixote theme. Father Quixote (Alec Guinness) is an old Spanish village priest traveling throughout Spain with his friend Sancho (Leo McKern), the village's mayor and his car called Rosinante. On their travels he has the similar adventures as his ancestor.

**567. Montecassino.** Superfilm. Italy. 1946. 93m. B&W. *Producer & Director:* Arturo Gemmiti *Writer:* Arturo Gemmiti, Virgillo Sabel, Giovanni Paolucci *Cast:* Alberto C. Lolli, Gilberto Severi, Ubaldo Lay, Zora Piazza, Pietro Bigerna, Silverio Blasi, Vira Silenil, Rudolf H. Neuhaus, Livio Bussa, Giuseppe Forli

Semi-documentary about the incidents that led up to the bombing of Monte Cassino Abbey during the Italian campaign of World War II. A dramatic battle against the German troops is being waged by the abbot, monks and brothers of the abbey. The Germans seek to stop them from caring for women, children, the elderly, and the sick. The film begins in October 1943, when the fighting first started, to the following March when the Abbey was destroyed by American bombs.

**568. Mool-Dori Village.** Happ Dong Films. South Korea. 1979. 105m. C. *Producer:* Jeong-hwan Kwak *Director:* Doo-yong Lee *Writer:* Su-jung Yeo *Cast:* Yeong-ran Kim, So-ryong Han, Kil-su Hyeon, Wu-cheol Shin, Seong-kwan Choi

Based on an old Korean legend about the origins of a mask festival. A young priest (So-ryong Han receives a divine message that tells him to make masks and send his woman (Yeong-ran Kim) away while he is working. She is determined to spend her waiting time praying before a shrine, but monks force her away and try to rape her. She falls down a hill trying to escape an evil monk. Later, as she lies dying, her wish is to see her love one last time. Also known as *Muldori dong* and *Muldori Village.*

**569. A Mormon Maid.** Friedman Enterprises, Inc. US. 1917. B&W. *Director:* Robert Z. Leonard *Writer:* Paul West, Charles Sarver *Cast:* Mae Murphy, Frank Borzage, Hobart Bosworth, Edythe Chapman, Noah Beery, Richard Cummings

The film is set in 1848 and begins with the migration of the Mormons to Salt Lake City. John Hogue (Hobart Bosworth), his wife and daughter live along the roadside where the Mormon caravan is traveling. Tom Rigdon (Frank Borzage), a young convert and an elder, Darius Burr (Noah Beery) both are attracted to the Hogue's daughter. The Indians attack and the Hogue's hut is burned down. The family is rescued by the Mormons. They join the Utah colony and Hogue becomes prosperous and influential. Burr plots to add the Hogue's daughter to his list of wives, but she claims to be impure and therefore ineligible for marriage with the Mormon.

**Morning Mist** *see* **Manhã Submersa**

**570. Mort, où est ta victoire?** Gaumont. France. 1964. 135m. B&W. *Director:* Hervé Bromberger *Writer:* Daniel-Rops, Frederic Grendel, Hervé Bromberger *Cast:* Pascale Audret, Laurent Terzieff, Michel Auclair, Olivier Despax, Elizabeth Ercy, Jacques Monod, Philippe Noiret

An orphan is falsely accused of lesbian advances by a boy, when she would not give in to his advances. She then goes to work for an old priest, who tries to help her find herself. She sacrifices her virginity to a shady doctor. She faces one bad thing after another for this poor person until she decides to become a nun. Also known as *Death, Where Is Your Victory?*

**571. Morte in Vaticano.** Film International. Spain/Italy/Mexico. 1982. 105m. C. *Producer:* Fabián Arnaud, Enzo Gallo, J. M. Reyzabal *Director:* Marcello Aliprandi *Writer:* Max Savigny (novel), Maurice Serral (novel), Marcello Aliprandi, Lucio Battistrada, Alberto Fioretti, Enzo Gallo, Pedro Mario Herrero *Cast:* Terence Stamp, Fabrizio Bentivoglio, Paula Molina, José Luis López Vázquez, Antonio Marsina, Roberto Antonelli, Patrick La Place, Adriano Amidei Migliano, Eduardo Fajardo, Franco Ferri, Pep Munné

Fictionalized version of the alleged murder of Pope John Paul I. An idealistic young priest Father Bruno Martello (Fabrizio Bentivoglio) becomes a Fascist and breaks his vows with a female terrorist and learns of a magical mixture. He plots the poisoning of his old friend and mentor the Pope (Terence Stamp) who was once Father Andreani. Also known as *Death in the Vatican* and *The Vatican Conspiracy.*

**Mother Mary** *see* **Mat Mariya**

**572. Mother Teresa: In the Name of God's Poor.** The Family Channel. (TV). US /UK/Germany. 1997. 95m. C. *Producer:* Peter Shepherd *Director:* Kevin Connor *Writer:* Jan Hartman, Dominique LaPierre, Carol Kaplan *Cast:* Geraldine Chaplin, Keene Curtis, Helena Carroll, David Byrd, William Katt

Tells the true story of Mother Teresa (Geraldine Chaplin) and her missionary work with the very poor in India.

**573. Mother Teresa of Calcutta.** Alfred Haber Distribution. (TV). Italy. 2003. 180m. C. *Producer:* Luca Bernabei, Pete Maggi *Director:* Fabrizio Costa *Writer:* Massimo Cerofolini, Francesco Scardamaglia *Cast:* Olivia Hussey, Sebastiano Somma,

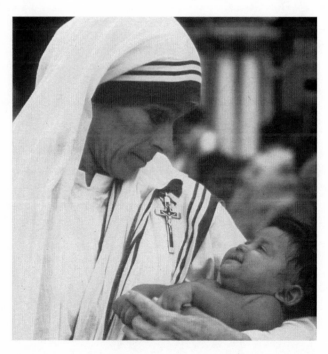

In *Mother Teresa* (1997), the missionary nun (Geraldine Chaplin) devotes her life to helping the sick and poor in India.

Michael Mendl, Laura Morante, Ingrid Rubio, Guillermo Ayesa, Neil Stuke, Emily Hamilton

The story of Mother Teresa (Olivia Hussey). Also known as *Madre Teresa*.

**574. The Mountain.** EB. UK. 1935. B&W. *Producer, Director & Writer:* Travis Jackson *Cast:* Maurice Jones, Hope Sharpe, Alan F. Elliott, J. Vyne Clarke, Rosemary Lee Booker, Sydney Dench

Jealous cleric, Reverend Brian Goodhall (Alan F. Elliott), goes mad and kills wife's mountaineering lover.

**575. The Mummy.** UI. UK. 1959. 88m. C. *Producer:* Michael Carreras *Director:* Terence Fisher *Writer:* Jimmy Sangster *Cast:* Peter Cushing, Christopher Lee, Yvonne Furneaux, Eddie Byrne, Felix Aylmer, Raymond Huntley, George Pastell, John Stuart, Harold Goodwin, Dennis Shaw

Egyptian priest brings revived mummy to England to kill three archaeologists, who had disturbed the grave of an important Egyptian female priest.

**576. Murder in the Cathedral.** Classic Pictures. UK. 1952. 140m. B&W. *Producer& Director:* George Hoellering *Writer:* George Hoellering, T. S. Eliot (play) *Cast:* Father John Groser, Alexander Gauge, Donald Bisset, Clement McCallin, Michael Groser, Mark Dignam, Michael Aldridge, Leo McKern, Paul Rogers, GeorgeWoodbridge

Film version of T.S. Eliot's play of the same name, about the murder and martyrdom of Archbishop Thomas Becket (Father John Groser).

**577. Murder Ordained.** (TV). US. 1987. C. *Producer:* Zev Braun *Director:* Mike Robe *Cast:* Keith Carradine, Kathy Bates, Guy Boyd, John Goodman, Terry Kinney, M. Emmet Walsh, George McDaniel, Margot Rose, Terence Knox, Annabella Price, Jo-Beth Williams

Lutheran minister Pastor Tom Bird (Terry Kinney) and church secretary Lorna Anderson (JoBeth Williams) are having an affair and pray that God will make it work out. When God doesn't cooperate, the couple decides to have their respective spouses murdered. When Pastor Tom's wife dies in an auto accident, Kansas highway trooper John Rule (Keith Carradine) suspects that something is not right. A few months later, Lorna's husband ends up dead.

**578. Mutiny in the Big House.** Monogram. US. 1939. 83m. B&W. *Producer:* Grant Withers *Director:* William Nigh *Writer:* Robert Hardy Andrews *Cast:* Charles Bickford, Barton MacLane, Pat Moriaity, Dennis Moore, William Royle, Charles Foy, George Cleveland, Nigel De Bruller, Eddie Foster, Richard Austin, Russell Hopton

Based on the actual incident of Father Patrick O'Neil, who was awarded the Carnegie medal for his bravery in halting a prison break in 1929, where prisoners and guards died. Prison chaplain Father Joe (Charles Bickford) tries to save Johnny (Dennis Moore) who has been sentenced to 1 to 14 years for forging a $10 check. Tough guy prisoner Red (Barton MacLane) works to toughen him up.

**579. My Buddy.** Republic. US. 1944. 67m. B&W. *Director:* Steve Sekely *Writer:* Arnold Manoff *Cast:* Don 'Red' Barry, Ruth Terry, Lynne Roberts, Alexander Granach, Emma Dunn, John Litel, George E. Stone, Jonathan Hale, Ray Walker, Joe Devlin, Matt McHugh

Father Jim Donnelly (John Litel) tells the story of Eddie Ballinger, a World War I veteran, in testimony during Congressional Hearings to Senator Bill Henry's Post-War Planning Committee to illustrate his view that World War II veterans should have jobs awaiting them when they return from combat.

**580. Myrkrahöfðinginn.** Icelandic Film. Iceland/Sweden/Norway/Germany. 2000. 100m. C. *Producer:* Friðrik Þór Friðriksson *Director:* Hrafn Gunnlaugsson *Writer:* Bo Jonsson, Hrafn Gunnlaugsson, Thorarinn Eldjarn *Cast:* Hilmir Snær Guðnason, Sara Dögg Ásgeirsdóttir, Guðrún Kristín Magnúsdóttir, Hallgrímur H. Helgason, Alexandra Rapaport, Jón Sigurbjörnsson, Jón Tryggvason

At the end of the 17th century a dying old man comes to a remote monastery in the Icelandic wilderness and tells his story to one of the priests. The movie then uses flashbacks to take the viewer to 1643. The man is Jón Magnússon (Hilmir Snær Guðnason), a young priest. He is told he can take over a small, remote parish if he marries the previous priest's widow who is 30 years older than him. At the same time he lusts for a beautiful young girl, Thurildur (Sara Dögg Ásgeirsdóttir). He decides to rid the parish of all worshipers of Satan and targets Thurildur's father and brother and accuses them of witchcraft. After Thurildur refuses to sleep with him, the two men are burned alive and Thurildur is accused of being a disciple of Satan. The story has a tragic conclusion. Also known as *Witchcraft* and *Flames of Paradise*.

**Nachtwache** *see* **Keepers of the Night**

**581. Nachtwache.** Casino Film. Germany. 1953. 109m. *Producer:* Hans Abich, Jacob Geis *Director:* Harald Braun *Writer:* Paul Alvardes, Harald Braun *Cast:* Luise Ullrich, Hana Nielsen, René Deltgen, Dieter Borsche, Käthe Haack, Angelika Meissner, Gertrud Eysoldt

The film's theme is about a Protestant pastor and a Catholic priest both struggling to retain their faith. Pastor Heger (Hans Nielsen) falls in love with a female doctor at a sisterhood hospital, but she rejects him. His faith is shaken when his daughter dies in an accident. His faith is uplifted again when he prevents the actor who was responsible for the accident from committing suicide. It ends with the pastor and the priest Reverend von Imhoff (Dieter Borsche) sharing one church. Also known as *Keepers of the Night*.

**582. The Name of the Rose.** TCF. Germany/France/Italy. 1986. 130m. C. *Producer:* Bernd Eichinger *Director:* Jean-Jacques Annaud *Writer:* Umberto Eco (novel), Andrew Birkin, Gérard Brach, Howard Franklin, Alain Godard *Cast:* F. Murray Abraham, Elya Baskin, Feodor Chaliapin Jr., Sean Connery, William Hickey, Michael Lonsdale, Ron Perlman, Volker Prechtel, Helmut Qualtinger, Christian Slater, Valentina Vargas

Franciscan friars assemble at a Benedictine abbey to discuss what the poverty of Christ means to the life of the Catholic Church. At the same time the abbey is the scene of a series of murders and the abbot asks one of the visiting friars William of Baskerville (Sean Connery) to investigate. The friar discovers a plot to conceal a manuscript copy of Aristotle's treatise on comedy. He must race to solve the crimes before the innocent accused face the wrath of the Holy Inquisitor Bernardo Gui (F. Murray Abraham). Also known as *Der Name der Rose*.

**583. Nasty Habits.** Brut. UK/US. 1977. 96m. C. *Producer:* Robert Enders *Director:* Michael Lindsay-Hogg *Writer:* Robert Enders, Muriel Spark (novel) *Cast:* Glenda Jackson, Melina Mercouri, Geraldine Page, Sandy Dennis, Anne Jackson, Anne Meara, Susan Penhaligon, Edith Evans, Jerry Stiller, Rip Torn, Eli Wallach, Suzanne Stone, Peter Bromilow

Conflict ensues when dying Abbess fails to nominate her successor in a Philadelphia Abbey. The film is a parody of the Watergate scandal with would-be head Sister Alexandra (Glenda Jackson) plotting with others to break into her competition's sewing box. The box contains letters from a lover. Nothing will stand in this Sister's way.

**584. Nat's Conversion.** Cricks & Martin. UK. 1909. B&W. *Director:* A.E. Coleby

Fighting parson converts brutal drunkard.

**585. Nattvardsgästerna.** Janus Films. Sweden. 1963. 81m. B&W. *Producer:* Allan Ekelund *Director & Writer:* Ingmar Bergman *Cast:* Ingrid Thulin, Gunnar Björnstrand, Max von Sydow, Allan Edwall, Kolbjörn Knudsen, Olof Thunberg, Elsa Ebbesen

On a cold wintry Sunday, widowed village pastor Tomas Ericsson (Gunnar Björnstrand), empty of faith and unloved, reveals his bitter failures to his flock to try and offer spiritual consolation to his parishioners. After services he attempts to help others but can only talk about his troubled relationship with God. A school teacher offers her love but he resists. Part of a film trilogy dealing with man's relationship with God. Also known as *Winter Light*.

**586. Nazarín.** Altura Films. Mexico. 1958. 94m. B&W. *Producer:* Manuel Barbachano Ponce *Director:* Luis Buñuel *Writer:* Julio Alejandro, Luis Buñuel, Emilio Carballido, Benito Pérez Galdós *Cast:* Francisco Rabal, Marga López, Rita Macedo, Jesús Fernández, Ignacio López Tarso, Luis Aceves Castañeda, Ofelia Guilmáin, Noé Murayama, Rosenda Monteros

Father Nazarín (Francisco Rabal) tries to live by following strict Christian principles even though others treat him with disgust and hatred. He wants to live the life of a priest in Mexico as he imagined Jesus lived. Unlike Jesus he is detached from everything human. While in prison, waiting for trial for a minor crime of harboring a prostitute wanted for murder, he meets two thieves. He is unable to forgive the bad thief and the good thief, makes him realize that he is of no use. A single act of kindness by a fruit-selling woman may open the door to a better future for Father Nazarín.

Buñuel said "I am very much attached to Nazarín. He is a priest. He could as well be a hairdresser or a waiter. What interests me about him is that he stands by his ideas, that these ideas are unacceptable to society at large, and that after his adventures with prostitutes, thieves and so forth, they lead him to being irrevocably damned by the prevailing social order."

**587. The Nervous Curate.** Clarendon. UK. 1910. B&W. *Director:* Percy Stow

Cleric's young brother changes labels on presents.

**588. Never Take No for an Answer.** Souvaine Selective Films. UK. 1951. 82m. B&W. *Producer:* Anthony Havelock-Allen *Director:* Maurice Cloche, Ralph Smart *Writer:* Paul Gallico (novel), Pauline Gallico, Maurice Cloche, Ralph Smart *Cast:* Vittorio Manunta, Denis O'Dea, Frank Coulson, Guido Celano, Nerio Bernardi, Robert Adamina, John Murphy, Harry Weedon

Seven-year old Italian orphan Peppino (Vittorio Manunta) has been befriended by United States troops and lives in a hut with his invaluable donkey. Kindly Father Damico (Denis O'Dea) keeps an eye on him. A note with food from America tells him to never take no for an answer. When his donkey falls ill he begs to be allowed him to bring the donkey into the church where lies the tomb of St. Francis. The authorities say no

so he goes to Rome to plead his case to the Pope. His commitment and faith induce the Pope to grant his wish. An old church wall is brought down so the donkey may enter and a treasure is discovered. Also known as *The Small Miracle.*

**Night Creatures** *see* **Captain Clegg**

**589. The Night of the Hunter.** UA. US. 1955. 93m. B&W. *Producer:* Paul Gregory *Director:* Charles Laughton *Writer:* James Agee, Charles Laughton, Davis Grubb (novel) *Cast:* Robert Mitchum, Shelley Winters, Lillian Gish, James Gleason, Evelyn Varden, Peter Graves, Don Beddoe, Billy Chapin, Sally Jane Bruce, Gloria Castillo, Mary Ellen Clemons, Cheryl Callaway, Gloria Pall, Paul Bryar, Kay La Velle, Corey Allen, Michael Chapin, John Hamilton, James Gleason

During the Depression a self-proclaimed "man of the cloth" preacher Harry Powell (Robert Mitchum) travels throughout West Virginia killing rich widows, thinking he is doing the Lord's work. While in prison he learns that a condemned man has hidden $10,000. When he gets out, he marries the now dead man's widow Willa in his quest for the money. The preacher has "LOVE" tattooed on his right hand and "HATE" on his left hand. Willa's children are very weary of their new father. When Willa realizes what preacher is really after, he silts her throat and tells the kids she ran away. After some harrowing experiences, the preacher is captured.

**590. The Night of the Hunter.** ABC. (TV). US. 1991. 100m. C. *Director:* David Greene *Writer:* Davis Grubb (novel), Edmond Stevens *Cast:* Richard Chamberlain, Diana Scarwid, Reid Binion, Amy Bebout, Ray McKinnon, Mary Nell Santacroce, Burgess Meredith, Ed Grady, Joe Inscoe, Bobby McLamb

Remake of the 1955 film with Robert Mitchum. A false preacher Harry Powell (Richard Chamberlain) involves himself with a dead man's family in order to discover where he hid the money from a robbery.

**591. The Night of the Iguana.** MGM. US. 1964. 125m. B&W. *Producer:* Ray Stark, John Huston *Director:* John Huston *Writer:*

During the Depression, preacher Harry Powell (Robert Mitchum), travels throughout West Virginia killing rich widows, thinking he is doing the Lord's work. The preacher has "love" tattooed on his right hand and "hate" on his left hand; *The Night of the Hunter* (1959).

Anthony Veiller, John Huston, Tennessee Williams (play) *Cast*: Richard Burton, Ava Gardner, Deborah Kerr, Sue Lyon, Grayson Hall, Cyril Delevanti, Mary Boylan, Gladys Hill, Billie Matticks, Fidelmar Duran, Roberto Leyva, C. G. Kim, Eloise Hardt, Skip Ward

The Reverend T. Lawrence Shannon (Richard Burton), a defrocked clergyman, is now a bus guide on cheap tours. His new group consists of complaining female American teachers traveling through Mexico. The women don't believe that he was ever a minister and some of the women are very attracted to him.

**592. Nøglen til Paradis.** A/S Asa Filmudlejning. Denmark. 1970. 76m. C. *Producer*: Ole Mølgaard *Director*: Sven Methling *Writer*: Aage Stentoft *Cast*: Lone Hertz, Dirch Passer, Jørgen Ryg, Preben Mahrt, Vera Gebuhr

A rural vicar happens to run a travel agency specializing in charter holidays to Spain. Strict church officials are upset when he travels to open a new nightclub. An angel accompanies him for a possible attempt at his seduction. Also known as *The Key to Paradise*.

**None but the Brave** *see* **For the Love of Mike**

**593. None Shall Escape.** Columbia. US. 1944. 85m. B&W. *Producer*: Samuel Bischoff *Director*: André De Toth *Writer*: Lester Cole *Cast*: Marsha Hunt, Alexander Knox, Henry Travers, Erik Rolf, Richard Crane, Dorothy Morris, Richard Hale, Ruth Nelson, Kurt Kreuger, Shirley Mills, Frank Jaquet

Father Warecki (Henry Travers) is the first witness to tell the story of Wilhelm Grimm (Alexander Knox) to a Tribunal of War Crimes after World War II. Father Warecki recalls the spring of 1919 when Wilhelm, a crippled German soldier, returns from World War I and resumes teaching in a small Polish village. He has become bitter and turns to the Nazi ideology. He is forced to leave the village when he violates a student. He rises in the Nazi party and returns to the village as a commandant. His reign is full of terror. For example, Rabbi Levin (Richard Hale) dies for his convictions rather than suffer under Nazis. When Wilhelm orders Jewish people to be herded into cattle cars for deportation to concentration camps, the Rabbi urges them to resist and he is shot and killed. Person after person testifies to tell his evil story.

**594. Nonnen fra Asminderod.** Nordisk and Great Northern Films. Denmark. 1911. B&W.

When a young girl's lover comes to visit his love, a monk, who lusts after his love, convinces her father to have her enter a convent. Just before she is to take her vows she meets her lover. After they are discovered together, the lover is thrown in jail and the monk attacks the girl. When she fends him off with a crucifix, he accuses her of blasphemy and orders her to be walled up alive in a tomb. When the lover tells a prince of their situation, the girl is released. The girl and the lover marry and the monk is punished. Also known as *The Nun* and *The Life of a Nun*.

**595. The North Avenue Irregulars.** Buena Vista. US. 1979. 99m. C. *Producer*: Ron Miller, Tom Levich *Director*: Bruce Bilson *Writer*: Rev. Albert Fay Hill (book), Don Tait *Cast*: Edward Herrmann, Barbara Harris, Susan Clark, Karen Valentine, Michael Constantine, Cloris Leachman, Patsy Kelly, Douglas Fowley Virginia Capers, Steve Franken

Presbyterian minister Michael Hill (Edward Herrmann) is a young reverend on his first assignment at the North Avenue Church and has plans to give his new parish responsibility. When the reverend gives money to one of the townspeople she invests it in a horserace. When he tries to retrieve the money from the bookie he discovers that there is evil in the town and vows to save the city. Housewives become cohorts in his plan to expose the crooks.

**596. Nos miran.** Columbia TriStar. Spain. 2002. 104m. C/B&W. *Producer*: César

Benítez *Director*: Norberto López Amado *Writer*: Javier García Sánchez (novel), Jorge Guerricaechevarría *Cast*: Carmelo Gómez, Icíar Bollaín, Manuel Lozano, Carolina Petterson, Margarita Lozano, Massimo Ghini, Francisco Algora, Roberto Álvarez, Karra Elejalde

Juan (Icíar Bollain) is a married cop with two children. He has been assigned to reopen a three year old kidnapping case. His partner Munoz (Francisco Algora) uncovers shelves of documentation on the case. The ex-cop responsible for compiling the information is now in a mental institution and can only mutter "They're watching us." Juan becomes so obsessed with the case that his office walls are covered with other people that have disappeared. He starts having flashbacks and his mother warns him to stop investigating the case. They soon find themselves talking to a priest (Roberto Álvarez). He explains supernatural matters, the theory of different planes of reality, and that children have perceptions that adults have lost. Juan finds out that his sister went missing as a child. Also known as *They're Watching Us*.

**Not of This World** *see* **Fuori dal mondo**

**The Novice** *see* **La Suora giovane**

**597. Les Novices.** Parafrance. France. 1970. 91m. C. *Producer*: André Génovès *Director*: Guy Casaril *Writer*: Paul Gégauff, Guy Casaril *Cast*: Brigitte Bardot, Annie Girardot, Jacques Jouanneau, Jean Carmet, Jess Hahn, Jacques Duby, Marc Deus, Lucien Barjon

Agnes (Brigitte Bardot) is a novice nun who one day flees the convent when they all go for a swim. She swims off, goes to another beach, steals clothes and a motorbike and starts her adventures. She meets an earthy prostitute with a heart of gold Lisa (Anne Girardot). Agnes tries the profession but remains chaste. They encounter a few more situations. Eventually, they swim over to the nuns' beach and end up in nuns' clothing.

**598. Nu Börjar Livet.** Svensk Filmindstri. Sweden. 1948. 91m. B&W. *Director*: Gustaf Molander *Writer*: Rune Lindström, Gustaf Molander *Cast*: Mai Zetterling,

George Rydeberg, Wanda Rothgardt, Hugo Björne, Bengt Ekelund, Åke Grönberg, Ivar Kåte, Jan Molander, Sven-Erik Gamble, Helge Hagerman

The plot follows minister Tore Gerhard (George Rydeberg) who is unhappily married and wants a divorce, but is afraid of the scandal. He makes love to a young girl who later realizes her mistake and rejects him. Disappointed, the minister commits suicide. Also known as *Life Starts Now.*

**599. Nugel Bujan.** Mongolfilm. Mongolia. 1964. 70m. *Director & Writer*: D. Cimit-Oser *Cast*: D. Icinchorloova, B. Dulamsurenova, L. Terble

A young monk (L. Terble) is attracted to a girl living with a sinful mother who is trying to sell her to rich men. A real friendship grows between them while she fights off men. When the monk learns that his teacher is a liar he leaves as does the girl. Also known as *Vice and Virtue.*

**The Nun** *see* **Nonnen fra Asminderod**

**The Nun** *see* **La Religieuse**

**600. The Nun.** Hepworth. UK. 1907. B&W. *Director*: Lewin Fitzhamon

Girl saved from convent by lover posing as abbot.

**601. The Nun and the Bandit.** Roadshow Entertainment. Australia. 1992. 92m. C. *Producer*: Paul Ammitzboll, Paul Cox *Director*: Paul Cox *Writer*: Paul Cox, E. L. Grant Watson (novel) *Cast*: Gosia Dobrowolska, Chris Haywood, Victoria Eagger, Charlotte Haywood, Tommy Lewis, Norman Kaye

Kidnappers abduct a rich man's young granddaughter for ransom. The child is taken when she is with her unworldly aunt Sister Lucy (Gosia Dobrowolska), a Polish nun visiting her sister, the girl's mother. The leader of the kidnappers Michael Shanley (Chris Haywood) is a bandit who refuses to rape the nun and wants her to be nice to him.

**The Nun and the Devil** *see* **Le Monache di Sant'Arcangelo**

**602. The Nun and the Sergeant.** UA. US. 1962. 74m. B&W. *Producer*: Eugene Frenke *Director*: Franklin Adreon *Writer*:

Don Cerveris *Cast*: Robert Webber, Anna Sten, Leo Gordon, Hari Rhodes, Robert Easton, Dale Ishimoto, Linda Wong, Linda Ho, Tod Windsor, Valentin de Vargas

During the Korean War, Sergeant McGrath (Robert Webber) takes along men from the brig on a dangerous mission. Behind enemy lines they meet a nun (Anna Sten) and a group of Korean schoolgirls whose bus has been destroyed by a bomb. When it becomes apparent that the nun will die of her leg wound, McGrath permits the schoolgirls to take her to a nearby village. McGrath leads his men into action.

**A Nun at the Crossroads** *see* **Encrucijada para una monja**

**The Nun of Monza** *see* **La Monaca di Monza**

**603. Nuns on the Run.** TCF. UK. 1990. 89m. C. *Producer*: Michael White *Director &Writer*: Jonathan Lynn *Cast*: Eric Idle, Robbie Coltrane, Camille Coduri, Janet Suzman, Doris Hare, Lila Kaye, Robert Patterson, Robert Morgan, Winston Dennis, Tom Hickey, Colin Campbell

Brian Hope (Eric Idle) and Charlie McManus (Robbie Coltrane) decide to leave the gangster business but when their boss finds out he sets them up to be killed. While on the job they steal money and while escaping they take refuge in a convent. The boys disguise themselves as Sister Inviolata and Sister Euphemia.

**604. The Nun's Story.** Warner. US. 1959. 149m. C. *Producer*: Henry Blanke *Director*: Fred Zinnemann *Writer*: Robert Anderson, Kathryn Hulme (book) *Cast*: Audrey Hepburn, Peter Finch, Edith Evans, Peggy Ashcroft, Mildred Dunnock, Dean Jagger, Beatrice Straight, Colleen Dewhurst, Patricia Collinge, Rosalie Crutchley, Ruth White, Barbara O'Neil

Young nurse/nun Sister Luke (Audrey Hepburn) enters a nursing order that is semi-cloistered. She wants to be a nurse because her father is a famous surgeon. The order stresses being a good nun first which leads to inner conflict.

Sister Luke is sent to work in the Congo just before World War II. She is torn between her religious vows, her nursing abilities, and an attraction to a physician (Peter Finch). When she contracts tuberculosis, the strong-willed physician brings her back to health. Sister Luke returns to Belgium just as World War II begins. When her father is killed by the Nazis, she decides to help the underground against the wishes of her superiors. Eventually, she leaves the convent in pursuit of greater freedom. She realizes that she can accomplish more outside an institution. She puts on street clothes and walks outside to an unknown future.

**605. Nunsense.** A&E. (TV). US. 1993. 111m. C. *Producer:* Jim McGinn, Neil Rosen *Director:* Dan Goggin, David Stern *Writer:* Dan Goggin *Cast:* Rue McClanahan, Christine Anderson, Semina De Laurentis, Christine Toy, Terri White

A cooking accident causes most of the order of the Little Sisters of Hoboken to die of botulism. The Reverend Mother Superior Mary Regina (Rue McClanahan) buys a camcorder and VCR for the convent. As a result they don't have enough money to bury the remaining sisters. Therefore in order to raise money the sister put on a revue with song and dance numbers. Following in 1994 was *Nunsense 2: The Sequel*. Filmed version of the Off-Broadway musical comedy.

**606. Of Human Hearts.** MGM. US. 1938. 103m. B&W. *Producer:* John W. Considine Jr., Clarence Brown *Director:* Clarence Brown *Writer:* Bradbury Foote *Cast:* Walter Huston, James Stewart, Gene Reynolds, Beulah Bondi, Guy Kibbee, Charles Coburn, John Carradine, Ann Rutherford, Leatrice Joy Gilbert, Charley Grapewin, Gene Lockhart

In the early 1850s, Reverend Ethan Wilkins (Walter Huston) moves his family from a prosperous parish in Maryland to a poor village on the banks of the Ohio River. Even though he is promised $400 a year, he receives only $250 and cast-off clothing. His son Jason (James Stewart) cannot accept their poor lifestyle and when he is old enough he leaves to study medicine in Virginia. His devoted mother Mary (Beulah Bondi) sells anything she can to send Jason money. Mary writes to tell him that Ethan is dying but Jason arrives too late. He leaves

again and she sells her wedding ring for Jason. Jason fights in the Civil War and one day receives a summons from the White Head. President Lincoln has received a letter from Mary asking where her son was buried since she hadn't heard from him in a very long time. Finally Jason and Mary are reunited.

**607. The Omen.** TCF. UK. 1976. 111m. C. *Producer:* Harvey Bernhard *Director:* Richard Donner *Writer:* David Seltzer *Cast:* Gregory Peck, Lee Remick, David Warner, Billie Whitelaw, Harvey Stephens, Leo McKern, Patrick Troughton, Martin Benson, Robert Rietty, Tommy Duggan

An American ambassador (Gregory Peck) in Rome adopts the antichrist Damien, when an Italian priest convinces him to substitute another hospital baby for the one his wife lost in childbirth. When the child turns five years old, he realizes that something is wrong with the child and he finds an exorcist Carl Bugenhagen (Leo McKern). The child can only be killed with a dagger of Meggado. First film in the *Omen* trilogy.

**Omen III: The Final Conflict** *see* **The Final Conflict**

**608. On the Waterfront.** Columbia. US. 1954. 108m. B&W. *Producer:* Sam Spiegel *Director:* Elia Kazan *Writer:* Malcolm Johnson, Budd Schulberg *Cast:* Marlon Brando, Karl Malden, Lee J. Cobb, Rod Steiger, Eva Marie Saint, Pat Henning, Leif Erickson, James Westerfield, Tony Galento, Tami Mauriello, John F. Hamilton, Arthur Keegan

Longshoreman and ex-prize fighter Terry Malloy (Marlon Brando) confronts the corrupt labor unions led by Johnny Friendly (Lee J. Cobb). Headstrong Father Barry (Karl Malden) is so outraged by the corruption that he causes a revolt. Terry's brother Charlie (Rod Steiger) is brutally murdered when he can't prevents Terry from talking to the authorities. One of the highpoints of the film is when Father Barry gives a speech in the hold of a ship where a longshoreman has been murdered.

**609. One Foot in Heaven.** Warner. US. 1941. 108m. B&W. *Producer & Director:* Irving Rapper *Writer:* Casey Robinson,

The Reverend William Spence (Frederic March) and his wife Hope (Martha Scott) are seen praying to God in their struggle to balance family and religion; *One Foot in Heaven* (1941).

Hartzell Spence (book) *Cast*: Frederic March, Martha Scott, Beulah Bondi, Gene Lockhart, Elisabeth Fraser, Harry Davenport, Laura Hope Crews, Grant Mitchell, Moroni Olsen, Ernest Cossart

Originally a medical student, William Spence (Frederic March) turns to religion after listening to an evangelist. Now a Methodist minister Reverend Spence, takes his fiancée Hope (Martha Scott) from her beautiful home to his first parish in small town in rural Iowa. They struggle to provide for their three children as they are transferred from one small parish to another. The film climaxes with his attempt to build a new church for his flock and with a stirring sermon.

**610. One Man's Way.** UA. US. 1964. 105m. B&W. *Producer:* Frank Ross *Director:* Denis Sanders *Writer:* Eleanore Griffin, John Bloch, Arthur Gordon (book) *Cast:* Don Murray, Diana Hyland, William Windom, Virginia Christine, Carol Ohmart, Veronica Cartwright, Liam Sullivan, June Dayton, Hope Summers, Virginia Sale

Based on the biography "Norman Vincent Peale: Minister To Millions" by Arthur Gordon. The film begins with twelve-year-old Norman Vincent Peale declaring that he will never become a clergyman because of the insults he has suffered as the son of a minister. Years later he changes his mind when as a Detroit crime reporter he becomes frustrated that he cannot relieve the suffering of those he reports on. In the seminary he is thought of as a rebel because he believes in a God of love, rather than of vengeance. However his enthusiasm increases church attendance everywhere he preaches. He marries and accepts a position at New York City's Marble Collegiate Church. Through radio, magazine articles, and a syndicated newspaper column he develops his thesis that God helps those who help themselves. The publication of his book "The Power of Positive Thinking" causes condemnation of his theological attitudes. He is about to resign when a critically ill child rallies after he keeps a nighlong prayer vigil. He has renewed faith and remains with the church.

**611. The One Woman.** Select Pictures.

US. 1918. B&W. *Director*: Reginald Barker *Writer*: Reverend Thomas Dixon Jr. (book), Richard Schayer, Harry Chandlee *Cast*: Lawson Butt, Clara Williams, Herschell Mayall, Adda Gleason, Ben Alexander, Mary Jane Irving

A manic married clergyman, Reverend Frank Gordon (Lawson Butt), preaches about the brotherhood of man and is made to resign. He falls in love with a wealthy woman and wants to leave his wife. He tries to get money from a banker to build a church. The vamp donates enough money for the preacher to build his church and he abandons his family. He finds his new woman with the banker and kills him in a fight. The vamp testifies against him and he is convicted. The preacher's wife gains him a pardon.

**Open City** *see* **Roma, città aperta**

**612. L'Ora di religione: il sorriso di mia madre.** Istituto Luce. Italy. 2002. 103m. C. *Producer*: Marco Bellocchio, Sergio Pelone *Director & Writer*: Marco Bellocchio *Cast*: Sergio Castellitto, Jacqueline Lustig, Chiara Conti, Alberto Mondini, Gianni Schicchi, Maurizio Donadoni, Gigio Alberti

This drama deals with artist Ernesto Picciafuoco (Sergio Castellitto), an atheist who is confronted with lingering ties to the church. One scene that demonstrates Ernesto's disdain for the church is evident when he receives a visit from a clerical emissary summoning him to an audience with a cardinal. He learns the purpose of the visit is to involve him in his family's bid for the canonization of his mother. Also known as *The Religion Hour (My Mother's Smile)*.

**Orange-Colored Bells** *see* **Hoi Duiong Mau Da Cam**

**613. The Order.** TCF. US/Germany. 2003. 102m. C. *Producer*: Craig Baumgarten, Brian Helgeland *Director & Writer*: Brian Helgeland *Cast*: Heath Ledger, Shannyn Sossamon, Benno Fürmann, Mark Addy, Peter Weller, Francesco Carnelutti, Mattia Sbragia, Mirko Casaburo, Giulia Lombardi, Richard Bremmer, Christina Maccà, Paola Emilia Villa

When the head of an order of priests known as Carolingians dies, Father Alex Bernier (Heath Ledger) is sent to Rome to investigate the mysterious circumstances. The body has signs of a Sin Eater. A sin eater is an individual who swallows the souls of the damned in to clear order their passage to heaven. Accompanying him is an escaped mental patient Mara (Shannyn Sossamon). In Rome, Father Alex teams up with an Irish priest Father Thomas (Mark Addy) who is also trying to find the Sin Eater.

**614. Ordet.** Kingsley-International. Denmark. 1955. 126m. B&W. *Producer*: Carl Theodor Dreyer, Erik Nielsen, Tage Nielsen *Director* Carl Theodor Dreyer *Writer*: Carl Theodor Dreyer, Kaj Munk (play) *Cast*: Henrik Malberg, Emil Hass Christensen, Preben Lerdorff Rye, Cay Kristiansen, Brigitte Federspiel, Ove Rud, Gerda Nielsen

Film concentrates the conflict between Catholic and Protestant views towards life and religion. Dreyer shows two families, one with a fundamentalist faith and the other with a Christian faith but lacking conviction. In one family, there are three brothers-one married with a child on the way has no faith, another brother wants to marry the daughter of a fundamentalist preacher, and the third brother believes he is Jesus reincarnated, who is obsessed by the belief that he is Christ. A little girl's faith finally enables him to work a miracle. Kaj Munk was a Danish pastor murdered by the Nazis for speaking out. Filmed previously in 1943 with Gustaf Molander as the director. Also known as *The Word*.

**615. Az Örök Titok.** Alfa. Hungary. 1938. B&W. *Director*: István György *Writer*: Gyula Czapik, Gyula Somogyváry, J. S. Spillmann (novel) *Cast*: Rezsö Harsányi, Sári Fedák, Lojas Gáárday, Árpád Lehotay, Zoltán Greguss, Gyuri Dévényi, Panni Kéry, László Földényi, Aranka Laczkó

The setting for the story is a small town in France during the 1870s. The parish priest (Rezsö Harsányi) is accused of murdering a rich old woman. He can only prove his innocence by betraying the secret of the confessional since the real murderer has confessed his crime. The priest chooses to keep silent and is divested of the symbols of priesthood and sentenced to death. The real murderer finally confesses his guilt and the priest returns in triumph to his village. Also known as *Eternal Secret.*

**616. Oscar and Lucinda.** Fox Searchlight. US/Australia/UK. 132m. C. *Producer:* Robin Dalton, Timothy White *Director:* Gillian Armstrong *Writer:* Peter Carey (novel), Laura Jones *Cast:* Ralph Fiennes, Cate Blanchett, Ciarán Hinds, Tom Wilkinson, Richard Roxburgh, Clive Russell, Bille Brown, Josephine Byrnes, Barnaby Kay, Barry Otto

In mid-1800's England, a young misfit Anglican priest, Oscar (Ralph Fiennes), finds a soul mate in a teenage heiress Australian girl Lucinda (Cate Blanchett). As a youth God told him to leave his Pentecostal family and join the Church of England. Lucinda buys a glass factory and wishes to build a church of glass and move it to Australia. Since Oscar and Lucinda both love to gamble Lucinda bets her fortune that he cannot move the church safely to Australia.

**617. Otete Sergiy.** Corinth. Russia. 1978. 95m. C. *Director:* Igor Talankin *Writer:* Igor Talankin, Leo Tolstoy (novel) *Cast:* Sergei Bondarchuk, Irina Skobtseva, Georgi Burkov, Alla Demidova, Valentina Titova, Vladislav Strzhelchik, Nikolai Gritsenko

Tale about a nobleman's attempt to find faith and meaning in life. The film is divided into episodes from his life. Taking place in turn-of-the-century Russia it shows him as a traveler on a ferryboat and then his story is told in flashbacks. We see him as a boy in military school and as a man troubled by his feelings and his decision to become a priest. His sexual desires were so strong that he gave up the priesthood. Also known as *Otyets Sergei* and *Father Sergius.*

**The Other Canterbury Tales** *see* **Gli Altri racconti di Canterbury**

**The Other Hell** *see* **L'Altro inferno**

**618. The Other Side of Heaven.** Excel. US. 2001. 113m. C. *Producer:* John Garbett, Gerald Molen *Director:* Mitch Davis *Writer:* Mitch Davis, John Groberg (book) *Cast:* Christopher Gorham, Anne Hathaway, Joe Folau, Miriama Smith, Nathaniel Lees, Whetu Fala, Alvin Fitisemanu, Peter Sa'ena Brown, Apii McKinley, John Sumner

During the 1950s, a farm kid John Groberg (Christopher Gorham) from Idaho becomes a missionary in the Tongan islands.

**Otyets Sergei** *see* **Otete Sergiy**

**619. Outrage.** RKO. US. 1950. 75m. B&W. *Producer:* Collier Young *Director:* Ida Lupino *Writer:* Ida Lupino, Malvin Wald, Collier Young *Cast:* Mala Powers, Tod Andrews, Robert Clarke, Raymond Bond, Lillian Hamilton, Rita Lupino, Hal March, Kenneth Patterson, Jerry Paris, Angela Clarke, Roy Engel

After working late one night, Ann Walton (Mala Powers) is raped while going home. The attitude of her small town and her fiancé cause her to flee. She stops in a small California town where an understanding preacher Reverend Bruce Fergunson (Tod Andrews) and his rancher friends help to recover her faith in people. Now, she is ready to face her family.

**620. Over the Wall.** Warner Bros. US. 1938. 67m. B&W. *Director:* Frank McDonald *Writer:* Lewis E. Lawes, Crane Wilbur, George Bricker *Cast:* Dick Foran, June Travis, John Litel, Dick Purcell, Veda Ann Borg, George E. Stone, Ward Bond, John Hamilton, Jonathan Hale, Tommy Bupp, Robert Homans, Mabel Hart, Raymond Hatton, Alan Davis, Eddie Chandler

An arrogant fighter Jerry Davis (Dick Foran) is railroaded into prison for a murder he did not commit. Prison chaplain Father Connor (John Litel) takes him under his wing. While on an outside work detail Jerry manages to prove his innocence.

**621. O Padre e a moça.** Difilm. Brazil. 1965. 90m. B&W. *Producer:* Luiz Carlos Barreto, Joaquim Pedro de Andrade *Director:* Joaquim Pedro de Andrade *Writer:* Joaquim Pedro de Andrade, Carlos Drummond de Andrade *Cast:* Helena Ignez, Paulo José, Mário Lago, Fauzi Arap, Rosa Sandrini

A young priest (Paulo José) arrives in a small poverty stricken village in Minas Gerais and falls in love with a young woman. He helps her escape from a would-be suitor only to be trapped by the villagers. Also know as *The Priest and the Girl.*

**622. Padre on Horseback.** Key International Pictures. US. 1977. 116m. C. *Producer*: Arthur E. Coates *Director & Writer*: Ken Kennedy *Cast*: Ricardo Montalban, Richard Egan, Cesar Romero, John Ireland, Joseph Campanella, Stephen McNally, Anthony Caruso, Rory Calhoun, Keenan Wynn, Aldo Ray

Father Eusebio Kino (Richard Egan) is a Jesuit missionary in the old Southwest. Also known as *Mission to Glory* and *The Father Kino Story*.

**623. Padre Pio.** Mediaset. (TV). Italy. 2000. 200m. C. *Producer*: Angelo Rizzoli Jr. *Director*: Carlo Carlei *Writer*: Renzo Allegri (book), Carlo Carlei, Massimo De Rita, Mario Falcone *Cast*: Sergio Castellitto, Gianni Bonagura, Raffaele Castria, Roberto Chevalier, Tosca D'Aquino, Mario Erpichini, Pierfrancesco Favino, Flavio Insinna, Adolfo Lastretti, Camillo Milli, Rosa Pianeta

The film is a detailed depiction of the life and mission of the recently canonized in 2002 of Padre Pio (Sergio Castellitto) from San Giovanni Rotondo. Padre Pio carries the stigmata, makes prophesies, and has a strong cult following. His actions make the Vatican very uneasy.

**624. A Pair of Desperate Swindlers.** Warwick Trading Co. UK. 1906. B&W. *Director:* Charles Raymond

Thieves escape the police, pose as nuns and are caught.

**Palm Sunday** *see* **Virágvasárnap**

**625. Il Pap'occhio.** Cinematográfica/ Titanus. Italy. 1981. 110m. C. *Producer*: Mario Orfini *Director*: Renzo Arbore *Writer*: Renzo Arbore, Luciano De Crescenzo *Cast*: Luciano De Crescenzo, Renzo Arbore, Roberto Benigni, Isabella Rossellini, Andy Luotto, Flag Sisters, Diego Abatantuono, Milly Carlucci

The Pope has an idea of how to get youth out of the discos and back into the fold of the church. He opens a Vatican television station. The first program is a variety show. Also known as *In the Pope's Eye*.

**626. Parallels.** Group 3. Canada. 1980. 92m. C. *Producer:* Jack Wynters, Mark Schoenberg *Director:* Mark Schoenberg *Writer:* Mark Schoenberg, Jaron Summers *Cast:* David Fox, Judith Mahbey, Gerard Lepage, Kyra Harper, David Ferry, Walter Kaasa, Howard Dallin, Jennifer Riach, Stephen Walsh

Father Robert Dane (David Fox) is a Catholic priest and the rector of a boys' college. A complication enters the plot with a new student whose mother was once the girlfriend of the priest before he entered the priesthood.

**627. The Parson and the Outlaw.** Columbia. US. 1957. 71m. C. *Producer*: Charles 'Buddy' Rogers *Director*: Oliver Drake *Writer*: Oliver Drake, John Mantley *Cast*: Anthony Dexter, Sonny Tufts, Marie Windsor, Charles 'Buddy' Rogers, Jean Parker, Robert Lowery, Madalyn Trahey

Billy the Kid (Anthony Dexter) is trying to stay away from violence of killing. But when his old friend the parson Reverend Jericho Jones (Charles 'Buddy' Rogers) gets shot while standing up to the bad guys, Billy steps in and in return gets shot himself.

**The Parson of Kirchfeld** *see* **Der Pfarrer von Kirchfeld**

**628. The Parson of Panamint.** Paramount. US. 1916. B&W. *Director:* William Desmond Taylor *Writer:* Julia Crawford Ivers, Peter Kyne (novel) *Cast:* Dustin Farnum, Winifred Kingston, Pomeroy Cannon, Howard Davies, Colin Chase, Ogden Crane, Jane Keckley, Tom Bates

Dustin Farnum plays the role of the fighting parson Philip Pharo in a wild-west mining town. In the end he dies saving one of his enemies from burning to death. The story of the parson and the camp is told by an old western character sitting on a pile of empty tin cans that was once the spot where Panimint stood.

**629. The Parson of Panamint.** Paramount. US. 1941. 84m. B&W. *Producer:* Harry Sherman *Director:* William C. McGann *Writer:* Harold Shumate, Adrian Scott, Peter Kyne (novel) *Cast:* Charles Ruggles, Ellen Drew, Phillip Terry, Joseph Schildkraut, Porter Hall, Henry Kolker, Janet Beecher, Clem Bevans, Douglas Fowley, Paul Hurst, Frank Puglia, Minor Watson, Harry Hayden, Russell Hicks

Young minister Reverend Philip Pharo (Phillip Terry) finds himself in the rough tough mining town of Panamint. He works on being a spiritual guide and gaining the respect of the lawless. He reforms a Mexican bandit Joaquin (Frank Puglia), romances a dance hall woman, and wins the town over, especially since he is willing to use his fists.

**630. The Parson's Cookery Lesson.** Hepworth. UK. 1904. B&W. *Director:* Lewin Fitzhamon

Girls smother parson with eggs, milk and flour.

**631. The Parson's Prayer.** New York Motion Pictures Co. US. 1909. B&W.

A villain coaxes a girl under his power with a false note. He intends to force her to marry him, but when she pleads her situation to the parson, he refuses to perform the ceremony. There is a fight and the villain loses.

**632. The Parson's Umbrella.** Edison Mfg. Co. US. 1910. B&W.

In the beginning a congregation is seen leaving church during a rainstorm. The first comers take the best umbrellas while the rest are left without. Someone has taken the parson's umbrella. At the next service he announces that the culprit who took the umbrella will be exposed unless they return the umbrella by throwing it in his backyard that night. Everyone in the congregation who did not take their own umbrella is seized with fear and at nightfall there is a procession of umbrellas being thrown into the parson's backyard until they cover the ground.

**633. The Parson's Wife.** Hepworth. UK. 1911. B&W. *Director:* Lewin Fitzhamon

Wife spies on parson and catechism in indiscretion.

**634. Pass the Ammo.** New Century Vista Film. US. 1988. 93m. C. *Producer:* David Streit *Director:* David Beaird *Writer:* Joel Cohen, Neil Cohen *Cast:* Bill Paxton, Linda Kozlowski, Tim Curry, Annie Potts, Dennis Burkley, Glenn Withrow, Anthony Geary, Brian Thompson, Logan Ramsey, Leland Crooke

Corrupt television evangelist Reverend Ray Porter (Tim Curry) and his wife Darla (Annie Potts) are fleecing the public. One day he and his congregation are held hostage by a woman, her lover, and her cousins trying to avenge the theft of her dying grandmother-in-law's money. Film was released at the time of television evangelist Jim Baker and Tammy Faye scandal.

**635. Passage West.** Paramount. US. 1951. 80m. C. *Producer:* William H. Pine, William C. Thomas *Director:* Lewis R. Foster *Writer:* Nedrick Young (story), Lewis R. Foster *Cast:* John Payne, Dennis O'Keefe, Arleen Whelan, Frank Faylen, Mary Anderson, Peter Hansen, Richard Rober, Griff Barnett, Dooley Wilson, Mary Field, Richard Travis, Mary Beth Hughes, Arthur Hunnicutt, Lillian Bronson, Ilka Grüning, Estelle Carr, Susan Whitney, Paul Fierro, Clint Stuart

Parson Jacob Karns (Dennis O'Keefe) leads a wagon train headed to California to establish a religious community. A group of hardened escape convicts take over the group and subject the people to cruel abuse. The people's simple faith and courageous leaders hold them together.

**636. Passing Glory.** TNT. (TV). US. 1999. 100m. C. *Producer:* Gordon Wolf *Director:* Steve James *Writer:* Harold Sylvester *Cast:* Andre Braugher, Rip Torn, Sean Squire, Ruby Dee, Bill Nunn, Daniel Hugh Kelly, Tony Colitti, Anderson Bourell, Khalil Kain, Tony Bond

Based on the true story of the first integrated basketball game in the history of New Orleans. The game is between all-black St. Augustine High School and all-white Jesuit High. The film focuses on Father Joseph Verette's (Andre Braugher) struggles in pulling the game off and earning respect for his team. Father Verette goes against the wishes of Father Robert Grant (Rip Torn) as he strives to achieve his goal.

**637. La Passion de Bernadette.** France. 1989. 106m. *Director:* Jean Delannoy *Writer:* Jean Aurenche, Jean Delannoy *Cast:* Sydney Penny, Emmanuelle Riva, Catherine de Seynes, Malka Ribowska, Georges Wilson, Michèle André, Maurice Jacquemont, Roland Lesaffre, Michel Ruhl, Michèle Simonnet

The adult life of Bernadette and her life in the Convent of Saint-Gildard de Nevers.

**638. La Passion de Jeanne d'Arc.** Jason Film. France. 1928. 114m. B&W. *Direc-*

tor: Carl Theodor Dreyer *Writer:* Carl Theodor Dreyer, Joseph Delteil *Cast:* Maria Falconetti, Eugene Silvain, André Berley, Maurice Schutz, Antonin Artaud, Michel Simon, Jean d'Yd, Louis Ravet, Armand Lurville, Jacques Arnna, Alexandre Mihalesco, Léon Larive

The film centers on the last day of the trial of Joan (Maria Falconetti) and her burning at the stake. Dreyer's original cut of the film was found in a janitor's closet after nearly fifty years. Joan of Arc was canonized in 1920, only a few years before film was released. The film was based directly on trial manuscripts. Film is notable for its use of close-ups and unique camera angles. A silent masterpiece ranking among the best films ever made. Falconetti was never able to make another film. Also known as *The Passion of Joan of Arc.*

**The Passion of Joan of Arc** *see* **La Passion de Jeanne d'Arc**

**Passion of St. Francis** *see* **Frate Francesco**

**639. Pastor Hall.** UA. UK. 1940. 95m. B&W. *Producer:* John Boulting *Director:* Roy Boulting *Writer:* Leslie Arliss, Anna Reiner, Haworth Bromley, John Boulting, Roy Boulting *Cast:* Nova Pilbeam, Seymour Hicks, Wilfrid Lawson, Marius Goring, Percy Walsh, Brian Worth, Peter Cotes, Hay Petrie, Eliot Makeham, Edmund Willard, Manning Whiley, Lina Barrie J. Fisher White, Barbara Gott, Bernard Miles, D. J. Williams, George Street

Benevolent village pastor, Pastor Frederick Hall (Wilfrid Lawson), denounces Nazism and is sent to a concentration camp. After very brutal torture he escapes and returns to the pulpit where he is shot down. Story based on true story of Pastor Martin Neimuller who was sent to Dachau for speaking against the Nazis.

**Pastoral Symphony** *see* **La Symphonie pastorale**

**Path to the Kingdom** *see* **Sor Intrepida**

**640. Pavilion of Women.** UI. China/US. 2001. 116m. C. *Producer:* Yan Luo *Director:* Ho Yim *Writer:* Pearl S. Buck (novel), Yan Luo, Paul Collins *Cast:* Willem Dafoe, Yan Luo, Shek Sau, John Cho, Yi Ding, Chieng Mun Koh, Anita Loo, Amy Hill, Kate McGregor-Stewart, Jia Dong Liu

Under the Japanese invasion in World War II, a Chinese woman Nadame Wu (Yan Luo) finds her husband a second wife so she may have respite from sex. She soon catches the eye of and falls in love with European missionary Father Andre (Willem Dafoe) who is helping her son with western education.

**641. The Peacemaker.** UA. US. 1956. 82m. B&W. *Producer:* Hal R. Makelim *Director:* Ted Post *Writer:* Hal Richards, Jay Ingram, Richard Poole (novel) *Cast:* James Mitchell, Rosemarie Stack, Jan Merlin, Jess Barker, Hugh Sanders, Herbert Patterson, Dorothy Patrick, Taylor Holmes, Robert Armstrong, Philip Tonge, David McMahon, Wheaton Chambers

Newly-arrived parson Terrall Butler (James Mitchell) is an ex-gunfighter turned preacher in a town torn by war between farmers and ranchers. Parson Butler tries to bring the groups together. The railroad representative arrives supposedly to protect the farmers but in reality is trying to personally acquire cheap land. The plot is exposed by the parson just in time, before war really breaks out.

**642. Pecata minuta.** United International y Cía. Spain. 1999. 95m. C. *Producer:* José María Lara *Director:* Ramón Barea *Writer:* Ramón Barea, Felipe Loza *Cast:* Ane Gabarain, Loli Astoreka, Aitzpea Goenaga, Itziar Lazkano, Ione Irazábal, Ramón Ibarra, Elena Irureta

Comedy, which centers on a group of nuns digging a tunnel under the confession box in order to escape from the convent. The nuns include Sister Rufina (Elena Irureta) who has always wanted to be a priest; Sister Asun (Loli Astoreka) who believes she is pregnant and then believes she has had the baby; Sister Remedios (Aitzpea Goenaga) who talks to a statue of Jesus as though he were alive, and Rosarito (Ane Gabarain) whose innocence verges on simple-mindedness. Also known as *Venial Sins.*

**643. Peggy.** Triangle. 1916. B&W. *Director:* Charles Giblyn, Thomas H. Ince

*Writer*: C. Gardner Sullivan *Cast:* Billie Burke, William H. Thompson, William Desmond, Charles Ray, Nona Thomas, Gertrude Claire, Truly Shattuck

A young American Peggy Cameron (Billie Burke) visits her uncle in Scotland. Her American ways surprise the villagers, especially handsome Reverend Donald Bruce (William Desmond).

**644. The Penitentes.** Triangle. US. 1915. B&W. *Director*: Jack Conway *Writer*: R. Ellis Wales (novel), Mary H. O'Connor *Cast*: Orin Johnson, Seena Owen, Paul Gilmore, Irene Hunt, Josephine Crowell, F.A. Turner, Charles Clary, Allen Sears, Dark Cloud

Indians attack and kill everyone in a 17th century New Mexico village except two monks and a baby named Manuel. A violent, fanatical Catholic sect laid claim to all the property. Years later, Father David notices Manuel and asks about him. Fearing exposure Manuel is selected to be sacrificed and crucified on the upcoming Good Friday. Father David has the army stop the ceremony and Manuel escapes a horrible death. Later an old monk reveals the truth about Manuel's origins.

**Penn of Pennsylvania** *see* **Courageous Mr. Penn**

**645. The Persuader.** AA. US. 1957. 72m. B&W. *Producer & Director*: Dick Ross *Writer*: Curtis Kenyon, Dick Ross *Cast*: William Talman, James Craig, Kristine Miller, Darryl Hickman, Georgia Lee, Alvy Moore, Gregory Walcott, Rhoda Williams, Paul Engle, Jason Johnson, Nolan Leary, John Milford, Frank Richards

Preacher Matt Monham (William Talman) arrives in a small Oklahoma town to find out his brother has been murdered for resisting gang leader, Rick Justin (James Craig). With his preaching Monham wins over the townspeople and Rick Justin, impressed by the new solidarity, passes on a chance to burn down the new church and moves on.

**646. Die Pest in Florenz.** Germany. 1919. 96m. B&W. *Producer*: Erich Pommer *Director*: Otto Rippert, Fritz Lang *Writer*: Fritz Lang, Edgar Allan Poe *Cast*: Erich Bartels, Theodor Becker, Julietta Brandt, Erner

Huebsch, Marga von Kierska, Otto Mannstaedt, Hans Walter

In medieval Florence, an evil courtesan seduces a devout monk and both die of the plague brought by Death. Also known as *The Plague in Florence.*

**647. Le Petit monde de Don Camillo.** Dear Film. France/Italy. 1951. 96m. B&W. *Director*: Julien Duvivier *Writer*: Julien Duvivier, Giovanni Guareschi, René Barjavel *Cast*: Fernandel, Gino Cervi, Franco Interlenghi, Vera Talchi, Clara Auteri Pepe, Charles Vissière

Priest Don Camillo (Fernandel) and the Communist mayor Peppone (Gino Cervi) of a small village in the Po Valley struggle for leadership while maintaining a friendship. At the end they get in a fist fight and Don Camillo is transferred. First in the Don Camillo film series. Also known as *The Little World of Don Camillo* and *Don Camillo.* (See illustration next page.)

**648. La Petite soeur des pauvres.** Pathè Rural. France. 1928. B&W. *Producer*: George Pallu *Writer*: Marcel Priollet *Cast*: Desdemona Mazza, Ducette Martell, De Saint Andre, Georges Melchoir, Frédéric Mariotti

Two sisters Christiane and Pauline are very different from each other. Christiane is a flirt and Pauline very religious. Their neighbors Daniel and his cousin Roger have designs on the girls. The treachery of Roger causes Pauline to enter a convent. Christiane marries Daniel but Roger's trick causes her to write a letter to the Mother Superior of Pauline's convent that she became a nun because of unrequited love. Pauline falls very ill and when Christiane learns of this, she rushes to her. The truth is exposed and Daniel and Pauline are united. Christiane devotes her life to charity. Also known as *Sister of Mercy.*

**649. Der Pfarrer von Kirchfeld.** Constantin. Germany. 1955. 94m. C. *Producer*: Hans Deppe, Johnannes J. Frank *Director*: Hans Deppe *Writer*: Ilse Lotz-Dupont, Tibor Yost, Ludwig Anzengruber (play) *Cast*: Claus Holm, Ulla Jacobsson, Kurt Heintel, Annie Rosar, Heinrich Gretler, Helen Vita, Hansi Knoteck, Fritz Genschow

In this first film of the series, Don Camillo (Fernandel) and the Communist mayor Peppone (Gino Cervi) disagree about life in their village while maintaining a friendship, in *Le Petit monde de Don Camillo* (1951; also known as *The Little World of Don Camillo* and *Don Camillo*).

Anna Birkmaier (Ulla Jacobsson) comes to work for the parson of Kirchfeld (Claus Holm) because she has an illegitimate son living nearby. The parson and Anna attend a concert at another town and miss the last train home. Their reputations are tarnished but the parson doesn't love her and performs the marriage between Anna and the village blacksmith. The parson is shown as a regular guy from drinking to bowling with the guys. This classic plot of a parson torn between love of a woman or serving God is seen across cultures and time. Other versions were filmed in 1914, 1926, and 1937. Also known as *The Parson of Kirchfeld*.

**650. Der Pfarrer von St. Pauli.** Exportfilm. Germany. 1970. 103m. C. *Producer:* Heinz Willeg *Director & Writer:* Rolf Olsen *Cast:* Curt Jürgens, Heinz Reincke, Barbara Lass, Corny Collins, Günther Stoll, Dieter Borsche, Horst Naumann, Christine Diersch, Klaus Hagen Latwesen, Ilse Peternell

World War II German submarine Commander Konrad Johannsen (Curt Jürgens) whose boat was sunk towards the end of World War II. After escaping he made a promise to God that he would become a clergyman. The war is now over and we find him performing clerical duty in the Reeperbahn district. His enemies try to trap him with the help of a prostitute, but he emerges victorious. Also known as *The Priest of St. Pauli*

**651. Phörpa.** Fine Line Features. Bhutan/Australia.1999. 93m. C. *Producer:* Raymond Steiner, Malcolm Watson *Director & Writer:* Khyentse Norbu *Cast:* Orgyen Tobgyal, Neten Chokling, Jamyang Lodro, Lama Chonjor, Godu Lama, Thinley Nudi, Kunsang, Kunsang Nyima, Pema Tshundup, Dzigar Kongtrul

Based on a true story of a couple of newcomers to a Buddhist monastery in Tibet, who also happen to be soccer fanatic.

The young monks plot on how to watch the World Cup finals between France and Brazil by renting a satellite dish. Film shows the struggle between the spiritual and the secular worlds. Since there are no actors in Bhutan, Norbu had no choice but to cast real monks in the film. Also known as *The Cup*.

**652. Pianese Nunzio, 14 anni a maggio.** Medusa Distribuzione. Italy. 1996. 114m. C. *Producer:* Gianni Minervini *Director & Writer:* Antonio Capuano *Cast:* Fabrizio Bentivoglio, Flavio Brunetti, Rosaria De Cicco, Emanuele Gargiulo, Beppe Gatta, Manuela Martinelli, Vincenzo Pirozzi, Teresa Saponangelo

Young compassionate priest Don Lorenzo Borrelli crusades against the Camorra crime syndicate that has haunted Naples since the 19th century. Don Borrelli readily speaks out and the gangsters take notice. The gangsters don't want to kill him and make him a martyr so then try to expose his sexual relationship with a troubled 14-year-old boy Nunzio. Nunzio is so happy to have the priest's attention that he doesn't mind the sexual nature of their relationship. Nunzio doesn't want to betray the priest no matter what.

**653. Pieces of Dreams.** UA. US. 1970. 100m. C. *Producer:* Robert F. Blumofe *Director:* Daniel Haller *Writer:* William E. Barrett (novel), Roger O. Hirson, John McCollam *Cast:* Robert Forster, Lauren Hutton, Will Greer, Ivor Francis, Richard O'Brien, Edith Atwater, Mitzi Hoag, Rudy Diaz, Sam Javis, Gail Bonney, Helen Westcott, Joanne Moore Jordan, Miriam Martínez, Kathy Baca, Eloy Casados, Robert McCoy

Father Gregory Lind (Robert Forster) is a young parish priest in an ethnically mixed urban area. The day to day problems of his parishioners challenge his own beliefs. Examples include a dangerous pregnancy and a housewife troubled by the dilemma of birth control devices. To complicate things further, he falls in love with Pamela Gibson (Lauren Hutton), a rich social worker.

**654. Pieces of Silver: a Story of Hearts and Souls.** The Helgar Corp. US.1914. B&W. *Director & Writer:* Charles L. Gaskill *Cast:* Helen Gardner

A woman who is left a fortune by her dying uncle (on the condition that she either get married or the money will go to her aunt) is convinced to enter a convent by her aunt. Heartbroken by the girl's decision her sweetheart becomes a priest. The aunt tells of the deception on her death bed, but because of her sweetheart's vows she cannot marry him. She returns to the convent and becomes a nun.

**655. The Pilgrim.** First National. US. 1923. 59m. B&W. *Producer, Director & Writer:* Charles Chaplin *Cast:* Charles Chaplin, Edna Purviance, Kitty Bradbury, Mack Swain, Loyal Underwood, Mai Wells, Sydney Chaplin, Charles Reisner, Tom Murray, Monta Bell, Henry Bergman, Raymond Lee

A man escapes from prison, steals a minister's clothes and is welcomed by his new congregation. He knows that the minister has been delayed and continues the impersonation. From the pulpit he pantomimes the story of David and Goliath.

**656. Pink Tights.** Universal. US. 1920. B&W. *Producer & Director:* B. Reeves Eason *Writer:* Philip Hurn, J. U. Giesy *Cast:* Jack Perrin, Gladys Walton, David Dyas, Stanton Heck, Rosa Gore, Dorothea Wolbert, B. Reeves Eason Jr.

A circus is stranded in a small town and its crew is snubbed by the townspeople, except for young Reverend Jonathon Meek (Jack Perrin). He doesn't get the girl Mazie (Gladys Walton) though because her old boyfriend shows up.

**The Plague in Florence** *see* **Die Pest in Florenz**

**657. Plunging Hoofs.** Universal. US. 1929. B&W. *Producer:* William Lord Wright *Director:* Henry MacRae *Writer:* George Morgan, Basil Dickey *Cast:* Rex and Starlight (horses), Jack Perrin, Barbara Worth, J.P. McGowan, David Dunbar

Parson Jed Campbell (Jack Perrin) marries the dancehall girl and they move to a better environment, after the horses knock-off the cruel saloon owner.

**658. Poison Pen.** Republic. UK. 1940. 66m. B&W. *Producer:* Walter C. Mycroft *Director:* Paul L. Stein *Writer:* Doreen Montgomery, William Freshman, N. C. Hunter,

Esther McCracken, Richard Llewellyn (play) *Cast:* Flora Robson, Robert Newton, Ann Todd, Geoffrey Toone, Reginald Tate, Belle Chrystall, Edward Chapman, Edward Rigby, Athole Stewart, Mary Hinton, Cyril Chamberlain, Catherine Lacey, Wally Patch, Ella Retford, Jean Clyde, Wilfrid Hyde-White, Marjorie Rhodes, Esma Cannon, Kenneth Connor

Village vicar Reverend Rider (Reginald Tate) finds his spinster sister is the writer of poison pen letters. These horrid letters are causing villagers to turn against each other. In addition, a suicide, a love almost dies, and a shooting result from these vindictive letters.

**659. Polly of the Circus.** Goldwyn. US. 1917. B&W. *Director:* Charles Horan, Edwin L. Hollywood *Writer:* Adrian Gil-Spear, Emmett Campbell Hall, Margaret Mayo (play) *Cast:* Mae Marsh, Vernon Steele, Charles Eldridge, Wellington A. Playter, George S. Trimble, Lucille La Verne, Dick Lee, Charles Riegel, Lucille Southerwaite, Jack B. Hollis, Helen Sallinger, Isabel Vernon, Viola Compton, John Carr, Stephen Carr, Mildred Call

Circus rider Polly (Mae Marsh) is badly hurt during a dangerous horse riding trick and taken to a minister's home. She falls in love with the handsome young minister John Douglas (Vernon Steele), despite strong objections of the church's deacon. The deacon's daughter has her eye on the minister. Remade in 1932 starring Clark Gable and Marion Davies.

**660. Pope Joan.** Columbia/Warner. UK. 1972. 132m. *Producer:* Kurt Unger *Director:* Michael Anderson *Writer:* John Briley *Cast:* Liv Ullmann, Olivia de Havilland, Lesley-Anne Down, Trevor Howard, Jeremy Kemp, Patrick Magee, Franco Nero, Maximilian Schell, Natasa Nicolescu, Sharon Winter, Richard Bebb

Joan (Liv Ullmann) is a midwestern preacher who identifies with a woman who supposedly became Pope. She goes to a psychiatrist who has her regress to a former life that of a 9th century raped German girl who poses as a monk and is ultimately nominated Pope. Legend has it that a woman served as a Pope from 855 until 858, until she was stoned to death for giving birth. It turns out that Joan the preacher has been trying to hide her own pregnancy and she dies giving birth.

**661. The Pope Must Die.** Miramax. UK. 1991. 95m. C. *Producer:* Stephen Wooley *Director:* Peter Richardson *Writer:* Peter Richardson, Pete Richens *Cast:* Robbie Coltrane, Alex Rocco, Adrian Edmondson, Paul Bartel, Damir Mejovsek, Bozidar Smiljanic, Salvatore Cascio, Annette Crosbie, Marc Smith, Peter Richardson, Ranko Zidaric, Beverly D'Angelo, Balthazar Getty, Herbert Lom

Father Dave Albinizi (Robbie Coltrane) is a car mechanic/rock musician priest who runs a rural Italian orphanage. When the pope dies, Father Dave's name comes up as the next Pope, due to a clerical error. Now as Pope he must deal with a corrupt Vatican and the mob. One day his ex-lover Veronica Dante (Beverly D'Angelo) shows up with his long-lost rock star son. Also known as *The Pope Must Diet.*

**The Pope Must Diet** *see* **The Pope Must Die**

**662. La Portentosa vida del Padre Vincente.** Ascle Films. Spain. 1978. 82m. C. *Director & Writer:* Carles Mira *Cast:* Albert Boadella, Ovidi Montllor, Ángela Molina, Quico Carbonell, Rafael Miró, Cuca Aviñó, Fernando Mira, Carmen Platero

Spoof of the life in 15th century Valencia, Saint Vincent Ferrer. The story has Father Vincente (Albert Boadella) traveling through villages during the time of the Catholic Monarchs performing miracles and resisting temptations. Also known as *The Prodigious Life of Father Vincent.*

**663. A Portrait of the Artist as a Young Man.** Contemporary Films. UK. 1977. 92m. C. *Producer & Director:* Joseph Strick *Writer:* Judith Rascoe, James Joyce (novel) *Cast:* Bosco Hogan, T.P. McKenna, John Gielgud, Rosaleen Linehan, Maureen Potter, Niall Buggy, Brian Murrary, Desmond Cave, Leslie Lalor, Desmond Perry, Susan Fitzgerald, Luke Johnston, Danny Figgis, Cecil Sheehan, Brendan Cauldwell, Aden Grenell

The film is based on author James Joyce's life from Jesuit school days to University. Stephen Dedalus' (Bosco Hogan) childhood is dominated by the clergy and fighting the flesh as he ages. In one scene, a hellfire and damnation priest (John Gielgud) preaches such a graphic sermon that Stephen rushes to the confessional.

**664. The Poseidon Adventure.** TCF. US. 1972. 117m. C. *Producer:* Irwin Allen, Steve Broidy *Director:* Ronald Neame *Writer:* Wendell Mayes, Stirling Silliphant, Paul Gallico (novel) *Cast:* Gene Hackman, Ernest Borgnine, Red Buttons, Carol Lynley, Roddy McDowall, Stella Stevens, Shelley Winters, Jack Albertson, Pamela Sue Anderson, Eric Shea, Arthur O'Connell, Leslie Nielsen

A luxury ocean liner completely capsizes, when struck by a huge tidal wave, at sea during a New Years' Eve party. Reverend Frank Scott (Gene Hackman) leads a group of trapped passengers struggling to survive and escape their upside down world. Before the trouble starts, the Reverend has a conversation about God with the Chaplain (Arthur O'Connell) of the ship. Scott is portrayed as a troubled man but a true leader.

**665. The Possessed.** NBC. (TV). US. 1977. 76m. C. *Producer*: Philip Mandelker *Director*: Jerry Thorpe *Writer*: John Sacret Young *Cast*: James Farentino, Joan Hackett, Claudette Nevins, Eugene Roche, Harrison Ford, Ann Dusenberry, Diana Scarwid, Dinah Manoff, Carol Jones, P. J. Soles, Ethelinn Block

A defrocked minister (and now a freelance exorcist) battles evil forces that are apparently responsible for a rash of mysterious fires at an isolated girl's school.

**666. La Poupée.** Ward. UK. 1920. B&W. *Director:* Meyrick Milton *Writer:* Meyrick Milton, Edmond Audran (opera) *Cast:* Fred E. Wright, Flora le Breton, Richard Scott, William Farren, Gladys Vicat

Monk fulfills will by marrying doll, not knowing the maker's daughter has taken its place.

**Poussière d'empire** *see* **Hon vong phu**

**667. The Power of the Cross.** American Mutoscope and Biograph Co./Georges Méliès. France. 1900. B&W.

Shows the interior of a convent with nuns and a priest where during the audience's observations the devil, imps, and Satan appear. Ghosts of nuns appear and chase everything away except Satan. The nuns and priests can't drive him away but suddenly it is overturned by an apparition of St. George.

**668. Prästänkan.** Denmark/Sweden. 1920. 80m. B&W. *Director:* Carl Theodor Dreyer *Writer:* Kristofer Janson, Carl Theodor Dreyer *Cast:* Einar Rod, Greta Almroth, Hildur Carlberg, Olav Aukrust, Kurt Welin

In Norway, there is an old custom that the newly elected parson had to take over the widow of the dead leader before he could become parson. In this tale three men are in contention for being the new parson. Two of the competitors bribe the judges with food but when they see the widow they run away. She looks and acts like a witch. The one man left takes a drink of something and then proposes to the widow. Soon the old woman dies and the new parson marries his true love. Also known as *The Witch Woman*.

**669. Prästen.** Sweden. 1914. B&W. *Director*: Victor Sjöström *Writer*: Peter Lykke-Seest *Cast*: Carl Borin, Egil Eide, Justus Hagman, William Larsson, Richard Lund, Clara Pontoppidan, Carlo Wieth

A minister takes in a young woman and her son when they are discarded by a squire. Sometimes the minister's sermons cause his congregation to be upset. When he beats up the town bully, they accept him. The minister sends the woman to college and finds himself falling in love with her. He realizes that she loves a college boy and accepts the loss and marries them. Also known as *Saints and Their Sorrows*.

**670. A Prayer for the Dying.** Samuel Goldwyn Co. US. 1987. 105m. C. *Producer*: Samuel Goldwyn Jr., Peter Snell *Director*: Mike Hodges *Writer*: Jack Higgins (novel), Edmund Ward, Martin Lynch *Cast*: Mickey Rourke, Alan Bates, Bob Hoskins, Sammi Davis, Liam Neeson, Christopher Fulford, Leonard Termo, Camille Coduri, Maurice O'Connell, Alison Doody

Martin Fallon (Mickey Rourke) is a burnt out Irish Republican Army terrorist who attempts to blow up a troop truck but accidentally hits a bus load of school kids. He gets his payment and travels to London. In order to escape the IRA he needs the help of Jack Meehan (Alan Bates), a London mob boss, who wants Martin to make one last hit. Martin does the hit on a rival crime boss but he is seen by a priest Father Michael Da Costa (Bob Hoskins). Father Michael has a blind and lovable niece Anna (Sammi Davis) who Martin falls in love with. Father Michael has a shady past and was once a soldier who still can fight. His niece has plays the organ in his church. Martin doesn't want to kill any more innocent people so he must try to escape without harming Father Michael.

**671. The Preacher's Wife.** Buena Vista. US. 1996. 124m. C. *Producer:* Samuel Goldwyn Jr *Director:* Penny Marshall *Writer:* Robert Nathan (novel), Nat Mauldin, Allan Scott *Cast:* Denzel Washington, Whitney Houston, Courtney B. Vance, Gregory Hines, Jenifer Lewis, Loretta Devine, Justin

Pierre Edmund, Lionel Richie, Paul Bates, Lex Monson

A young black preacher Reverend Henry Biggs (Courtney B. Vance) becomes frustrated when his church is going broke and the neighborhood is being developed. The preacher's neglected wife and choir leader Julia (Whitney Houston) becomes angry when she learns that her husband is backing the developer in exchange for a new church. Dudley (Denzel Washington) an angel enters the picture. Remake of *The Bishop's Wife*.

**672. The Price He Paid.** Regal Films. UK. 1916. B&W. *Director & Writer:* David Aylott *Cast:* George Keene, Lettie Paxton, George Foley, Wingold Lawrence, Lionel d'Aragon, Charles Ashwell

Tibetan priest kills blackmailer for stealing jewel from idol.

**673. Priest.** Miramax. UK. 1995. 98m. C. *Producer:* George Faber, Josephine Ward *Director:* Antonia Bird *Writer:* Jimmy McGovern *Cast:* Linus Roache, Tom Wilkinson, Robert Carlyle, Cathy Tyson, Lesley Sharp, Robert Pugh, James Ellis, Christine Tremarco, Paul Barber, Rio Fanning

Father Greg Pilkington (Linus Roache) struggles with his vows and sexuality, in *Priest* (1995).

This film takes on many religious taboos—celibacy, incest, sexual abuse, homosexuality, and secrecy of the confessional. The story centers on two priests—conservative Father Greg Pilkington (Linus Roache) and the older and more practical Father Matthew Thomas (Tom Wilkinson). Soon after arriving, Father Greg learns that Father Matthew openly sleeps with his black housekeeper. Father Greg wrestles with his own demons. Father Greg secretly picks up men at the local gay pub. Adding to his dilemma, during confession a young girl confides that her father is sexually abusing her.

When the film was being released, John Cardinal O'Connor, the Roman Catholic Archbishop of New York, compared the movie to scrawling on the walls of men's rooms. He condemned the film even though he had not seen *Priest*. The film generated boycotts and rallied many religious organizations to attack it.

**The Priest and the Girl** *see* **O Padre e a moça**

**674.　The Priest Killer**. NBC. (TV). US. 1971. 120m. C. *Producer*: David Levinson *Director*: Richard A. Colla *Writer*: Robert Van Scoyck, Joel Oliansky, David Devy *Cast*: Raymond Burr, George Kennedy, Don Galloway, Don Mitchell, Louise Latham, Anthony Zerbe, Peter Brocco, Robert Sampson, Robert Shayne, Kermit Murdock, Fred Slyter, Max Gail

Wheelchair-bound police chief Robert Ironside and cop-turned-priest, Sarge (George Kennedy) work together to solve a series of murders among the clergy. This is the second pilot for *Sarge* which ran for several months in late 1971. The first pilot is *Sarge: The Badge or the Cross*.

**The Priest of St. Pauli** *see* **Der Pfarrer von St. Pauli**

**The Priest's Wife** *see* **La Moglie del prête**

**675.　Primal Fear**. Paramount. US. 1996. 129m. C. *Producer*: Gary Lucchesi *Director*: Gregory Hoblit *Writer*: Steve Shagan, Ann Biderman, William Diehl (novel) *Cast*: Richard Gere, Laura Linney, John Mahoney, Alfre Woodard, Frances McDormand, Edward Norton, Terry O'Quinn, Andre

Braugher, Steven Bauer, Joe Spano, Tony Plana, Stanley Anderson, Maura Tierney, Jon Seda, Reginald Rogers

Hotshot lawyer Martin Vail (Richard Gere) is faced with the task of defending altar boy Aaron Stampler (Edward Norton), who is accused of the brutal murder of an eminent bishop who had taken him in. Aaron is seen running away from the grisly scene. After being examined by a psychiatrist, it is concluded that the boy suffers from multiple personality disorder. Or is it just a great job of acting?

**676.　Prince of Darkness**. Universal. US. 1987. 102m. C. *Producer*: Larry J. Franco *Director & Writer*: John Carpenter *Cast*: Donald Pleasence, Jameson Parker, Victor Wong, Lisa Blount, Dennis Dun, Susan Blanchard, Anne Marie Howard, Ann Yen, Ken Wright, Dirk Blocker, Robert Grasmere

Father Loomis (Donald Pleasence) discovers a vat containing green liquid underneath an abandoned church in the middle of the city. The vat had been protected since the 15th century by a secret society. Even the Vatican knows nothing of its existence. Father Loomis contacts a professor who gathers a group of graduate students to investigate. The group's expertise covers physics, theology, microbiology, chemistry and other fields. They discover that the liquid contains the essence of Satan.

**677.　The Prisoner**. Columbia. UK. 1955. 95m. B&W. *Producer*: Vivian Cox *Director*: Peter Glenville *Writer*: Bridget Boland (play) *Cast*: Alec Guinness, Jack Hawkins, Wilfrid Lawson, Raymond Huntley, Jeanette Sterke, Ronald Lewis, Kenneth Griffin, Mark Dignam, Gerard Heinz

The Interrogator's (Jack Hawkins) torture methods eventually make the Cardinal (Alec Guinness), held on a phony charge of treason, confess to treason. The Cardinal is reprieved within minutes of execution to face a bigger punishment by going into world after his admission of guilt.The setting is never stated but assumed to be Eastern Europe. It bears a resemblance to the real trial of a Cardinal behind the Iron Curtain.

**678. The Private Secretary.** TFD. UK. 1935. 70m. B&W. *Producer:* Julius Hagen *Director:* Henry Edwards *Writer:* Geoge Broadhurst, Arthur Macrae, H. Fowler Mear, Van Moser (play) *Cast:* Edward Everett Horton, Barry MacKay, Judy Gunn, Oscar Asche, Sydney Fairbrother, Michael Shepley, Alastair Sim, Aubrey Dexter, O. B. Clarence, Davina Craig

Rich man's nephew dupes meek cleric, Reverend Robert Spalding (Edward Everett Horton), into protecting him from creditors.

**679. The Private War of Major Benson.** UI. US. 1955. 105m. C. *Producer:* Howard Pine *Director:* Jerry Hopper *Writer:* Richard Alan Simmons, Joe Connelly, Bob Mosher, William Roberts *Cast:* Charlton Heston, Julie Adams, William Demarest, Tim Hovey, Nana Bryant, Tim Considine, Sal Mineo, Milburn Stone, Mary Field

Tough career army office Major Bernard Benson (Charlton Heston) is assigned to a post at Sheraton Military Academy in Santa Barbara about to lose its ROTC rating because he complained about how easy troops have it in the army. To his horror, the academy turns out to be a Catholic institution run by nuns and his troops range from ages 6 to 15. Mother Redempta (Nana Bryant) the very wise Mother Superior and the school doctor Kay Lambert (Julie Adams) help soften his approach.

**Proces au Vatican** *see* **Miracle of Saint Therese**

**680. Le Procès de Jeanne d'Arc.** Pathé Contemporary. France. 1962. 65m. B&W. *Producer:* Agnès Delahaie *Director &Writer:* Robert Bresson *Cast:* Florence Delay, Jean-Claude Fourneau, Roger Honorat, Marc Jacquier, Jean Gillibert, Michel Herubel, André Règnier, Arthur Le Bau, Marcel Darbaud, Philippe Dreux, Paul-Robert Mimet, Gérard Zingg

The film reconstructs the trial of Joan of Arc (based on transcripts of the real-life trial). Also known as *Trial of Joan of Arc.*

**681. A Prodigal Parson.** Essanay Films. 1908. 20m. B&W.

The theme of this film is the ruin and regeneration of the parson and his wife. Two villains have a blackmail proposition and husband and wife are separated. The two villains fight and one kills the other and the parson is blamed. His wife becomes a concert hall singer. The surviving villain turns up and accuses the parson of the murder, but the wife fails to back him up. He attempts suicide, but his blind child prevents it. The couple is reunited and all ends well.

**The Prodigious Life of Father Vincent** *see* **La Portentosa vida del Padre Vincente**

**682. Proibito.** Union Générale Cinematografica. France/Italy. 1954. 100m. C. *Producer:* Jacques Bar *Director:* Mario Monicelli *Writer:* Mario Monicelli, Suso Cecchi d'Amico, Giuseppe Mangione *Cast:* Mel Ferrer, Amedeo Nazzari, Lea Massari, Henri Vilbert, Germaine Kerjean, Eduardo Ciannelli, Decimo Cristiani, Paola Ferrara

Priest Don Paolo (Mel Ferrer) returns to his home village where townspeople are split by old family rivalries. Don Paolo struggles to bring peace to the village and after a few setbacks he succeeds. Also known as *Forbidden.*

**683. The Prophecy.** Miramax. US. 1995. 98m. C. *Producer:* Joel Soisson *Director& Writer:* Gregory Widen *Cast:* Christopher Walken, Elias Koteas, Virginia Madsen, Eric Stoltz, Viggo Mortensen, Amanda Plummer, Moriah 'Shining Dove' Snyder, Adam Goldberg, Steve Hytner, J.C. Quinn

Thomas (Elias Koteas) is a priest who has lost his faith and becomes a cop. The archangel Gabriel (Christopher Walken) has started a war in heaven and searches the earth for souls to use in his army. Thomas joins forces with Simon (Erich Stoltz) to try to stop Gabriel. Followed by sequels.

**684. The Proposition.** Polygram Films. US. 1998. 110m. C. *Producer:* Ted Field, Diane Nabatoff, Scott Kroopf *Director:* Lesli Linka Glatter *Writer:* Rick Ramage *Cast:* Kenneth Branagh, Madeleine Stowe, William Hurt, Neil Patrick Harris, Robert Loggia, Blythe Danner, Bronia Wheeler, Ken Cheeseman, Jim Chiros, Dee Nelson, Josef Sommer, David Byrd

Father Michael McKinnon (Kenneth Branagh) isn't exactly who he pretends to be. New to a Boston parish in 1930's, he has been avoiding the influential Barrets. Arthur

(William Hurt) is a lawyer and madly in love with his wife Eleanor (Madeline Stowe). They are unable to have children so they hire Roger Martin (Neil Patrick Harris) to impregnate the wife for $25,000. Roger falls madly in love with Eleanor and wants to tell the truth. Mysteriously, Roger ends up dead. Eleanor happens to be near an open grave with Father Michael, when she sees Roger as the corpse in the grave she collapses into the grave and loses the baby. Father McKinnon happens to be the son of Arthur's ruthless brother. More secrets clog up the plot. Father McKinnon has an affair with Eleanor, who gives birth to his twins and dies giving birth.

**685. Puckoon.** UA. UK/Ireland. 2002. 82m. C. *Producer:* Ken Tuohy, Terence Ryan *Director:* Terence Ryan *Writer:* Spike Milligan (novel), Terence Ryan *Cast:* Sean Hughes, Elliott Gould, Daragh O'Malley, John Lynch, Griff Rhys Jones, Nickolas Grace, B. J. Hogg, David Kelly, Milo O'Shea, Freddie Jones, Richard Rickings, Richard Attenborough

In 1924, the village of Puckoon is divided in half when the border between Irish Free State and Northern Ireland is drawn up. The film centers on the cemetery which is on Catholic ground and the church is in Northern Ireland. The local priest Father Rudden (Daragh O'Malley) faces the fact that deceased parishioners must secure a British passport in order to be buried. Father Rudden must conspire to have the bodies exhumed and reburied in Ireland. He is unaware that bumbling IRA members have been using the coffins to smuggle explosives.

**686. Putování Jana Amose.** Ceskoslovensky Filmexport. Czechoslovakia. 1983. 147m. C. *Director:* Otakar Vávra *Writer:* Milos Václav Kratochvil, Otakar Vávra *Cast:* Ladislav Chudík, Jana Brezinová, Marta Vancurová, Zuzana Cigánová, Jirí Adamíra, Mikulás Huba, Oldrich Kaiser, Citbor Filcik, Leopold Haverl, Radovan Lukavský

The story of Comenius (Jan Amos Komensky 1592–1670), a priest in the Church of the Brethren, which was under Catholic persecution. Comenius advocated for over forty years that education be universally available to men and women, rich or poor. He traveled through Poland, England, Sweden, France, and the Netherlands pleading his case and the doctrine of Jan Hus, a martyr burned at the stake in 1415. Also known as *Jan Amos' Peregrination.*

**The Quarry** *see* **La Faille**

**687. The Quiet Man.** Republic. US. 1952. 129m. C. *Producer:* Merian C. Cooper, G. B. Forber, John Ford, L.T. Rosso *Director:* John Ford *Writer:* Frank S. Nugent, Maurice Walsh *Cast:* John Wayne, Maureen O'Hara, Barry Fitzgerald, Ward Bond, Victor McLaglen, Mildred Natwick, Francis Ford, Eileen Crowe, Arthur Shields

Sean Thornton (John Wayne) has returned from America to reclaim his Irish homestead and escape his past of accidentally killing a man during a prizefight. Mary Kate Danaher (Maureen O'Hara) catches the eye of Sean. Michaleen Flynn (Barry Fitzgerald) is the matchmaker that watches over their courtship. Red Will Danaher (Victor McLaglen) is Sean's rival for Mary Kate's attention. Father Peter Lonergan (Ward Bond) is a pragmatic, down-to-earth and very likable priest who says it like it is.

**688. Quills.** TCF. US. 2000. 124m. C. *Producer:* Julia Chasman, Nick Wechsler, Peter Kaufman *Director:* Philip Kaufman *Writer:* Doug Wright *Cast:* Geoffrey Rush, Kate Winslet, Joaquin Phoenix, Michael Caine, Billie Whitelaw, Patrick Malahide, Amelia Warner, Jane Menelaus, Stephen Moyer

Tells the story of the Marquis de Sade's (Geoffrey Rush) compulsive creativity during his long imprisonment at the Charenton asylum. He smuggles his writings to the outside world through a young laundress, Madeleine (Kate Winslet). A liberal-minded priest Abbe de Coulmier (Joaquin Phoenix) has a progressive notion to allow the Marquis to write and stage theatricals featuring the asylum's residents. A lurid new play gives the repressive Doctor Royer-Collard (Michael Cain) cause to shut down the theatre and take away the writer's quills, but the Marquis cannot be stopped as he composes on his bed sheets with wine and blood and then by shouting to fellow inmates. The

Abbe is fighting for the soul of de Sade and fighting his desires for Madeleine.

**The Ragpickers of Emmaus** *see* **Les Chiffonniers d'Emmaüs**

**689. Rain.** UA. US. 1932. 92m. B&W. *Director*: Lewis Milestone *Writer*: John Colton (play), Clemence Randolph (play), Maxwell Anderson, W. Somerset Maugham *Cast*: Joan Crawford, Walter Huston, Fred Howard, Ben Hendricks Jr., William Gargan, Mary Shaw, Guy Kibbee, Kendall Lee, Beulah Bondi, Matt Moore, Walter Catlett

Prostitute Sadie Thompson (Joan Crawford) is quarantined with other passengers on Pago Pago Island. She does not get along with the missionaries. One missionary, Reverend Alfred Davidson (Walter Huston) forces Sadie to repent. He can not control his lust for her so he rapes her and then he commits suicide. In the end, Sadie ends up with Sergeant O'Hara (William Gargan).

**690. Rappresaglia.** National General Pictures. Italy/France. 1973. 110m. C. *Producer*: Carlo Ponti *Director*: George P. Cosmatos *Writer*: Robert Katz *Cast*: Richard Burton, Marcello Mastroianni, Leo McKern, John Steiner, Anthony Steel, Robert Harris, Peter Vaughan, Renzo Montagnani, Giancarlo Prete, Renzo Palmer

The Italian resistance plants a bomb that kills 33 German soldiers in Rome. The Germans demand revenge and that 10 Italians for every German soldier be killed in retribution. The Nazi Colonel Herbert Kappler (Richard Burton) in charge of Rome during the World War II debates the plan with an outraged priest Father Pietro Antonelli (Marcello Mastroianni). Based on a true incident known as the Ardeatine Massacre. Also known as *Massacre in Rome*.

**691. Rasputin: The Mad Monk.** TCF. UK. 1966. 91m. C. *Producer:* Anthony Nelson Keys *Director:* Don Sharp *Writer*: Anthony Hinds *Cast*: Christopher Lee, Barbara Shelley, Richard Pasco, Francis Matthews, Suzan Farmer, Disdale Landen, Renée Asherson, Joss Ackland, Robert Duncan, John Bailey

Russian ex-monk mystic Rasputin (Christopher Lee) uses hypnotism to attain power at court of tsar.

**692. The Ravagers.** Hemisphere Pictures. Philippines/US. 1965. 88m. B&W. *Producer*: Kane W. Lynn, Eddie Romero *Director*: Eddie Romero *Writer*: Cesar Amigo, Eddie Romero *Cast*: John Saxon, Fernando Poe Jr., Bronwyn Fitzsimmons, Mike Parsons, Kristina Scott, Robert Arevalo, Vic Diaz, Vic Silayan, Jose Dagumboy

In the Philippines, 1945, the Japanese take over a convent in order to obtain a shipment of gold bullion stored at the convent. An American officer and an ex-convict lead a group of native guerrillas to defeat the Japanese.

**693. The Reckoning.** Paramount Classics. US. 2004. 112m. C. *Producer*: Caroline Wood *Director*: Paul McGuigan *Writer*: Barry Unsworth (novel), Mark Mills *Cast*: Paul Bettany, Willem Dafoe, Brian Cox, Gina McKee, Ewen Bremner, Vincent Cassel, Elvira Minguez, Tom Hardy, Mark Benton

Set in 14th century England, Nicholas (Paul Bettany) is a disgraced priest on the lam who joins a troupe of itinerant actors who stage biblical plays from town to town. In one town there has been a series of killing of young boys and the villagers are planning to hang a deaf-mute faith healer accused of the murders. The acting troop decides to dramatize the murders and ends up getting at the truth.

**694. The Red Danube.** MGM. US. 1949. 119m. B&W. *Producer*: Carey Wilson *Director*: George Sidney *Writer*: Bruce Marshall (novel) Gina Kaus, Arthur Wimperis *Cast*: Walter Pidgeon, Ethel Barrymore, Peter Lawford, Angela Lansbury, Janet Leigh, Louis Calhern, Francis L. Sullivan, Melville Cooper, Robert Coote, Alan Napier

Post World War II Vienna is the backdrop for a love story which takes place at a convent where four soldiers are living while completing their mission in Vienna. Colonel Michael Nicobar (Walter Pidgeon) verbally duels with the Mother Superior (Ethel Barrymore) about pros and cons of organized religion. A mysterious dancer Maria Buhlen (Janet Leigh) is also at the convent. Only the Mother Superior knows the true identity of Olga Alexandrova. Maria fears that she will be forced back to Russia.

**695. The Red Flame of Passion.** State Rights. 1914. B&W.

A hunter Hardy is accidentally shot and rescued by a taxidermist Jim. The taxidermist's wife Ada falls in love with the hunter and runs off with him with the couple's property and baby daughter. Jim overcomes depression and becomes a prominent physician. Jim gets revenge ten years later. Their daughter learns the truth after Jim forces Ada to tell her in order to save Hardy's life. Ada becomes a nun when Hardy leaves her

**The Red Inn** *see* **L'Auberge rouge**

**696. La Religieuse.** Altura Films International. France. 1966. 135m. C. *Producer:* Georges de Beauregard *Director:* Jacques Rivette *Writer:* Denis Diderot (novel), Jean Gruault, Jacques Rivette *Cast:* Anna Karina, Liselotte Pulver, Micheline Presle, Francine Bergé, Francisco Rabal, Christiane Lénier, Yori Bertin, Catherine Diamant, Gilette Barbier, Annik Morice, Danielle Palmero

In 18th century France, a young girl Suzanne Simonin (Anna Karina) is forced into a convent because she is seen as a burden to her family. The convent is a cruel and strict place where her spirit is continually beaten down. It is pure torture for her until a sympathetic clergyman helps her leave. Her next convent is liberal and permissive. Unfortunately, the Mother Superior makes night visits and sexual advances all of which frightens her. A priest helps her leave but once free he accosts her. Finally on the outside, an apparently nice woman takes her in and feeds her. This woman happens to be a madam of a brothel. Suicide seems to be her only answer. Also known as *The Nun*.

**The Religion Hour (My Mother's Smile)** *see* **L'Ora di Religione: il sorriso di mia madre**

**697. The Reluctant Saint.** Davis-Royal. US/Italy. 1962. 105m. B&W. *Producer & Director:* Edward Dmytryk *Writer:* John Fante, Joseph Petracca *Cast:* Maximilian Schell, Ricardo Montalban, Lea Padovani, Akim Tamiroff, Harold Goldbatt, Arnoldo Foá, Mark Damon, Luciana Paluzzi, Giulio Bosetti, Elisa Cagani

Giuseppe (Maximilian Schell) is a simple minded peasant thought by many to be an idiot. His mother sends him to his brother in a monastery, where he ends up being sent to the stables. His love of horses attracts the attention of the Bishop, who encourages him to become a priest. Giuseppe surprises everyone when he passes the entrance examination. When he prays to a statue of the Madonna he floats. Don Raspi (Ricardo Montalban) doesn't believe in his floating until he sees a vision of the Madonna. This vision relieves the hysteria of the villagers that thought Giuseppe is possessed by demons. This man would become Saint Joseph of Cupertino.

**698. Repossessed.** New Line Cinema. US. 1990. 80m. C. *Producer:* Steve Wizan *Director & Writer:* Bob Logan *Cast:* Linda Blair, Ned Beatty, Leslie Nielsen, Anthony Starke, Thom Sharp, Lana Schwab, Benj Thall, Dove Dellos, Jacquelyn Masche, Melissa Moore

In this parody of *The Exorcist* the possessed child now plays mother and housewife Nancy Aglet (Linda Blair) with a family who becomes possessed when Satan comes out of the television during evangelists Ernest Weller (Ned Beatty) and Fanny Ray Weller (Lana Schwab)'s show. Young timid priest Father Luke Brophy (Anthony Starke) can't deal with the devil so Father Jebedaiah Mayii (Leslie Nielsen) comes out of retirement.

**699. Resurrection.** Universal. US. 1980. 103m. C. *Producer:* Renée Missel, Howard Rosenman *Director:* Daniel Petrie *Writer:* Lewis John Carlino *Cast:* Ellen Burstyn, Sam Shepard, Richard Farnsworth, Roberts Blossom, Clifford David, Pamela Payton-Wright, Jeffrey DeMunn, Eva LeGallienne, Lois Smith, Madeleine Sherwood, Richard Hamilton, Carlin Glynn, Lane Smith, Penelope Allen, Ebbe Roe Smith

An affluent Los Angeles husband and wife Edna McCauley (Ellen Burstyn) are involved in a car accident in the car she just gave him for his birthday. He dies and her legs are left paralyzed. During her recovery in Kansas she finds that her brush with death has given her the miraculous power of healing by the laying on of hands.

**700. Le Retour de Don Camillo.** Cinedis. France/Italy. 1953. 115m. B&W. *Director:* Julien Duvivier *Writer:* René Barjavel, Julien Duvivier *Cast:* Fernandel, Gino Cervi, Edouard Delmont, Alexandre Rignault, Paolo Stoppa, Thomy Bourdelle, Tony Jacquot

Takes off where *The Little World of Don Camillo* ends with Don Camillo in exile after fighting Mayor Peppone. Don Camillo (Fernandel) is now at another parish in a remote village. His old town really misses him – old people refuse to die and young people refuse to marry. Camillo soon returns to his old parish. Mayor Peppone (Gino Cervi) and Camillo start fighting again but unite when a flood threatens the town. Also known as *Return of Don Camillo.*

**The Return of Don Camillo** *see* **Le Retour de Don Camillo**

**701. Revelation.** First Look. UK. 2001. 111m. C. *Producer:* Jonathan Woolf, Stuart Urban *Director & Writer:* Stuart Urban *Cast:* Terence Stamp, James D'Arcy, Natasha Wightman, Udo Kier, Liam Cunningham, Derek Jacobi, Heathcote Williams, Ron Moody, Celie Imrie

Satanic adventure-drama about four people on a trail from France through Malta to Greece in search of the Loculus, a sacred box once held by the Knights Templar. On the journey is reclusive billionaire mogul Magnus Martel (Terence Stamp), his estranged son, Jake (James D'Arcy), a cryptographer, alchemist Mira (Natasha Wightman) and shadowing them is the Grand Master (Udo Kier), a satanic immortal. Father Ray Connolly (Liam Cunningham) seems to aid and thwart their search. Cloning and Jesus' descendants enter the plot.

**702. Rhubarb.** Warner-Pathe. UK. 1969. 37m. C. *Producer:* Jon Penington *Director & Writer:* Eric Sykes *Cast:* Harry Secombe, Eric Sykes, Jimmy Edwards, Hattie Jacques, Gordon Rollings, Graham Stark, Kenneth Connor, Johnny Speight

Slapstick golf match between village vicar (Harry Secombe) and police inspector (Eric Sykes). The police inspector cheats any way he can until the vicar asks for help from the Lord. His prayers are answered by a bolt of lightning and a storm.

**Ring Around the Clock** *see* **Vogliamoci bene**

**703. The Rip-Tide.** Arrow. US. 1923. 50m. B&W. *Director:* Jack Pratt *Writer:* J. Grubb Alexander *Cast:* Stuart Holmes, Rosemary Theby, J. Frank Glendon, Dick Sutherland, George Regas, Russell Simpson, Diana Alden

A young Hindu prince renounces his religion to become an Episcopal priest. When he is to return home for missionary work, his father disowns him when he learns that he plans to convert his own people.

**704. A River Runs Through It.** Columbia. US. 1992. 123m. C. *Producer:* Patrick Markey, Robert Redford *Director:* Robert Redford *Writer:* Richard Friedenberg, Norman Maclean *Cast:* Craig Sheffer, Brad Pitt, Tom Skerritt, Brenda Blethyn, Emily Lloyd, Edie McClurg, Stephen Shellen

This is the story of two brothers growing up in Montana with their Presbyterian minister father Reverend Maclean (Tom Skerritt). One son is rebellious and the other is sensible but they all have the same love of fly fishing in common.

**The Road Home** *see* **Boys Town**

**705. Rolling Home.** Screen Guild Productions. 1946. 71m. B&W. *Producer & Director:* William A. Berke *Writer:* William A. Berke, Edwin V. Westrate *Cast:* Jean Parker, Russell Hayden, Raymond Hatton, Pamela Blake, Jo Ann Marlowe, Jimmy Conlin, Jimmie Dodd, Robert 'Buzz' Henry, Jonathan Hale, George Tyne, Harry Carey Jr.

An old time rodeo performer and his grandson arrive in a small town with an injured horse. Local minister Reverend David Owens (Russell Hayden) treats the horse's bad leg. The church happens to be in debt but when the horse wins a race all is saved. A wealthy widow is also softened up by the men.

**706. Roma, città aperta.** Mayer-Burstyn. Italy. 1945. 100m. B&W. *Director:* Roberto Rossellini *Writer:* Sergio Amidei, Federico Fellini, Roberto Rossellini, Alberto Consiglio *Cast:* Anna Magnani, Aldo Fabrizi, Marcello Pagliero, Vito Annichiarico, Nando Bruno, Harry Feist, Giovanna Galletti, Francesco Grandjacquet

Key film of the Italian Neo-Realism period which was shot largely during the Nazi occupation of Rome. Two resistance leaders, one a priest Don Pietro Pellegrini (Aldo Fabrizi), the other a Communist, work against the Germans. The priest smuggles items under his robes across lines. He gives his life for the cause and dies blessing neighborhood children standing outside the prison. Also known as *Roma, città aperta*.

**707. Romance.** MGM. US. 1930. 76m. B&W. *Producer & Director:* Clarence Brown *Writer:* Edwin Justus Mayer, Bess Meredyth, Edward Sheldon (play) *Cast:* Greta Garbo, Lewis Stone, Gavin Gordon, Elliott Nugent, Florence Lake, Clara Blandick, Henry Armetta, Mathilde Comont, Rina De Liguoro

Harry wants to marry an actress but his family disapproves of the relationship. Harry turns to his grandfather Bishop Armstrong for advice. The elderly Bishop tells the story of French opera star Madame Rita Cavallini (Greta Garbo) the woman he loved and wanted to marry when he was a young minister. Rita, a woman with a past, realizes that she cannot marry him and the relationship ends. He marries a good girl, whose uncle had a relationship with Rita.

**708. Romeo and Juliet.** UA. Italy/UK. 1954. 138m. C. *Producer:* Joseph Janni, Sandro Ghenzi *Director & Writer:* Renato Castellani *Cast:* Laurence Harvey, Susan Shentall, Flora Robson, Mervyn Johns, Bill Travers, Enzo Fiermonte, Ubaldo Zollo, Giovanni Rota, Sebastian Cabot, Lydia Sherwood, Norman Wooland, Giulio Garbinetto, Nietta Zocchi, Dagmar Josipovitch, Luciano Bodi, Thomas Nicholls

British version of Shakespeare's classic. Friar Laurence (Mervyn Johns) always plays a key part in the story.

**709. Romeo and Juliet.** Paramount. Italy/UK. 1968. 138m. C. *Producer:* Anthony Havelock-Allan, John Brabourne *Director:* Franco Zeffirelli *Writer:* Franco Brusati, Maestro D'Amico, Franco Zeffirelli *Cast:* Leonard Whiting, Olivia Hussey, Milo O'Shea, Michael York, John McEnery, Pat Heywood, Natasha Parry, Paul Hardwick,

Robert Stephens, Keith Skinner, Roberto Bisacco, Bruce Robinson

The Shakespeare's play has been produced a number of time throughout the cinematic history. Friar Laurence (Milo O'Shea) always plays a key part in the story.

**710. Romero.** Four Square. US. 1989. 102m. C. *Producer:* Ellwood Kieser *Director:* John Duigan *Writer:* John Sacret Young *Cast:* Raul Julia, Richard Jordan, Ana Alicia, Eddie Velez, Alejandro Bracho, Tony Plana, Harold Gould, Lucy Reina, Al Ruscio, Tony Perez, Robert Viharo

The true story of Salvadoran Archbishop Oscar Arnulfo Romero (Raul Julia), who was assassinated in the 1980s for supporting the struggle for the liberation of El Salvador. Romero speaks out against the death squads the tyrannical government is using against the guerillas. This was the first feature film made in the United States by a Roman Catholic organization, Paulist Pictures.

**711. Rosa de América.** Distribuidora Panamericana. Argentina. 1946. 105m. B&W. *Director:* Alberto De Zavalia *Writer:* Ulises Petit de Murat, Homero Manzi *Cast:* Delia Garcés, Orestes Caviglia, Antonia Herrero, Elsa O'Connor, Enrique Diosdado, Angelina Pagano, Domingo Sapelli, Francisco López Silva, Rafael Frontaura, Ernesto Vilches

Tells the story of Rosa de Lima, the high-born Peruvian lady, who became a saint. Also known as *Rose of America*.

**712. The Rosary.** Associated First National Pictures. US. 1922. B&W. *Producer:* William Nicholas Selig, Sam E. Rork *Director:* Jerome Storm *Writer:* Bernard McConville, Edward E. Rose (play) *Cast:* Lewis Stone, Jane Novak, Wallace Beery, Robert Gordon, Eugenie Besserer, Dore Davidson, Pomeroy Cannon, Bert Woodruff, Mildred June, Harold Goodwin

After the death of his uncle, Kenwood Wright (Wallace Beery) is cut off while his nephew, Bruce Wilton (Robert Gordon), inherits most of the estate. Wright is also angered by the engagement between Vera Mather (Jane Novak), whom he loves, and Bruce. Bruce's sister Alice becomes Wright's victim and Vera gets involved in the scandal trying to save her. Bruce takes back the rosary he had given her to pledge his love. Wright constructs an explosion at the cannery which Bruce narrowly escapes. Father Brian Kelly (Lewis Stone) names Wright as a conspirator and the posse sets out to capture him. He seeks refuge in the church. He draws a pistol against Father Kelly, but Bruce's mother gets shot instead. Wright plunges to his death while crossing an old bridge trying to escape. Previously filmed in 1915 with Charles Clary as Father Brian Kelly.

**713. The Rosary Murders.** New Line Cinema. US. 1987. 105m. C. *Producer:* Robert G. Laurel *Director:* Fred Walton *Writer:* William Kienzle (novel), Elmore Leonard, Fred Walton *Cast:* Donald Sutherland, Josef Sommer, Charles Durning, B. Constance Barry, Belinda Bauer, John Danelle, Rex Everhart, Cordis Heard, Tom Mardirosian, Robert C. Maxwell, Addison Powell, Kathleen Tolan, Peter Van Norden

A serial killer with a grudge is striking the Catholic Church of the Holy Redentor in Detroit. All the victims are priests or nuns and all found with a black rosary in their hands. Father Robert Koesler (Donald Sutherland) collaborates with the police that is until the killer confesses to him.

**Rose of America** *see* **Rosa de América**

**714. The Ruling Class.** AVCO Embassy Pictures. UK. 1972. 154m. C. *Producer:* Jules Buck, Jack Hawkins *Director:* Peter Medak *Writer:* Peter Barnes *Cast:* Peter O'-Toole, Alastair Sim, Arthur Lowe, Harry Andrews, Coral Browne, Michael Bryant, Nigel Green, William Mervyn Carolyn Seymour, James Villiers, Hugh Burden, Graham Crowden

When a member of the House of Lords dies, in a silly way, he leaves his estate to his son Jack Arnold Alexander ... 14th Earl of Gurney (Peter O'Toole) who thinks he is Jesus Christ. The other members of the family plot to steal the estate from him causing murder and mayhem. Jack is considered too religious for normal society. Bishop Lampton (Alastair Sim) is pulled into the plot.

**715. The Runner Stumbles.** TCF. US. 1979. 109m. C. *Producer & Director:* Stanley Kramer *Writer:* Milan Stitt (play) *Cast:* Dick Van Dyke, Kathleen Quinlan, Maureen Stapleton, Ray Bolger, Tammy Grimes, Beau Bridges, Allen Nause, John Procaccino, Sister Marguerite Morrissey, Zoaunne LeRoy, Jock Dove

Based on an actual murder case in 1927 where a priest is accused of murdering the nun he has fallen in love with. The story is told in three parts, Father Rivard (Dick Van Dyke) in jail, the story of the relationship between Father Rivard and Sister Rita (Kathleen Quinlan) and then the trial. Father Rivard is a lonely and depressed priest stuck in a small poor mining town. With the arrival of young perky Sister Rita, Father Rivard cheers up and soon falls in love.

**716. Russicum—i giorni del diavolo.** Columbia TriStar. Italy. 1989. 111m. C. *Producer:* Mario Cecchi Gori, Vittorio Cecchi Gori *Director:* Pasquale Squitieri *Writer:* Enzo Russo (novel), Robert Balchus, Valerio Riva, Pasquale Squitieri *Cast:* Treat Williams, F. Murray Abraham, Danny Aiello, Rita Cecchi Gori, Robert Balchus, Rossano Brazzi, Nigel Court, Leopoldo Mastelloni, Luigi Montini, Martin Sorrentino

The Roman Catholic Pope and the head of the Ukrainian Orthodox Church are planning a reconciliatory meeting. Suddenly, while the Pope is speaking to the crowds, a nun is assassinated by a Ukrainian. A young man is assigned to investigate and is lead to the Russicum, a center for the study of Russia within the Vatican City. He finds himself caught up in intrigue with agents and double agents, and ending with a revelation. Also known as *The Third Solution*.

**717. Ryan's Daughter.** MGM. UK. 1970. 206m. C. *Producer:* Anthony Havelock-Alan *Director:* David Lean *Writer:* Robert Bolt *Cast:* Robert Mitchum, Trevor Howard, Sarah Miles, Christopher Jones, John Mills, Leo McKern, Barry Foster, Archie O'Sullivan, Marie Kean, Evin Crowley

In 1916 Ireland the immature wife Rosy (Sarah Miles) of the village's schoolmaster Charles (Robert Mitchum), who is much older then her, falls in love with a shell-shocked soldier Randolph (Christopher Jones). He is to take charge over a British garrison and an affair develops. The sub-plot involves rebel gun running and betrayal. Father Collins (Trevor Howard) is the knowing village priest.

**718. Rys.** Poland. 1981. 84m. *Director:* Stanislaw Rózewicz *Writer:* Jaroslaw Iwaszkiewicz, Stanislaw Rózewicz *Cast:* Piotr Bajor, Ryszarda Hanin, Franciszek Pieczka, Jerzy Radziwilowicz, Maria Klejdysz, Henryk Machalica, Hanna Mikuc, Anna Skuratowicz

During the German occupation of Poland during World War II, Father Konrad (Jerzy Radziwilowicz) first meets Satan/Lynx (Piotr Bajor) in the confessional. The Lynx is Satan incarnate sent to assassinate a collaborator. Also known as *Lynx.*

**719. El Sacerdote.** Award Films. Spain. 1979. 115m. C. *Director:* Eloy de la Iglesia *Cast:* Simón Andreu, Queta Claver, Amparo Climent, José Franco, Emilio Gutiérrez Caba, Esperanza Roy

The film is set in a strict Catholic parish house. Father Miguel is so obsessed by images and fantasies of sex that it triggers a suicidal mid-life crisis. Should he surrender to his fantasies or stay and fight the demons of temptation? The conflict between celibacy and human nature plays out in this film.

**720. Sacred Hearts.** Channel Four Films. UK. 1985. 95m. C. *Producer:* Dee Dee Glass *Director & Writer:* Barbara Rennie *Cast:* Anna Massey, Katrin Cartlidge, Oona Kirsch, Fiona Shaw, Anne Dyson, Annette Badland, Sadie Wearing, Ann-Marie Gwatkin, Kathy Burke

A portrayal of life in a repressive convent school set during World War II. Tyrannical Sister Thomas (Anna Massey) ignores the fears and feelings of her charges during the bombings. Newcomer Doris (Katrin Cartlidge) confides in her friend that she is not a Catholic and we learn that she is Jewish.

**721. Sadie Thompson.** UA. US. 1928. 97m. B&W. *Producer & Director:* Raoul Walsh *Writer:* Raoul Walsh, W. Somerset Maugham (story), John Colton (play), Clemence Randolph (play) *Cast:* Gloria Swanson, Lionel Barrymore, Blanche Frederici, Charles Lane, Florence Midgley, James A. Marcus, Sophia Artega, Will Stanton, Raoul Walsh

Sadie Thompson (Gloria Swanson) arrives in Pago-Pago to start a new life but extremist missionary Alfred Davidson (Lionel Barrymore) tries to force her away. In a lustful rage, he rapes her and then slits his own throat. This was the first version of the W. Somerest Maugham story "Rain," which was remade in 1932 with the title *Rain* and again in 1953 as *Miss Sadie Thompson.*

**722. Sagebrush Gospel.** Arrow Film Corp. US. 1924. B&W. *Director:* Richard Hatton *Writer:* Carl Coolidge *Cast:* Neva Gerber, Harry von Meter, Richard Hatton, Nellie Franzen

An evangelist and his daughter arrive in the western town of Sagebrush. Finding no church they decide to stay. His daughter falls in love and her new beau puts a gang in jail. The dancehall becomes a church on the day of Lucy's wedding to her beau.

**723. St. Elmo.** State Rights/Box Office Attraction. US. 1914. B&W. *Producer:* William Fox *Director:* J. Gordon Edwards *Writer:* William Jossey, Augusta Jane Evans Wilson (novel) *Cast:* Augusta Jane Evans Wilson

St. Elmo, a troublemaker, meets Agnes, the daughter of the town blacksmith. She goes away after her father dies. St. Elmo follows her and has some near disasters. When he hears the Lord's voice he decides to reform. He becomes a minister and gets Agnes. Versions filmed before and after this film.

**724. St. Elmo.** Capitol. UK. 1923. B&W. *Director & Writer:* Rex Wilson *Cast:* Shayle Gardner, Gabrielle Gilroy, Madge Tree, Harding Thomas

Widow's son kills clerical rival in duel and becomes possessed by devil.

**Saint Francis** *see* **San Francesco il poverello d'Assisi**

**Saint Hans' Celebration** *see* **Sankt Hans Fest**

**Saint Jerome** *see* **São Jerônimo**

**725. Saint Joan.** UA. UK. 1957. 110m. B&W. *Producer & Director:* Otto Preminger *Writer:* Graham Greene, George Bernard Shaw (play) *Cast:* Jean Seberg, Richard Widmark, Richard Todd, Anton Walbrook, John Gielgud, Felix Aylmer, Harry Andrews,

Barry Jones, Finlay Currie, Bernard Miles, Patrick Barr

Peasant girl Joan (Jean Seberg) has been told by God to lead the French army against the English. Joan is betrayed, tried for heresy and witchcraft, and burned at the stake. Graham Greene's screenplay was an adaptation of George Bernard Shaw's play. In 1927, Sybil Thorndike performed the cathedral scene from Shaw's play. There was British television production in 1958 with Siobhan McKenna as Saint Joan.

**726. Saint Joan.** NBC. (TV). US. 1967. 120m. *Producer & Director:* George Schaefer *Writer:* Robert Hartung George Bernard Shaw (play) *Cast:* Geneviève Bujold, Roddy McDowall, Maurice Evans, James Donald, James Daly, Theodore Bikel, Raymond Massey, Leo Genn, David Birney, George Ross

George Bernard Shaw's drama traces the life of Joan of Arc (Geneviève Bujold) from her first attempt to save France to her trial and burning at the stake. This production is part of the *Hallmark Hall of Fame* drama series.

**Saint Joan the Maid** *see* **La Merveilleuse vie de Jeanne d'Arc**

**727. St. Patrick: The Irish Legend.** Fox. (TV). US. 2000. 100m. *Producer:* Robert Hughes *Director:* Robert Hughes *Writer:* Martin Duffy, Robert Hughes *Cast:* Patrick Bergin, Luke Griffin, Alan Bates, Susannah York, Malcolm McDowell, Eamonn Owens, Chris McHallem, Michael Cavern, Stephen Brennan, Adam Goodwin

With the English Church looking to remove his influence over Christians in Ireland Patrick (Patrick Bergin) records his tale of being captured as a young boy and then made a slave in Ireland. When he escapes back to England, he discovers God. He has a great desire to return to Ireland to convert the Irish to Christianity. He gets his wish when he returns to Ireland as a missionary. He endures many hardships including political differences while fulfilling his mission.

**St. Simon of the Desert** *see* **Simón del desierto**

**The Saint that Forged a Country** *see* **La Virgen que forjó una patria**

**St. Theresa, the Little Flower** *see* **Glory of Faith**

**Saint Therese of Lisieux** *see* **Little Flower of Jesus**

**Saints and Their Sorrows** *see* **Prästen**

**728. Sally and Saint Anne.** UI. US. 1952. 90m. B&W. *Producer:* Leonard Goldstein *Director:* Rudolph Mate *Writer:* James O'Hanlon, Herb Meadow *Cast:* Ann Blyth, Edmund Gwenn, John McIntire, Hugh O'Brian, Jack Kelly, Frances Bavier, Otto Hulett, Kathleen Hughes, George Mathews, Lamont Johnson

Story of Sally O'Moyne (Ann Blyth) who prays to a statue of Saint Anne for help for her neighbors. Although she does not pray for herself, she makes an exception and appeals to St. Anne that her family will be able to keep their house.

**San Francesco d'Assisi** *see* **Frate Sol**

**729. San Francesco il poverello d'Assisi.** Cines. Italy. 1911. B&W. *Director:* Enrico Guazzoni *Cast:* Emilio Ghione, Italia Manzini

In a dream, Francis has a vision of poverty. He gives up his rich family and founds an order of monks. The Pope accepts his order. The film closes with Francis' death surrounded by his monks and his friend Clare and her order of nuns. Also known as *Saint Francis.*

**730. San Francisco.** MGM. US. 1936. 115m. B&W. *Producer:* John Emerson, Bernard H. Hyman *Director:* W. S. Van Dyke *Writer:* Robert Hopkins, Anita Loos *Cast:* Clark Gable, Jeanette MacDonald, Spencer Tracy, Jack Holt, Jessie Ralph, Ted Healy, Shirley Ross, Margaret Irving, Harold Huber, Edgar Kennedy, Al Shean, William Ricciardi, Kenneth Harlan, Roger Imhof, Charles Judels, Russell Simpson, Bert Roach, Warren Hymer

In early 1900s San Francisco, Blackie Norton (Clark Gable) owner of the Paradise a gambling club, fights with childhood friend Father Tim Mullin (Spencer Tracy) over the future of singer Mary Blake (Jeanette MacDonald). Blackie actually hits Father Tim when Mary must choose between opera and Blackie. Mary wins a singing competition and gives her winnings to Blackie so he can

re-open his club after its closing. Blackie refuses the money and then the famous San
Francisco earthquake destroys the city.
Blackie, Father Tim, and Mary are reunited
at a Salvation Army camp and prepare for
the new city.

**731. San Francisco de Asís.** Azteca.
Mexico. 1944.119m. B&W. *Producer:* Pedro
A. Calderón *Director:* Alberto Gout *Writer:*
Juan Antonio Vargas, Luis White Morque-
cho *Cast:* Crox Alvarado, Antonio Bravo,
Alicia de Phillips, Elene D'Orgaz, José Luis
Jiménez, Carmen Molina, Elia Ortiz, Luis
Alcoriza, Salvador Quiroz, Crox Alvarado

Francis is born into a rich family and
enjoys wine, women, song, and fighting. He
gives up everything and starts an order of
monks and becomes Saint Francis.

**732. Sanctuary of Fear.** NBC. (TV).
UK. 1979. 100m. C. *Producer:* Philip Barry, Jr.
*Director:* John Llewellyn Moxey *Writer:* Don
Mankiewicz, Gordon Cotler, G. K. Chester-
ton *Cast:* Barnard Hughes, Kay Lenz,
Michael McGuire, George Hearn, Robert
Schenkkan, David Rasche, Fred Gwynne,
Elizabeth Wilson, Donald Symington, Saul
Rubinek, Peter Maloney, Jeffrey DeMunn,
Maureen Silliman, Alice Drummond

A Manhattan parish priest Father
Brown (Barnard Hughes) comes to the aid of
a young actress who is innocently involved
in a series of bizarre incidents.

**733. The Sandpiper.** MGM. US. 1965.
117m. C. *Producer:* Martin Ransohoff *Director:* Vincente Minnelli *Writer:* Dalton
Trumbo, Michael Wilson *Cast:* Elizabeth
Taylor, Richard Burton, Eva Marie Saint,
Charles Bronson, Robert Webber, James Edwards, Torin Thatcher, Tom Drake, Douglas Henderson, Morgan Mason

The story of an affair between single,
would-be artist, Laura Reynolds (Elizabeth
Taylor) and a married Episcopalian minister, Dr. Edward Hewitt (Richard Burton),
who is headmaster of a private school for
boys attended by her son.

**734. Sankt Hans Fest.** Snorre Films.
Norway. 1947. 88m. B&W. *Producer & Direc-
tor:* Toralf Sandø *Writer:* Victor Borg, Toralf
Sandø, Per Schrøder-Nilsen, Alex Kielland
(novel) *Cast:* Tore Foss, Johannes Eckhoff,
Jon Lennart Mjøen, Erling Drangsholt,
Sigrun Otto, Sigurd Magnusson, Else-
Merete Heiberg

A tyrannical priest (Tore Foss) seeks to
control all human souls. He desires to play
God on earth. Also known as *Saint Hans'
Celebration.*

**735. São Jerônimo.** Rio Filme. Brazil.
1999. 75m. C. *Producer, Director & Writer:*
Julio Bressane *Cast:* Everaldo Pontes, Hamilton Vaz Pereira, Balduíno Léllis, Helena
Ignez, Bia Nunes, Silvia Buarque

Biographical film about Saint Jerome
(Everaldo Pontes), the monk who first trans-
lated the Bible into Latin. Also known as
*Saint Jerome.*

**736. Sarge: The Badge or the Cross.**
NBC. (TV). US. 1971. 120m. C. *Producer:*
David Levinson *Director:* Richard A. Colla
*Writer:* Don Mankiewicz *Cast:* George
Kennedy, Ricardo Montalban, Nico Minar-
dos, Diane Baker, Stewart Moss, Sallie
Shockley, Larry Gates, Harold Sakata,
Naomi Stevens, Henry Wilcoxon, Stanley
Livingston, Dana Elcar, Ramon Bieri, Wal-
ter Brooke, Charles Tyner, David Huddle-
ston

A veteran cop (George Kennedy) turns
to the priesthood after his wife is shot to
death. Three years later he is assigned to a
parish where he encounters the assassin.
First of two pilots for the TV series *Sarge.*
The second pilot *The Priest Killer* aired in
September 1971.

**Satan Never Sleeps** *see* **The Devil
Never Sleeps**

**737. Saving Grace.** Columbia. US.
1985. 112m. C. *Producer:* Herbert F. Solow
*Director:* Robert M. Young *Writer:* Richard
Kramer, Joaquin Montana, Celia Gittelson
(novel) *Cast:* Tom Conti, Fernando Rey, Erland Josephson, Giancarlo Giannini, Donald Hewlett, Edward James Olmos, Patricia
Mauceri, Angelo Evans, Marta Zoffoli,
Guido Alberti

Newly-elected Pope Leo XIV (Tom
Conti) gets accidentally locked out of the
Vatican. Still an unknown to the world, he
finds himself in a small and poor Italian village. His adventures amongst Italian peasants teach the Pope lessons about friendship

and self-esteem. A trio of Cardinals covers for the Pope in his absence.

**738. The Sawdust Paradise**. Paramount. US. 1928. 68m. B&W. *Producer:* Adolph Zukor, Jesse L Lansky *Director:* Luther Reed *Writer:* Louise Long, George Manker Watters *Cast:* Esther Ralston, Reed Howes, Hobart Bosworth, Tom Maguire, George B. French, Alan Roscoe, Mary Alden, Jack W. Johnston, Frank Brownlee, Helen Hunt

Hallie (Esther Ralston), who works in a cheap street carnival, is arrested for gambling. Vowing to reform she is paroled into the custody of Isaiah (Hobart Bosworth), an evangelist whose tent is across the street from the carnival. Soon she helps the older man make his revival meetings a success. Butch, her old beau, buys a carnival and sees the meetings as a threat. When he sees Hallie, Butch can't go through with his plan. Butch and Hallie reunite at the end.

**739. Say One for Me**. TCF. US. 1959. 120m. C. *Producer & Director:* Frank Tashlin *Writer:* Robert O'Brien *Cast:* Bing Crosby, Debbie Reynolds, Robert Wagner, Ray Walston, Les Tremayne, Frank McHugh, Joe Besser, Stella Stevens, Connie Gilchrist, Sebastian Cabot, David Leonard, Thomas Browne Henry

Father Conroy's (Bing Crosby) parish serves the New York City acting and performance community. The daughter, Holly, of one of his parishioners must find work when her father becomes too sick to work. She finds a job working at a dance club. Father Conroy looks after Holly. A televised benefit show hosted by the Father comes at the end of the film.

**740. Scandal at Scourie**. MGM. US. 1953. 90m. C. *Producer:* Edwin H. Knopf *Director:* Jean Negulesco *Writer:* Leonard Spigelgass, Karl Tunberg, Norman Corwin, Mary McSherry *Cast:* Greer Garson, Walter Pidgeon, Anges Moorehead, Donna Corcoran, Arthur Shields, Philip Ober, Rhys Williams, Margalo Gillmore, John Lupton, Philip Tonge

When a little girl accidentally starts a fire that destroys a Catholic orphanage, the nuns and their charges travel to seek homes for some of the children. They stop in a Scottish-Canadian province of Scourie, Ontario. The local priest Father Reilly (Arthur Shields) tells the nuns that most of the residents are Protestant. Patsy, the little girl who started the fire finds a home with the wife, Mrs. Victoria McChesney (Greer Garson), of the local shopkeeper and mayor with some controversy because they are Protestant.

**Scapegrace** *see* **Balarrasa**
**The Scarecrow of Romney Marsh** *see* **Dr. Syn, Alias the Scarecrow**

**741. The Scarlet and the Black**. CBS. (TV). Italy/US. 1983. 143m. C. *Producer:* Bill McCutchen *Director:* Jerry London *Writer:* J. P. Gallagher (book), David Butler *Cast:* Gregory Peck, Christopher Plummer, John Gielgud, Raf Vallone, Kenneth Colley, Walter Gotell, Barbara Bouchet, Julian Holloway, Angelo Infanti, Olga Karlatos

True story of Monsignor Hugh O'Flaherty (Gregory Peck) who hides downed pilots, escaped prisoners of war and Italian resistance families from the Nazi's from 1943–45. His diplomatic immunity prevents his arrest so the Nazi's decide to assassinate him. In order to continue his work, he must disguise himself.

**742. The Scarlet Letter**. Fox. US. 1917. B&W. *Director:* Carl Harbaugh *Writer:* Carl Harbaugh, Nathaniel Hawthorne (novel) *Cast:* Stuart Holmes, Mary Martin, Edward Hoyt, Robert Vivian, Dan Mason, Florence Ashbrook, Kittens Reichert

The classic tale of Hester Prynne (Mary Martin), the wife of the doctor who has disappeared. She falls in love with the village pastor Reverend Arthur Dimmesdale (Stuart Holmes) and bears his child, both keeping the secret since it would ruin his life. Hester must wear a scarlet A for years rather than reveal the secret. The husband returns, and the pastor tortured by guilt confesses to the congregation and dies. Nathaniel Hawthorne's novel has been filmed numerous times.

**743. The Scarlet Letter**. MGM. US. 1926. 98m. B&W. *Producer & Director:* Victor Sjöström *Writer:* Frances Marion, Nathaniel Hawthorne *Cast:* Lillian Gish, Lars

Hanson, Henry B. Walthall, Karl Dane, William H. Tooker, Marcelle Corday, Fred Herzog, Jules Cowles, Mary Hawes, Joyce Coad, James A. Marcus, Chief Yowlachie, Polly Moran

Another version of the classic tale of Hester Prynne (Lillian Gish) and Reverend Arthur Dimmesdale (Lars Hanson).

**744. The Scarlet Letter.** Buena Vista. US. 1995. 135m. C. *Producer*: Roland Joffé, Andrew G. Vajna *Director*: Roland Joffé *Writer*: Nathaniel Hawthorne (novel), Douglas Day Stewart *Cast*: Demi Moore, Gary Oldman, Robert Duvall, Lisa Joliffe-Andoh, Edward Hardwicke, Robert Prosky, Roy Dotrice, Joan Plowright, Malcolm Storry, James Bearden

Retelling of the classic story of Hester (Demi Moore) and Reverend Dimmesdale (Gary Oldman), only instead of Hawthorne's climax with the minister revealing his own scarlet letter carved on his flesh, an Indian raid ends the film and the lovers ride off happily into the sunrise.

**745. The Scarlet Sin.** Universal Film. US. 1915. B&W. *Director:* Otis Turner *Writer:* James Dayton, Olga Printzlau Clark *Cast*: Hobart Bosworth, Jane Novak, Hart Hoxie, Grace Thompson, Frank Elliott, Ed Brown, Wadsworth Harris, Helen Wright, Ed Clark

Reverend Eric Norton (Hobart Bosworth) leaves his position in a fashionable New York church to clean up a mining town. His bored wife leaves the minister and their child for an old lover. Trouble strikes the mines. Eric remarries thinking his wife has committed suicide. She appears and rescues their child from a fire and soon dies.

**746. Scene Nun, Take One.** Columbia. UK. 1964. 26m. *Producer*: Tim Pitt Miller, Maurice Hatton *Director*: Maurice Hatton *Writer*: Maurice Hatton, Michael Wood *Cast*: Susannah York

Film actress dresses as nun and has various adventures.

**747. Le Scomunicate di San Valentino.** Italy. 1973. C. *Producer*: Gino Mordini *Director*: Sergio Grieco *Writer*: Sergio Grieco, Max Vitali *Cast*: Françoise Prévost, Jenny Tamburi, Paolo Malco, Franco Ressel, Corrado Gaipa, Gino Rocchetti, Pier Giovanni

Anchisi, Calisto Calisti, Aldina Martano, Bruna Beani, Barbara Herrera, María Luisa Sala, Adriana Facchetti, Dada Gallotti, Cinzia Greco, Eleonora Spinellí, Attilio Dottesio, Teresa Passante, Carla Mancini

Lucita's family has had her locked away in a convent to keep her away from her lover, Esteban. Lucita and Esteban make plans to elope, but Esteban is accused of heresy before Lucita can escape. He seeks sanctuary in the convent where she is being held and discovered it is ruled by wicked Abbess. He must try to save Lucita before taking Orders and clear his own name before being captured and executed. Lucita is also arrested for murdering a fellow nun. Also known as *The Sinful Nuns of Saint Valentine.*

**The Sea** *see* **El Mar**

**748. Sea Wife.** TCF. UK. 1957. 82m. C. *Producer*: André Hakim *Director*: Bob McNaught *Writer*: George Burke, J. M. Scott (novel) *Cast*: Joan Collins, Richard Burton, Basil Sydney, Cy Grant, Ronald Squire, Harold Goodwin, Gibb McLaughlin, Roddy Hughes, Lloyd Lamble, Ronald Adams, Joan Hickson

Story of four survivors from a ship torpedoed doing World War II after it left Singapore. Biscuit (Richard Burton) is a RAF officer nicknamed because he is in charge of rations. Sea Wife (Joan Collins) is a nun nicknamed because she swims like a mermaid. Bulldog (Basil Sydney) is a ruthless businessman and Number Four (Cy Grant) named because he is the fourth person and the last person in the dinghy. Only Number Four knows of Sea Wife's true occupation. Biscuit starts to fall in love with Sea Wife but she is promised to another. They land on an island where Number Four builds a raft. Bulldog tricks Number Four and he is attacked by a shark. The three survivors are rescued. The film begins with Biscuit going on a hunt for Sea Wife by placing ads. We learn through flashbacks the story of the survivors. Bulldog is now in a mental hospital.

**The Seal of God** *see* **Das Siegel Gottes**

**Sealed Lips** *see* **The Silence of Dean Maitland**

**749. Sebastiane.** Libra Films. UK. 1976. 90m. C. *Producer*: Howard Malin,

James Whaley *Director:* Paul Humfress, Derek Jarman *Writer:* Paul Humfress, Derek Jarman, James Whaley *Cast:* Leonardo Treviglio, Barney James, Richard Warwick, Ken Hicks, Janusz Romanov, Neil Kennedy, Donald Dunham, Lindsay Kemp

Officer of the Imperial Guard, Sebastiane, is banished to a remote outpost of the Roman Empire by Emperor Diocletian, when he learns of Sebastiane's Christian sympathies. Sebastian spends most of the time tortured and haunted by the sexually advances of his commander. Little is known of this martyr and saint.

**The Secret Conclave** *see* **Gli Uomini non guardano il cielo**

**Secrets of a Women's Temple** *see* **Hiroku onnadera**

**750. See How They Run.** BL. UK. 1955. 84m. B&W. *Producer:* Bill Luckwell *Director:* Leslie Arliss *Writer:* Leslie Arliss, Philip King, Val Valentine *Cast:* Ronald Shiner, Greta Gynt, James Hayter, Wilfrid Hyde-White, Dora Bryan, Richard Wattis, Viola Lyel, Charles Farrell, Michael Brennan, Roddy Hughes, Ballard Berkeley

A British corporal seeking a promotion to fulfill will, poses as a vicar and catches a fugitive convict.

**751. La Señora de Fátima.** Suevia Films. Spain/Portugal. 1951. 90m. B&W. *Producer:* Aníbal Contreiras, Manuel J. Goyanes *Director:* Rafael Gil *Writer:* Vicente Escrivá, Fernando Garcia, Tibor Reves *Cast:* Inés Orsini, Fernando Rey, Tito Junco, Ángel Álvarez, Rafael Bardem, Francisco Bernal. Mario Berriatúa, Julia Caba Alba, Juan Espantaleón, María Rosa Salgado

The story takes place on Portugal and tells of the 1917 miracle of Fatima in which the Virgin Mary appears to three children (two girls and one boy).

**Serious Charge** *see* **Immoral Charge**

**752. The Servant.** BBC. (TV). UK. 1953. *Director:* Douglas Allen *Cast:* Pamela Alan, Peter Copley, John Glen, Marjorie Manning, Jonathan Meddings, Philip Ray, Arthur Young

The story of Joan of Arc.

**753. The Servant in the House.** FBO. US. 1920. B&W. *Producer:* H. O. Davis *Director:* Jack Conway *Writer:* Lanier Bartlett *Cast:* Jean Hersholt, Jack Curtis, Claire Anderson, Clara Horton, Edward Peil, Harvey Clark, Zenaide Williams, John Gilbert, Mrs. George Hernandez

Vicar William Smythe (Edward Peil) hopes to obtain funds to restore his church from his rich brother-in-law, the Bishop of Lancaster (Harvey Clark). Meanwhile Vicar Smythe's brother, the Bishop of Benares enters the house disguised as a servant named Manson. William's other brother has sacrificed much for the education of his brothers and received nothing in return. He is also bitter about the church because he blames it for the death of his wife. Through his generous spirit, Manson is able to bring the family together.

**754. Seven Cities of Gold.** TCF. US. 1955. 103m. C. *Producer:* Robert D. Webb, Barbara McLean *Director:* Robert D. Webb *Writer:* Richard L. Breen, John C. Higgins, Isabelle Gibson Ziegler (novel) *Cast:* Richard Egan, Anthony Quinn, Michael Rennie, Jeffrey Hunter, Rita Moreno, Eduardo Noriega, Leslie Bradley, John Doucette, Victor Junces, Pedro Galván

Story of Father Junipero Serra's (Michael Rennie) attempt at establishing a string of missions in California under early Spanish rule. The military and the Church end up in conflict during their journey from Mexico City to the California coast near the Bay of San Diego in the 1700's. Father Serra must overcome many hardships to establish his first mission.

**755. Seven Women.** MGM. US. 1966. 87m. C. *Producer:* Bernard Smith *Director:* John Ford *Writer:* Janet Green, John McCormick, Norah Lofts *Cast:* Anne Bancroft, Sue Lyon, Margaret Leighton, Flora Robson, Mildred Dunnock, Betty Field, Anna Lee, Eddie Albert, Mike Mazurki, Woody Strode, Jane Chang

In the 1930s, Tunga Khan and his bandits are terrorizing the isolated mission located near the Chinese border. Also in that area is a group of missionaries led by a woman. A cynical worldly female, Dr. Cartwright (Anne Bancroft), finds herself in conflict with the rigid mission's head Agatha

Andrews (Margaret Leighton) and soon must make great sacrifices to help the group survive the invasion of Tunga Khan.

**756. Seven Years in Tibet.** Columbia Tristar. US. 1997. 139m. C. *Producer*: Jean-Jacques Annaud, John H. Williams, Iain Smith *Director*: Jean-Jacques Annaud *Writer*: Heinrich Harrer (book), Becky Johnston *Cast*: Brad Pitt, David Thewlis, B. D. Wong, Mako, Danny Denzongpa, Victor Wong, Ingeborga Dapkunaite, Jamyang Jamtsho Wangchuk, Lhakpa Tsamchoe, Jetsun Pema

Heinrich Harrer (Brad Pitt) runs from trouble in World War II Austria to climb a mountain in the Himalayas. He and his fellow climber, Peter Aufschnaiter (David Thewlis) wind up to be the only two foreigners in the Tibetan Holy City of Lhasa. Heinrich's life changes when he becomes a close confidant to the Dalai Lama.

**757. The Seventh Commandment.** Crown International Pictures. US. 1960. 82m. B&W. *Producer & Director*: Irvin Berwick *Writer*: Jack Kevan, Irvin Berwick *Cast*: Jonathan Kidd, Lyn Statten, Frank Arvidson, John Harmon, Johnny Carpenter, Wendy Berwick, Wayne Berwick

Ted Mathews (Jonathan Kidd) and his girl friend Terry James are involved in a car accident in which Ted believes that he has killed the driver of the other car. He develops amnesia and wanders about until he is befriended by Reverend Noah Turnbull (Frank Arvidson), a traveling evangelist. Ted becomes a world-renowned preacher Reverend Tad Morgan. Learning of Ted's new identity Terry decides to blackmail him and then tricks him into a phony marriage. As Terry's demands increase Ted pushes her off a bridge and returns to his congregation. However, she survives the fall and mistakenly kills the wrong person. She becomes obsessed with killing Ted. Ted strangles her to death, goes to his tabernacle and suffers a fatal heart attack.

**758. Sexton Blake.** Gaumont. UK. 1909. B&W. *Director:* C. Douglas Carlile *Writer:* C. Douglas Carlile, W. Murray Graydon

Detective poses as a cleric to save squire's daughter from marrying murderer.

**759. Shadow on the Land.** ABC. (TV). US. 1968. 100m. C. *Producer*: Matthew Rapf *Director*: Richard C. Sarafian *Writer*: Nedrick Young *Cast*: Jackie Cooper, John Forsythe, Gene Hackman, Carol Lynley, Marc Strange, Janice Rule, Mike Margotta, Bill Walker, Scott Thomas, Myron Healey, Frederic Downs, Jonathan Lippe

The film attempts to show America under a totalitarian government. There is also a secret underground force battling a dictator and his henchmen. To continue ministering, the churches are also forced underground. Reverend Thomas Davis (Gene Hackman) sees to spiritual needs.

**760. Shadows.** Al Lichtman Corp. US. 1922. B&W. *Producer*: B. P. Schulberg *Director*: Tom Forman *Writer*: Wilbur Daniel Steele, Eve Unsell, Hope Loring *Cast*: Lon Chaney, Marguerite De La Motte, Harrison Ford, John Sainpolis, Walter Long, Buddy Messenger, Priscilla Bonner, Frances Raymond

John Malden (Harrison Ford) is the newly arrived minister to a small conservative fishing village. A brutal fishing fleet captain is lost at sea leaving his nice wife Sympathy (Marguerite De La Motte) to marry the new minister. Other suitors of the wife are very upset and one blackmails the minister by supposedly sending letters from the dead husband implying bigamy. Yen Sin (Lon Chaney), an immigrant Chinese laundry man who the minister befriended, solves the mystery of the blackmailer. Yen Sin expects John to take revenge on the man but instead John forgives the blackmailer. Yen Sin is overwhelmed by this sincere act and decides to convert to Christianity.

**761. Shanghai Surprise.** MGM. UK. 1986. 97m. C. *Producer*: John Kohn *Director*: Jim Goddard *Writer*: John Kohn, Robert Bentley, Tony Kenrick (novel) *Cast*: Sean Penn, Madonna, Paul Freeman, Richard Griffiths, Philip Sayer, Clyde Kusatsu, Kay Tong Lim, Sonserai Lee, Victor Wong

Missionary Gloria Tatlock (Madonna) enlists the down-and-out would-be adventurer Glendon Wasey (Sean Penn) to help her find opium which she will sell for medicine for the mission.

**762. Shao Lin ying xiong bang.** Shaw Bros. Hong Kong. 1979. 95m. C. *Producer:* Shaw Brothers *Director:* Meng-Hwa Ho *Writer:* Kuang Yi *Cast:* David Chiang, Lieh Lo, Li-Li Li, Shao-chiang Hsu, Kuan-chung Ku, Sze Wei, Pin-chang Pan, Yung Yu, Yin-charn Tang, Hang-sheng Wu, Jamie Luk

The Ching dynasty government wipes out Shaolin monks because they violated and order against having arms. One survivor Chi San (David Chiang) uses kung fu to get rid of his enemies. A nun (Li-Li Li) and Chih don't have much time for romance. Also known as *Shaolin Abbot.*

**Shaolin Abbot** *see* **Shao Lin ying xiong bang**

**763. Shattered Vows.** TV. US. 1984. 94m. C. *Producer:* Robert Lovenheim *Director:* Jack Bender *Writer:* Mary Gilligan Wong *Cast:* Valerie Bertinelli, David Morse, Caroline McWilliams, Tom Parsekian, Millie Perkins, Leslie Ackerman, Lisa Jane Persky, Elayne Heilveil, Patricia Neal, Matt Adler, Robert Clotworthy

During the 1960's, at the age of 16, Mary Gilligan (Valerie Bertinelli) becomes a nun. She faces demanding times at the convent. She never gets used to life in a convent and falls in love with a priest, Father Tim (David Morse). Her desire to raise a family overwhelms her so she leaves before taking her final vows. Based on a true story.

**764. Sheepdog of the Hills.** Butch. UK. 1941. 76m. B&W. *Producer:* F. W. Baker *Director:* Germain Burger *Writer:* Vera Allinson, Kathleen Butler *Cast:* David Farrar, Philip Friend, Helen Perry, Dennis Wyndham, Leonard Sharp, Jack Vyvian, Arthur Denton, Philip Godfrey, Johnnie Schofield

Village vicar of rural Devon, Reverend Michael Verney (David Farrar), is in love with a local woman. The vicar loses her to the new doctor Dr. Peter Hammond (Philip Friend). Reverend Verney adopts a evil farmer's sheepdog, who was trained to steal sheep.

**The Sheriff of Tombstone** *see* **Galloping Gallagher**

**765. The Shoes of the Fisherman.** MGM. US. 1968. 162m. C. *Producer:* George Englund *Director:* Michael Anderson *Writer:* James Kennaway, John Patrick, Morris L. West (novel) *Cast:* Anthony Quinn, Laurence Olivier, Oskar Werner, David Janssen, Vittorio De Sica, Leo McKern, John Gielgud, Barbara Jefford, Rosemarie Dexter, Frank Finlay

Kiril Lakota (Anthony Quinn), an archbishop of the Russian Catholic Church, is released from a Siberian prison camp after being held for twenty years as a political prisoner. Soviet Premier Piotr Lylich Kamenev (Laurence Olivier) hopes to establish a Russian influence in Rome. Lakota is made a cardinal by the Pope, hoping to bridge the East West gap. Soon the Pope dies and against his will Lakota is named Pope. Lakota chooses the name Pope Kiril I, first non-Italian pope in 400 years. He is befriended by a younger troubled priest Father David Telemond (Oskar Werner). The new Pope dons normal priest clothes and travels around Rome. He is brought back to the Vatican and soon journeys to Mongolia to meet with the Chinese. He pledges to help the poor and back at the Vatican he offers the Church's wealth to the hungry.

**766. Shooting Straight.** RKO. US. 1930. 72m. B&W. *Director:* George Archainbaud *Writer:* J. Walter Ruben, Barney A. Sarecky *Cast:* Richard Dix, Mary Lawlor, James Neill, Mathew Betz, George Cooper, William Janney, Robert Emmett O'Connor, Clarence Wertz, Eddie Sturgis, Dick Curtis

City gambler Larry Sheldon (Richard Dix) is sharing a Pullman section with Mr. Walters, an evangelist when the train is wrecked. He later awakes as the guest of Reverend Powell (James Neill) who has mistaken him for Mr. Walters; he keeps his identity a secret. He is attracted to the minister's daughter. His true identity is discovered and his innocence in a murder is proven. Larry gets the girl and goes straight.

**767. Das Siegel Gottes.** Casino Film Exchange. Austria. 1949. 87m. B&W. *Producer:* Walter Tjaden *Director:* Alfred Stöger *Writer:* Alexander Lix, Peter Rosegger (novel) *Cast:* Josef Meinard, Hilde Mikulicz, Alexander Trojan, Hugo Gottschlich, Robert Lindner, Karl Günther, Elisabeth Markus

A priest knows all about a crime but cannot tell anyone because he is bound by his oath. Also known as *The Seal of God*.

**768. Signs.** Buena Vista. US. 2002. 106m. C. *Producer:* Frank Marshall, Sam Mercer, M. Night Shyamalan *Director & Writer:* M. Night Shyamalan *Cast:* Mel Gibson, Joaquin Phoenix, Rory Culkin, Abigail Breslin, Cherry Jones, Patricia Kalember, M. Night Shyamalan

Widower Graham Hess (Mel Gibson), an Episcopalian minister who loses his faith after the sudden death of his wife, finds crop circles on his Pennsylvanian farm. He lives on the farm with his two children and his brother. The dramatic focal point is Hess' loss of faith in God because of his wife's death in a car accident. Initially, he dismisses the crop circles as a hoax that is until strange things start happening world-wide. During the alien invasion, Hess regains his faith in God. He and his family survive the alien attack. Hollywood never seems to make a film about someone who loses their faith and does not get it back by the end.

**769. The Silence of Dean Maitland.** World Film Corp. US. 1915. B&W. *Director:* John Ince *Writer:* Frank Condon *Cast:* William Courtenay, Arthur Ashley, Mary Charleson, Adele Ray, Marie E. Wells, Edward N. Hoyt

Minister Cyril Maitland (Arthur Ashley) confesses at the pulpit of his past sins-leading an innocent girl astray and the killing of her father. Another man went to prison for his crimes. After serving nearly 20 years of imprisonment, the man came to Dean Maitland and forgave him. Maitland is going to turn himself and serve his time. Also known as *Sealed Lips*.

**770. Simón del desierto.** Altura Films. Mexico. 1965. 40m. B&W. *Producer:* Gustavo Alatriste *Director:* Luis Buñuel *Writer:* Julio Alejandro, Luis Buñuel *Cast:* Claudio Brook, Silvia Pinal, Hortensia Santovaña, Jesús Fernández, Enrique Álvarez Félix, Enrique del Castillo, Luis Aceves Castañeda, Francisco Reiguera, Antonio Bravo

Film deals with the temptations of 5th century Saint Simeon Stylite of Antioch (Claudio Brook), who withdrew from the world to commune with God atop a pillar in the desert for about 27 years, it is said. A temptress shows her breasts to him, an evil priest tempts Simon with food, homosexuality is suggested by a young monk, and other temptations are all rejected by Simon. Also known as *St. Simon of the Desert*.

**771. Simple Simon.** Hepworth. UK. 1922. B&W. *Director:* Henry Edwards *Writer:* Henry Edwards, Walter Courtenay Rowden *Cast:* Henry Edwards, Chrissie White, Mary Dibley, Hugh Clifton, Henry Vibart, Esme Hubbard, E. C. Matthews

Falsely accused monk flirts with authoress but realizes he loves islander.

**772. The Sin That Was His.** Select Pictures. US. 1920. B&W. *Producer & Director:* Hobart Henley *Writer:* Edmund Goulding *Cast:* William Faversham, Lucy Cotton, Pedro de Cordoba, Miss Sherman, Lulu Warrenton, Robert Conville, John Barton

Former priest and now gambler Raymond Chapelle (William Faversham) is asked by a dying friend to bring a bag of gold to his mother. While traveling to the mother, he meets Father Aubert (Pedro de Cordoba). During a storm another son tries to take the money from Raymond but is shot by the mother. Raymond escapes and finds the priest felled by a tree. Raymond takes his clothes and pretends to be a priest. The real priest has lost his memory and is blamed for the shooting. Raymond feels extreme guilt for his impersonation and confesses to a Bishop. Eventually the dying mother confesses to the shooting.

**The Sinful Nuns of St. Valentine** *see* **Le Scomunicate di San Valentino**

**773. The Singer Not the Song.** Warner. UK. 1961. 132m. C. *Producer:* Roy Ward Baker, Jack Hanbury *Director:* Roy Ward Baker *Writer:* Nigel Balchin, Audrey Erskine-Lindop (novel) *Cast:* Dirk Bogarde, John Mills, Mylène Demongeot, Laurence Naismith, John Bentley, Leslie French, Eric Pohlmann, Nyall Florenz, Roger Delgardo, Laurence Payne, Lee Montague

In an isolated Mexican village bandit Anacleto (Dirk Bogarde) kills villagers alphabetically to spite the newly arrived Irish priest, Father Keogh (John Mills), who secretly loves a landowner's daughter. Unbeknownst to the priest, Anacleto has forbidden church services. When Father Keogh says mass, Anacleto starts the killing. Keogh doesn't back down and Anacleto offers him a deal- determine which inspires goodness "the singer" (the priest) or "the song" (religion). When Anacleto learns of the attraction between Father Keogh and the girl, he puts the priest in a moral dilemma.

**774. The Singing Nun.** MGM. US. 1966. 98m. C. *Producer:* John Beck *Director:* Henry Koster *Writer:* John Furia, Sally Benson *Cast:* Debbie Reynolds, Ricardo Montalban, Greer Garson, Agnes Moorehead, Chad Everett, Katharine Ross, Ed Sullivan, Juanita Moore, Ricky Cordell, Michael Pate, Tom Drake.

Belgian Dominican nun Sister Ann (Debbie Reynolds) becomes involved with helping little Dominic (Ricky Cordell) and his sister Nicole (Katharine Ross). Meanwhile Father Clementi (Ricardo Montalban) hears Sister Ann singing and enters her into a talent contest against the wishes of Mother Prioress (Greer Garson). A record deal comes her way as well as an old boyfriend. Sister Ann is unprepared for her new found fame. At first she doesn't embrace a musical career. After a series of actions that alienate the local people, she realizes that perhaps music is her way to make a contribution and share God's gift with others. Soon she finds herself on the Ed Sullivan show. Sister Ann is a good-hearted nun struggling with her commitment to religious life. Her experiences create personal crises whenever she is drawn into the world. A personal crisis develops when Dominic is hit by a car. The experience shocks her into the realization that she really wants to be a missionary nun rather than a singer. At the conclusion, she

Belgian Dominican nun Sister Ann (Debbie Reynolds) performs for Father Clementi (Ricardo Montalban), Mother Prioress (Greer Garson; in all-white at left front) and the other sisters, in *The Singing Nun* (1966).

follows her feelings and becomes a missionary in Africa. This film is based on the real-life of a nun turned recording artist. She gave up her habit to pursue a singing career, which didn't take off. She then failed at running a school for autistic children. Unfortunately, the she eventually committed suicide.

**775. Sister Act.** Buena Vista. US. 1992. 100m. C. *Producer:* Teri Schwartz *Director:* Emile Ardolino *Writer:* Joseph Howard *Cast:* Whoopi Goldberg, Maggie Smith, Kathy Najimy, Wendy Makkena, Mary Wickes, Harvey Keitel, Bill Nunn, Robert Miranda, Ellen Albertini Dow, Carman Zapata, Pat Crawford Brown

When lounge singer Deloris Van Cartier (Whoopi Goldberg) witnesses her Mafia boyfriend killing someone, she winds up in the witness protection program. The police hide her in one place that her boyfriend would never look a convent and in conflict with the Mother Superior (Maggie Smith). Soon she becomes Sister Mary Clarence. Against the wishes of Mother Superior, Sister Mary Clarence is assigned to the convent's choir. She soon makes friends with Sister Mary Robert (Wendy Makkena), Sister Mary Lazarus (Mary Wickes), and Sister Mary Patrick (Kathy Najimy). She ends up coaching the choir and making it a big success. Followed by *Sister Act 2: Back in the Habit.*

**776. Sister Act 2: Back in the Habit.** Buena Vista. US. 1993. 107m. C. *Producer:* Scott Rudin, Dawn Steel *Director:* Bill Duke *Writer:* Joseph Howard, James Orr, Jim Cruickshank, Judi Ann Mason *Cast:* Whoopi Goldberg, Kathy Najimy, Barnard Hughes, Mary Wickes, James Coburn, Michael Jeter, Wendy Makkena, Sheryl Lee Ralph, Robert Pastorelli, Thomas Gottschalk, Maggie Smith

The sisters ask Deloris Van Cartier/Sister Mary Clarence (Whoopi Goldberg) to once again don the nun's habit to teach music in their parochial school, presided over by Mother Superior (Maggie Smith), which is doomed for closure. The choir has made it to the state championship, but the most talented girl's mother has forbidden her to sing.

**777. Sister Angelica.** Pathé Frères. France. 1909. B&W.

Story of a long ago tale of a nun and a warrior. The warrior who had been a lover of the nun before she became a nun has been wounded in battle. He sends a message to the nun that he wants to see her. She gets the message and admits to the Mother Superior that she is torn about what to do. The Mother Superior tells her she cannot go. She is in turmoil about what to do when the figure of the Virgin Mary comes to life and tells her to go. The Virgin takes her place at the altar and assumes her place. The nun goes to the warrior and stays with him until he dies. She returns to the convent and the Virgin Mary becomes a statue once again.

**Sister of Mercy** *see* **La Petite soeur des pauvres**

**Sisters of Satan** *see* **Le Monache di Sant'Arcangelo**

**Skid Road** *see* **Journey into Light**

**778. The Sky Pilot.** First National. US. 1921. B&W. *Producer:* Catherine Curtis *Director:* King Vidor *Writer:* Faith Green, John McDermott, Ralph Conner (novel) *Cast:* John Bowers, Colleen Moore, David Butler, Harry Todd, James Corrigan, Donald MacDonald, Kathleen Kirkham

Tale of a college-bred young minister (John Bowers) assigned to a ranch community. In this story the heroine is pronounced a cripple who will never walk again. She is faced with the task of rescuing the minister from a burning building. She drags herself to where he is lying, pulls herself to an upright position and drags him out. His first service is in the saloon. When the ranch foreman shows his disapproval of the sermon, the minister gives him a thrashing.

**779. Sleepers.** Warner. US. 1996. 147m. C. *Producer:* Steve Golin, Barry Levinson *Director:* Barry Levinson *Writer:* Lorenzo Carcaterra (book), Barry Levinson *Cast:* Brad Pitt, Jason Patric, Joseph Perrino, Brad Renfro, Geoffrey Wigdor, Jonathan Tucker, Robert De Niro, Kevin Bacon, Billy Crudup, Ron Eldard, Dustin Hoffman, Terry Kinney, Minnie Driver, Vittorio Gassman, Bruno Kirby

Four boys growing up in New York's Hell's Kitchen during the 1960's are sent to Wilkinson Home for the Boys when a prank goes deadly. While imprisoned they are raped repeatedly and tortured by the guards. Later, as adults they are connected by that shame. When two of the men see one of their old tormentors they shoot him. One of the boys is now an assistant DA and will makes every attempt so they will walk. Father Bobby (Robert De Niro) is a tough guy priest who drinks, smokes and threatens. He knew the men as kids and lies on the stand to help them.

**780. The Small Miracle.** NBC. (TV). US. 1973. 73m. C. *Director:* Jeannot Szwarc *Writer:* Paul Gallico *Cast:* Vittorio de Sica, Raf Vallone, Marco Della Cava, Guidarini Guidi, Jan Larsson

A young boy Pepino (Marco Della Cava) believes that St. Francis of Assisi will cure his hurt donkey. Father Superior (Raf Vallone) will not allow the donkey into the church so the boy travels to get the Pope's permission. Kindly Father Damico (Vittorio de Sica) is his only hope. Based on a story by Paul Gallico and previously filmed as *Never Take No for an Answer.*

**781. Smith's Wives.** Fox British. UK. 1935. 59m. B&W. *Producer:* Ernest Gartside *Director:* H. Manning Haynes *Writer:* Con West, Herbert Sargent, James Darnley (play) *Cast:* Ernie Lotinga, Beryl de Querton, Tyrell Davis, Richard Ritchie, Kay Walsh, Jean Gillie, Vashti Taylor

Bookie and parson, Reverend James Smith (Richard Ritchie), both named Smith, live in opposite flats.

**782. Il Sole di Montecassino.** Harris-Wolper. Italy. 1945. 87m. *Director:* Giuseppe Maria Scotese *Writer:* Diego Fabbri, Giovanna Soria, Giuseppe Maria Scotese, Arnaldo Genoino, Glorgia Lastricato, Mario Monocelli *Cast:* Fosco Giachetti, Nino Pavese, Alfredo Varelli, Liliane Laine, Manoel Roero, Adriana Benetti, Virgilio Tomassini, Anna Maria Padoan

The film is based on the life of St. Benedict, founder of the Benedictine order and the Benedictine Monastery at Monte Cassino. Benedict da Norca (Fosco Giachetti), a member of a rich family in Rome, dedicates his life to prayer and helping the poor. Also known as *Fear No Evil.*

**Some Kind of Saint** *see* **Ein Komischer Heiliger**

**783. Somewhere in France.** YCC. UK. 1915. B&W. *Director:* Tom Watts *Writer:* Ruby M. Ayres *Cast:* Vera Cornish

Soldier poses as a priest to save wife from Uhlan.

**784. A Son of David.** Walturdaw. UK. 1920. B&W. *Producer:* Walter West *Director:* Hay Plumb *Writer:* Benedict James, Charles Barnett *Cast:* Poppy Wyndham, Ronald Colman, Arthur Walcott, Constance Backner, Robert Vallis, Joseph Pacey, Vesta Sylva

Rabbi adopts orphan Maurice Phillips (Ronald Coleman), who becomes boxer and fights man he thinks killed his father. He learns that his father died of a heart-attack.

**785. The Song and the Silence.** Cloverhouse Films. US. 1969. 80m. B&W. *Producer, Director & Writer*: Nathan Cohen *Cast*: Harry Rubin, Jim Murphy, Nana Austin, Mary Antoinette, Jonathon Scott, Harry Leshner, Felix Fiebich

In 1939 a group of Hasidic Jews are living in a small Polish community. Rabbi Shlomo (Harry Rubin) is apprehensive about his son, but delighted for the love his daughter has for Fievi (Jim Murphy), a rabbinical student. Fievi consents to marry the rabbi's daughter. Without warning the Nazi's arrive and shoot the members of the community.

**786. Song for a Raggy Boy.** Lolafilms/Subotica Entertainment. Ireland/Denmark/UK/Spain. 2003. 100m. C. *Producer*: Tristan Lynch, Dominic Wright, John McDonnell, Kevin Byron Murphy *Director*: Aisling Walsh *Writer*: Patrick Galvin, Aisling Walsh, Kevin Byron Murphy *Cast*: Aidan Quinn, Iain Glen, Marc Warren, Dudley Sutton, Alan Devlin, Stuart Graham, John Travers, Chris Newman

After returning to Ireland in 1939, William Franklin (Aidan Quinn) takes a teaching job as the only non-cleric on staff at St. Jude's, an Irish Catholic reform school for boys. He disagrees with Brother John's (Iain Glen) strict disciplinarian style and befriends the boys and in particular student Liam Mercier (John Travers). He intervenes to stop Brother John's viscous punishment and tries to instill a sense of achievement, self-worth and future possibility in the boys. One boy confesses to having been raped by Brother Mac (Marc Warren). Based on an autobiographical account of Patrick Galvin's life at an Irish Catholic reform school.

**787. The Song of Bernadette.** TCF. US. 1943. 156m. B&W. *Producer:* William Perlberg *Director:* Henry King *Writer:* Franz Werfel (novel), George Seaton *Cast:* William Eythe, Charles Bickford, Vincent Price, Lee J. Cobb, Gladys Cooper, Anne Revere, Roman Bohnen, Mary Anderson, Patricia Morison, Aubrey Mather, Jennifer Jones, Charles Dingle

Bernadette Soubirous (Jennifer Jones) is a French peasant whose visionary experience at Lourdes in 1858 resulted in the cre-ation of one of the greatest pilgrim shrines. Linda Darnell (pregnant at the time) played the Virgin Mary. No one else sees the Virgin Mary but Bernadette and soon word of the vision begins to spread. Some of the townspeople see her as an idiot and a fraud. Water at the spring is found to have curing powers. A commission is formed to investigate the miracles and the grotto is kept open. Bernadette is vindicated and she becomes a novice and accepts a hard life. Bernadette, on her death bed from tuberculosis, sees the Virgin for the last time. The film won four Oscars, including one for Jennifer Jones.

**The Song of Sister Maria** *see* **Sor intrépida**

**788. Sor intrépida.** Master Films. Spain. 1953. 85m. B&W. *Producer:* Manuel J. Goyanes *Director:* Rafael Gil *Writer:* Vicente Escrivá, Ramón D. Faraldo *Cast:* Dominique Blanchar, Julia Caba Alba, José Nieto, Margarita Robles, Francisco Rabel

The crowds grow when they learn that Bernadette Soubirous (Jennifer Jones) has had a visionary experience at Lourdes, in *The Song of Bernadette* (1943).

Trials and tribulations of successful singer turned nun Sister Maria (Domnique Blanchar). She sings six records in order to raise money for the Order, teaches a paralytic boy to walk, redeems a cynic on his deathbed, and convinces a rich aunt to leave her money to the church. Also known as *The Song of Sister Maria.*

**Sorceress** *see* **Le Moine et la sorcière**

**Il Sorriso del grande tentatore** *see* **The Devil Is a Woman**

**789. The Sorrows of Love.** Triangle. US. 1916. B&W. *Producer*: Thomas H. Ince *Director*: Charles Giblyn *Writer*: Elaine Sterne, J. G. Hawks *Cast*: Bessie Barriscale, William Desmond, Ora Carew, Herschel Mayall, Wedgwood Nowell

In Italy, Sister Beatrice (Bessie Barriscale) becomes the confidante of the Contessa Angelica de Vecchio (Ora Carew). Her brother has placed her in the convent for having an affair with a radical. When Angela dies, Beatrice leaves the convent and joins a group of revolutionaries and marries one of its leaders. When she hears of a plan to rise up against Angelica's brother Beatrice alerts him. Her husband is killed during the fighting, but before he dies he forgives Beatrice for betraying him. Beatrice returns to the convent.

**790. Souls Aflame.** First Division. US. 1928. 60m. B&W. *Producer*: James Ormont *Director*: Raymond Wells *Writer*: Raymond Wells, Jack Kelly *Cast*: Gardner James, Buddy Barton, Raymond Wells, Edward Lackey, Gael Kelton

A feud between the Bucks and the Lillys begins over the death of a Lilly by five Bucks, who are acquitted of the crime because they are Bucks. The son of the dead Lilly becomes a preacher and wants peace in the mountains. He falls in love with a Buck girl and is beaten up by the Bucks for enticing her to the church. His mother and kin decide to wipe out the Bucks. After a terrible fight the Bucks are killed and the Buck girl refuses to continue the feud and marries the preacher.

**791. Souls in Conflict.** Great Commission. UK. 1955. 75m. C. *Producer*: Billy Graham, Dick Ross *Director*: Dick Ross *Writer*: Dick Ross, Leonard Reeve *Cast*: Billy Graham, Colleen Townsend, Joan Winmill Brown, Eric Micklewood, Charles Leno, Hilda Fenemore, Frederick Leister, Neal Arden, Daphne Abbott

American evangelist (Billy Graham) converts vicar's daughter, test pilot, and factory hand.

**792. The Sound of Music.** TCF. US. 1965. 174m. C. *Producer & Director*: Robert Wise *Writer*: Ernest Lehman, Maria Augusta Trapp (book) *Cast*: Julie Andrews, Christopher Plummer, Eleanor Parker, Richard Haydn, Peggy Wood, Charmian Carr, Heather Menzies, Nicholas Hammond, Duane Chase, Angela Cartwright, Debbie Turner, Kym Karath, Anna Lee, Portia Nelson, Ben Wright, Daniel Truhitte, Norma Varden, Gilchrist Stuart, Marni Nixon, Evadne Baker

Musical adaptation of the life of Maria von Trapp. Set in the 1930s when the Nazis are just beginning to occupy Austria. Tells the story of Maria (Julie Andrews), a novice at the abbey in Salzburg, and her adventures as a governess to the seven motherless von Trapp children and her eventual romance and marriage to their father. Mother Abbess (Peggy Wood) is very understanding and supportive of Maria. At the beginning Maria finds the father, a retired naval officer, to be a strong disciplinarian and the children to be hostile, but she eventually wins them all over. After their marriage the sisters at the abbey help the von Trapp family escape from the Nazis, who want the Captain to serve in their navy.

**793. Sous le soleil de Satan.** Alive Films. France. 1987. 93m. C. *Director*: Maurice Pialat *Writer*: Sylvie Danton, Maurice Pialat, Georges Bernanos (novel) *Cast*: Gérard Depardieu, Maurice Pialat, Sandrine Bonnaire, Alain Artur, Yann Deder, Brigitte Legendre, Jean-Claude Bourlat, Jean-Christophe Bouvet, Philippe Pallat, Marcel Anselin

Young priest Donissan (Gérard Depardieu) is consumed with an agony of self-double and fears that he is losing the struggle against Satan. One of his parishioners is a neurotic teenager Mouchette (Sandrine Bonnaire) who is also agonized by life and passions. She kills her wealthy lover and turns to another lover, a doctor, for an abortion. He refuses and she turns to the priest for guidance. He is unable to help her and eventually she kills herself. Even when he is transferred to another parish, he continues to be tormented. His health declines and he prays asking God to let him live longer. He dies very soon while hearing a confession. Also known as *Under Satan's Sun.*

**794. La Sposa bella.** MGM. Italy/US. 1960. 99m. B&W. *Producer*: Goffredo Lombardo *Director*: Nunnally Johnson *Writer*: Bruce Marshall (novel), Nunnally Johnson, Giorgio Prosperi *Cast*: Ava Gardner, Dirk Bogarde, Joseph Cotton, Vittorio De Sica, Aldo Fabrizi, Arnoldo Foa, Finlay Currie, Rosanna Rory, Enrico Maria Salerno

During the Spanish Civil War a voluntarily defrocked priest Arturo Carrera (Dirk Bogarde) travels to Spain to join the Loyalist side and finds himself attracted to Soledad (Ava Gardner) an entertainer/prostitute. He is being hunted by the leftist and anti-fascist fighters. He is trapped by forces trying to obtain a holy relic. Also known as *The Angel Wore Red.*

**Spring, Summer, Fall, Winter…and Spring** *see* **Bom yeoreum gaeul gyeoul geurigo bom**

**795. Squeeze a Flower.** BEF Film. Australia. 1970. 102m. C. *Producer*: George Willoughby, Howard G. Barnes, Bill Harmon *Director*: Marc Daniels *Writer*: Charles Isaacs *Cast*: Walter Chiari, Jack Albertson, Dave Allen, Rowena Wallace, Kirrily Nolan, Alec Kellaway, Michael Lawrence, Alan Tobin, Charles McCallum, Harry Lawrence, Franz Zavier Zach, Ricky Cilona, Roger Ward, Alex Mozart, Sandy Harbutt, Amanda Irving, Jeff Ashby, Penny Sugg, Sue Lloyd, Barry Crocker, Lea Denfield, Pat Sullivan, Beryl Cheers

Monk Brother George (Walter Chiari) knows the secret ingredients to an exotic liquor. When the abbot orders him to reveal the secret he flees to Australia where he goes into partnership with Alfredo Brazzi (Jack Albertson) who is unaware that he is a monk. Brother George is sending his share of the money back to his monastery. Most of the film deals with Brazzi and his son-in-law trying to obtain the secret formula from the monk.

**796. Stanley and Livingstone.** TCF. US. 1939. 101m. B&W. *Producer*: Darryl F. Zanuck *Director*: Henry King *Writer*: Hal Long, Sam Hellman, Philip Dunne, Julien Josephson *Cast*: Spencer Tracy, Nancy Kelly, Richard Greene, Walter Brennan, Charles Coburn, Cedric Hardwicke, Henry Hull, Henry Travers, Miles Mander, David Torrence, Holmes Herbert, C. Montague Shaw, Brandon Hurst, Hassan Said, Paul Harvey, Russell Hicks, Frank Dae

American newspaperman and adventurer Henry M. Stanley (Spencer Tracy) is sent to Africa by his editor to find Dr. David Livingstone (Cedric Hardwicke), the missing Scottish missionary. He finds Dr. Livingstone in a native village practicing medicine and preaching the gospel. Back in London, Stanley prints his findings creating a world sensation with his stories of Livingstone. However, the British Geographical Society refuses to accept Stanley's evidence. Word comes that Livingstone has died of a fever and as his last request he asks that Stanley carry on with his work. Stanley resigns from his job and returns to Africa.

**The Star and the Cross** *see* **Hand in Hand**

**Star Knight** *see* **El Caballero del dragón**

**797. Stars in My Crown.** Metro. US. 1950. 89m. B&W. *Producer*: William H. Wright *Director*: Jacques Tourneur *Writer*: Margaret Fitts, Joe David Brown (novel) *Cast*: Joel McCrea, Ellen Drew, Dean Stockwell, Alan Hale, Lewis Stone, James Mitchell, Amanda Blake, Juano Hernandez, Charles Kemper, Connie Gilchrist, narrated by Marshall Thompson, Ed Begley

Upon his arrival in a small Tennessee town just after the Civil War, Parson Josiah Doziah Grey (Joel McCrea) begins preaching to the townspeople. His first sermon is held in the saloon with gun in hand. He leads an effort so build the town's first church and marries the church organist. A recent medical graduate Daniel is planning to leave town because townspeople don't accept his modern ways. Typhoid strikes the town and Daniel asks Josiah to quarantine himself because he may be spreading the illness. Faith, the love of Daniel, is struck by the illness. Daniel can't help her but Josiah cures her with prayer. Daniel now becomes a believer. Josiah also with prayer saves an innocent man from an angry mob.

**798. State of Wonder.** UK. 1984. 113m. C. *Producer, Director & Writer:* Martin Donovan *Cast:* Nigel Court, David Meyer, Tony Meyer, James Telfer, Annie Chaplin, Martin Donovan, Barrie Smith, Tony Edridge, Anja Schute, Michael Halphie, David Capri

In a tiny Irish village, the village simpleton Pichirica (Nigel Court) mistakes the leader of a peace activist group for Jesus (Tony Meyer). While, a group of soldiers are looking for members of a militant peace movement. Local priest Father Daniel (Martin Donovan) is first seen writing his sermon and listening to trendy music on his Walkman. Father Daniel is also devoted to rehearsing a local song for the finals of the Eurovision Song Contest.

**799. The Stealers.** Robertson-Cole Distributing. US. 1920. B&W. *Director & Writer:* William Christy Cabanne *Cast:* William H. Tooker, Robert Kenyon, Myrtle Morse, Norma Shearer, Ruth Dwyer, Walter Miller, Eugene Borden, Jack Crosby, Matthew Betz, John O'Brien, Downing Clarke

The film begins with a traveling preacher Reverend Robert Martin (William H. Tooker) who is really just a cover for a gang of crooks. While he preaches they steal. His daughter Julia discovers what her father does and confronts him. His explanation is that he steals because God cheated him in his youth. He loses his sight. Steve, part of the gang, gets arrested and is sent away. Mary, also a member of the gang, reforms and marries a rich young man. Steve reforms and leaves Mary to her husband. The preacher's eyesight is restored when his runaway wife appears.

**800. Stealing Heaven.** Scotti Brothers. UK/Yugoslavia. 1989. 115m. C. *Producer:* Simon MacCorkindale *Director:* Clive Donner *Writer:* Chris Bryant, Marion Meade

(novel) *Cast:* Patsy Byrne, Kenneth Cranham, Derek de Lint, Denholm Elliott, Bernard Hepton, Mark Jax, Rachel Kempson, Angela Pleasence, Kim Thompson

Abelard (Derek de Lint), director of the cathedral school at Notre Dame, falls in love with Heloise (Kim Thompson) despite his vow of chastity. Her uncle, however, has plans to marry her into money. Her uncle takes revenge with the approval of the Bishop of Paris by having Ableard castrated. Abelard becomes a monk and Heloise becomes a nun. Their love continues on a platonic level and from a distance. They are reunited before they die.

**Stephen** *see* **Esthappan**

**801. Stigmata.** MGM. US. 1999. 103m. C. *Producer:* Frank Mancuso Jr. *Director:* Rupert Wainwright *Writer:* Tom Lazarus, Rick Ramage *Cast:* Patricia Arquette, Gabriel Byrne, Jonathan Pryce, Nia Long, Thomas Kopache, Rade Serbedzija, Enrico Colantoni, Dick Latessa, Portia de Rossi, Patrick Muldoon, Ann Cusack, Shaun Toub

Father Andrew Kiernan (Gabriel Byrne) is sent by the Vatican to investigate claims that a small town church in Brazil has a statue that bleeds from the eyes. After he returns, he is sent to investigate Frankie Paige (Patricia Arquette), who may be experiencing the stigmata.

**802. The Stolen Sacrifice.** Gerrard. UK. 1916. B&W. *Director & Writer:* Sidney Morgan *Cast:* Peggy Richards

Detective saves girl, who attempted suicide, from being sacrificed by priest of an Indian sect.

**803. Stolen Summer.** Miramax. US. 2002. 91m. C. *Producer:* Matt Damon, Ben Afleck, Chris Moore *Director & Writer:* Pete Jones *Cast:* Aidan Quinn, Bonnie Hunt, Kevin Pollak, Adiel Stein, Mike Weinberg, Eddie Kaye Thomas, Brian Dennehy

The story is told through the eyes of an 8-year-old Catholic boy named Pete O'Malley (Adiel Stein). At the end of the school year a nun tells him to pursue God's path, which he takes literally and embarks on a quest to convert Jews to Catholicism. The rabbi's son Danny Jacobsen (Michael Weinberg), who's in remission from leukemia, seems to be the perfect candidate for conversion. The parish priest Father Kelly (Brian Dennehy) instructs the boy that certain tests are required before admission into heaven, so Pete devises a trial for Danny. Pete's fireman dad Joe (Aidan Quinn) disapproves and orders Danny to stop bothering the rabbi's family. Rabbi Jacobsen (Kevin Pollak) creates further hostility when he rewards the fireman's bravery in saving Danny from a fire, the Jewish community selects his eldest son for a medical scholarship, which he is too proud to accept.

**804. A Strange Meeting.** Biograph Co. US. 1909. 11m. B&W. *Director*: D. W. Griffith *Writer*: D. W. Griffith, Stanner E.V. Taylor *Cast*: Charles Avery, Kate Bruce, John R. Cumpson, Arthur V. Johnson, James Kirkwood, Florence La Badie, Stephanie Longfellow, Wilfed Lucas, Owen Moore, Anthony O'Sullivan, Lottie Pickford, Mary Pickford, Frank Powell, Billy Quirk, Mack Sennett, George Siegmann, Henry B. Walthall, Dorothy West

A good preacher Reverend John Stanton (Arthur V. Johnson) tries to rescue a fallen young woman Mary Rollins (Stephanie Longfellow) from a saloon. She must decide between remaining a thief and doing the right thing. When fellow thieves break into the preacher's home, the preacher discovers them. She stops the thieves from shooting him. Mary continues her wicked ways until she goes to church to see the preacher to return the watch that was stolen. He offers her a bible and she accepts it.

**805. Stranger at My Door.** Republic. US. 1956. 85m. B&W. *Director*: William Witney *Writer*: Barry Shipman *Cast*: Macdonald Carey, Patricia Medina, Skip Homeier, Stephen Wootton, Louis Jean Heydt, Howard Wright, Slim Pickens, Malcolm Atterbury

Outlaw Clay Anderson (Skip Homeier) and his gang rob a bank and then flee in separate directions. Clay's horse goes lame and he is forced to hide at a nearby farm. He soon discovers that the place belongs to country preacher Hollis Jarret (Macdonald Carey), his second wife Peg (Patricia Medina), and his son Dodie (Stephen Wootton).

Clay, posing as a weary traveler, tries to hide his identity to secure a hideout at the farm for a few days. Reverend Jarret knows exactly what is going on but he agrees to allow Clay to remain at the farm for a few days. Jarret welcomes the chance to convince Clay to reform and convert.

**806. A Stranger in the Kingdom.** Ardustry Home Entertainment. US. 1998. 112m. C. *Producer & Director*: Jay Craven *Writer*: Howard Frank Mosher (novel) *Cast*: David Lansbury, Ernie Hudson, Martin Sheen, Bill Raymond, Sean Nelson, Jean Louise Kelly, Jordan Bayne, Henry Gibson, Carrie Snodgress, Rusty De Wees, Larry Pine, Michael Ryan Segal, George Dickerson

During the 1950's the service record of former Army chaplain Walter Andrews (Ernie Hudson) make such an impression on a Vermont town that they hire him as minister over the telephone. The townspeople are shocked to find out he is black. Despite some initial resistance, he becomes accepted by the people. When young Claire LaRivierre is found murdered, Andrew becomes a suspect because he had sheltered the girl.

**807. Strictly Illegal.** Gaumont. UK. 1935. 69m. B&W. *Producer*: Joe Rock *Director*: Ralph Ceder *Writer*: Syd Courtenay, Georgie Harris, Herbert Sargent (play), Con West (play) *Cast*: Leslie Fuller, Betty Astell, Georgie Harris, Cissy Fitzgerald, Glennis Lorimer, Mickey Brantford, Ernest Sefton, Alfred Goddard, Humberston Wright

Street bookie poses as a cleric to hide from the law. He performs the mass at a wedding for a rich young woman. At the same time, another crook is disguised as a priest but he is trying to steal jewels. A chase occurs and they end up at a clergyman's convention and the bookie saves the Lady's gems from theft.

**808. The Sunday School Treat.** Clarendon. UK. 1907. B&W. *Director*: Percy Stow

The troubles of cleric and children on a picnic are portrayed.

**809. Sunshine After Storm.** Williamson. UK. 1908. B&W. *Director*: James Williamson

Salvationist reforms suicidal drunkard, who is later wrecked while escorting emigrants, and saved from sea by ex-wife.

**810. La Suora giovane.** Italapettacolo. Italy. 1964. 97m. B&W. *Director:* Bruno Paolinelli *Writer:* Giovanni Arpino (novel), Bruno Paolinelli *Cast:* Laura Efikian, Jonathan Elliott, Maria Sarduch, C. M. Picardi, Aid Aste, Emilio Esposito, Marcella Rovena

Tells the love story between a middle-aged man Antonio (Jonathan Elliott) and a young novice nun Salina (Laura Efikian), who meet while she is caring for an invalid. They confess their love and he is ready to abandon his mistress when a misunderstanding between them occurs. He tracks her down but isn't sure about what to do about their relationship. Also known as *The Novice.*

**811. Superstar.** Paramount. US. 1999. 81m. C. *Producer:* Lorne Michaels *Director:* Bruce McCulloch *Writer:* Steven Wayne Koren *Cast:* Molly Shannon, Will Ferrell, Elaine Hendrix, Harlan Williams, Mark McKinney, Glynis Johns, Emmy Laybourne

Mary Katherine Gallagher (Molly Shannon), a character from *Saturday Night Live*, is a clumsy, geeky 17-year-old whose dream is to become a superstar. She plans to enter the school's talent contest (a Catholic Teenage Magazine-sponsored Let's Fight Venereal Disease fundraiser). Her second goal is to secure her first kiss from campus football star Sky (Will Ferrell) who is already going out with a perfect blonde. Father Ritley (Mark McKinney) is the kindly priest principal of the school.

**The Surf** *see* **Branningar**

**812. La Symphonie pastorale.** Janus Films. France. 1946. 110m. B&W. *Director:* Jean Delannoy *Writer:* Jean Aurenche, Jean Delannoy, Pierre Bost, André Gide (novel) *Cast:* Michèle Morgan, Pierre Blanchar, Line Noro, Jacques Louvigny, Jean Desailly, Andrée Clément, Rosine Luguet

A well-meaning Swiss pastor Jean Martens (Pierre Blanchar) takes a blind orphan Gertrude (Michèle Morgan) into his home in a mountain village. As she grows into a beautiful woman, his passion for her destroys the happiness of his wife and son. His son wishes to marry Gertrude but the pastor stops that as well as an operation to restore her sight. Gertrude does have the operation and sees the misery around her. Gertrude ends her confusion by suicide. Also known as *Pastoral Symphony.*

**813. Tarnished Angel.** RKO. US. 1938. 67m. B&W. *Producer:* B. P. Fineman *Director:* Leslie Goodwins *Writer:* Jo Pagano, Saul Elkins *Cast:* Sally Eilers, Lee Bowman, Ann Miller, Alma Kruger, Paul Guilfoyle, Jonathan Hale, Cecil Kellaway, Janet Dempsey, Hamilton MacFadden, Byron Foulger, Barry Macollum, Helen Jerome Eddy

Showgirl Carol Vinson (Sally Eilers) helps a jewel thief escape from the police then she flees the city with her best friends. Chased from town to town the trio finally stops at a shelter where a preacher is giving a sermon. Inspired with an idea Carol dyes her hair blonde, renames herself Sister Connie, and travels throughout New England with a revival show. When she spies someone in the audience, who recognizes her, she decides to add her past into the show. The wealthy founder Mrs. Stockton (Alma Kruger) of a children's hospital invites Sister Connie to her home for the weekend where she plots to steal a necklace from Mrs. Stockton. During a revival where the theft is to take place, Sister Connie actually cures a crippled child and is reformed.

**814. Le Tartuffe.** Connoisseur. France. 1984. 140m. C. *Producer:* Margaret Ménégoz *Director:* Gérard Depardieu *Writer:* Molière (play) *Cast:* Gérard Depardieu, François Périer, Yveline Ailhaud, Paule Annen, Paul Bru, Elisabeth Depardieu, Dominique Ducos, Noureddine El Ati, Bernard Freyd

Tartuffe (Gérard Depardieu) pretends to be a pious priest in order to get ahead with a rich merchant and his family, especially the daughter. Molière's play was banned for five years until he changed the ending so that Tartuffe did not 'win.' This made the French clergy happy.

**815. Tawny Pipit.** Universal Pictures. UK. 1944. 81m. B&W. *Producer:* Bernard Miles *Director & Writer:* Bernard Miles, Charles Saunders *Cast:* Bernard Miles, Rosamund John, Niall MacGinnis, Jean Gillie, George Carney, Christoher Steele,

Lucie Mannheim, Brefni O'Rorke, Wylie Watson, John Salew, Marjorie Rhodes, Ernest Butcher, Grey Blake, Joan Sterndale Bennett, Johnnie Schofield, Katie Johnson

During wartime, a convalescent pilot, nurse, and village vicar Reverend Kingsley (Christopher Steele) save pair of rare nesting birds (tawny pipits) as they to give birth to quintuplets. As the plot progresses the whole countryside rallies to this cause.

**Temptation** *see* **Tentação**
**The Tempter** *see* **The Devil Is a Woman**
**The Temptress** *see* **Byakuya no yojo**
**The Temptress and the Monk** *see* **Byakuya no yojo**

**816. The Tender Years.** TCF. US. 1948. 81m. B&W. *Producer:* Edward L. Alperson *Director:* Harold Schuster *Writer:* Arnold Belgard, Jack Jungmeyer *Cast:* Joe E. Brown, Richard Lyon, Noreen Nash, Charles Drake, Josephine Hutchinson, James Millican, Griff Barnett, Jeanne Gail, Harry Cheshire, Blayney Lewis, Jimmie Dodd

During the 1880s in a small town, Minister Will Norris (Joe E. Brown) becomes aware of vicious dog fighting. When one of the injured dogs escapes, it finds itself in the minister's home. The minister is forced by the law to return the dog to its owner. With his son, he steals the dog and preaches to outlaw dog fighting because of his son's love for this particular dog.

**817. Tentação.** Filmes Lusomundo. Portugal. 1997. 115m. C. *Producer:* Tino Navarro *Director & Writer:* Joaquim Leitão *Cast:* Joaquim de Almeida, Cristina Câmara, Diogo Infante, Ana Bustorff, Sofia Leite, Ana Hortelão, José Eduardo, António Capelo, João Lagarto

Father Antonio (Joaquim de Almeida) is a well-liked charismatic priest in a small town in remote northern Portugal. He befriends junkie Lena (Cristina Câmara). The relationship starts with Father Antonio giving Lena swimming lessons and the two become close friends. They become close friends and Cristina starts to clean up her act. Of course, the town people do not approve of their relationship. Just when it looks as if Lena is cleaning up her act, her daughter dies in a car accident and she falls off the wagon. Father Antonio is gradually pulled into Lena's demise with tragic results. Gradually Father Antonio is drawn into her world of drugs and gives up everything to use heroin. Also known as *Temptation*.

**818. Teresa de Jesús.** Spain. 1927. B&W. *Director:* Arturo Beringola, Francisco Beringola

Life of Teresa of Ávila

**819. Teresa de Jesús.** CEA Distribución. Spain. 1961. 131m. B&W. *Director:* Juan de Orduña *Writer:* Manuel Mur Oti, José María Pemán, Antonio Vich *Cast:* Aurora Bautista, José Bódalo, Roberto Camardiel, Antonio Durán, Alfredo Mayo, José Moreno, Jesús Tordesillas, Eugenia Zúffoli

Life of Teresa of Ávila

**820. Teresa de Jesús.** (TV-miniseries). Spain. 1984. 480m. C. *Producer:* Ramón Salgado *Director:* Josefina Molina *Writer:* Carmen Martín Gaite, Victor García de la Concha, Josefina Molina *Cast:* Concha Velasco, Francisco Rabal, María Massip, Héctor Alterio, Lina Canalejas, José María Muñoz, Carmen Lozano, Emilio Guitérrez Caba, Patricia Adriani

Series based on the life of Santa Teresa de Jesus (Concha Velasco). She was a daughter of a Jew who converted to Catholicism. She became a mystic nun who lived in a monastery in Spain. The series takes up from her early twenties and goes through her death.

In 2003, the film was shortened to 222 minutes for television and released under *Teresa de Jesús*.

**821. Thais.** Sawyer, Inc. US. 1914. B&W. *Director:* Arthur Maude, Constance Crawley *Writer:* Anatole France (novel), Arthur Maude *Cast:* Arthur Maude, Constance Crawley, George Gebhardt

Thais is a courtesan in ancient Alexandria and loved by a young Roman Paphnuce, who has converted to Christianity. When Thais' affections towards Paphnuce cool he becomes a monk and preaches in the desert for five years. Upon his return to Alexandria he converts Thais to Christianity and she becomes a member of the White Sisters. Paphnuce still loves Thais and he goes to the convent, but instead of leaving with him, she dies in his arms.

**822. Thais.** Goldwyn Distributing Corp. US. 1917. B&W. *Director*: Hugo Ballin, Frank Hall Crane *Writer*: Edfrig A. Bingham, Anatole France (novel) *Cast*: Mary Garden, Hamilton Revelle, Crauford Kent, Lionel Adams, Alice Chapin, Margaret Townsend, Charles Trowbridge

Thais is an Egyptian courtesan who was converted to a life of a penitent by a holy man Paphnutius. She is taken to a convent in the desert and lives her life in the care of the abbess. Paphnutius is attacked by a rival and in self-defense slays him. Overcome with grief he travels to the desert and joins a Christian colony. He returns to Thais and convinces her to follow him into the desert where she becomes a nun. She is haunted by visions of her former life and attempts to return, but she is exhausted and repents. The nuns purge her of sins. Meanwhile Paphnutius has returned to his old life, but comes back and confesses to a dying Thais. There have been other versions from 1916 and 1984.

**823. Thérèse.** Circle Films. France. 1986. 94m. C. *Producer*: Maurice Bernart *Director*: Alain Cavalier *Writer*: Camille de Casabianca, Alain Cavalier *Cast*: Catherine Mouchet, Hélène Alexandridis, Aurore Prieto, Clémence Massart-Weit, Sylvie Habault, Nathalie Bernart, Mona Heftre, Beatrice De Vigan, Jean Pèlégri, Jean Pieuchot, Armand Meppiel

The life of Saint Thérèse of Lisieux told in minimalist vignettes. The 15-year-old girl (Catherine Mouchet) must fight to enter the Carmelite order, in the same convent where two of her sisters are cloistered. Initially, she is denied entry because of her age but finally she is admitted. The film portrays the everyday life of her and the other nuns in a Carmelite convent. The mother superior gives her a notebook and asks her to fill it with her thoughts. This autobiography is the basis of this film. The film follows her simple short life and makes an attempt to make goodness interesting. She died in 1897 at the age of 24, and in 1925 she became Saint Thérèse of Lisieux. She is also known as "The Little Flower of Jesus." This film won the Jury award at Cannes and 8 Cesars (French Oscars.) Other versions include Julien Duvivier's from 1929 and two by French directors in 1939 and 1951.

**824. Thèrése: The Story of Saint Thèrése of Lisieux.** US. 2002. C. *Director*: Leonardo Defilippis *Writer*: Patti Defillipis, Saint Thèrése of Lisieux (writings) *Cast*: Lindsay Younce, Melissa Sumpter, Leonardo Defilippis, Maggie Rose Fleck, Susan Funk, Linda Hayden, Samantha Kramer, Jen Nikolaisen, Kaycherie Rappaport

At an early age Thèrése (Lindsay Younce) fights to become a nun and goes all the way to the Vatican. The Pope grants her permission to become a Carmelite nun.

**825. They Call Me Mister Tibbs!** UA. US. 1970. 108m. C. *Producer*: Herbert Hirschman *Director*: Gordon Douglas *Writer*: Alan Trustman, James R. Webb *Cast*: Sidney Poitier, Martin Landau, Barbara McNair, Anthony Zerbe, Juano Hernandez, George Spell, Jeff Corey, David Sheiner, Beverly Todd, Edward Asner

Sequel to *In the Heat of the Night*. Virgil Tibbs (Sidney Poitier), now a San Francisco homicide lieutenant investigates the murder of a prostitute. Last seen leaving her apartment is Reverend Logan Sharpe (Martin Landau), a politically crusading minister and close friend of Tibbs. Reverend Sharpe is in the middle of a campaign to pass a measure to reform local government. Reverend Sharpe is the prime suspect because he admits that he had been sleeping with the prostitute. It turns out that he is the killer.

**They're Watching Us** *see* **Nos miran**
**They've Kidnapped Anne Benedict** *see* **The Abduction of Saint Anne**

**826. The Third Miracle.** Sony. US. 1999. 119m. C. *Producer*: Fred Fuchs, Steven Haft, Elie Samaha *Director*: Agnieszka Holland *Writer*: John Romano, Richard Vetere (novel) *Cast*: Ed Harris, Charles Haid, Anne Heche, Susan Henley, Ken James, James Gallanders, Ron Gabriel, Barbara Sukowa, Armin Mueller-Stahl, Arthur Eng, Aron Tager, Jade Smith, Michael Risploi, Jean-Louis Roux, Caterina Scorsone

A skeptical Bishop (Charles Haid) sends a struggling and tormented priest

Frank Shore (Ed Harris) as Postulator to investigate the possible Beatification of a dead Austrian immigrant Helen (Barbara Sukowa) who devoted herself to good works in Chicago. Frank is sent to investigate a statue of the Virgin Mary that is rumored to bleed tears of blood on the anniversary of Helen's death. Tests reveal that blood from the statue is the same as Helen's. He begins an affair with Helen's daughter Roxanne (Anne Heche). Roxanne is an atheist who was abandoned by her mother and feels no obligation to help him. Archbishop Werner (Armin Mueller-Stahl) arrives from the Vatican to stop any talk of making Helen a saint. Brother Gregory (James Gallenders) uncovers information that explains why the Archbishop is so against Helen.

**The Third Solution** see **Russicum—i giorni del diavolo**

**827. Third Time Lucky.** W&F. UK. 1930. 85m. B&W. *Producer*: Michael Balcon *Director*: Walter Forde *Writer*: Angus Macphail, H. Fowler Mear, Arnold Ridley (play) *Cast*: Bobby Howes, Gordon Harker, Dorothy Boyd, Garry Marsh, Henry Mollison, Gibb McLaughlin, Clare Greet, Margaret Yarde, Viola Compton, Marie Ault, Alexander Field, Harry Terry, Philip Godfrey, Matthew Boulton

Timid vicar Reverend Arthur Fear (Bobby Howes) steals back ward's letters from blackmailer.

**This Age Without Pity** see **Anthracite —cet âge est sans pitié**

**828. The Thorn Birds.** ABC. (Miniseries-TV). US. 1983. 477m. C. *Producer*: Stan Margulies *Director*: Daryl Duke *Writer*: Colleen McCullough (novel), Carmen Culver, Lee Stanley *Cast*: Richard Chamberlain, Rachel Ward, Barbara Stanwyck, Christopher Plummer, Jean Simmons, Richard Kiley, Ken Howard, Piper Laurie, Earl Holliman, Mare Winningham, Bryan Brown

The television miniseries chronicles sixty years in the lives of the Cleary family who traveled from New Zealand to Australia to run their aunt's ranch. The story centers on the romance between their daughter Meggie Cleary (Rachel Ward) and the family priest Ralph de Bricassart (Richard

Chamberlain) which has tragic consequences in the end. Meggie tries to forget her true love by marrying Luke (Bryan Brown) as Father Ralph ascends the church hierarchy. Their love cannot be denied. They have an affair and Ralph fathers a child, who grows up to be a priest. In 1996, *Thorn Birds: The Missing Years* aired.

**829. Thou Shalt Not Kill.** Republic. US. 1939. 67m. B&W. *Producer*: Robert North *Director*: John H. Auer *Writer*: Robert Presnell, George Carleton Brown *Cast*: Charles Bickford, Owen Davis Jr., Doris Day, Paul Guilfoyle, Granville Bates, Charles Waldron, Sheila Bromley, George Chandler, Charles Middleton, Emmett Vogan, Leona Roberts, Ethyl May Halls, Edmund Elton, Elsie Prescott

Reverend Chris (Charles Bickford) influences a youth Allen Stevens (Owen Davis Jr.) who faces a murder charge while trying to go straight. As the youth is convicted, Reverend Chris learns the real killer's identity. In the absence of a Catholic priest he takes the confession of the real killer. Reverend Chris must make the confessor tell the truth to the police.

**830. Thou Shalt Not Steal.** US. 1915. B&W.

The treasurer of a young minister's church is caught stealing and since it isn't his first time he is barred from any duty. He joins a gang and convinces a girl thief to deliver a letter to the minister stating that she is having the minister's baby. She goes to deliver the letter and decides to take his watch. He gives her a bible with Thou Shalt Not Steal. She reforms. He is falsely implicated in other crimes, but all ends well with a marriage.

**Three Nights of Love** see **Tre notti d'amore**

**831. Thunder on the Hill.** UI. US. 1951. 84m. B&W. *Producer*: Michel Kraike *Director*: Douglas Sirk *Writer*: Oscar Saul, Andrew Solt, Charlotte Hastings (play) *Cast*: Claudette Colbert, Ann Blyth, Robert Douglas, Anne Crawford, Philip Friend, Gladys Cooper, Michael Pate, John Abbott, Connie Gilchrist, Gavin Muir

Sister Mary Bonaventure (Claudette

Colbert) runs a hospital ward in a convent in Norfolk County, England. One stormy night, a woman Valerie Carns (Ann Blyth), who is accused of murdering her brother, and her guard seek refuge at the convent due to flooding. Townspeople also seek shelter at the convent. The woman confides her innocence to Sister Mary, who comes to believe that she is indeed innocent. Sister Mary is able to clear her by finding the real killer who turns out to be a doctor. It turns out that Dr. Jeffreys (Robert Douglas) poisoned Valerie's brother because he was jealous of his attention to his wife. Also known as *Bonaventure.*

**832. Ti ritrovera.** Lux Film. Italy. 1949. 82m. B&W. *Producer:* Valentino Brosio *Director:* Giacomo Gentilomo *Writer:* Giacomo Gentilomo, Nicola Manzari, Guido Pala, Alberto Vecchietti *Cast:* Enrico Viarisio, Delia Scala, Val du Bois, Peter Ford, Gaio Visconti, John Kitzmiller, Enzo Turco, Renata Nassi, Robert Stevens

During her honeymoon in Italy, a young bride becomes separated from her husband. He happens to be a British Intelligence officer tracking smugglers. With the help of the village priest Don Giuseppe (Enrico Viarsio), they are reunited. Also known as *I'll Find You Again.*

**833. Tierra del Fuego.** EMPA. Argentina. 1948. 120m. B&W. *Director:* Mario Soffici *Writer:* Ulises Petit de Murat *Cast:* Pedro López Lagar, Sabina Olmos, Alberto Closas, Orestes Caviglia, Ricardo Duggan, Norma Giménez

A Catholic priest of the Salesian order, Father Paul (Pedro López Lagar), and his martyred attempts to bring Christianity into the lives of the Patagonian Indians is the focus of this film. The natives are persecuted by the whites. He also tries to redeem the motley crew of white adventurers.

**834. Till We Meet Again.** Paramount. US. 1944. 88m. B&W. *Director:* Frank Borzage *Writer:* Lenore J. Coffee, Alfred Maury (play) *Cast:* Ray Milland, Barbara Britton, Walter Slezak, Lucile Watson, Konstantin Shayne, Vladimir Sokoloff, Marguerite D'Alvarez, Mona Freeman, William Edmunds, George Davis

During World War II in France, the Mother Superior (Lucile Watson) of a convent and the convent's gardener help escaping prisoners of war with the help of the French underground. Young innocent nun Sister Clothilde (Barbara Britton) unintentionally reveals one prisoner but redeems herself when she accompanies downed pilot John (Ray Milland) on his journey to freedom. She pretends to be his wife and he is to be her mute husband. Sister Clothilde has always loathed men because of her father's infidelities, during the journey she realizes she is wrong. One reason is hearing how much John loves his wife and son. In exchange for John's life, she makes a deal with a German. John escapes and Sister Clothilde returns but without the papers she had promised. For punishment she will be forced to "service" German officers. The mayor is so upset by this punishment that he fights with a soldier, and Sister Clothilde is accidentally shot and killed.

**835. Tilly and the Mormon Missionary.** Hepworth. UK. 1911. B&W. *Director & Writer:* Lewin Fitzhamon *Cast:* Alma Taylor, Chrissie White, Frank Denton

Girls posing as gypsies chased by uncle and Mormon missionary.

**836. A Time for Miracles.** ABC. (TV) US. 1980. 100m. C. *Producer:* Beverlee Dean *Director:* Michael O'Herlihy *Writer:* Henry Denker *Cast:* Kate Mulgrew, Jean-Pierre Aumont, Rossano Brazzi, John Forsythe, Lorne Greene, Jean LeClerc, Leonard Mann, Robin Clarke, William Prince, Dominic Chianese

The story of United States' first native born saint St. Elizabeth Bayley Seton (Kate Mulgrew) who founded the American Sisters of Charity and the first American Catholic schools.

**Time of Favor** *see* **Ha-Hesder**

**837. Tiresia.** Haut et Court. France/Canada. 2003. 116m. C. *Producer:* Carole Scotta, Simon Arnal *Director:* Bertrand Bonello *Writer:* Bertrand Bonello, Luca Fazzi *Cast:* Laurent Lucas, Clara Choveaux, Thiago Telès, Célia Catalifo, Lou Castel, Alex Descas, Fred Ulysse

Tiresia is a Brazilian transsexual living with her brother when she meets Terranova who drives through the woods near Paris where transsexual prostitutes work. He convinces Tiresia to accompany him to his house in the suburbs. He says he only wants to sleep chastely beside her. Without hormone injections Tiresia masculine traits come back. Terranova is upset about what he has done so he mutilates her by poking out her eyes and dumping her. A mute girl finds her and nurses back to health. Tiresai now has reverted back to his masculine self and has attained psychic abilities. He starts muttering predictions all of which prove true. People come far and wide to hear what he has to say. The parish priest Father Francois finds that his prophet status is against the church beliefs.

**To Hell with This Priest** *see* ¡Al diablo con este cura!

**838. To Kill a Priest.** Columbia. US/France. 1989. 117m. C. *Producer*: Jean-Pierre Alessandri *Director*: Agnieszka Holland *Writer*: Michael Cooper, Agnieszka Holland, Jean-Yves Pitoun *Cast*: Christopher Lambert, Ed Harris, Joss Ackland, Tim Roth, Timothy Spall, Pete Postlethwaite, Cherie Lunghi, Joanne Whalley, David Suchet, Charlie Condou, Tom Radcliffe, Wojciech Pszoniak

Story centers around Father Alek (Christopher Lambert) who isn't afraid to go against the system in 1981's Poland. On the other side is Stefan (Ed Harris), a secret police officer, who loves his country and supports communism. He thinks that if Alek were eliminated the Solidarity movement would disappear. The film is loosely based on Father Jerzy Popieluszko, a martyr of the Polish trade union Solidarity.

**839. Todo sobre mi madre.** Sony Pictures Classics. France/Spain. 2000. 101m. C. *Director & Writer:* Pedro Almódovar *Cast:* Cecilia Roth, Marisa Paredes, Candela Peña, Antonia San Juan, Penélope Cruz, Rosa María Sardà, Eloy Azorín, Fernando Fernán Gómez, Fernando Guillén, Toni Cantó, Carlos Lozano

Nurse Manuela Coleman Echevarría (Cecilia Roth) has lost her son Esteban (Eloy Azorín) in an accident and travels to Barcelona in search of Esteban's father in order to tell him about their son. Her husband was also named Esteban. A pregnant Manuela had left him when he had breast implants and changed his name to Lola. In Barcelona, she befriends Sister Maria Rosa Sanz (Penélope Cruz) a pregnant nun infected with HIV by Lola. Sister Rosa is both beautiful and very kind. Manuela also meets her long lost friend Agrado (Antonia San Juan) a transvestite hooker. Manuela ends up caring for Rosa and eventually adopting Rosa's baby when Rosa dies. Also known as *All About My Mother.*

**840. Tomorrow Will Be Friday.** Williamson. UK. 1901. B&W. *Director:* James Williamson *Cast:* John Macauley

Fishing monk drains his bottle and drinks brother's bottle.

**841. Tongues of Men.** Paramount. US. 1916. B&W. *Director:* Frank Lloyd *Writer:* E. J. Clawson **Cast:** Constance Collier, Forrest Stanley, Herbert Standing, Lamar Johnstone, Lydia Yeamans Titus, Helen Eddy, Elizabeth Burbridge, Miss Marlborough, Charles Marriot, John McKinnon, Howard Davies

Reverend Penfield Sturgis (Forrest Stanley), a holier-than-thou minister, condemns stage performers such as Jane Bartlett (Constance Collier) an opera singer. He even writes an editorial against her for the newspaper. To prove the minister wrong, Jane uses her charms and Penfield falls in love with Jane. She accepts his marriage proposal which causes trouble within his congregation. Jane realizes she does not love him, cancels the engagement, and unites Penfield with his true love Georgine (Elizabeth Burbridge).

**842. Die Trapp-Familie.** Hispano Foxfilms. Germany. 1956. 106m. C. *Producer:* Wolfgang Reinhardt, Utz Utermann *Director:* Wolfgang Liebeneiner *Writer:* George Hurdalek *Cast:* Ruth Leuwerik, Hans Holt, Maria Holst, Josef Meinard, Agnes Windeck, Friedrich Domin, Hilde von Stolz, Liesl Karlstadt, Alfred Balthoff, Hans Schumm, Gretl Theimer

Adapted from the memoirs of Baroness Maria Trapp of her life as a young novice (Ruth Leuwerik), who leaves the convent to teach a family of seven motherless children.

Soon she falls in love with their father Baron Trapp and they marry. Another more famous version of the story *The Sound of Music* which is very well known.

**843. Travelin' On.** Paramount. US. 1922. B&W. *Director*: Lambert Hillyer *Writer*: William S. Hart, Lambert Hillyer *Cast*: William S. Hart, Jim Farley, Ethel Grey Terry, Brinsley Shaw, Mary Jane Irving, Bob Kortman, Willis Marks

A preacher Hi Morton (Brinsley Shaw) and his beautiful wife Mary Jane (Mary Jane Irving) meet a prospector J.B. (William S. Hart) The preacher has come to build a church to fight the viciousness of a mining camp. Morton is so determined to build this church that he must deal with crooked businessman and lack of funds. He tricks gamblers by having his wife sell books that are actually bibles. Morton is so obsessed with the church that he robs a stage coach. He is caught and about to be hanged when J.B. declares that he robbed the stage and rides off. Morton completes his church and hangs a sign over the door claiming that the church was built by an unbeliever. The man of God is mean and contemptible!

**844. Tre notti d'amore.** Magna Pictures Distribution Corp. Italy. 1964. 112m. C. *Producer*: Silvio Clementelli *Director*: Luigi Comencini, Renato Castellani, Franco Rossi *Writer*: Marcello Fondato, Franco Castellano, Massimo Franciosa *Cast*: Catherine Spaak, John Phillip Law, Renato Salvatori, Aldo Puglisi, Enrico Maria Salerno, Diletta D'Andrea

La Faterbenefratelli is one part of a trilogy which deals with a religious theme. When Ghiga (Catherine Spaak), a high-class call girl, is injured in an automobile accident she is taken to a hospital run by friars. Brother Felice (John Phillip Law) who is preparing for his final vows, tries to save Ghiga's soul but she attempts to seduce him. She later becomes a nun and he leaves the order. Also known as *Three Nights of Love*.

**845. The Trial of Chaplain Jensen.** ABC. (TV). US. 1975. 73m. C. *Producer*: Ron Preissman *Director*: Robert Day *Writer*: Loring Mandel, Martin Abrahamson (book) *Cast*: James Franciscus, Joanna Miles, Lynda Day George, Dorothy Tristan, Charles Durning, Harris Yulin, Howard Platt, Alan Manson, Dennis Larson, Steven Kunz, Betty Urich, Sally Carter Ihnat

The true account of Chaplain Andrew Jensen (James Franciscus), who was the first U.S. naval court-martialed solely on charges of adultery.

**Trial of Joan of Arc** *see* **Le Procès de Jeanne d'Arc**

**846. Tried in the Fire.** Hepworth. UK. 1913. B&W. *Director*: Warwick Buckland *Cast*: Alec Worcester, Alma Taylor, Harry Royston

Cleric saves spoilt rich girl from kidnappers.

**847. Tristar.** Hong Kong. 1996. C. *Producer, Director & Writer*: Hark Tsui *Cast*: Moses Chan, Sunny Chan, Leslie Cheung, King-fai Chung, Paul Fonoroff, Wai-Hung Fung, Catherine Hung Yan, Alvina Kong, Radium Cheung, Anita Yuen, Xin Xin Xiong

A priest Father Zhong Guoqiang (Leslie Cheung) hears a prostitute's confession. She accidentally leaves an envelope with her address and a large sum of money in the confessional. He goes undercover, becomes her neighbor, and tries to straighten out her life. Also known as *Da san yuan*.

**848. Trouble Along the Way.** Warner. US. 1953. 110m. B&W. *Producer*: Melville Shavelson *Director*: Michael Curtiz *Writer*: Melville Shavelson, Jack Rose, Robert Hardy Andrews, Douglas Morrow *Cast*: John Wayne, Donna Reed, Charles Coburn, Tom Tully, Sherry Jackson, Marie Windsor, Tom Helmore, Dabbs Greer, Leif Erickson, Douglas Spencer, Lester Matthews, Chuck Connors, Bill Radovich

Father Burke (Charles Coburn) heads the bankrupt St. Anthony's College in New York which has been ordered closed due to debt. He thinks that a football team is needed. Father Burke hires Steve Williams (John Wayne), a cynical ex-coach, who has lost many jobs because of his inability to conform. He accepts the job to keep custody of his daughter Carol (Sherry Jackson). Steve stacks the team with ringers but Father Burke forgives him. Father Burke decides to resign and let the young take over.

**849. The Trouble with Angels.** Columbia. US. 1966. 112m. C. *Producer*: William Frye *Director*: Ida Lupino *Writer*: Jane Trahey (novel), Blanche Hanalis *Cast*: Rosalind Russell, Binnie Barnes, Camilla Sparv, Mary Wickes, Marge Redmond, Dolores Sutton, Margalo Gillmore, Portia Nelson, Marjorie Eaton, Barbara Bell Wright, Judith Lowry, Hayley Mills, June Harding, Gypsy Rose Lee, Barbara Hunter

Mother Superior (Rosalind Russell) battles two juvenile pranksters-extrovert Mary Clancy (Hayley Mills) and sensitive Rachel Devery (June Harding) at an all-girl's Catholic boarding school St. Francis' Academy. Some of the girls' pranks include smoking cigars in the boiler room which causes the fire department or secretly entering the cloister. In one touching scene, Mother Superior stays up all night helping Rachel finish her sewing project while recalling her own dream of being a fashion designer. The film treats the nuns with respect and very positively. In fact, Mary Clancy decides to remain and join the order herself. Followed by *Where Angels Go Trouble Follows*.

**850. True Confessions.** UA. US. 1981. 108m. C. *Producer*: Irwin Winkler, Robert Chartoff *Director*: Ulu Grosbard *Writer*: John Gregory Dunne (novel), Joan Didion, Gary S. Hall *Cast*: Robert De Niro, Robert Duvall, Charles Durning, Ed Flanders, Burgess Meredith, Rose Gregorio, Cyril Cusack, Kenneth McMillan, Dan Hedeya, Jeannette Nolan

Police homicide Tom Spellacy (Robert Duvall) investigates two murders- a priest found in a brothel and a mutilated girl in 1940s Los Angeles. His brother Monsignor Spellacy (Robert De Niro), a corrupt priest embroiled in money laundering and collaborating with drug lords, may be involved. The Monsignor is the protégé of Cardinal Danaher (Cyril Cusack).

**851. The Trygon Factor.** Warner/Seven Arts. UK. 1969. 87m. C. *Producer*: Brian Taylor *Director*: Cyril Frankel *Writer*: Derry Quinn *Cast*: Stewart Granger, Susan Hampshire, Robert Morley, Cathleen Nesbitt, Brigitte Horney, Sophie Hardy, James Robertson-Justice, Eddi Arent, Diane Clare, James Culliford

In order to save their English manor, Livia Emberday (Cathleen Nesbitt) and her daughter Trudy (Susan Hampshire) turn to a life of crime. Livia, Luke (James Culliford), her dumb son, and Trudy set up a phony order of nuns and a convent on their property as a front for receiving stolen goods. When a man from Scotland Yard disappears while investigating the convent, Superintendent Cooper-Smith (Stewart Granger) is on the case.

**852. The Twinkle in God's Eye.** Republic. US. 1955. 73m. B&W. *Producer*: Mickey Rooney *Director*: George Blair *Writer*: P.J. Wolfson *Cast*: Mickey Rooney, Coleen Gray, Hugh O'Brian, Joey Forman, Don 'Red' Barry, Mike Connors, Jil Jarmyn, Kem Dibbs, Tony Garcen, Raymond Hatton, Ruta Lee

A young recently-ordained parson Reverend William Macklin II (Mickey Rooney) is determined to bring religion to a wild frontier community. He wants to rebuild the church destroyed by an Indian raid. The local gambling hall owner doesn't want the church near his establishment. He reforms key townspeople and gains the support of the other townspeople.

**853. Two Mules for Sister Sara.** Universal. US. 1970. 116m. C. *Producer*: Martin Rackin, Carroll Case *Director*: Don Siegel *Writer*: Albert Maltz, Budd Boetticher *Cast*: Shirley MacLaine, Clint Eastwood, Manuel Fábregas, Alberto Morin, Armando Silverstre, John Kelly, Enrique Lucero, David Estuardo

An American mercenary/gunfighter Hogan (Clint Eastwood) hooks up with Sister Sara (Shirley MacLaine) in French occupied Mexico. He thinks Sister Sara is a nun when he kills some men about to rape her. He soon discovers she is disguised as a nun. She is really a prostitute with a heart of gold in this western.

**854. The Two Natures Within Him.** US. 1915. B&W. *Cast*: Thomas Santschi, Bessie Eyton, Franklin Paul

A young minister/social worker Reverend William Morris (Thomas Santschi) is hit over the head with a brick by a thief. He changes from a good man to a criminal. He begins a life of crime and attempts to rob his old home. His sweetheart catches him, but not recognizing her he strangles her. During his trial the truth about his injury comes out and after an operation by Dr. Bishop, he returns to his good self.

**855. Uccellacci e uccellini.** Brandon Films. Italy. 1966. 91m. B&W. *Producer*: Alfredo Bini *Director & Writer*: Pier Paola Pasolini *Cast*: Totó, Ninetto Davoli, Femi Benussi, Rossana Di Rocco, Lena Lin Solaro, Rosina Moroni, Renato Capogna, Pietro Davoli, Gariele Baldini, Ricardo Redi, Francisco Leonetti

While strolling down a highway, a man and his son encounter a talking crow who asks them where they are going and what they are doing. When they are unable to answer the questions, the bird begins a philosophical discourse and while the bird is talking the father becomes a monk and the son a young friar in the year 1200 where they are met by St. Francis of Assisi. When they return to the present they continue on their journey. Very offbeat film where Pasolini sees human survival via co-existence. Also known as *Hawks and Sparrows*.

**856. Uforia.** Universal. US. 1980. 93m. C. *Producer*: Gordon Wolf *Director & Writer*: John Binder *Cast*: Cindy Williams, Harry Dean Stanton, Fred Ward, Robert Gray, Darrell Larson, Beverly Hope Atkinson, Harry Carey Jr., Ted Harris

A drifter Sheldon Bart (Fred Ward) meets up with Arlene Stewart (Cindy Williams) in a small desert town where he has gone to link up with an old friend Brother Bud Sanders (Harry Dean Stanton), who is a tent preacher. The romance between the drifter and Arlene is complicated by her intense belief in UFOs. She believes that aliens will be arriving any minute. Sheldon and Brother Bud see this has a way to make some money off those that believe in aliens

**Um Asilo muito louco** *see* **O Alienista**

**Under the Moonlight** *see* **Zir-e noor-e maah**

**857. Under the Red Robe.** TCF. US/UK. 1937. 80m. B&W. *Producer*: Robert T. Kane *Director*: Victor Sjöström *Writer*: Lajos Biró, Philip Lindsay, J. L. Hudson, Arthur Wimperis, Stanley J. Weyman (novel), Edward E. Rose (play) *Cast*: Conrad Veidt, Annabella, Raymond Massey, Romney Brent, Sophie Steward, Lawrence Grant, Wyndham Goldie, Balliol Holloway, Shale Gardner, Edie Martin Haddon Mason, J. Fisher White, Graham Soutten, Anthony Eustrel, Ralph Truman

Cardinal Richelieu (Raymond Massey) persuades a nobleman, by sparing his life, to unmask the mastermind behind a conspiracy. The Cardinal's emissary happens to fall in love with the revolutionary's sister.

**Under the Sun of Satan** *see* **Sous le soleil de Satan**

**The Unfrocked One** *see* **Le Défroqué**

**858. The Unholy.** Vestron Pictures. US. 1988. 102m. C. *Producer*: Mathew Hayden *Director*: Camilo Vila *Writer*: Philip Yordan, Fernando Fonseca *Cast*: Ruben Rabasa, Nicole Fortier, Peter Frechette, Phil Becker, Ned Beatty, Susan Bearden, Xavier Barquet, Lari White, Jeff D'Onofrio, Ben Cross, Hal Holbrook, Trevor Howard, William Russ, Jill Carroll

Horror film about a demon that preys on priests caught sinning. Father Michael (Ben Cross) is assigned a church in New Orleans. The church was the scene of two brutal murders. Father Michael must fight the demon in a haunted church.

**859. Gli Uomini non guardano il cielo.** Italian Film Export. Italy. 1951. 90m. B&W. *Director*: Umberto Scarpelli *Writer*: G. De Mori, E. Bacchion *Cast*: Henry Vidon, Tullio Carminati, Luigi Tosi, Filippo Scelzo, Sandro Ruffini, Corrado Annicelli, Antonio Centa, Mario Pisu

Tale of a simple priest who becomes Pope Pius X (Henry Vidon) told through a series of flashbacks. Also known as *The Secret Conclave*.

**860. Vacanze in America.** Columbia. Italy. 1984. 98m. C. *Producer*: Mario and Vittorio Cecchi Gori *Director*: Carlo Vanzina *Writer*: Enrico and Carlo Vanzina *Cast*: Jerry Calà, Christian De Sica, Claudio Amendola, Antonella Interlenghi, Edwige Fenech, Fabio Ferrari, Giacomo Rosselli, Gianmarco Tognazzi

A parochial boys' academy is on a trip across the United States for vacation. A picky young cleric Don Burro (Christian De Sica) is supervising their journey. Also helping out is the beautiful mother, Signora De Romanis (Edwige Fenech), of one of the boys. The couple almost ends up in bed together but the priest remains chaste. Also known as *Vacation in America.*

**861. Valentina.** Moreno Film. Spain. 1982. 85m. C/B&W. *Producer:* Carlos Escobedo, Javier Moro *Director:* Antonio José Betancor *Writer:* Lautaro Murúa, Antonio José Betancor, Carlos Escobedo, Javier Moro, Ramón J. Sender (novel) *Cast:* Anthony Quinn, Jorge Sanz, Paloma Gómez, Saturno Cerra, Concha Leza, Antonio Canal

Childhood memories of a narrator who will die as a prisoner of war in a French prison camp in 1939. He tells stories about his youth to raise the spirits of the other prisoners. Set in an Aragonese village around 1910 it is a look at a mischievous childhood. Paternal village priest Mosen Joaquin (Anthony Quinn) befriends the boy José (Antonio Canal) and tutors him. The priest tells him about brave men, saints, heroes, and the poets. The boy is in love with Valentina (Paloma Gómez), a neighbor girl.

**862. Valley of Song.** Pathé. UK. 1953. 80m. B&W. *Producer:* Vaughan N. Dean *Director:* Gilbert Gunn *Writer:* Cliff Gordon, Phil Park *Cast:* Mervyn Johns, Clifford Evans, Maureen Swanson, John Fraser, Rachel Thomas, Betty Cooper, Rachel Roberts, Hugh Pryse, Edward Evans, Kenneth Williams, Alun Owen

Minister Griffiths (Mervyn Johns) and the new choirmaster Geraint Llewelyn (Clifford Evans) are in the middle of a choir feud which divides their town. When the choirmaster replaces the solo for the past 30 years, chaos erupts and a young couple is torn apart.

**The Vatican Conspiracy** *see* **Morte in Vaticano**

**Venial Sins** *see* **Pecata minuta**

**863. Das Verlangen.** Filmakademic Baden. Germany. 2002. 94m. C. *Producer:* Till Schmerbeck *Director:* Iain Dilthey *Writer:* Iain Dilthey, Silke Parzich *Cast:* Susanne-Marie Wrage, Klans Grünberg, Robert Lohr, Heidemarie Rohweder, Manfred Kranich, Peter Lerchbaumer, Wolfgang Packhäuser, Sigrid Skoetz, Eva Loebau

Relates the story of Lena (Susanne-Marie Wrage), the plain wife of a protestant minister Johannes (Klaus Grünberg) living in a village in southern Germany. The film shows her routine wifely duties like playing the organ at the church. That is until their car develops a problem and she gets to know mechanic Paul (Robert Lohr) and an attraction blossoms between them. Also known as *The Longing.*

**864. The Vernon Johns Story.** (TV). US. 1994. 100m. C. *Producer:* Mitchell Galin, David R. Kappes *Director:* Kenneth Fink *Writer:* Leslie Lee, Kevin Arkadie *Cast:* James Earl Jones, Mary Alice, Joe Seneca, Tommy Hollis, Nicole Leach, Ashanti Nailah Blaize, Lashayla Logan, Clifton James, Shelby Ware, Cissy Houston, Moses Gibson

The film tells the story of Reverend Vernon Johns (James Earl Jones) pastor of the Dexter Avenue Baptist Church in Montgomery, Alabama during the turbulent 1960's.

**865. Der Veruntreute Himmel.** UFA. Germany. 1958. 105m. C. *Producer:* Georg M. Reuther *Director:* Ernst Marischka *Writer:* Franz Werfel (novel), Ernst Marischka *Cast:* Annie Rosar, Hans Holt, Viktor de Kowa, Vilma Degischer, Fred Liewehr, Kurt Meisel, Kai Fischer, Rudolf Vogal, Lotte Lang, Jane Tilden

Teta Linek (Annie Rosar) is a naive and religious aunt who believes that God will give her a place in heaven if she sends all her money to her nephew so he can become a priest. She unburdens her heart to Chaplain Kaplan Seydel (Hans Holt), who gives her last rites. The spoiled nephew embezzles all of her money. Also known as *The Embezzled Heaven.*

**Vessel of Wrath** *see* **The Beachcomber**

**866. The Vicar of Bray.** ABPC. UK. 1937. 68m. B&W. *Producer:* Julius Hagen *Director:* Henry Edwards *Writer:* H. Fowler Mear, Anson Dyer *Cast:* Stanley Holloway, Margaret Vines, Esmond Knight, Eve Gray, Felix Aylmer, Hugh Miller, Garry Marsh, Martin Walker, George Merritt, K. Hamilton Price, Fred O'Donovan

The tutor for the future King Charles I is an Irish priest. When the prince becomes king, the priest persuades him to pardon one of his parishioners now imprisoned for treason.

**The Vicar of Olot** *see* **El Vicario de Olot**

**867. The Vicar of Wakefield.** Motion Picture Distributors. US. 1910. B&W. *Writer:* Oliver Goldsmith (novel from 1766) *Cast:* Martin Faust, William Garwood, Bertha Blanchard, Frank Hall Crane, William Russell, Marie Eline

Troubles of a vicar and his family. One of the first of many versions of the novel *The Vicar of Wakefield* by Oliver Goldsmith.

**868. The Vicar of Wakefield.** Pathé. UK. 1912. B&W. *Director:* Frank Powell *Writer:* Oliver Goldsmith (novel) *Cast:* Florence Barker

Squire has vicar jailed for debt and fakes marriage to daughter.

**869. The Vicar of Wakefield.** Hepworth. UK. 1913. B&W. *Director:* Frank Wilson *Writer:* Blanche McIntosh, Oliver Goldsmith (novel) *Cast:* Violet Hopson, Harry Royston, Warwick Buckland, Chrissie White, Harry Gilbey, Marie de Solla, Jack Raymond, Harry Buss, John McAndrews, Jamie Darling, Claire Pridelle

Squire has poor vicar jailed for debt and fakes marriage to his daughter.

**870. The Vicar of Wakefield.** Pathé Exchange. US. 1917. B&W. *Director:* Ernest C. Warde *Writer:* Emmett Mixx, Oliver Goldsmith (novel) *Cast:* Frederick Warde, Carey L. Hastings, Boyd Marshall, Kathryn Adams, Gladys Leslie, William Parke Jr., Tula Belle, Barbara Howard, Thomas A. Curran, Robert Vaughn

The Vicar of Wakefield (Frederick Warde) has big family troubles. First, his eldest son leaves home spurned by love, his daughter Olivia (Kathryn Adams) elopes with unscrupulous squire, and finally on son sent to sell their colt squanders the money on green glasses. The Vicar sets out to find his daughter, soon to have his horse and money stolen. He joins a group strolling players and soon finds Olivia who has been left by the squire. They find their home

ablaze and the squire has the Vicar thrown in jail because of debts. The squire's superior comes and frees the Vicar and marries the daughter.

**871. El Vicario de Olot.** Profilmar. Spain. 1980. 101m. C. *Director:* Ventura Pons *Writer:* Emili Teixidor *Cast:* Enric Majó, Juan Monleon, Rosa María Sardá, Maria Aurèlia Capmany, Nuria Feliu, Marina Rossell, Anna Lizaran

The story revolves around a handsome young vicar. He and his uncle, a high church official, decide to organize a congress dedicated to Catholic Sexology. The campaign is countered by some Barcelona prostitutes and gays. Film ends with the vicar giving a sermon regarding the variety of sexual behavior. Also known as *The Vicar of Olot* and *El Vicari d'Olot.*

**872. The Vicar's Garden Party.** Pathé Fréres. France. 1905. B&W.

No description available.

**Vice and Virtue** *see* **Nugel Bujan**

**873. Vietnam, Texas.** Top Tape. US. 1990. 92m. C. *Producer:* Robert Ginty, Ron Joy *Director:* Robert Ginty *Writer:* Tom Badal, C. Courtney Joyner *Cast:* Robert Ginty, Haing S. Ngor, Kieu Chinh, Tamlyn Tomita, John Pleshette, David Chow, Bert Remsen, Chi Moui Lo, Michele B. Chan, Sachi Parker

A priest Father Thomas McCann (Robert Ginty) learns that he had fathered a child during his tour of duty in Vietnam. He has great guilt that he had abandoned his pregnant lover. He learns that the mother and child have relocated to Houston, Texas. He also discovers that his former lover is now married to a vicious drug runner. With the help of an old soldier buddy, he tries to reach his daughter. While searching for them he finds a great deal of prejudice against the Vietnamese people, particularly in the fishing community. He sets out to right the wrongs.

**874. Virágvasárnap.** Hungarofilm. Hungary. 1969. 83m. B&W. *Producer:* Ottó Föld *Director:* Imre Gyöngyössy *Writer:* Péter Bascó, Imre Gyöngyössy *Cast:* Frantisek Velecký, Benedek Tóth, Gábor Koncz, Mária Medgyesi, Teri Horváth

Film is set in 1919 Hungary based on some historical facts. The central character, priest Simon (Frantisek Velecký) really existed. The young secretary of a Bishop is searching for mysterious man called Simon the Priest, whose brother is a teacher and is said to be a leader of a Communist group. National terrorists are after both, but the peasants have hidden them. Also known as *Palm Sunday.*

**875. La Vírgen morena.** Soria & Santandar. Mexico. 1943. 98m. B&W. *Director:* Gabriel Soria *Writer:* Gabriel Soria, Alberto Santandar *Cast:* José Luis Jiménez, Amparo Morillo, Abel Salazar, Arturo Soto Rangel, María Luisa Zea, Antonio Bravo, Tito Junco

The cruelty of the conquistadors clash against the Aztecs, while the church tries to peacefully convert the Indians to Christians. Juan Diego (José Luis Jiménez) is an Indian peasant who sees the visions of Virgin of Guadalupe. This miracle brings the Spanish and Aztecs together. Also known as *The Virgin of Guadalupe.*

**876. La Virgen que forjó una patria.** Clasa Films. Mexico. 1942. 110m. B&W. *Producer:* Agustín J. Fink, Emilio Gómez Muriel *Director:* Julio Bracho *Writer:* Julio Bracho, René Capistrán Garza *Cast:* Ramon Novarro, Domingo Soler, Gloria Marín, Paco Fuentes, Felipe Montoya, Julio Villarreal, Ernesto Alozo, Victor Urruchúa, Fanny Schiller

Film covers both 1531 and 1810 in Mexico's history. Juan Diego (Ramon Novarro) is a peasant who sees the Virgin of Guadalupe and builds a church on the hill where he saw the Virgin. Other prominent clerics portrayed are Brother Martin (Domingo Soler) and Father Hidalgo (Julio Villarreal). Also known as *Saint That Forged a Country.*

**The Virgin of Guadalupe** *see* **La Vírgen morena**

**877. Viridiana.** Kingsley International Films. Spain/Mexico. 1961. 90m. B&W. *Director:* Luis Buñuel *Writer:* Luis Buñuel, Julio Alejandro, Benito Pérez Galdós (novel) *Cast:* Silvia Pinal, Francisco Rabal, Fernando Rey, Margarita Lozano, Victoria Zinny, José Calvo, Teresa Rabal

Viridiana (Silvia Pinal), about to take her vows as a nun, gives up her vows and turns to a pure Christian life by organizing a haven for an assortment of odd people. Her uncle sees in her a perfect image of his long-dead wife but she is repelled by his affections. He hangs himself in remorse. She returns to his farm with an assortment of beggars and odd people. Film ends in a famous orgy of destruction, containing Buñuel's blasphemous scene of the Last Supper. This film got Buñuel kicked out of Spain.

**878. The Vision Beautiful.** US. 1912. B&W. *Director:* Colin Campbell *Cast:* Herbert Rawlinson, Tom Santschi, Hobart Bosworth, Betty Harte

A young monk is struggling with his vocation. He would rather be an artist and loves to daydream. In a vision Christ appears and reminds him that whatever he does for the least of his brethren he does for his savior. The monk embraces his demanding religious life.

**879. La Viuda negra.** Alameda. Mexico. 1977. 78m. C. *Director:* Arturo Ripstein *Writer:* Vicente Armendáriz, Francisco del Villar, Ramón Obón, Raphael Solana (play) *Cast:* Hilda Aguirre, Eduardo Alcaraz, Mário Almada, René Casados, Jorge Fegán, Sergio Jiménez, Leonor Llausás

A priest shares what he hears in the confessional with his mistress. The film caused controversy because of its subject matter. Also known as *Black Widow.*

**880. La Voce.** F. J. Lucas. Italy/Yugoslavia. 1982. 122m. C. *Producer:* Oscar Brazzi *Director:* Brunello Rondi *Writer:* Tullio Pinelli, Brunello Rondi *Cast:* Liliana Tari, Marisa Belli, Bekim Fehmiu, Margaret Mazzantini, Rossano Brazzi

Biographical picture on the childhood of Mother Teresa of Calcutta (Liliana Tari). She is portrayed as a normal girl with a beautiful voice. She contracts tuberculosis and is sent to a mountain convent to recover. She hates the stifling life of nuns until a priest (Rossano Brazzi) just returned from India sparks her interest. Also known as *The Voice.*

**881. Vogliamoci bene.** International Film Associates. Italy. 1949. 88m. B&W. *Producer:* Sonio Coletti, Paolo William Tamburella *Director:* Paolo William Tamburella

*Writer*: G. Collegare, Jacopo Corsi *Cast*: Nando Bruno, Lauro Gazzolo, Mario Nicotra, Peppino Spadaro, Arturo Bragaglia, Paolo Stoppa, Patrizia Mangano

The historic clock of a small town needs to be repaired but there is no money to pay fro the repairs. Priest Don Paolo (Peppino Spadaro) is so committed to fixing the clock that he raises the money by running a lottery. The Communist and Socialist townspeople are unhappy that the priest will get the credit. Also in question is what will happen to the extra money. The mayor forms committees to answer the concerns. One day a mechanic, who has no love of either the cleric or the politicians, fixes the clock himself. Also known as *Ring Around the Clock*.

**The Voice** *see* **La Voce**

**882. The Vow.** US. 1918. B&W.

Love story of a priest and nun told in song. At the beginning of the film we learn that the songs of the repentant monk were buried. Both the priest and the nun were devout to the end—wedded to the church.

**883. Vredens Dag.** George J. Schaefer & Son. Denmark. 1943. 110m. B&W. *Producer*: Carl Theodor Dreyer, Tage Nielsen *Director*: Carl Theodor Dreyer *Writer*: Hans Wiers-Jenssens (novel), Carl Theodor Dreyer, Poul Knudsen, Paul La Cour, Mogens Skot-Hansen *Cast*: Thorkild Roose, Lisbeth Movin, Sigrid Neiiendam, Preben Lerdorff Rye, Anna Svierkier, Albert Hoeberg, Olaf Ussing

In a 17th century Danish village, the young wife of the town's aging pastor falls in love with the pastor's son. Her confession of this affair brings on her husband's death. The pastor's mother accuses the widow of being a witch. In the background an old woman is accused of witchcraft and is eventually burnt at the stake. Also known as *Day of Wrath*.

**884. The Waifs.** Triangle. US. 1916. B&W. *Producer*: Thomas H. Ince *Director*: Scott Sidney *Writer*: J. G. Hawks *Cast*: Jane Grey, William Desmond, Robert Kortman, Carol Holloway, J. Frank Burke, Fannie Midgley, Lewis Durham, Truly Shattuck, Harry Keenan

During graduation at a theological seminary, Arthur Rayburn (William Desmond) drinks from a spiked punch and the Bishop defrocks him. He loses his fiancée and ends up in the slums. Rags (Jane Grey) a piano player saves him from suicide. Arthur redeems himself by opening a mission in the slums. The Bishop reinstates him and he gets his love back.

**885. A Walk to Remember.** Warner. US. 2002. 101m. C. *Producer*: Denise Di Novi, Hunt Lowry *Director*: Adam Shankman *Writer*: Karen Janszen, Nicholas Sparks (novel) *Cast*: Shane West, Mandy Moore, Peter Coyote, Daryl Hannah, Lauren German, Clayne Crawford, Al Thompson, Paz de la Huerta, Jonathan Parks Jordan, Matt Lutz, David Andrews, David Lee Smith

Moody youth Landon Carter (Shane West) and his buddies cause a classmate's injury during an initiation ritual. He takes the blame and is forced to tutor younger students at a nearby school and in the school play. He is upset because only loser, nerds, and do-gooders do such things. He meets Jamie Sullivan (Mandy Moore) daughter of the town's Baptist minister Reverend Sullivan (Peter Coyote) also tutoring there. At first, they dislike each other but slowly fall in love. Her father doesn't approve of their relationship because boys like Cater have expectations. A dark cloud descends but their love remains true.

**886. The Walls Come Tumbling Down.** Columbia. US. 1946. 82m. B&W. *Producer*: Albert J. Cohen *Director*: Lothar Mendes *Writer*: Jo Eisinger (novel), Wilfrid H. Petitt *Cast*: Lee Bowman, Marguerite Chapman, Edgar Buchanan, George Macready, Lee Patrick, Jonathan Hale, J. Edward Bromberg, Elisabeth Risdon, Miles Mander, Moroni Olsen, Katherine Emery, Noel Cravat, Bob Ryan, Charles La Torre

The story of a well known columnist Gilbert Archer (Lee Bowman) whose friend, an aged priest, is found hanged in the rectory. The police think it is suicide but Gilbert suspects foul play. Gilbert decides to investigate and find the killer.

**887. The War of the Worlds.** Paramount. US. 1953. 85m. C. *Producer*: George Pal

*Director*: Byron Haskin, George Pal *Writer*: Barre Lyndon, H. G. Wells (novel) *Cast*: Gene Barry, Ann Robinson, Les Tremayne, Lewis Martin, Robert Cornthwaite, Sandro Giglio, William Phipps, Paul Frees, Ann Codee, Jack Kruschen, Vernon Rich, Cedric Hardwicke (commentary)

Film adaptation of H.G. Wells' tale of alien invasion of Earth by Martians. In one scene before the aliens attack, Pastor Dr. Matthew Collins (Lewis Martin) approaches the alien ships reciting the Lord's Prayer. He feels that the aliens are also God's creatures and therefore are not evil. The aliens greet him with a ray blast and death. A scientist Dr. Clayton (Gene Barry) and the pastor's niece Sylvia (Ann Robinson) fall in love amidst the alien invasion. At the end of the film churches are used as refuge against the aliens.

**Warrior of Russia** *see* **Aleksandr Nevsky**

**Ways of Love** *see* **Il Miracolo**

**Wedding Night** *see* **I Can't...I Can't**

**888. The Weekend Nun.** ABC. (TV). US. 1972. 90m. C. *Producer*: Thomas L. Miller, Edward K. Milkis *Director*: Jeannot Szwarc *Writer*: Ken Trevey *Cast*: Joanna Pettet, Vic Morrow, Ann Sothern, James Gregory, Beverly Garland, Kay Lenz, Michael Clark, Tina Andrews, Judson Pratt

Based on the true life of a nun who was a probation officer. Sister Mary Damian/Marjorie Walker (Joanna Pettet) is a young nun torn between her secular job as a daytime juvenile probation officer and the vows she has taken with the church. Based on the life of Louisiana nun Sister Fabian/Joyce Duco.

**889. Weekend of Terror.** ABC. (TV). US. 1970. 90m. C. *Producer*: Joel Freeman *Director*: Jud Taylor *Writer*: Lionel E. Siegel *Cast*: Robert Conrad, Lee Majors, Carol Lynley, Lois Nettleton, Jane Wyatt, Kevin Hagen, Todd Andrews, Ann Doran, Gregory Sierra

Three nuns on a weekend trip are kidnapped by two desperate men. Soon realize that their abductors only need one of them alive to substitute for a hostage that they accidentally killed.

**Welcome Reverend!** *see* **Benvenuto, Reverendo!**

**890. We're No Angels.** Paramount. US. 1989. 101m. C. *Producer*: Art Linson *Director*: Neil Jordan *Writer*: David Mamet *Cast*: Robert De Niro, Sean Penn, Demi Moore, Hoyt Axton, Bruno Kirby, Ray McAnally, James Russo, Wallace Shawn, John C. Reilly, Jay Brazeau

Two escaped convicts (Robert De Niro, Sean Penn) on the run are mistaken for priests. They use the monastery as a refuge while disguised as priests.

**891. What Love Will Do.** Fox Film Corp. US. 1921. B&W. *Director*: William K. Howard *Writer*: John Stone, Gordon Rigby *Cast*: Edna Murphy, Johnnie Walker, Glen Cavender, Barbara Tennant, Richard Tucker, Edwin B. Tilton

Goldie Rowan (Barbara Tennant) elopes with Herbert Dawson (Richard Tucker) leaving her husband and 3-year-old son, Johnny. Upon hearing that her husband has died she marries Dawson, only to be deserted by him. Johnny grows up and falls in love with the minister's daughter. Now a traveling evangelist, Dawson, comes to town and delegates Johnny to act as treasurer of his funds. He plans to have Johnny beaten and robbed, but tries to alter his plans when he sees Goldie in the congregation, but is killed by his cohorts. Goldie is reunited with her lost son.

**892. What Money Can Buy.** Gaumont. UK. 1928. B&W. *Producer*: Maurice Elvey, Gareth Gundrey *Director*: Edwin Greenwood *Writer*: Edwin Greenwood, Ben Landeck (play), Arthur Shirley (play) *Cast*: Madeleine Carroll, Humberston Wright, John Longden, Cecil Barry, Alf Goddard, Maudie Dunham, Ante Sharp Bolster, Judd Green

Cleric alibis ex-convict when she is blamed for death of wealthy husband.

**893. When Dawn Came.** State Rights. US. 1920. 85m. B&W. *Producer*: Hugh Dierker *Director*: Colin Campbell *Writer*: Mrs. Hugh E. Dierker *Cast*: Lee Shumway, James Barrows, William Conklin, Kathleen Kirkham, Colleen Moore, Master Isadore Cohen

Dr. John Brandon (Lee Shumway), a young and ambitious physician, devotes his knowledge to the poor until he meets a newspaper woman. She convinces another doctor to take him as a partner. Dr. Brandon's success causes him to become a drunk, fortunately a priest Father Michael Farrell (James Barrows) helps him find his way. The physician performs an operation on a blind girl and discovers love.

**894. When in Rome.** MGM. US. 1952. 78m. B&W. *Producer & Director*: Clarence Brown *Writer*: Dorothy Kingsley, Robert Buckner, Charles Schnee *Cast*: Van Johnson, Paul Douglas, Joseph Calleia, Carlo Rizzo, Tudor Owen, Dino Nardi, Aldo Silvani, Mario Siletti, Argentina Brunetti, Mimi Aguglia

On a trip to Rome for the 1950 Holy Year celebrations, Father John X. Halligan (Van Johnson) befriends Joe Brewster (Paul Douglas). Unknown to John is that Joe is an escaped convict from San Quentin. When the boat docks, Joe steals John's cassock and avoids the waiting police. He fools two priests who think he is John. They whisk him away on a bus full of clerics bound for Rome. John is forced to wear Joe's street clothes and he is arrested. The police soon realize that they have the wrong man. Meanwhile Joe finds himself at The Monastery of the Three Saints. The police follow John thinking that he will lead them to Joe. John ends up at the monastery and finds Joe. During a fire at the monastery Joe saves John's life. John hears Joe's confession and knows that he feels repentant. John and Joe separate and go their own ways. When he doesn't turn himself in, John feels that perhaps Joe has not seen the light. John finds himself at the monastery and sees Joe. Joe decides to a take a vow of silence and wishes to stay at the monastery. An elderly monk tells that he knows the truth about Joe and believes him. John gives Joe his prized possession his mother's rosary. John promises to try and get him a pardon in America.

**895. Where Angels Go, Trouble Follows.** Columbia. US. 1968. 93m. C. *Producer*: William Frye *Director*: James Neilson *Writer*: Blanche Hanalis *Cast*: Rosalind Russell, Stella Stevens, Binnie Barnes, Mary Wickes, Dolores Sutton, Susan Saint James, Barbara Hunter, Milton Berle, Arthur Godfrey, Van Johnson, Robert Taylor, William Lundigan, Michael Christian, John Findlater, Alice Rawlings

Sequel to the 1966 film *The Trouble With Angels*. Rosalind Russell is again cast as the conservative Mother Superior. This time around the nuns and students, from the Catholic school St. Francis Academy in Pennsylvania, are on a cross-country bus trip to an inter-faith youth rally in California. Mother Superior clashes with the younger and more progressive Sister George (Stella Stevens).

**896. Where the River Runs Black.** MGM. US. 1986. 92m. C. *Producer*: Harry J. Ufland *Director*: Christopher Cain *Writer*: David Kendall (book), Peter Silverman, Neal Jimenez *Cast*: Charles Dunning, Alessandro Rabelo, Ajay Naidu, Divana Brandao, Peter Horton, Castulo Guerra, Conchata Ferrell, Dana Delany, Chico Díaz, Marcelo Rabelo, Ariel Coelho, Paulo Sergio Oliveira, Mario Borges

A boy is born to a strange woman who lives along on the banks of a river in Brazil. He is conceived when a missionary priest happens upon the woman, makes love to her and then leaves in his canoe. The wild boy lives with nature and is a friend of the dolphins. When his mother is murdered, he ends up in a city with Father O'Reilly (Charles Dunning) who knew his father. This fatherly priest must determine the fate of the boy.

**897. Which Way Is Up?** UI. US. 1977. 94m. C. *Producer*: Steve Krantz *Director*: Michael Schultz *Writer*: Cecil Brown, Carl Gottlieb *Cast*: Lonette McKee, Margaret Avery, Richard Pryor, Morgan Woodward, Marilyn Coleman, Bebe Drake, Gloria Edwards, Ernesto Hernández, DeWayne Jessie, Morgan Roberts, Diane Rodriguez

Richard Pryor plays three roles an orange picker Leroy Jones, Leroy's father (a dirty old man), and Reverend Lenox Thomas, who has impregnated his Leroy's wife. Leroy tries to seduce the reverend's wife. Americanized remake of the Italian film *The Seduction of Mimi*.

**898. While Satan Sleeps.** Paramount. US. 1922. B&W. *Director*: Joseph Henabery *Writer*: Albert S. Le Vino, Peter B. Kyne *Cast*: Jack Holt, Wade Boteler, Mabel Van Buren, Fritzi Brunette, Will Walling, J. P. Lockney, Fred Huntley, Bobby Mack, Sylvia Ashton, Herbert Standing

The son of an Anglican bishop (Jack Holt) escapes from prison, assumes the disguise of an Episcopalian clergyman, and heads west. He wins many converts with his fists and plots bank robberies in the town of Panamint. He repents, confesses his past to the congregation, and returns to prison. Based on the story "The Parson of Panamint."

**899. Whispering Devils.** Equity Pictures. US. 1920. B&W. *Producer*: Harry Garson *Director*: John M. Voshell *Writer*: Henry Arthur Jones *Cast*: Conway Tearle, Rosemary Theby, Sam Sothern, Esther Ralston, Warren Millais, Lenore Lynard

Puritanical minister Reverend Michael Faversham (Conway Tearle) shows no tolerance towards Rose when he commands her to confess that she has an illegitimate child. He has no room in his heart for compassion. He secretly loves Audrey Lesden (Rosemary Theby) but won't admit it. One night he finds himself on a lonely island with her and their love is unstoppable. During the next sermon he removes his robes and confesses his crime. Suddenly he awakens and learns that it was all a dream to show him compassion.

**900. White Hands.** Wid Gunning. US. 1922. B&W. *Producer*: Max Graf *Director & Writer*: Lambert Hillyer, C. Gardner Sullivan *Cast*: Hobart Bosworth, Robert McKim, Freeman Wood, Al Kaufman, Muriel Frances Dana, Elinor Fair, George O'Brien

This is the story of the love between a sea captain Hurricane Hardy (Hobart Bosworth) and a missionary woman Helen Maitland (Elinor Fair). Hardy feels regenerated by her and when he realizes, he can't have Helen, he leaves. Now she is free to rehabilitate a handsome young man addicted to drink.

**901. The White Rose.** UA. US. 1923. 100m. B&W. *Producer, Director & Writer*: D. W. Griffith *Cast*: Mae Marsh, Carol Demp-

ster, Ivor Novello, Neil Hamilton, Lucille La Verne, Porter Strong, Jane Thomas, Kate Bruce, Erville Alderson, Herbert Sutch, Joseph Burke, Mary Foy, Charles Emmett Mack, Uncle Tom Jenkins

Joseph Beaugarde (Ivor Novello) graduates from the seminary and decides to experience the worldly side of life to see what he must battle. Joseph has an affair with a sweet young girl Bessie (Mae Marsh). He feels guilty and rushes home to repent and marry the girl he left behind. Meanwhile, Bessie loses her job and finds herself pregnant and ill. From the pulpit he preaches about the sin of the flesh. One day Bessie shows up with the baby. He confesses his sin and decides to marry Bessie.

**902. The White Sister.** V-L-S-E, Inc. US. 1915. B&W. *Director*: Fred E. Wright *Writer*: Francis Marion Crawford (novel), Walter C. Hackett *Cast*: Viola Allen, Richard Travers, Florence Oberle, Thomas Commerford, Emilie Melville, John Thorn, Sidney Ainsworth, Ernest Maupain, Camille D'Arcy, John Cossar, Frank Dayton

When Donna Angela Chiaromonte's (Viola Allen) father dies in an auto accident her deceiving aunt burns the will and inherits everything. After hearing the news that her lover, Giovanni (Richard Travers), has been killed in battle in Egypt she joins the Convent of the White Sisters. After being held prisoner for five years he returns and tries to get Angela to renounce her vows, but she refuses. He is then injured when a powder magazine explodes, but refuses to have his arm amputated to save his life. A sympathetic Monsignor obtains a special order from the Pope for Angela to leave the sisterhood. Giovanni has the operation and the two are reunited.

**903. The White Sister.** Metro. US. 1923. 143m. B&W. *Producer & Director*: Henry King *Writer*: Francis Marion Crawford (novel) George V. Hobart, Charles E. Whittaker *Cast*: Lillian Gish, Ronald Colman, Gail Kane, J. Barney Sherry, Charles Lane, Juliette La Violette, Sig Serena, Alfredo Bertone, Roman Ibanez, Alfredo Martinelli, Ida Carloni Talli, Giovanni Viccola, Antonio Barda

Angela Chiaromonte (Lillian Gish) is left penniless and homeless when her father dies. Her fiancé goes to war in Africa and when she hears reports of his death she joins a convent. When he returns after being taken prisoner he tries to persuade her to renounce her vows, but she refuses. He later dies helping the townspeople escape an erupting volcano.

**904. The White Sister.** MGM. US. 1933. 110m. B&W. *Producer & Director*: Victor Fleming *Writer*: F. Marion Crawford (novel), David Ogden Stewart, Walter C. Hackett *Cast*: Helen Hayes, Clark Gable, Lewis Stone, Louise Closser Hale, May Robson, Edward Arnold, Alan Edwards, Nat Pendleton, Sarah Padden

Tells the story of a forbidden romance between Angela Chiaromonte (Helen Hayes), the daughter of an Italian prince and a soldier named Giovanni (Clark Gable). One day on her way to Giovanni's home her automobile collides with her father's and the prince dies instantly. Grief stricken Angela arranges with Father Saracinesca (Edward Arnold) to enter a convent and she becomes a nun. During World War I, Giovanni becomes a fighter and is presumed dead. Giovanni discovers that Angela is now a nun. He tries to persuade her to join him but he realizes that she is committed to God. He is hit and dies in Angela's arms.

**Who Killed Fen Markham** *see* **The Angelus**

**Why Did Bodhi-Dharma Leave for the East?** *see* **Dharmaga tongjoguro kan kkadalgun**

**905. Wide Awake.** Miramax. US. 1998. 88m. C. *Producer*: Cathy Konrad, Cary Woods *Director & Writer*: M. Night Shyamalan *Cast*: Joseph Cross, Timothy Reifsnyder, Dana Delany, Denis Leary, Robert Loggia, Rosie O'Donnell, Camryn Manheim, Vicki Giunta, Heather Casler, Dan Lauria, Julia Stiles

A grief stricken fifth grader Joshua Beal (Joseph Cross) goes in search of God after his beloved grandfather dies. While attending an all-boy school Waldron Academy, he runs into many growing pains and trouble. A sports loving nun Sister Terry (Rosie O'-

Donnell) befriends the boy and helps him in his quest for God.

**The Wild Heart** *see* **Gone to Earth**

**906. Wild Honey.** William L Sherry Service. US. 1918. B&W. *Director*: Francis J. Grandon *Writer*: Louis Joseph Vance, Vingie E. Roe *Cast*: Doris Kenyon, Frank Mills, Edgar Jones, Jack Hopkins, Joe Mack, Howard Kyle, Henry Hebert, Herbert Standing, Nellie King, Vinnie Burns, Ruth Taylor, Mildred Leary

Young Clergyman Dr. David Warwick (Herbert Standing) calls on Pastor Holbrook (Frank Mills) and his wife in the company of an actress. They wish to marry but are afraid of the effect of her profession on his career. Pastor Holbrook tells the story of Wild Honey. Young clergyman Jim Brown (Frank Mills) goes to a camp intending to reform and save souls. He falls in love with a young dance hall woman. She falls in love with him and takes a lot of verbal abuse. We switch back to Pastor Holbrook where we learn that he is Jim Brown and his wife is Wild Honey and they have been married for 30 years.

**Winter Light** *see* **Nattvardsgästerna**

**907. The Wisdom of Brother Ambrose.** Hepworth. UK. 1911. B&W. *Director*: Lewin Fitzhamon

Monk tricks highwayman into using his bullets.

**908. Wise Blood.** New Line Cinema. US/German. 1979. 108m. C. *Producer*: Kathy Fitzgerald, Michael Fitzgerald *Director*: John Huston *Writer*: Benedict Fitzgerald, Michael Fitzgerald, Flannery O'Connor (story) *Cast*: Brad Dourif, Ned Beatty, Harry Dean Stanton, Dan Shor, Amy Wright, Mary Nell Santacroce, John Huston

A young man Hazel Motes (Brad Dourif) home from the war sheds his uniform for clothes that make him look like a preacher. He goes to the city and is attracted to a blind preacher and his teenage daughter. We learn that his grandfather was a brimstone preacher. He is driven to preach himself. His church is without Christ since there is no sin and no need for a redeemer but only a trust in oneself. He discovers that the blind preacher can see and is a fake. He blinds himself to see what it means and becomes a prisoner of his landlady.

**The Witch Woman** *see* **Prästänkan**
**Witchcraft** *see* **Häxan**
**Witchcraft** *see* **Myrkrahöfðinginn**
**Within a Cloister** *see* **Interno d'un convento.**
**Within the Gates** *see* **Miraklet**

**909. Woman in the Dark.** Republic. US. 1952. 60m. B&W. *Director*: George Blair *Writer*: Albert DeMond, Nicolas Cosentino (play) *Cast*: Penny Edwards, Ross Elliott, Rick Vallin, Richard Benedict, Argentina Brunetti, Martin Garralaga, Edit Angold, Peter Brocco, Barbara Billingsley, John Doucette, Richard Irving, Luther Crockett, Carl Thompson, Charles Sullivan

Story of three sons of an Italian-American family caught up in a jewel robbery. The three sons are a priest Father Tony Morello (Ross Elliott), a lawyer Phil Morello (Rick Vallin), and a ne'er-do-well Gino Morello (Richard Benedict). The third son is used as a patsy in a jewel robbery and with the help of his two brothers is gotten out of the jam. He is later shot by the crooks and the lawyer brother takes revenge with help from the police.

**910. The Woman Who Came Back.** Republic. US. 1945. 68m. B&W. *Producer& Director*: Walter Colmes *Writer*: Dennis Cooper, Lee Willis, John H. Kafka *Cast*: John Loder, Nancy Kelly, Otto Kruger, Ruth Ford, Harry Tyler, Jeanne Gail, Almira Sessions, J. Farrell MacDonald, Emmett Vogan

Lorna Webster (Nancy Kelly) returns to the New England village her family has lived in for generations. She believes she is bewitched by a 300-year-old curse. Strange things happen and the townspeople all believe in the curse. Her doctor fiancé Dr. Matt Adams (John Loder) and the village minister Reverend Jim Stevens (Otto Kruger) find evidence clearing her of the curse.

**911. A Woman Who Sinned.** F.B.O. US. 1924. 70m. B&W. *Producer, Director &Writer*: Finis Fox *Cast*: Morgan Wallace, Irene Rich, Lucien Littlefield, Mae Busch, Dick Brandon, Cissy Fitzgerald, Rex Lease

The plot revolves around two contrasting couples, one, a Wall Street broker and his neglected wife; the other a New-England minister Reverend Hillburn (Lucien Littlefield) and his contented wife (Mae Busch). The city playboy sails into the small town on his yacht and awakens interest in the preacher's wife. He lures her aboard his boat. She is afraid to face her husband and child, but gets her revenge by sending him to prison. Years later she has become cold and calculating. She is reformed by a young evangelist, who turns out to be the son she left years before.

**912. Won by Losing.** Initial. UK. 1916. B&W. *Director*: Bertram Philips *Cast*: Queenie Thomas, Frank McClellan

Cleric weds woman to reform her but she takes to drink and dies.

**The Word** *see* **Ordet**

**913. The Worldly Madonna.** Equity Pictures. US. 1922. 62m. B&W. *Director*: Harry Garson *Writer*: Sada Cowan *Cast*: Clara Kimball Young, William P. Carleton, Richard Tucker, George Hackathorne, Jean de Limur, William Marion, Milla Davenport

Twin sisters trade places. Janet Trevor (Clara Kimball), a convent novitiate trades places with her twin sister Lucy, a cabaret dancer, because she believes she has killed a politician named John McBride. Janet falls in love with McBride and the two are implicated in the murder of Toni Lorenz, but it is revealed that restaurateur Alan Graves bribed Lorenz to leave the country. Janet remains with McBride and Lucy becomes a nun.

**914. The World's Greatest Sinner.** Frenzy Productions. US. 1962. 82m. B&W/C. *Producer, Director & Writer*: Timothy Carey *Cast*: Timothy Carey, Gil Baretto, Betty Rowland, James Farley, Gail Griffen, Grace De Carolis, Gitta Maynard, Gene Pollock, Whitey Jent, Carolina Samario

Insurance salesman Clarence Hillard (Timothy Carey) declares himself God and forms the Eternal Man Party. He becomes a rock and roll evangelist to gain converts. An elderly woman finances his operation and he thinks of politics. His mother dies and his wife and daughter leave him. Upset and doubting himself, he challenges God to reveal himself. A miracle occurs and he repents.

**915. The Wrath of God.** MGM. US. 1972. 111m. C. *Producer:* Peter Katz *Director:* Ralph Nelson *Writer:* James Graham (novel), Jack Higgins, Ralph Nelson *Cast:* Robert Mitchum, Frank Langella, Rita Hayworth, John Colicos, Victor Buono, Ken Hutchison, Paula Pritchett, Gregory Sierra, Frank Ramírez, Enrique Lucero

Defrocked priest Van Horne (Robert Mitchum) aids a terrorized Latin American town during the 1920s and becomes a reluctant hero.

**The Year of Maria** *see* **Año Mariano**

**916. Yo, la peor de todas.** First Run Features. Argentina. 1990. 105m. C. *Producer:* Lita Stantic *Director:* María Luisa Bemberg *Writer:* María Luisa Bemberg, Antonio Larreta *Cast:* Assumpta Serna, Dominique Sanda, Héctor Alterio, Lautaro Murúa, Graciela Araujo, Alberto Segado, Gerardo Romano, Franklin Caicedo

Story of 17th century real-life Mexican poet and writer Sister Juana Ines de la Cruz (Assumpta Serna) a target of the Spanish Inquisition. A viceroy's wife protects the nun so she may continue to write. When she leaves, Sister Juana is without support and will be betrayed. As the Sister's reputation grows the Church tries to silence her. The title of the film comes from the last documents known to have been written by her. Also known as *I, the Worst of All.*

**The Young Monk** *see* **Der Junge Mönch**

**Z dalekiego Kraju** *see* **From a Far Country**

**917. Zapomenuté světlo.** Asociace Ceských Filmových Klubu. Czechoslovakia. 1996. 105m. C. *Producer:* Alice Nemanska, Jana Tomsova, Ivana Kacirkova *Director:* Vladimír Michálek *Writer:* Jakub Deml (novel), Milena Jelínek *Cast:* Bolek Polívka, Veronika Zilková, Petr Kavan, Jirì Pecha, Simona Pekova, Antonin Kinsky, Jirì Lábus, Richard Metznarowski

Father Holy (Bolek Polívka) is a village priest who battles against the state and religious bureaucracies in 1980's Czechoslovakia. He is trying to raise money for a new church roof. In his losing battle, he is ordered transferred from his parish and his allies. With the help of a local sculptor he is able to make a copy of a statue and sell the original to repair the church. He is also able to counsel and comfort a dying woman. Film was adapted from the novel *The Forgotten Light* by the 1930's Czech writer/poet and Catholic priest Jakub Deml. Also known as *Forgotten Light.*

**918. Zir-e noor-e maah.** Iran. 2001. 96m. C. *Producer:* Manouchehr Mohammadi *Director & Writer:* Seyyed Reza Mir-Karimi *Cast:* Hossein Pour Sattar, Hamed Rajabali, Mehran Rajabi, Mahmud Nazar-Alian, Fereshteh Sadr-Orafai, Ashar Heidari

Look at Iran's Islamic clergy in this tale of a young man troubled by doubts. After completing his theological studies, a young man hesitates to wear the turban and robes of a mullah. One day a street boy steals the materials he has purchased to make his robe and turban. While searching for the boy, he discovers a community of homeless men living under a bridge. His contact with these spiritually honest outcasts fulfills him more than religious life. Also known as *Under the Moonlight.*

**919. Zulu.** Paramount. UK. 1964. 138m. C. *Producer:* Joseph Levine, Stanley Baker *Director:* Cy Endfield *Writer:* John Prebble, Cy Endfield *Cast:* Stanley Baker, Jack Hawkins, Ulla Jacobsson, James Booth, Michael Caine, Nigel Green, Ivor Emmanuel, Paul Daneman, Neil McCarthy

There is news that 4,000 Zulu warriors are on their way. Unfortunately, there is no chance for reinforcements because they have already been wiped out. Reverend Otto Witt (Jack Hawkins) is a missionary who pleads in vain with Lt. John Chard (Stanely Baker) to evacuate the garrison. He also pleads for the commandment not to kill but lay down your arms. Chard sends the missionary and his daughter away because he is afraid that Witt's talk may demoralize the soldiers. A handful of British soldiers withstand the onslaught of the 4,000 Zulu warriors.

# Television Series

**920. Aftermash.** CBS. US. 1983–84. 30m. *Cast:* Harry Morgan, Jamie Farr, William Christopher, Barbara Townsend, Ann Pitoniak, Rosalind Chao, John Chappell, Peter Michael Goetz, Jay O. Sanders, Brandis Kemp, Lois Foraker, Wendy Schaal, Patrick Cranshaw, Shirley Lang, David Ackroyd, Carolsue Walker, Susan Luck

The Korean War is over and Dr. Sherman Potter (Harry Morgan), Max Klinger (Jamie Farr), and Father Mulcahy (William Christopher) of the 4077th M.A.S.H. unit are now on the staff of the General Pershing Veteran's Administration Hospital in River Bend, Missouri, where Dr. Potter is chief of staff. Father Mulcahy serves as the hospital chaplain. Other characters include Mildred Potter (Barbara Townsend), his wife, Dr. Gene Pfeiffer (Jay O. Sanders), surgical resident, Nurse Coleman (Lois Foraker), patients, and Mike D'Angelo (John Chappell), a bureaucratic hospital administrator. This is a spin-off of the television series *M*A*S*H.*

**921. Aggigma psyhis.** Antenna Entertainment. Greece. 1998. *Cast:* Stavros Zalmas, Theofania Papathoma, Elena Nathanael, Petros Fyssoun, Christoforos Papakaliatis, Babis Alatzas, Yannis Voglis, Christopher Alexander King

A priest falls in love with a female artist. A popular Greek television series. Also known as *Touch of a Soul.*

**922. All Gas and Gaiters.** BBC. UK. 1967–71. 33 episodes *Cast:* Derek Nimmo, William Mervyn, Robertson Hare, John Baron, Ernest Clark

One of the first British television series to poke fun at the church. Comedy in which the Dean of Cathedral of St. Ogg tries unsuccessfully to bring order and sanity to the church's daily events. The Bishop (William Mervyn), the Archdeacon (Robertson Hare) and the chaplain Noote (Derek Nimmo) lead lazy and enjoy life's pleasures. Reverend Mervyn Noote is a naive and bumbling chaplain at this 13th century cathedral. Helping Noote are the Bishop (William Mervyn) and the aging Archdeacon (Robertson Hare) all of whom cross paths with Dean (John Baron).

**923. Amazing Grace.** NBC. US. 1995. 60m. *Cast:* Patty Duke, Marguerite Moreau, Justin Garms, Dan Lauria, Joe Spano, Gavin Harrison, Lorraine Toussaint, Robin Gammell

Hannah Miller (Patty Duke) was a small town nurse with a difficult life and failed marriage. All of which contributes to her drug addiction that almost kills her. Hannah Miller turns her life around and starts a new life as a minister. Her two children—a young son who accepts her decision to preach and her agnostic daughter- complicate her life. Also, causing problems is the church deacon, who opposed her hiring. Also known as *Wing and a Prayer.*

**924. Amen.** NBC. US.1986–1991. 30m. *Cast:* Sherman Hemsley, Clifton Davis, Anna Maria Horsford, Babrbara Montgomery, Roz Ryan, Jester Hairston, Franklyn Seales, Rosetta LeNoire, Elsa Raven, Tony T. Johnson, Bumper Robinson

Deacon Ernest Frye (Sherman Hemsley) whose father founded the First Community Church in Philadelphia. He intends to keep control of the church, that is until the new minister Reverend Reuben Gregory (Clifton Davis) is hired. They clash on a regular basis but both care about the church. Frye's unmarried daughter Thelma (Anna

Maria Horsford) eventually dates and then marries the Reverend. Guest appearances included a 13-year-old preacher Reverend Johnny Tolbert (played by real-life child minister Reverend William Hudson III). Actor Clifton Davis was a real-life minister and served as assistant pastor of a church in California while filming the show.

**925. Bless Me, Father.** UK. 1978–1981. 21 episodes. *Cast:* Arthur Lowe, Daniel Abineri, Gabrielle Daye, Derek Francis, Patrick McAlinney, Sheila Keith

Father Charles Clement Duddleswell (Arthur Lowe), a Roman Catholic priest, gets a new curate Father Neil Boyd (Daniel Abineri). They live in the London suburb of Fairwater with their housekeeper Mrs. Pring (Gabrielle Daye).

**926. Cadfael.** PBS. UK. 1994–1996. 13 episodes. 75m. *Cast:* Derek Jacobi, Mark Charnock, Peter Copley, Michael Culver, Julian Firth, Sean Pertwee, Terrence Hardiman, Anthony Green, Eoin McCarthy

A crusader returns to England and becomes a crime-solving monk by the name of Brother Cadfael (Derek Jacobi). At Shrewsbury Abbey, he is assigned the position of herbalist. He uses his knowledge to solve mysteries around the Abbey. Based on four novels from the series of Cadfael mysteries by Ellis Peters.

**927. The Cavanaughs.** CBS. US. 1986. 30m. *Cast:* Barnard Hughes, Christine Ebersole, Peter Michael Goetz, Mary Tanner, John Short, Danny Cooksey, Parker Jacobs

Francis 'Pop' Cavanaugh (Barnard Hughes) is the Irish patriarch of the Cavanaugh family. His daughter Kit (Christine Ebersole) returns after 20 years to help raise her widowed brother's family. Chuck's kids include Father Chuck Cavanaugh Jr. (John Short) a young priest, Mary Margaret (Mary Tanner) a shy teenager, and obnoxious twins Kevin and John.

**928. Christy.** CBS. US. 1994–1995. 60m. *Cast:* Kellie Martin, Tyne Daly, Randall Batinkoff, Tess Harper, Annabelle Price, Stewart Finlay-McLennan, Emily Schulman, Andy Nichols, Frank Hoyt Taylor, Clay Jeter, LaVar Burton

In 1912, nineteen year old Christy Huddleston (Kellie Martin) leaves her comfortable home to teach at a missionary school in a remote Appalachian mountain community. She was motivated by a speech at her church by Quaker Alice Henderson (Tyne Daly) who runs the school with her son-in-law Reverend David Grantland (Randall Batinkoff). Christy encounters many hardships and misgivings about teaching in such a poor community but she perseveres.

**929. Coronet Blue.** CBS. US. 1967. 60m. *Cast:* Frank Converse, Brian Bedford, Joe Silver

Michael Alden (Frank Converse) has total amnesia and remembers nothing except that when he was found in the water he was mumbling the words 'coronet blue.' In his quest to try to discover what happened and his true identity, he is assisted by a monk Anthony (Brian Bedford) and Max (Joe Silver).

**930. Dead Zone.** USA. US. 2002- . 60m. *Cast:* Anthony Michael Hall, Nicole deBoer, Chris Bruno, John L. Adams, David Ogden Stiers, Kristen Dalton

Johnny Smith (Anthony Michael Hall) was a respected science teacher with a fiancée until he had a horrible car accident. He was in a coma for six years and when he awoke he had special psychic powers. Johnny can see the past, present, and future lives of anyone he touches. His mother had died and left his inheritance in the care of unscrupulous Reverend Gene Purdy (David Ogden Stiers) head of the ultraconservative Faith Heritage Alliance. Johnny's psychic abilities are very much in demand.

**931. The Family Holvak.** NBC. US. 1975. 60m. *Cast:* Glenn Ford, Julie Harris, Lance Kerwin, Elizabeth Cheshire, Ted Gehring, Cynthia Howard, William McKinney

Reverend Tom Holvak (Glen Ford) and his family face tough times during the Depression in the South. He sells produce grown on church land to help supplement his meager salary. His wife Elizabeth (Julie Harris) and two children, Julie Mae (Elizabeth Cheshire) and Ramey (Lance Kerwin), are there to support him also.

**932. The Fanelli Boys.** NBC. US.

Father Frank Dowling (Tom Bosley) and Sister Stephanie (Tracy Nelson) solve many mysteries. Also in the series are Marie (Mary Wickes) as their busybody housekeeper and Father Prestwick (James Stephens) as a young priest; *Father Dowling Mysteries* (TV, 1989–1991).

1990–1991. 30m. *Cast:* Ann Morgan Guilbert, Ned Eisenberg, Andy Hirsch, Chris Meloni, Joe Pantoliano, Richard Libertini, Nick De-Mauro, Vera Lockwood

Widow Theresa Fanelli is ready to sell her home and move to Florida when her four grown sons return home to have her straighten out their lives. Her brother Father Angelo (Richard Libertini) offers his opinion now and then.

**933. Father Brown.** PBS. UK. 1974. 13 episodes. 60m. *Cast:* Kenneth More, Dennis Burgess

Mystery series with Father Brown (Kenneth More) solving cases based on the stories of G. K. Chesteron.

**934. Father Dowling Mysteries.** NBC/ABC. US. 1989–1991. 60m. *Cast:* Tom Bosley, Tracy Nelson, James Stephens, Mary Wickes, Regina Krueger

Father Frank Dowling (Tom Bosley) with the help of young and savvy Sister Stephanie (Tracy Nelson) solves many murder mysteries. Their home base is St. Michael's in Chicago. The unthreatening team never intimidates people and they are able to get their foot in almost every door. Marie (Mary Wickes) is their busybody housekeeper and Father Prestwick (James Stephens) is a young priest who doesn't realize that the Father and Sister are solving mysteries.

**935. Father Murphy.** NBC. US. 1982–1984. 60m. *Cast:* Merlin Olsen, Moses Gunn, Katherine Cannon, Timothy Gibbs, Lisa Trusel, Scott Mellini, Chez Lister, Charles Tyner, Ivy Bethune, Richard Bergman, Warren Munson, Charles Cooper

Drifter John Michael Murphy (Merlin Olsen) tries to rally the miners to rise against the town boss. For revenge, the boss' henchmen blow up the miners' camp. Murphy feels so guilty that he starts and then runs an orphanage for the now parentless children. He poses as a priest Father Murphy to make it appear legitimate. Later in the series, his deception is uncovered and he marries the schoolteacher and adopts the orphans.

**936. Father Ted.** Channel 4. UK. 1995–1998. 25 episodes. *Cast:* Dermot Morgan, Ardal O'Hanlon, Frank Kelly, Pauline McLynn, Jim Norton

1990s television situation comedy set on the remote fictional Craggy Island off the west coast of Ireland. Three priests Father Ted Crilly (Dermot Morgan), moronic Father Dougal McGuire (Ardal O'Hanlon), and drunken swearing elderly Father Jack Hackett (Frank Kelly) run the remote parish, with Mrs. Doyle (Pauline McLynn) as their tea-addicted housekeeper. Bishop Len Brennan (Jim Norton) is their boss who encouraged their "banishment." Father Ted was in trouble for misappropriating church funds, perhaps dealing with Las Vegas. Father Jack had some unspecified offense against nuns and Father Dougal for a mysterious incident were their offenses. Various parishioners also appear in the series. The show probably would have more episodes except for the death of Dermot Morgan.

**937. The Flying Nun.** ABC.US. 1967–1970. 30m. *Cast:* Sally Field, Marge Redmond, Madeleine Sherwood, Alejandro Rey, Shelley Morrison, Linda Dangcil, Vito Scotti, Manuel Padilla Jr.

Elsie Ethington (Sally Field) is so impressed by the mission work of her aunt that she decides to become a nun. Now as Sister Bertrille she is assigned to the Convent San Tanco near San Juan Puerto Rico. As a nun she has to wear coronets-headgear which has sides that look like wings. That combined with the San Juan trade winds, help ninety-pound Sister Bertrille soar around town. Being a nice person she puts her ability to good use for the community. Her landings are a bit bumpy though. She clashes with Mother Superior (Madeleine Sherwood) but gets along well with Sister Jacqueline (Marge Sherwood) and Sister Sixto (Shelley Morrison).

The show is based on the book *The Fifteenth Pelican* by Tere Rios. At first ABC was afraid of insulting Catholics with the show, but it went on to become approved and actually received the blessings of a religious order who thought it humanized nuns.

**938. Going My Way.** ABC. US. 1962– 1963. 60m. B&W. *Cast:* Gene Kelly, Leo G. Carroll, Dick York, Nydia Westman.

Father Chuck O'Malley (Gene Kelly) is a progressive young priest who is assigned to a parish in the slums of New York to aid crotchety old pastor Father Fitzgibbon (Leo G. Carroll). Boyhood pal Tom Clowell (Dick York) runs the local community center. Mrs. Featherstone (Nydia Westman) is the rectory's housekeeper. The series lasted only one season and was based on the 1944 film *Going My Way.*

**939. Good Morning Miami.** NBC. US. 2002–2003. 30m. *Cast:* Mark Feuerstein, Ashley Williams, Jere Burns, Matt Letscher, Tessie Santiago, Brooke Dillman, Constance Zimmer, Stephon Fuller, Suzanne Pleshette

Hotshot Boston producer Jake Silver (Mark Feuerstein) takes the position as director of the lowest rated morning talk-show in the country Good Morning Miami. A crazy nun in full habit Sister Brenda Trogman (Brooke Dillman) is the weathercaster. During weather forecasts she is always alluding to the guy up there.

**940. Good News.** UPN. US. 1997–1998. 30m. *Cast:* David Ramsey, Roz Ryan, Alexia Robinson, Tracey Cherelle Jones, Guy Torry, Jazsmin Lewis, Billy Preston

Pastor David Randolph (David Ramsey) is the new acting pastor at the Church of Life in Compton, California. Just as he arrives the staff is leaving to start their own congregation. Some church members do stay and help him cope with running the church.

**941. Hack.** CBS. US. 2002–2004. 60m. *Cast:* David Morse, Andre Braugher, George Dzundza, Donna Murphy, Matthew Borish, Bebe Neuwirth, Jacqueline Torres

Mike Olshansky (David Morse) is a Philadelphia cop who was kicked off the force for taking money from a crime scene. Now he drives a cab where he also helps people in need. Father Tom Grizz Grzelak (George Dzundza) is Mike's best friend and spiritual advisor. Sometimes he turns to ex-partner Marcellus Washington (Andre Braugher) who owes him because he took money but Mike never told. Mike tries to be close to his son and ex-wife.

**942. Hail to the Chief.** ABC. US. 1985.

Sister Bertrille (Sally Field) and Sister Jacqueline (Marge Sherwood), in *The Flying Nun* (TV, 1967–70).

30m. *Cast:* Patty Duke, Ted Bessell, Dick Shawn, Glynn Turman, Herschel Bernardi, John Vernon, Murray Hamilton, Maxine Stuart, Ricky Paul Goldin, Quinn Cummings, Alexa Hamilton, Richard Paul

President of the United States Julia Mansfield (Patty Duke) encounters many crises including an attempt to impeach her by Reverend Billy Bickerstaff (Richard Paul) who believes that Satan is responsible for a woman being in the White House.

**943. Have Faith.** ABC. US. 1989. 30m.

*Cast:* Joel Higgins, Ron Carey, Stephen Furst, Frank Hamilton, Francesca Roberts, Todd Susman

Four very different priests reside at St. Catherine's an inner city church in Chicago. Monsignor MacKenzie (Joel Higgins) is the nontraditional leader, traditional Father Tuttle (Frank Hamilton), Father Paglia (Ron Carey) the accountant, and Father Gabe (Stephen Furst) as a new uncertain priest. Sally (Francesca Roberts) is their non-Catholic secretary.

**944. Hell Town.** NBC. US. 1985. 60m. *Cast:* Robert Blake, Whitman Mayo, Jeff Corey, Natalie Core, Vonetta McGee, Isabel Grandin, Tony Longo, Rhonda Dodson, Zitto Kazann, Eddie Quillan

Father Noah "Hardstep" Rivers (Robert Blake) is a dedicated priest in the poor East Los Angeles parish of St. Dominic's. Father Noah is an ex-con now serving his old tough neighborhood. He knows all about the players who may want to take advantage of his flock. You can think of the character as Baretta in a collar.

**945. Hell's Bells.** BBC. UK. 1986. 6 episodes. 30m. *Cast:* Penelope Horner, Susan Jameson, Milton Johns, Phyllida Law, Derek Nimmo, Robert Stevens

Selwyn Makepeace (Derek Nimmo) the Dean of Norchester Cathedral is a traditional clergyman. He's horrified when his new Bishop Godfrey Hethercote (Robert Stephens) turns out to be a socialist with modern ideas.

**946. Highcliffe Manor.** NBC. US. 1979. 30m. *Cast:* Shelley Fabares, Stephen McHattie, Eugenie Ross-Leming, Gerald Gordon, Audrey Landers, Jenny O'Hara, Christian Marlowe, David Byrd, Luis Avalos, Ernie Hudson, Harold Sakata

Setting is Highcliffe Manor a mansion on an island off the coast of Massachusetts where weird things happen such as the creation of a Frankenstein monster. Helen Blacke (Shelley Fabares) owes the mansion and hasn't a clue about what is going on around her. One resident is Reverend Ian Glenville (Stephen McHattie) a girl chasing clergyman from South Africa.

**947. Hope Island.** PAX. US. 1999–2000. 60m. *Cast:* Cameron Daddo, Suki Kaiser, Duncan Fraser, Haig Sutherland, Beverley Elliott, Gina Stockdale, Allison Hossack, David Lewis, Matthew Walker, Max Peters, Brian Jensen

Daniel Cooper (Cameron Daddo), the son of a famous televangelist, starts a new life as a minister on Hope Island in the Pacific Northwest. Initially, the townspeople are very suspicious of the new minister but soon they are singing in church. Even though it is a small community the people led complicated lives.

**948. In the Beginning.** CBS. US. 1978. 30m. 6 episodes. *Cast:* McLean Stevenson, Priscilla Morrill, Priscilla Lopez, Fredric Lehne, Bobby Ellerbee, Jack Dodson, Cosie Costa, Olivia Barash, Michael Anthony

Pompous Father Cleary (McLean Stevenson) keeps trying to get transferred to a more stable environment the conflict is between the Father and the streetwise nun assigned to him, Sister Agnes (Priscilla Lopez). They work in a storefront community center in the inner city of Baltimore-her home neighborhood. She loves it while he hates the hookers, hustlers and the winos. He calls Sister Agnes "Attila the nun." Also in the cast is Sister Lillian (Priscilla Morrill).

**949. Joan of Arcadia.** CBS, US, 2003–2005. 60m. *Cast:* Joe Mantegna, Mary Steenburgen, Amber Tamblyn, Jason Ritter, Michael Welch

16-year-old Joan Girardi (Amber Tamblyn) is visited by God, who is seen in various disguises and asks her to do many different seemingly unrelated tasks. Her family doesn't realize what is going on but do show love and understanding. She has a wheelchair-bound older brother and another brainy brother.

**950. Just the Ten of Us.** ABC. US. 1988–1990. 30m. *Cast:* Bill Kirchenbauer, Deborah Harmon, Heather Langenkamp, Jamie Luner, Brooke Theiss, JoAnn Willette, Frank Bonner, Maxine Elliott, Heidi Zeigler, Matt Shakman

Coach Graham Lubbock (Bill Kirchenbauer) accepts a position at St. Augustine's Academy, a Catholic boys' school. He happens to have five young daughters who every boy wants to date. Father Robert Hargis

(Frank Bonner) is the absent minded head of the school. Sister Ethel (Maxine Elliott) is a scatterbrained elderly nun.

**951. Kate McShane.** CBS. US. 1975. 60m. *Cast:* Anne Meara, Sean McClory, Charles Haid

Female lawyer Kate McShane (Anne Meara) tends to become emotionally involved with her clients. Sometimes she turns to her father Pat (Sean McClory) or her Jesuit priest and law professor brother Ed (Charles Haid).

**952. Kristin.** NBC. US. 2001. 30m. *Cast:* Kristin Chenoweth, Jon Tenney, Larry Romano, Dale Godboldo, Ana Ortiz, Christopher Durang

Kristin fresh from Oklahoma is trying to make it on Broadway. She hasn't had much luck auditioning and needs a job. She meets Reverend Thornhill (Christopher Durang) the pastor of a small Lower East Side chapel. He advises her and helps her get a job with real estate developer Tommy Ballatine (Jon Tenney). Her down-home style clashes with his high power win at all costs style. He learns from this hick.

**953. Kumg Fu.** ABC. US. 1972–1975. 60m. *Cast:* David Carradine, Keye Luke, Philip Ahn, Radames Pera, Season Hubley

Kwai Chang Caine (David Carradine) is a Buddhist monk and hunted man. He was born in China to Chinese and American parents and raised by monks of the Shaolin Temple. The monks taught him spiritual ways and kung fu. When he was forced to kill a royal member in China, he become a hunted man and traveled to the American west searching for a brother. In 1992, a series *Kung Fu— The Legend Continues* premiered. It takes place in present day with the grandson of Kwai Chang Caine as the main character, also played by David Carradine.

**954. Lanigan's Rabbi.** NBC. US. 1977. 60m. *Cast:* Art Carney, Bruce Solomon, Janis Paige, Janet Margolin, Barbara Carney, Robert Doyle

Police Chief Paul Lanigan (Art Carney) of a small town in California and Rabbi David Small (Bruce Solomon) work together to crack cases. *Lanigan's Rabbi* was based on a series of novels. This series rotated with

other shows under "The NBC Sunday Mystery Movie."

**955. Little House on the Prairie.** NBC. US. 1974–1983. 60m. *Cast:* Michael Landon, Karen Grassle, Melissa Sue Gilbert, Melissa Sue Anderson, Lindsay and Sidney Greenbush, Richard Bull, Katherine MacGregor, Jonathan Gilbert, Alison Arngrim, Dabs Greer, Kevin Hagen, Victor French, Matthew Laborteaux

The Ingalls family faced disappointment, trials, tribulations, and adventures in frontier life of Minnesota. Many cast changes occurred over the years, but one consistent character was Reverend Robert Alden (Dabs Greer) who provided spiritual guidance.

**956. Little Women.** NBC. US. 1979. 60m. *Cast:* Dorothy McGuire, William Schallert, Jessica Harper, Susan Walden, Ann Dusenberry, Cliff Potts, Richard Gilliland, David Ackroyd, Mildred Natwick, Eve Plumb, Virginia Gregg, Robert Young, Maggie Malooly

Reverend John March (William Schallert) heads the March clan which continues where Miss Alcott's novel left off.

**957. Mama Malone.** CBS. US. 1984. 30m. *Cast:* Lila Kaye, Randee Heller, Evan Richards, Don Amendolia Raymond Singer, Ralph Manza, Richard Yniguez, Pendleton Brown, Mitchell Group, Joey Jupiter, Sam Anderson

Mama Renate Malone (Lila Kaye) is the very Italian widow of an Irish policeman who has a New York cooking television show. Her divorced daughter, grandson, and lounge singer brother cause her troubles on the set of her show. Padre Guardiano (Ralph Manzo) is the elderly parish priest and Father Jose Silva (Richard Yniguez) is his good looking young assistant.

**958. Mariah.** ABC. US. 1987. 60m. *Cast:* Philip Baker Hall, John Getz, Tovah Feldshuh, Chris Wiggins, Kathleen Layman, Wanda de Jesus, William Allen Young, Renee Lippin

Mariah State Penitentiary is the setting for this grim drama. The focus is on the staff –Chaplain Father Timothy Quinlan (Chris Wiggins), Superintendent James Malone

(Philip Baker Hall), psychiatrist Dr. Hertz (Tovah Feldshuh), activist Brandis LaSalle (Kathleen Layman), and Deputy Ned Sheffield (John Getz).

**959. M*A*S*H.** CBS. US. 1972–1983. 30m. *Cast:* Alan Alda, Wayne Rogers, Loretta Swit, Larry Linville, Gary Burghoff, McLean Stevenson, William Christopher, Jamie Farr, Harry Morgan, Mike Farrell, David Ogden Stiers, Kellye Nakahara, Alan Arbus

The 4077th Mobile Army Surgical Hospital, which was located behind the lines during the Korean War, served as the setting for this popular and long-running series based on the film *M*A*S*H.* The characters include Dr. Benjamin Franklin "Hawkeye" Pierce (Alan Alda), Dr. John "Trapper John" McIntyre (Wayne Rogers), Nurse Margaret "Hot Lips" Houlihan (Loretta Swit), Dr. Frank Burns (Larry Linville), Dr. Henry Blake (McLean Stevenson), Dr. Sherman Potter (Harry Morgan), Dr. B. J. Hunnicut (Mike Farrell), Dr. Charles Emerson Winchester (David Ogden Stiers), and psychiatrist Dr. Sidney Freedman (Alan Arbus). Nonmedical personnel were Father Francis Mulcahy (William Christopher), Walter "Radar" O'Reilly (Gary Burghoff), and Maxwell Klinger (Jamie Farr). *Aftermash* was a spin-off series which reunited some of the characters after the war. The character Trapper John later had his own series, *Trapper John M.D.*

Once when a soldier had been wounded he refused to talk to Father Mulcahy because the Father didn't have first hand knowledge of war. So Father Mulcahy sneaked out on a mission with Radar to deliver a wounded soldier in order to see what the war was about. On his secret mission he had to perform an emergency tracheotomy. He learns about war! He is a gentle and dizzy character who helps humanize some of the situations.

**960. Miracles.** ABC. US. 2003. 60m. *Cast:* Skeet Ulrich, Angus MacFadyen, Marisa Ramirez, Hector Elizondo, Sean Galuszka

Young seminarian Paul Callan (Skeet Ulrich) is an investigator who works for the Catholic Church to explore supposed miracles such as stigmata or weeping statues. He grows disillusioned when explanations are all of natural causes. He decides to take a break until his life is saved by a young boy with the power to heal. The boy dies and Paul sees writing in blood. He joins forces with investigator of paranormal Alva Keel (Angus MacFadyen) and a former police officer Evelyn Santos (Marisa Ramirez) when the Church dismisses his findings.

**961. The Montefuscos.** NBC. US. 1975. 30m. *Cast:* Joe Sirola, Naomi Stevens, Ron Carey, John Aprea, Phoebe Dorin, Linda Dano, Bill Cort, Sal Viscuso, Jeffrey Palladini

The Montefuscos is a middle-class Italian family that lives in Connecticut. Tony and Rose have three sons and one daughter. One son Joseph (John Aprea) is a priest.

**962. The New Adventures of Robin Hood.** TNT. US.1996–1997. 60m. *Cast:* Matthew Porretta, John Bradley, Anna Galvin, Barbara Griffin, Martyn Ellis, Richard Ashton, Christie Woods, Hakim Alston, Christopher Lee

Update of the Robin Hood and his Merry Men story. Friar Tuck (Martyn Ellis) loves to eat while Maid Marion teaches self-defense. The role of Robin was recast after a few episodes. Fantasy elements were introduced into the plots.

**963. Nothing Sacred.** ABC. US. 1997–1998. 60m. *Cast:* Kevin Anderson, Brad Sullivan, Ann Dowd, Scott Michael Campbell, Bruce Altman, Jose Zuniga, Tamara Mello, David Marshall Grant, Jennifer Beals

Not your typical priest Father Ray (Kevin Anderson) wrestles with his parish St. Thomas a large urban church in an inner-city neighborhood, his beliefs, and his failings. In some ways he resembles Father Chuck O'Malley but in other ways he is the anti-Chuck. For example, he is willing to tackle abortion by his willingness to counsel on the topic. Others in the parish include older wise Father Leo (Brad Sullivan), newly ordained Father Eric (Scott Michael Campbell), feminist nun Sister Maureen (Ann Dowd), youth minister Oritz (Jose Zuniga), receptionist Rachel (Tamara Mello), and business manager Sidney (Bruce Altman). There were many protests against the series due to its handling of sensitive issues such as abortion.

**964. Oh, Brother!** BBC. UK. 1968–1970. 19 episodes. 30m. *Cast:* Derek Nimmo, Felix Aylmer, Derek Francis, Colin Gordon, Geoffrey Hibbert, Edward Malin, Patrick McAlinney

Brother Dominic (Derek Nimmo) is a novice monk at Mountacres Priory where he walks a thin line between acceptance and expulsion from the order. Father Matthew (Derek Francis) is not pleased with his bumbling and talkative nature while Father Anselm (Felix Aylmer) is more accepting. Derek Nimmo had one season as Father Dominic in *Oh, Father!*

**965. Oz.** HBO. US. 1997–2003. 60m. *Cast:* Rita Moreno, Terry Kinney, Ernie Hudson, B. D. Wong, Christopher Meloni, Adewale Akinnuoye-Agbaje, Chazz Menendez, John Palumbo, Austin Pendleton, Chuck Zito, Scott William Winters, Steven Wishnoff, Evan Seinfeld, Otto Sanchez, Robert Clohessy, Eamonn Walker, Dean Winters, George Morfogen, Lauren Vélez, Lee Tergesen, J. K. Simmons, Harold Perrineau Jr., Kirk Acevedo

This series details the daily activities of the prison facility Oswald Maximum Security Correctional Facility nicknamed Emerald City. Daily life for both staff and the inmates is full of power struggles, gang fighting, drugs, and violence. Sister Peter Marie Reimondo (Rita Moreno) is a nun-psychologist at the facility. Also appearing is Father Ray Mukada (B. D. Wong).

**966. Picket Fences.** CBS. US. 1992–1996. 60m. *Cast:* Tom Skerritt, Kathy Baker, Holly Marie Combs, Justin Shenkarow, Adam Wylie, Costas Mandylor, Lauren Holly, Ray Walston, Fyvush Finkel, Kelly Connell, Dabs Greer, Roy Dotrice, Don Cheadle, Zelda Rubinstein.

Rome, Wisconsin was the setting for this sometimes strange drama. The stories centered on the Brocks- Jimmy (Tom Skerritt), the sheriff, Jill (Kathy Baker), a physician at Thayer Hospital, one daughter from a previous marriage, and two sons. It also prominently featured a local parish priest Father Gary Barrett (Roy Dotrice) consumed by a foot fetish and Minister Henry Novotny (Dabs Greer).

**967. Poltergeist: The Legacy.** MGM. US. 1996–1999. 60m. *Cast:* Derek de Lint, Martin Cummings, Robbi Chong, Helen Shaver, Jordan Bayne, Patrick Fitzgerald, Alexandra Purvis, Kristin Lehman, Daniel J. Travanti

The Legacy is a secret society that was created many centuries ago to fight evil in the world. The Legacy consists of a network of teams scattered around the world. The series centers on the San Francisco castle-like house. The team there consists of their leader the Precept Dr. Derek Rayne (Derek de Lint), psychiatrist Rachel Corrigan (Helen Shaver), priest Father Philip Callahan (Patrick Fitzgerald), ex-Navy SEAL Nick Boyle (Martin Cummings), and researcher/psychic Alex Moreau (Robbi Chong).

**968. Un Prete tra noi.** Radiotelevisione Italiana. Italy/Germany. 1997. *Cast:* Massimo Dapporto, Julia Brendler, Giovanna Ralli, Marina Tagliaferri, Michael Lonsdale, Mattia Sbragia, Alessio Boni

Don Marco (Massimo Dapporto) is an intelligent priest who must take over a parish when his mentor dies. He also continues the late priest's work as a chaplain. He does what he can to help his new flock. The daughter of a prisoner, who became a prostitute to support her father, falls in love with him. A popular television series in Italy.

**969. Rachel Gunn, RN.** FOX. US. 1992. 30m. *Cast:* Christine Ebersole, Kevin Conroy, Megan Mullally, Bryan Brightcloud, Dan Tullis Jr., Kathleen Mitchell, Lois Foraker

Head nurse Rachel Gunn (Christine Ebersole) runs the elective surgery floor of Little Innocence Hospital in Nebraska. Perky black nun Sister Joan (Kathleen Mitchell) takes care of the spiritual needs of patients and staff. Dr. David Dunkle (Kevin Conroy) is an arrogant physician. Nurse Becky (Megan Mullally) is the new nurse on the floor. Zac (Bryan Brightcloud) is a Native American nurse who served in Vietnam.

**970. Sarge.** NBC. US. 1971–1972. 60m. *Cast:* George Kennedy, Sallie Shockley, Harold Sakata, Ramon Bieri

Sarge (George Kennedy) is a priest at St. Aloysius Parish in San Diego. An area of town he knows well because previously to becoming a priest he was a police office for nine years. He is known as Sarge because of his past, which also comes in handy when dealing with parishioners. Kenji (Harold Sakata) is the rectory cook and Valerie (Sallie Shockley) is the parish secretary. Chief of Detectives Barney Verick (Ramon Bieri) seeks Sarge's assistance on some of his cases that may involve his own parishioners.

**971. Seventh Heaven.** WB. US. 1996–. 60m. *Cast:* Stephen Collins, Catherine Hicks, Barry Watson, David Gallagher, Jessica Biel, Beverly Mitchell, MacKenzie Rosman, Adam LaVorgna, Lorenzo Brino, Nikolas Brino, Dorian Harewood, Jeremy London, Ed Begley Jr., Happy the dog

The series centers on the trails and tribulations of Reverend Eric Camden (Stephen Collins), his wife Annie (Catherine Hicks) and their seven children. Originally the family consisted of five children but in 1999 Annie gave birth to twins. They live in the fictional town of Glen Oak, California.

**972. Sister Kate.** NBC. US. 1989–1990. 30m. *Cast:* Stephanie Beacham, Jason Priestly, Erin Reed, Hannah Cutrona, Penina Segall, Harley Cross, Alexandria Simmons, Joel Robinson, Gordon Jump

Sister Katherine Lambert (Stephanie Beacham) is the new head of Redemption House, an orphanage full of unruly kids. The scheming kids had already driven out three nice priests. The kids are no match for Sister Kate, especially since her last assignment was an archaeological dig.

**973. Soul Man.** ABC. US. 1997–1998. 30m. *Cast:* Dan Aykroyd, Dakin Matthews, Kevin Sheridan, Courtney Chase, Brendon Ryan Barrett, Spencer Breslin, Helen Cates, Anthony Clark, Micheal Finiguerra, Bridgette Collins

Mike Weber (Dan Aykroyd) is a widowed Episcopal priest who must deal with his four children and his parish is in Royal Oak, Michigan. The wet-behind-the-ears curate happens to be the nephew of his bishop. Reverend Mike Weber is a down-to-earth cool guy. Bishop Jerome (Dakin Matthews) didn't approve of his nontraditional sermons and methods.

**974. Tales of the Gold Monkey.** ABC. US. 1982–1983. 60m. *Cast:* Stephen Collins, Jeff MacKay, Caitlin O'Heaney, Roddy McDowall, John Calvin, Marta DuBois, John Fujioka

Setting for the series is a 1938 South Pacific island and the Monkey Bar. Pilot Jake (Stephen Collins) has two sidekicks his loyal but drunk mechanic Corky (Jeff MacKay) and a one-eyed dog named Jack. Bon Chance Louis (Roddy McDowall) owns the bar and Sarah (Caitlin O'Heaney) sings at the bar. Reverend Willie Tenboom (John Calvin) is a pompous Dutch minister who is really a German spy.

**Touch of a Soul** *see* **Aggigma psyhis**

**975. Tough Cookies.** CBS. US. 1986. 30m. *Cast:* Robby Benson, Lainie Kazan, Adam Arkin, Matt Craven, Art Metrano, Elizabeth Pena, Alan North

Police detective Cliff Brady (Robby Benson) is assigned to a tough Southside Chicago precinct. He grew up in the area and now lives nearby. Father McCaskey (Alan North) is the understanding police chaplain.

**976. The Vicar of Dibley.** BBC. UK. 1994–2000. 16 episodes. *Cast:* Dawn French, Gary Waldhorn, Emma Chambers, James Fleet, Roger Lloyd-Pack, John Bluthal, Trevor Peacock, Liz Smith

Geraldine Granger (Dawn French) is the new female vicar in the village of Dibley. Alice Tinker (Emma Chambers) is the very dumb verger, David Horton (Gary Waldhorn) the pompous and very conservative parish councilor, Hugo (James Fleet) his hapless son, "No, no, no. no…yes" Jim Trott (Trevor Peacock), Frank Pickle (John Bluthal) the boring Church secretary, Owen Newitt (Roger Lloyd-Pack) a farmer, and Letitia Cropley (Liz Smith) a dreadful cook with bizarre recipes. The townspeople are initially shocked when the liberal female vicar shows up in their village but soon accept and respect her.

**977. The Waltons.** CBS. US. 1972–1981. 60m. 208 episodes *Cast:* Ralph Waite, Michael Learned, Will Greer, Ellen Corby, Richard Thomas, Robert Wightman, Judy Norton-Taylor, David W. Harper, Kami Colter, Jon Walmsley, Mary Elizabeth Mc-Donough, Eric Scott, Joe Conley, Ronnie Claire Edwards, John Crawford, Helen Kleeb, Mary Jackson, Lynn Hamilton, Tom Bower, Peter Fox, John Ritter

Walton's Mountain in the Blue Ridge Mountains of Virginia during the Depression is the setting for this drama of a very close-knit family. Time did not stand still on the mountain as WWII became a factor. John Boy (Richard Thomas) becomes a writer. One daughter, Mary Ellen (Judy Norton-Taylor), becomes a nurse and marries Dr. Curtis Willard (Tom Bower), who appears to die in Pearl Harbor. Throughout the series a minister played a part in some of the episodes. Reverend Matthew Fordwick 1972–1977 was played by John Ritter and Reverend Hank Buchanan 1977–1978 was played by Peter Fox. Reverend Fordwick enlisted in the army during WWII

**978. When Things Were Rotten.** ABC. US. 1975. 30m. *Cast:* Dick Gautier, Dick Van Patten, Bernie Kopell, Richard Dimitri, Henry Polic II, Misty Rowe, David Sabin, Ron Rifkin, Jane A. Johnston

A satire created by Mel Brooks about Robin Hood (Dick Gautier) and His Merry Men of Sherwood Forest. Friar Tuck (Dick Van Patten) is there to help out.

**A Wing and a Prayer** *see* **Amazing Grace**

**979. Winnetka Road.** NBC. US. 1994. 60m. *Cast:* Paige Turco, Kellen Hathaway, Harley Vernon, Josh Brolin, Megan Ward, Ed Begley Jr., Catherine Hicks, Meg Tilly, Eddie Bracken, Sandy McPeak, Jayne Frazer, Richard Gilliland, Kurt Deutsch

Set in the Chicago suburb of Oak Bluff, Illinois where kindly blind Father Burke (Eddie Bracken) looks after a little boy named Nicky (Kellen Hathaway) while everyone else pursues earthly pleasures.

# Annotated Bibliography

Allen, John L., Jr. "Father Ted Makes Sacred Look Tame." *National Catholic Reporter* 34 no. 4 (1997): 5. Discusses the success of the English hit television show *Father Ted*, which spoofs priests and the Vatican. Even though *Father Ted* could be seen as offensive, it draws little protest—unlike *Nothing Sacred* in the United States.

Attwater, Donald. *The Avenel Dictionary of Saints.* New York: Avenel, 1981. Alphabetical reference book on the lives and legends of more than 750 saints.

Bazin, Andre (translated and edited by Bert Cardullo). "Cinema and Theology: The Case of *Heaven Over the Marshes.*" *Journal of Religion and Film* 6 no. 2 (2002). Examines Augusto Genina's *Heaven Over the Marshes* and concludes that it is a good Catholic film because it looks at sainthood from the outside.

Blake, Robert. "Return of the Exorcist: After 27 years, the Film Provokes an Entirely Different Set of Reactions. *America* 183 no. 16 (2000): 6. A fresh review of *The Exorcist* after 27 years.

Boudreaux, Richard, and Lorenza Munoz. "Uproar Over Film About Fallen Priest. *The Los Angeles Times* August 16, 2002: A1. Reporting of the clerical outrage over *The Crime of Father Amaro.*

Brooks, Tim, and Earle Marsh. *The Complete Directory to Prime Time Network and Cable TV Shows: 1946–Present.* Eighth Edition. New York: Ballantine, 2003.

Carreras-Kuntz, Maria Elena de las. "The Catholic Vision in Hollywood: Ford, Capra, Borzage and Hitchcock." *Film History* 14 (2002): 121–35. Explores the ways in which a Catholic view is reflected in the films of John Ford, Frank Capra, Frank Borzage, and Alfred Hitchcock.

Connelly, Robert. *The Motion Picture Guide (Silent Films 1910–36).* Chicago: Cinebooks, 1986.

Corliss, Richard. "Stations of the Cross." *Time International* 153 no. 6 (1999): 68. A few of Robert Bresson's films are analyzed.

Courvares, Francis. "Hollywood, Main Street, and the Church: Trying to Censor the Movies Before the Production Code." *American Quarterly* 44 no. 4 (1992): 584–617. Hollywood turned to the Catholic clergy for advice on censorship in the late 1920s, after relations between Hollywood and Protestant organizations had deteriorated. Concludes the Catholic clergy cooperated because they wanted greater acceptance in Protestant-dominated America.

Crowdus, Gary. "Filming the Story of a Spy for God: An Interview with Costa-Gavras. *Cineaste* 28 no. 2 (2003): 14-. An interview with Costa-Gavras about his film *Amen.*

_____. "The Sisters of No Mercy: An Interview with Peter Mullan. *Cineaste* 28 no. 4 (2003): 26-. An interview with the director of *The Magdalene Sisters.*

Cunneen, Joseph. "Connecting Faith and Film." *National Catholic Reporter* 40 no. 4 (2003): 23. A profile of the works of French film director Robert Bresson.

De La Paz, Diane. "Film Festival Attendees Mesmerized by the Real Deal. *National Catholic Reporter* 37, no. 22 (March 30, 2001): 13. *Diary of a City Priest* played at the Sundance Film Festival. The film is based on a book by a real priest who attended the festival.

Eby, Lloyd. "Is Hollywood Hostile to Religion: A Matter of Perspective." *World and I* 13 no. 4 (1998): 92-. Hollywood has made good religious movies and movies mocking religion and clerics. Michael Medved believes that films are indicative of Hollywood's war against religion.

Erens, Patricia. *The Jew in American Cinema.* Bloomington: Indiana University Press, 1984. Study of the Jew in American movies from the beginning of cinema.

Feder, Don. "The Benevolent Universe of Filmmaker M. Night Shyamalan." *The American Enterprise* 14 no. 3 (2003): 43-. An examination of the director's work and ties to spiritualism.

Fister, Charles. "The Catholic Crusade Against the Movies, 1940–1975." *America* 179 no. 4 (1998): 19. Review of *The Catholic Crusade Against the Movies, 1940–1975* by Gregory D. Black.

Fuentes, Maria Jose Gamez. "Women in Spanish

Cinema: Raiders of the Missing Mother?" *Cineaste* 29 no. 1 (2003): 38–. Examination of the mother in contemporary Spanish cinema.

Gifford, Denis. *The British Film Catalogue, 1895–1985.* London: David and Charles, 1986.

Golfman, Noreen. "Salvation through Cinema." *Canadian Forum* 74 no. 847 (1996): 9–10. Article on the film *Le Confessional.*

Gordon, Mary. "Father Chuck: A Reading of *Going My Way* and *The Bells of St. Mary's,* or Why Priests Made Us Crazy." *The South Atlantic Quarterly* 91 no. 3 (1994): 591–601. Considers *Going My Way* and *The Bells of St. Mary's* with concentration on Father Chuck O'Malley.

_____. "Women of God." *The Atlantic Monthly* 289 no. 1 (2002): 57–62, 64+. Extensive examination of nuns by novelist and memoirist Mary Gordon. She sees nuns as an endangered species because their way of life is disappearing. The author cites her personal feelings and experiences. Includes a discussion of cinematic nuns and interviews with real nuns.

"Group Protest R-rated *Priest.*" *Christianity Today* 39 no. 6 (1995): 52. Reports on the boycott of the Walt Disney Company organized by Catholic League for Religious and Civil Rights and the American Life League because of the portrayal of Catholic clergy in *The Priest.*

Hanson, Patricia King, editor. *The American Film Institute of Motion Pictures Produced in the United States: Feature Films 1911–1920.* Berkeley: University of California Press, 1988.

Harty, Kevin. *The Reel Middle Ages.* Jefferson, North Carolina: McFarland, 1999. A listing of films about medieval Europe.

Heins, Marjorie. "The Bishops Go to the Movies: *The Miracle*: Film Censorship and the Entanglement of Church and State. *Conscience* 24 no. 1 (2003): 12. Article details how the release in late 1950 of the Italian film *The Miracle* caused quite an uproar with protests and legal battles by the Catholic church's Legion of Decency and New York's Cardinal Francis Spellman who demanded that the film's license be revoked. Article goes on to explain the entanglement of church and state with regards to censorship.

Hiersteiner, Catherine. "Saints or sinners? The Image of Social Workers from American Stage and Cinema before World War II. *Affilia Journal of Women and Social Work* 13 no. 3 (1998): 312–26. Concentrates on social workers, but a few films are relevant to religious figures.

Hulsether, Mark. "Sorting Out the Relationship Among Christian Values, US Popular Religion, and Hollywood Films." *Religious Studies Review* 25 no. 1 (1999): 3–11. Discusses numerous books about the topic.

James, Nick. "In a Harsh Light." *Sight & Sound* 10 no. 8 (2000): 28–30. Discusses the image of the Hasidic male in the movies.

Janosik, MaryAnn. "Madonnas in Our Midst: Representations of Religious Women in Hollywood Film." *U.S. Catholic Historian* 15.3 (1997): 75–98. Examines three character types which have generally defined nuns in Hollywood film: the Earth Mother Madonna, the Eccentric Aunt, and the Social Activist Sister.

Kasten, Patricia. "Bing and Father Ray—Going the Same Way." *National Catholic Reporter* 34 no. 10 (1998): 9. Comparison of Father O'Malley and the priest in *Nothing Sacred.*

Keller, Julia. "Altar Ego: The Priest Has Long Been a Staple of Popular Culture." *Knight Ridder/Tribune News Service* May 6 (2002): pK4171. Explores the future image of priests in light of recent sexual scandals.

Kelly, Allison. "A Girl's Best Friend Is Her Mother: The Exorcist as a Post-modern Oedipal Tale." *Journal of Evolutionary Psychology* 25 no. 1–2 (2004): 64–70. Why does Regan only kill men? Because she has an oedipal complex. A psychological interpretation of *The Exorcist.*

Knight, Arthur. *The Liveliest Art: A Panoramic History of the Movies.* New York: Macmillan, 1978. This history of the movies revisits the classics, reviews trends and the film industry.

Kozlovic, Anton Karl. "Saint Cinema: The Construction of St. Francis of Assisi in Franco Zeffirelli's *Brother Sun Sister Moon.*" *Journal of Religion and Popular Culture* 2 (Fall 2002). Extensive examination of a film that the author feels is a popular and accessible biopic of St. Francis of Assisi.

Lawson, Terry. "Hollywood's Relationship with Religion Always Has Been Turbulent. *Knight Ridder/Tribune News Service* Feb. 19 (2004): K1804. Comments on the long history of religious organizations upset with the treatment of their beliefs.

Lindvall, Terrence. "The Organ in the Sanctuary: Silent Film and Paradigmatic Images of the Suspect Clergy." In *Sex, Religion, Media.* Lanham, Maryland: Rowman & Littlefield, 2002. Investigates the variety of sex and clergy themes by analyzing silent American films.

Lopate, Phillip. "Films as Spiritual Life." *Film Comment* 27 no. 6 (1991): 26–30. Discusses how the film *Diary of a Country Priest* changed the life of the Jewish man. He says it put him "in contact with habit of mind that I may as well call spiritual and a mental process suspiciously like meditation."

Lyons, David. "Priests." *Film Comment* 31 no. 3 (1995): 80–84. Symbols and icons used in religious movies are discussed. Despite differences in religions, there is universality in most of the icons.

Maddox, Peggy. "Retiring the Maid: The Last Joan of Arc Movie." *Journal of Religion and Popular Culture* 3 Spring (2003). Joan of Arc films began in 1895 and are still being made today. The author feels that *The Messenger* reshapes the image of Joan of Arc.

Magill, Frank N., editor. *Magill's Survey of Cinema: English Language Films, First Series.* Volume 1. Englewood Cliffs, New Jersey: Salem, 1980.

_____, editor. *Magill's Survey of Cinema: English Language Films, Second Series.* Volume 2. Englewood Cliffs, New Jersey: Salem, 1981.

_____, editor. *Magill's Survey of Cinema, Foreign Language Films.* Englewood Cliffs, New Jersey: Salem, 1985.

Marill, Alvin. H. *Movies Made for Television: The Telefeature and the Mini-Series 1964–1984.* New York: New York Zoetrope, 1984.

Martin, James. "The Gospel According to Blockbuster." *America* 176 no. 15 (1997): 20–23. An analysis of seven popular biblical films.

_____. "Penguins, regular guys, idiots and Whoopi Goldberg." *America* 170 no. 4 (1994): 20–23. Discusses movie and television depictions of the clergy, stereotypes of priests and nuns, and their dramatized struggles.

_____. "A Strange Media Drama." *America* 177 no. 11 (1997):16–19. Another viewpoint on the television series *Nothing Sacred*.

_____. "Those Nutty Catholics. *America* 172 no. 21 (1995): 32. Catholics and their beliefs are becoming scapegoats of prime time.

Martin, Joel, and Conrad Ostwalt, Jr., editors. *Screening the Sacred.* Boulder: Westview, 1995. A discussion of religion, myth, and ideology in popular American film.

Mason, M.S. "Religious Themes Get Wider Play, More Nuanced Portrayal in Fall Shows." *The Christian Science Monitor*, October 14, 1997. Explains about the number of Christian shows on the fall television schedule.

May, John R., and Michael Bird, editors. *Religion in Film.* Knoxville: University of Tennessee Press, 1982. A collection of essays exploring the religious interpretation of film, particular genres and trends, and directors with religious concerns.

McCormick, Patrick. "Do Saints Make Good Cinema?" *U.S. Catholics* 61 no. 10 (1996): 38–41. Father Ellwood Kieser has made a film about Dorothy Day.

_____. "Something Sacred: Hollywood's New Men in Black." *U.S. Catholics* 63 January (1989): 46–9. Comments about the priests we see in the movies.

McNeil, Alex. *Total Television: A Comprehensive Guide to Programming from 1948 to the Present.* Third Edition. New York: Penguin Books, 1991.

Miles, Margaret. *Seeing and Believing: Religion and Values in the Movies.* Boston: Beacon, 1996. Explores what popular films of the 1980s and 1990s say about religion and the values by which we live.

Monahan, Matthew. "View from a Pew." *America* 172 April 15 (1995): 4. Talks about *The Priest*.

Mullen, Eve. "Orientalist Commercializations: Tibetan Buddhism in American Popular Film." *Journal of Religion and Film* 2 no. 2 (1998). Shows how misleading Tibetan characterizations make their way into contemporary films such as *Seven Years in Tibet, Kundun,* and *Little Buddha*.

Munden, Kenneth W., editor. *The American Film Institute Catalog of Motion Pictures Produced in the United States. Vol. 2: Feature Films, 1921–1930. Vol. 3: Feature Films, 1961–1970.* New York: R. R. Bowker, 1971–1988.

Munoz, Lorenza. "Movies; Director Deflects Fire and Brimstone; Carlos Carrera's Controversial Film. *The Los Angeles Times*, Nov. 15, 2002: E17. Interview with the director of *El Crimen del Padre Amaro*.

Musser, Charles. "Turning the Tables." *Film Comment* 36 no. 5 (2000): 67–70. Focuses on black filmmaker Oscar Micheaux's silent film *Body and Soul*.

Nash, Jay Robert, and Stanley Ralph Ross. *The Motion Picture Guide (1927–1983).* Chicago: Cinebooks, 1986.

Natale, Richard. "Nuns' Stories." *Variety* 373 no. 6 (1998): 70. Examines the film portrayals of nuns.

*The New York Times Film Reviews (1913–1980).* New York: *New York Times* and Arno Press.

O'Brien, George Dennis. "Going Which Way?" *Commonwealth* 122, Sept. 22, 1995: 10–15. Discusses the film *Going My Way* with Bing Crosby as Father O'Malley.

O'Brien, Tom. "Sin and the Small Screen." *World and I* 13 no. 4 (1998): 85-. Television shows on religion have been rare, and when they exist the shows are removed from real life. The television show *Nothing Sacred* has been controversial because it deals with such issues as abortion.

"O'Connor Criticizes a Film on Priests." *New York Times* April 8 (1995): A26. Archbishop of New York John Cardinal O'Connor condemns the film *The Priest*.

Pacatte, Rose. "Stumbling into Divinity at the Movies." *National Catholic Reporter* 38 no. 42 (2002): 42-4. Review of *Celluloid Saints: Images of Sanctity in Film* by Theresa Sanders.

Quart, Leonard. "A Second Look: Social Values in the Film *Boys Town*." *Cineaste* 21 no. 3 (1995): 55–56. Newt Gingrich cites *Boys Town* as an embodiment of his own conservative values. The author demonstrates that the film really espouses liberal values.

Rebeck, Victoria. "Soul Men." *Christian Century* 114 no. 32 (1997): 1046–48. Examines the depiction of clergy in selected United States television programs.

Richards, Sylvie. "Keeping Up with the Joans: The Maid of Orleans in Literature and Film." *West Virginia University Philological Papers* (Fall 2000): 37–47. This study looks at the role of literature and film in determining Joan's place in history and popular culture.

Robinson, James III. The Image of Christian Leaders in Fictional Television Programs." *Sociology of Religion* 55 no. 1 (1994): 75–85. An investigation into how Christian leaders are portrayed on television by calculating their frequency of appearance, identifying the types of behaviors in which they engage, and establishing the traits in two contexts.

Rothman, Stanley. "Is God Really Dead in Beverly Hills?" *The American Schola*r 65 (Spring 1996): 272–8. Some films have presented religious characters in a positive light, but on the whole religious themes have played poorly in movies for the past forty years.

Savada, Elias (compiler). *The American Film Institute Catalog of Motion Pictures Produced in the United States: Film Beginnings, 1893–1910; Indexes and Entries*. Metuchen, New Jersey: Scarecrow, 1995.

Smith, Jeffrey. "Hollywood Theology: The Commodification of Religion in Twentieth-Century Films." *Religion and American Culture* 11 no. 2 (2001): 191. Author concludes that audiences are willing to suspend disbelief and religious belief long enough to indulge in a pleasurable pastime. People have a natural interest in what God and God's opponents might be doing.

Stone, Bryan. "Religion and Violence in Popular Film." *Journal of Religion and Film* 3 no. 1 (1999). An analysis of the top grossing films during the 1990s shows that religion as either a force for justifying and legitimating violence or a device for enhancing the entertainment value of violence.

Sullivan, Rebecca. "Celluloid Sisters: Femininity, Religiosity, and the Postwar American Nun Film." *Velvet Light Trap* (Fall 2000): 56–73. Detailed essay on the American nun films of the late 1950s and the 1960s.

*Variety Film Reviews, 1907–1984*. New York: Garland, 1984.

Williams, Peter. "Religion Goes to the Movies." *Religion and American Culture* 10 no. 2 (2000): 225–239. Reviews books that discuss religion in the movies, such as *The Catholic Crusade Against the movies, 1940–1975* by Gregory Black (1998); *American Religious and Biblical Spectaculars* by Gerald Forshey (1992); *Screening the Sacred*, edited by Joel Martin and Conrad Ostwald, Jr., (1995); *Seeing and Believing* by Margaret Miles (1996); and *Hollywood Dreams and Biblical Stories* by Bernard Brandon Scott (1994).

Wilson, Sarah Hinlicky. *An Ecumenical Luther. Books & Culture* 10 no. 1 (2004): 14. Details the newest Luther film.

Wloszczyna, Susan. "Heavens! Nuns Have Become Quite the Habit." *USA Today*, April 14, 2000. Nuns are showing up in most unlikely places in the movies.

Wolff, R. "*The Flying Nun* and Post-Vatican II Catholicism." *Journal of Popular Film & Television* 19 no. 2 (1991): 72. The article traces the history of *The Flying Nun* and its relationship with the Catholic Church in context with historical consideration.

Woodward, Joe. "Sex and the Single Priest." *Alberta Report* 24 no. 36 (1997): 34–36. Discusses the portrayal of priests and ministers in film and television.

Woodward, Kenneth L. "Bing Crosby Had It Right." *Newsweek*, March 4, 2002: 53. He wants to believe that his children's children will find their own Father O'Malleys.

Yarri, Donna. "*The Crime of Father Amaro*," *Journal of Religion & Film* 8 no. 1 (2004). Review of *The Crime of Father Amaro*.

# Name Index

References are to entry number. The names of real people are italicized.

# Subject Index

References are to entry numbers.